T0305096

MERGERS AND ACQUISITIONS

MERGERS

AND

ACQUISITIONS

Managing Culture
and Human Resources

**Edited by Günter K. Stahl
and Mark E. Mendenhall**

STANFORD BUSINESS BOOKS   *An imprint of Stanford University Press*
Stanford, California

Stanford University Press
Stanford, California
© 2005 by the Board of Trustees
of the Leland Stanford Junior University.
All rights reserved.

Printed and bound by CPI Group (UK) Ltd, Croydon, CR0 4YY

Library of Congress Cataloging-in-Publication Data

Mergers and acquisitions : managing culture and human resources / edited
by Mark E. Mendenhall and Günter K. Stahl.
    p. cm.
   Includes bibliographical references and index.
   ISBN 0-8047-4661-3 (cloth : alk. paper)
   1. Consolidation and merger of corporations—Psychological aspects.
2. Consolidation and merger of corporations—Social aspects.   3.
Corporate culture. I. Mendenhall, Mark E., date- II. Stahl, Günter K., date-

   HD2746.5.M474 2005
   658.1'62'019–dc22   2004028542

Original Printing 2005

Typeset by TechBooks in 9.7/11.5 Sabon and StoneSans.

Contents

Contributors   ix

Preface   xiii

Introductory Comments
    Carlos Ghosn and Jean-Pierre Garnier   xvi

PART I Introduction

1   Sociocultural Integration in Mergers and Acquisitions
    Günter K. Stahl, Mark E. Mendenhall,
    Amy L. Pablo, and Mansour Javidan   3

2   Integration: The Critical Link in M&A Value Creation
    David M. Schweiger and Robert L. Lippert   17

   Executive Commentary
    Tae-Gyun Shin   46

PART II The Process of Sociocultural Integration in Mergers and Acquisitions

3   Organizational Learning in Cross-Border Mergers and Acquisitions
    Danna N. Greenberg, Henry W. Lane, and
    Keith Bahde   53

   Executive Commentary
    Jean Luc Scalabre   77

4   Trust in Mergers and Acquisitions
    Günter K. Stahl and Sim B. Sitkin   82

Executive Commentary
Hans-Peter Engeli   103

5   The Role of Corporate Cultural Diversity in
     Integrating Mergers and Acquisitions
     Georg Schreyögg   108

Executive Commentary
Albert Young   126

6   The Construction of Social Identities in Mergers
     and Acquisitions
     Stein Kleppestø   130

Executive Commentary
Bjørn Z. Ekelund and Aina Aske   152

7   A Learning Perspective on Sociocultural Integration in
     Cross-National Mergers
     *Ingmar Björkman, Janne Tienari, and
     Eero Vaara*   155

Executive Commentary
Bernd Ratzke and Tom Kelly   176

**PART III   The Management of Sociocultural Integration in
             Mergers and Acquisitions**

8   Synergy Realization in Mergers and Acquisitions:
     A Co-Competence and Motivational Approach
     Rikard Larsson   183

Executive Commentary
Shlomo Ben-Hur and L. Todd Thomas   202

9   The Neglected Importance of Leadership in Mergers
     and Acquisitions
     Sim B. Sitkin and Amy L. Pablo   208

Executive Commentary
Wilfried Meyer   224

10   Psychological Communication Interventions in
     Mergers and Acquisitions
     Angelo S. DeNisi and Shung Jae Shin   228

Executive Commentary
Mark Jones   250

11   Developing a Framework for Cultural Due Diligence
     in Mergers and Acquisitions: Issues and Ideas
     Susan Cartwright and Simon McCarthy   253

     Executive Commentary
     Max Otte   268

PART IV   Learning from Experience: Case Analyses of
          Sociocultural Processes in Mergers and Acquisitions

12   Managing Human Resources to Capture Capabilities:
     Case Studies in High-Technology Acquisitions
     Saikat Chaudhuri   277

13   The CNH Global Case: Building Social Capabilities
     to Win in Global Acquisitions, Joint Ventures, and
     Alliances
     Piero Morosini   302

14   Integration Processes in Cross-Border Mergers:
     Lessons Learned from Dutch–German Mergers
     René Olie   323

15   DaimlerChrysler: A Case Study of a Cross-Border
     Merger
     Torsten Kühlmann and Peter J. Dowling   351

16   The Importance of the Agreement Formation Process
     in Partnering with the Unfamiliar: The Case of Renault
     and Nissan
     *Harry Korine, Kazuhiro Asakawa, and
     Pierre-Yves Gomez*   364

17   Creating a New Identity and High-Performance
     Culture at Novartis: The Role of Leadership and
     Human Resource Management
     *Chei Hwee Chua, Hans-Peter Engeli, and
     Günter K. Stahl*   379

PART V   Lessons for Research and Practice

18   Research on Sociocultural Integration in Mergers and
     Acquisitions: Points of Agreement, Paradoxes, and
     Avenues for Future Research
     *Günter K. Stahl, Mark E. Mendenhall, and
     Yaakov Weber*   401

19   People and Cultural Aspects of Mergers and
     Acquisitions: What Are the Lessons ... and
     the Challenges?
     Paul Evans and Vladimir Pucik   412

     Index   423

Contributors

KAZUHIRO ASAKAWA is Professor of Multinational Management and Organization Theory at Keio University (Japan)

AINA ASKE is the Cultural Heritage Manager of Larvik Municipality (Norway)

KEITH BAHDE is Director of Business Development at Cooper Lighting (USA)

SHLOMO BEN-HUR is Chief Learning Officer at DaimlerChrysler Services Academy, DaimlerChrysler Services AG (Germany)

INGMAR BJÖRKMAN is Professor of Management at the Swedish School of Economics (Finland)

SUSAN CARTWRIGHT is Professor of Organisational Psychology at the Manchester School of Management (UK)

SAIKAT CHAUDHURI is Assistant Professor of Management at the Wharton School of the University of Pennsylvania (USA)

CHEI HWEE CHUA is a Doctoral Candidate at the Moore School of Business at the University of South Carolina (USA)

ANGELO S. DENISI is Department Head and Paul M. and Rosalie Robertson Chair in Business Administration at Texas A&M University (USA)

PETER J. DOWLING is Pro Vice-Chancellor of the Division of Business, Law and Information Sciences and Professor of International Management and Strategy at the University of Canberra (Australia)

BJØRN Z. EKELUND is Managing Director of Human Factors AS (Norway)

HANS-PETER ENGELI is Managing Director of I+M Assignments Ltd. and Lecturer of IHRM at the University of Applied Sciences – Solothurn (Switzerland)

PAUL EVANS is the Shell Chaired Professor of Human Resources and Organizational Development at INSEAD (France and Singapore)

JEAN-PIERRE GARNIER is CEO of GlaxoSmithKline (USA and UK)

CARLOS GHOSN is President and CEO of Nissan Motor Co., Ltd. (Japan)

PIERRE-YVES GOMEZ is Professor of Strategic Management at EM Lyon (France)

DANNA N. GREENBERG is Assistant Professor of Management at Babson College (USA)

MANSOUR JAVIDAN is Professor of Strategy and Management, and Director of the International Management Center at Thunderbird, the Garvin School of International Management (USA)

MARK JONES is Human Resources Director-Asia Pacific with the BOC Group (Singapore)

TOM KELLY is a trainer and consultant on the management education team at the HVB Akademie, HypoVereins Bank Group (Germany)

STEIN KLEPPESTØ is Assistant Professor in the Department of Business Administration at Lund University (Sweden)

HARRY KORINE is Teaching Fellow in Strategic and International Management at the London Business School (UK) and Senior Research Fellow in Corporate Governance at EM Lyon (France)

TORSTEN KÜHLMANN is Chair of Human Resource Management at the University of Bayreuth (Germany)

HENRY (HARRY) W. LANE is the Darla and Frederick Brodsky Trustee Professor in International Business at Northeastern University (USA)

RIKARD LARSSON is Professor of Strategic Change at the School of Economics and Management at Lund University and Partner of Decision Dynamics (Sweden)

ROBERT L. LIPPERT is Managing Director, Schweiger, Lippert & Associates (USA)

SIMON McCARTHY is a Doctoral Candidate at the Manchester School of Management (UK)

MARK E. MENDENHALL is the J. Burton Frierson Chair of Excellence in Business Leadership at the University of Tennessee, Chattanooga (USA)

WILFRIED MEYER is the Group Vice President of Human Resources for Siemens Power Generation (Germany)

PIERO MOROSINI is an Adjunct Professor of Strategy and Leadership at the European School of Management and Technology (Germany)

RENÉ OLIE is Associate Professor of Strategic Management at the Rotterdam School of Management at Erasmus University (Netherlands)

MAX OTTE is Managing Director of IFVE Institute for Asset Development Inc. and Professor of International Management at the University of Applied Sciences, Worms (Germany)

AMY L. PABLO is Associate Professor of Strategy and Global Management at the University of Calgary (Canada)

VLADIMIR PUCIK is Professor of International Human Resources and Strategy at IMD – International Institute for Management Development, Lausanne (Switzerland)

BERND RATZKE is Head of HVB Akademie, the human resources development and training division of HypoVereins Bank Group (Germany)

JEAN LUC SCALABRE is the former President of Syngenta Korea Ltd. and the founder of Premium Partners International consulting group in Korea

GEORG SCHREYÖGG is Professor of Organization and Leadership at the Freie Universität Berlin (Germany)

DAVID M. SCHWEIGER is the Buck Mickel/Fluor Daniel Professor of International Business at the Moore School of Business at the University of South Carolina (USA) and Managing Director of Schweiger, Lippert & Associates

SHUNG JAE SHIN is an Assistant Professor in the Department of Management and Information Sciences, Washington State University (USA)

TAE-GYUN SHIN is Vice President of Human Resources Development, Samsung (Korea)

SIM B. SITKIN is Associate Professor of Management and Faculty Director of the Center on Leadership and Ethics at the Fuqua School of Business, Duke University (USA)

GÜNTER K. STAHL is Assistant Professor of Organizational Behavior at INSEAD (France and Singapore)

L. TODD THOMAS is Senior Manager, Organizational Development Consulting, DaimlerChrysler Services Academy, DaimlerChrysler Services, AG (USA)

JANNE TIENARI is Professor of Management and Organization at the Department of Business Administration at Lappeenranta University of Technology (Finland)

EERO VAARA is Professor of Management and Organization at the Swedish School of Economics and Business Administration (Finland) and Visiting Professor at Ecole de Management de Lyon (France).

YAAKOV WEBER is the Head of International Business – MBA and Professor of Management at The College of Management, Rishon Lezion (Israel)

ALBERT YOUNG is General Manager, Strategy and Portfolio, Shell Oil Products East (Singapore)

Preface

The genesis of this book began in the Fall of 2001 when a small group of executives and scholars interested in the cultural and human resource processes associated with mergers and acquisitions (M&A) gathered at Thurnau Castle, Germany, to discuss the sociocultural and human resource implications of M&A. From these discussions it became clear that despite the extensive body of research on M&A that has accumulated over the last thirty years, the key factors for M&A success and the reasons why so many M&A fail remain poorly understood. A number of themes emerged from the conference that were seen as being critical to reaping integration benefits in M&A, but that were largely neglected in the M&A literature, including (1) managing the transition phase of M&A, (2) social and cultural integration processes, (3) leadership, (4) trust building, (5) retention and motivation of key talent, and (6) interorganizational knowledge transfer and learning.

The result of the Thurnau Conference was a set of writings that addressed these critical issues from rich, novel perspectives. Additionally, we invited well-known M&A scholars who were not part of the original group of scholars and executives that participated in the Thurnau Conference to contribute chapters to this book. The contributing authors of this book come from different disciplines, research domains, and geographic regions, and thus provide diverse insights into the sociocultural processes and human resource management issues inherent in M&A. To ensure relevance for practice, we have invited M&A-experienced executives to comment on the issues raised by the social scientists in the book chapters.

An overarching theme in this book is that the traditional variables used to predict and explain M&A performance, such as degree of "strategic fit," method of payment, or amount of acquisition premium paid, can only predict the success of a merger or an acquisition if integration process variables are taken into consideration. While the strategic and financial conditioning factors at the time of the legal combination form the upper bound on the degree of success that a merger or an acquisition can achieve, the management of the postcombination integration process will determine the extent to which that potential is realized. One of the executives at the Thurnau Conference put it more succinctly: "you can merge any two companies if you are good at managing the integration process." Although this view struck some of us as being somewhat extreme (how can a firm hope to achieve synergies if there is a lack of strategic fit?), the chapters in this book suggest that the "process perspective" on M&A, which has been advocated by scholars such as Philippe Haspeslagh, David Jemison, and Sim Sitkin, has become the dominant paradigm in M&A research. Consistent with this perspective, research attention has recently begun to shift to the "softer," less tangible social, cultural, and psychological aspects of M&A management (for example, Cooper and Gregory, 2000; Hitt, Harrison, and Ireland, 2001; Morosini, 1998; Pablo and Javidan, 2004).

The Thurnau Conference, and the on-going interaction of M&A scholars and executives after the meeting, could not have produced the writings that are published in this book without the generous support of many individuals and organizations. We gratefully acknowledge the contributions of the following organizations (in alphabetical order) who supported the efforts that have led to the publication of this book: Robert Bosch, DaimlerChrysler, DaimlerChrysler Services, Debitel, The Frierson Leadership Institute, the German Science Foundation, the Hornschuch'sche Allgemeine Wohlfahrtsstiftung, INSEAD, Siemens, the University of Bayreuth, and the University of Tennessee at Chattanooga. Further, we gratefully acknowledge the support for the final editing of the book that was provided by a research grant from INSEAD, where this book project was headquartered. We would also like to thank Claudia Einfalt, who did an excellent job in her role as conference organizer for the Thurnau Conference, and Chei Hwee Chua and Soma Chatterjee Rao, whose assistance in the final editing of the book was invaluable.

Without the patience and support of the Stanford University Press team, this book would have never seen the light of day. First, we wish to express our sincere thanks to Bill Hicks, who understood the vision of this project. His suggestions and excitement were key catalysts in turning our symposium into a book. Kate Wahl and Martha Cooley shepherded the lengthy process of manuscript preparation with skill and patience. We also wish to thank the reviewers, and all who have given us constructive criticism regarding this project. The quality of the contents of this book was enhanced by their input.

Finally, we wish to dedicate this book to our wives, Dorit and Janet; their love, and support of us in all our travel and work, is a rich blessing–one for which we are deeply grateful.

It is our hope that this book will act as a catalyst for scholars who work in the field of M&A by providing them with a wider scope of theoretical understanding regarding the complexity of the variables that influence long-term productivity and synergies in M&A. Also, we believe that executives involved in strategic planning of M&A will find this book invaluable in aiding them in constructing due diligence processes that go beyond financial analyses. Without a clearer understanding of the "gestalt" of M&A success, focusing solely on financial measures in making "merge" and "acquire" decisions is like playing a piano with only the white keys and ignoring the black keys and the pedal. It is our hope that this book will aid both scholars and executives to more clearly comprehend the complexity of the dynamics inherent in M&A processes.

Günter K. Stahl, Singapore and Fontainebleau (France)
Mark E. Mendenhall, Signal Mountain, Tennessee (USA)

References

Cooper, C. L., and Gregory, A. (eds.) (2000). *Advances in Mergers and Acquisitions*, Vol. 1. New York: JAI Press.

Hitt, M. A., Harrison, J. J., and Ireland, R. D. (2001). *Mergers and Acquisitions: A Guide to Creating Value for Stakeholders*. Oxford: Oxford University Press.

Morosini, P. (1998). *Managing Cultural Differences: Effective Strategy and Execution Across Cultures in Global Corporate Alliances*. New York: Pergamon.

Pablo, A. L., and Javidan, M. (eds.) (2004). *Mergers and Acquisitions: Creating Integrative Knowledge*. Oxford: Blackwell.

Introductory Comments

Managing Culture and Human Resources in Mergers and Acquisitions: The CEO's Point of View

CARLOS GHOSN AND JEAN-PIERRE GARNIER

Carlos Ghosn, President and CEO, Nissan Motor Co., Ltd.

I have always believed that an alliance, merger, or acquisition—in fact, any corporate combination—is about partnership and trust rather than power and domination. This is particularly true for alliances such as the Renault–Nissan Alliance, but the premise also applies to mergers and most acquisitions. Academic scholars and most business analysts tend to view these business ventures only from financial and operational perspectives. They are often surprised when mergers struggle or even fail when, on paper, they seemed sure to succeed.

It is my view that success in these types of ventures is not simply a matter of making fundamental changes to a company's organization and operations. Of critical importance is the necessity to protect the company's identity and the self-esteem of its people. Those two goals—making changes and safeguarding identity—could easily come into conflict; pursuing them both entails a difficult, yet vital balancing act.

My experience with Nissan has reconfirmed my conviction that the dignity of people must be respected even as you challenge them to overturn deep-seated practices and traditions. The most fundamental challenge of any alliance or merger is cultural: If one does not believe anything can be learned from one's new partners, the venture is doomed to fail. In the final analysis, the only real asset any company has is its people, and people perform well only if they are motivated. People will not give their best efforts if they feel that their identity is being consumed by a greater force. If any partnership or merger is to succeed, it must respect the identities and self-esteem of all the people involved.

The task is elevated when bridging cultures. I have been asked, "Is Renault–Nissan 'bicultural'?" My reply is that our alliance is both global and multicultural. We are French and Japanese, certainly, but our corporate culture also includes American, Chinese, Brazilian, Mexican, and many other cultures. We are always evolving, always adapting, always pursuing synergies that will create value and improve our performance, based on our internal learning from one another. The ability to comprehend and leverage global and cross-cultural processes is a critical core competency for any large company. Cross-cultural exchange is an integral part of basic, sustainable performance.

In this book, Professors Stahl and Mendenhall, working with a distinguished team of academic scholars and business executives, have highlighted many of the sociocultural and human resource processes that are critical for alliances, mergers, or acquisitions to succeed. This book rejects simplistic analyses and, instead, explores the human and social paradoxes, complexities, and challenges that are inherent when two or more business systems integrate or collaborate with one another.

Each corporate combination or partnership has a singular history and context. While there are "how-to" recommendations contained within this book, the writings of the various scholars and executives wisely do not offer a recipe approach to managing alliances and mergers. In business, as in life, solutions to challenging problems rarely come from overly simplistic recipes or formulas. Even so, a careful reading of this book may allow a thoughtful executive to combine his own experience, his own values, and his understanding of the crucial variables associated with success in alliances, mergers, and acquisitions to construct an effective approach to his own situation. That alone makes this book a useful addition to any executive's library.

Jean-Pierre Garnier, CEO, GlaxoSmithKline

In any merger or acquisition, investment banks and equity analysts will provide you with a plethora of figures quantifying the synergistic strategic benefits of the union. Yet, what determines whether a merger succeeds or fails is really its people. History has been, sadly, littered with far too many examples of failed acquisitions or mergers that did not create value for the companies involved. What lessons can we draw from them and how can we avoid this?

GlaxoSmithKline (GSK) has been fortunate in the sense that we have had a heritage of having managed a series of alliances and mergers. Each of these occasions has represented an opportunity for us to learn and improve. Perhaps most influential to our learning process were the two major successful mergers of Glaxo with Wellcome in 1995 and SmithKline with Beecham in 1989. One big lesson—build a truly new company that is different from either of its predecessors. After all, we can hardly hope to build a dynamic new company if we were duplicates of each other.

Thus, one of the key issues I faced with the GlaxoSmithKline merger was to have employees thinking and behaving as GSK people and not Glaxo people or SmithKline people. We had to decide and collectively answer some very fundamental questions from the start. Why did we exist as a business? How did we work and treat each other as colleagues? Where were we going as a business in the future? How were we going to get there? With input and in consultation with their various departments, the Corporate Executive Team (CET) did a remarkable job in distilling the essence of what the new GSK stood for and what our vision and guiding principles were. However, these principles would have remained little more than words unless each member of the GSK family adopted them and decided to act accordingly.

How then to win the buy-in of our people? In a diverse company with far-flung offices all around the world and more than one hundred thousand employees, this is certainly no easy task. Yet, there are some commonalities, upon which we focused our actions. Most people want to belong to a great organization. They want to belong to a company that is determined to play a leadership role. The merger of GlaxoWellcome and SmithKlineBeecham would create an entity with a combination of R&D excellence, unmatched marketing strength, and financial power to lead the industry. GSK would provide tremendous potential for society and if successful, an end product of great significance. This was something that everyone understood and it served to energize our people and create excitement for the new company. More importantly, employees would get a chance to participate in the process of executing the winning game plan that was being created.

Yet, this alone was not sufficient. In order to bring life to our values and principles, they had to be made real and human. Take for example, one of the key elements of the GSK spirit—performance with integrity. What did this really mean? I took it upon myself to describe this in a video communicated to all GSK employees. Performance with integrity for GSK meant not taking shortcuts and pride in the way we generated profits for shareholders. When faced with a choice of either maximizing profits for the company or to do good, we would choose to do good first. Of course, words had to be backed up by action in order to be credible and to demonstrate that we walk our talk. GSK was one of the earliest believers in providing low-cost drugs to poor, developing nations. We also committed ourselves to an ambitious program, in conjunction with the WHO and regional institutions, to eradicate lymphatic filiariasis, a grievous disease afflicting the poor in underdeveloped countries, as a public health problem by 2020.

Another issue common with mergers and acquisitions is a lack of continuity. Very often, different teams are involved with the initial target acquisition stage, the deal making stage, and the postintegration stage. Companies tend to spend a lot of time at each of these stages but what commonly happens is that not enough attention is spent on the interfaces between them. Sometimes, the team in charge of postmerger integration has only a vague idea of what the target acquisition team had in mind when deciding on the merger. It is the responsibility of those in charge to ensure that the key messages are not lost in the frenzied activity of every merger. This is something that Sir Richard Sykes and I paid a lot of attention to—staying aligned and forging a common vision, then trying to realize that vision and bringing everyone else along to understand it.

I am pleased to see a group of such distinguished academic scholars team up with business executives to discuss the sociocultural and human resource processes involved in integrating merged or acquired firms. Professors Stahl and Mendenhall have done a superb job putting together a book that focuses on one of the most important yet often neglected areas in the field of mergers and acquisitions, that of creating a common corporate culture and optimizing human capital, key assets that are essential for companies to create and maintain competitive advantage. It is way past time for a book such as this to be on the market.

MERGERS AND ACQUISITIONS

PART I *Introduction*

1 Sociocultural Integration in Mergers and Acquisitions

GÜNTER K. STAHL, MARK E. MENDENHALL, AMY L. PABLO, AND MANSOUR JAVIDAN

Mergers and acquisitions (M&A) have become an increasingly popular strategy for achieving corporate growth and diversification, with M&A activity in the 1990s smashing all existing records, both in terms of the number of transactions and the size of the deals. The worldwide value of M&A increased from US$462 billion in 1990 to over US$3.5 trillion in 2000 (Thomson Financial Services, 2001). Even though this unprecedented wave of M&A has subsided in the early 2000s as the global economy cooled off and slid into recession, the M&A volume worldwide remains at a much higher level than existed ten years ago. Most business observers believe that M&A activity will intensify again and more mega-deals can be expected in the long term (Evans, Pucik, and Barsoux, 2002).

Despite their popularity and strategic importance, the performance of most M&A has been disappointing (Datta and Puia, 1995; Hunt, 1990; Sirower, 1997). At the same time, companies such as General Electric, British Petroleum, and Cisco have been very successful in managing acquisitions. Although there is little doubt that M&A, particularly those that reach across borders, are difficult to manage, the key factors for M&A success and the reasons why so many M&A fail remain poorly understood.

The Importance of Sociocultural Integration

Over the recent decades, M&A research has branched along several paths:

- *Strategic Management* which examines strategic motives and drivers of M&A and their implications for merger performance. Bower (2002) identified five distinct strategic reasons for M&A: to reduce capacity, to implement geographic expansion, to extend product lines, to acquire R&D capability, and to exploit emerging convergence of industries. Bower suggested that different strategic drivers require different types of postmerger implementation plans and can have widely different outcomes. Other authors have suggested that mergers can take place to enhance learning (Ghoshal, 1987) and to gain access to improved resources (Barney, 1991). Acquiring firms may use M&A to achieve synergies in cost efficiency (Walter and Barney, 1990) or to increase their market power (Trautwein, 1990). Various authors have examined the consequences of various strategic drivers for the performance of the merger and have reached sometimes conflicting results (Lubatkin, 1983; Seth, 1990; Singh and Montgomery, 1987; Sirower, 1997).

– *Capital Markets* perspective which looks at M&A performance using stock-market-based measures. In this approach, M&A are viewed as investments that require a financial return for the purchaser rather than a windfall for shareholders of the acquired firm. Stock-market-based measures (so called "event studies") are commonly used to measure cumulative abnormal returns (CARs) a short time after announcement of the M&A in an effort to measure how markets perceive the deal (Chatterjee, 1992; Jensen, 1986; Seth, 1990). Sirower (1997), in a review of such studies, showed that the average acquirer's CAR measured over a two-day period ranges from −0.8 to −3.35 percent. He further showed that anywhere from 59 to 79 percent of acquiring firms have negative CARs. Datta and Puia (1995) also showed that acquiring firms in cross-border mergers do not create value for their shareholders. A few other studies, however, show more positive results. Shelton (1988) found that the acquisitions that provide access to new markets create shareholder value. Lubatkin (1987) concluded that mergers lead to permanent gains in value for both acquiring and target firms. Jensen (1988) estimated that during the period 1977–86, buying firm shareholders enjoyed at least $50 billion in gains while shareholders of acquired companies enjoyed gains totaling $346 billion.

– *Economic Performance* which examines accounting-based measures of M&A performance to measure relatively long-term performance of mergers. The literature typically uses cumulative excess returns (CERs) over industry average returns over a period of time to assess the success of M&A preferring realized profit measures over market expectation measures. As an alternative to using abnormal stock prices, in this approach the cumulative excess returns are based on such accounting-based measures like realized profit or additional sales after the acquisition date. Healy, Palepu, and Ruback (1997) assessed the operating cash flow of the acquiring firms in fifty of the largest U.S. industrial acquisitions from 1979 to 1984. They showed that on average, acquiring firms generated sufficient returns to cover the premiums paid. Morosini, Shane, and Singh (1998) used growth rate in sales over the two-year period following the acquisition in a sample of fifty-two Italian-based targets or acquiring firms. They showed that the bigger the cultural distance between the two merging companies, the higher the sales growth rate. Hitt et al. (1991) examined the impact of mergers on the R&D investment and output of the acquiring firms and concluded that acquisitions have a negative effect on both.

– *Organizational Theory* which seeks to understand the processes by which previously autonomous entities are combined into a cohesive whole. The main focus of this line of work is how the two companies integrate their structures, systems, and cultures to achieve synergy. The underlying premise of this literature is that integration is the mediating mechanism between acquisition potential and acquisition performance (Larsson, 1989; Pablo, 1994). Larsson's discussion of synergies points out the delicate balance that must be achieved in integration (Larsson, 1989). The concept of synergy, ubiquitous in acquisition literature, relates to the effect of the whole being greater than the sum of its parts (Fuller, 1975; Hitt, Harrison, and Ireland, 2001) as a result of interdependencies between the parts (Porter, 1985). The acquisition's impact on the organization and the people in it can occur in a number of ways including organizational structures and working relationships (Shanley and Correa, 1992), disruption of culture (Nahavandi and Malekzadeh, 1988; Sales and Mirvis, 1984), career disruption (Jick, 1979; Walsh, 1989), and loss of status in the organization (Hambrick and Cannella, 1993). Pablo and Javidan (2002) provide a conceptual framework and a detailed case study of how cultural differences can have dysfunctional effects on the merger. Napier (1989), Schweiger and Goulet (2000), and Schweiger and Walsh (1990) provide comprehensive reviews of organizational issues in M&A. For example, it has been shown that turnover of the top management of the acquired firm is usually higher than expected (Walsh, 1989) and is generally disruptive to performance (Hambrick and Canella, 1993).

– *Human Resources* (HR) focus that has emphasized psychological, communication, and leadership issues in M&A. The underlying theme in this stream of work is that the "human side" of mergers and acquisitions (Buono and Bowditch, 1989) is "frequently neglected by managers' intent on doing the deal and realizing operational synergies" (Birkinshaw, Bresman, and Hakanson, 2000, p. 398). Researchers have examined the impact of the communication and managerial actions and decisions on the success of mergers (Bastien, 1987; Cartwright and Cooper, 1993; Greenwood, Hinings, and Brown, 1994; Haspeslagh and Jemison, 1991; Hunt, 1990; Sales and Mirvis, 1984; Schweiger and DeNisi, 1991; Shrivastava, 1986). Recent writings by Morosini (1998) and Marks and Mirvis (1998) demonstrate similar ideas about CEO leadership, focusing on elements inherent in the transformational leadership paradigm. For example, Marks and Mirvis (1998) discuss the importance of positive vision coupled with an articulation of the principles, values, and priorities behind an M&A. Other authors have focused their attention on the stress accompanying an M&A (Birkinshaw, Bresman, and Hakanson, 2000; Cartwright and Cooper, 1993; Schweiger and DeNisi, 1991). They note that stress in an M&A is due to such factors as a highly uncertain future, job insecurity, a loss of personal control or autonomy, and simply the notion that change in and of itself is stressful, whether or not that change will ultimately evolve into something for the better. Larsson and Finkelstein (1999) suggest that the greatest stress and resistance should logically be seen on the part of the acquired company. It may suffer from the "merger syndrome" in which its employees "mourn a corporate death" and are more likely to not view change as a positive event (Marks and Mirvis, 1983, p. 41).

In general, the diverse streams of research described above have not been well integrated to enhance our understanding of what contributes to M&A success. Attempts to explain M&A success and failure have traditionally focused on strategic and financial factors, which reflect existing M&A practice where special emphasis is placed on the strategic and financial goals of the transaction, while the sociocultural implications are often ignored.

From a managerial perspective, the central question is one of M&A success and how value is created. Following the M&A transaction, some degree of interorganizational integration is necessary to achieve the intent of the deal. However, sociocultural integration, which we define as the combination of groups of people possessing established norms, beliefs, and values, can lead to sharp interorganizational conflict as different organizational cultures, managerial viewpoints, HR management systems, and other aspects of organizational life come into contact.

Recent work (Birkinshaw, Bresman, and Hakanson, 2000) taking a more fine-grained view of integration breaks the post-M&A integration process into subprocesses reflecting task integration and human integration. This approach suggests that overall effective integration is an interactive process whereby necessary interdependencies between acquired and acquiring units build in a cyclical manner. Attempts at task integration without the lubrication of successful human integration results in only a satisficing solution, whereas human integration resulting in a sense of community and respect paves the way for the efficacious task integration that is the basis of the synergy sought through M&A. In other words, poor human integration will often block successful task integration, and task integration cannot be driven faster than success with human integration (Bower, 2002).

A Process Perspective on M&A Integration

The purpose of this book is to delineate the dynamics of the socio-cultural processes inherent in M&A, and to discuss their implications for management, with a particular focus on postcombination integration management. One of the basic premises of this book is that though the strategic and financial factors are important *conditioning factors* of the subsequent integration process, these factors can only predict the success of a merger or an acquisition if *integration process variables* are taken into consideration (Haspeslagh and Jemison, 1991; Hunt, 1990; Morosini, 1998; Pablo, Sitkin, and Jemison, 1996).

The authors of the chapters in this book argue that integration process variables such as the degree of cultural tolerance and sensitivity exhibited by the acquiring firm, the quality of reward and job security changes for the members of the acquired firm, the social climate surrounding the M&A, the amount and quality of communication, and the visionary leadership and trust-building capabilities of top management are of paramount importance to the postcombination integration success. Although the initial conditioning factors, such as buyer strategy, price paid, and initial organizational fit, form the upper bound on the degree of success that a combination can achieve, the management of the postcombination integration process will likely determine the extent to which that potential is realized (Pablo, Sitkin, and Jemison, 1996).

The chapters that follow thus focus attention on the "people" issues of integrating merging firms, presenting new findings, identifying gaps in the current research, and generating new insights into important sociocultural issues and how to manage them. This book is divided into five parts:

I   Introduction
II The Process of Sociocultural Integration in Mergers and Acquisitions
III The Management of Sociocultural Integration in Mergers and Acquisitions
IV Learning from Experience: Case Analyses of Sociocultural Processes in Mergers and Acquisitions
V   Lessons for Research and Practice

Part I. Introduction

The chapter that follows provides the overall context for the rest of the chapters in the book by integrating the strategy, finance, and HR literatures on M&A. In "Integration: The Critical Link in M&A Value Creation," Dave Schweiger and Robert Lippert focus on the importance of effective HR management for synergy creation through integration and, ultimately, the holy grail of value creation. They suggest that there are a number of HR activities that play a key role through the various stages of the M&A process, and that during the transaction, transition, and integration phases, HR practices are critical in many ways in the decisions that must be made to ensure value preservation and realization.

Part II. The Process of Sociocultural Integration in Mergers and Acquisitions

In this part, contributors take a process perspective by applying new frameworks to suggest how M&A leaders can effectively focus their actions on the problems and facilitating factors arising in the M&A process.

Current theories of acquisition performance take into account not only those factors that indicate the *potential* for value creation, but also the processes through which value is *actually* created as synergistic benefits come to be realized. In these works, writers have taken a more fine-grained and multilevel approach to understanding the dimensions of this paradigmatic view in order to elucidate our understanding of key variables and the relationships among them.

In this part's first chapter, Danna Greenberg, Harry Lane, and Keith Bahde alert us to the intricacies of learning in M&A relationships, particularly in multinational settings. Their contention in "Organizational Learning in Cross-Border Mergers and Acquisitions" is that learning throughout the M&A process is hampered by failures in information and knowledge flow caused by differences and misunderstandings throughout the phases of the acquisition process. The specific knowledge outcomes that are expected to generate synergies do not materialize and thus limited learning about the M&A process is gained.

In "Trust in Mergers and Acquisitions," Günter Stahl and Sim Sitkin suggest that trust building is a central element in the success or failure of M&A. This chapter emphasizes that just as trust *within* organizations enhances relationships, improves performance, and decreases negative manifestations within these organizational dimensions, trust is also of critical importance to maintaining relationships *between* organizations in an M&A context. Furthermore, in this chapter, the authors build a model that delineates the antecedents to mutual trust in M&A relationships.

Georg Schreyögg leads us to consider how we deal with the issue of corporate cultures in M&A situations. In raising this issue in "The Role of Corporate Cultural Diversity in Integrating Mergers and Acquisitions," the author suggests that our focus should not be on characteristics of a corporate culture, but rather on what occurs when two (or more) cultures are thrust together and forced to interact. Primarily, he raises the question of whether, and to what degree, cultural consistency is needed for success in M&A.

Stein Kleppestø uses the concept of social identity to explore the role of culture in M&A in his chapter, "The Construction of Social Identities in Mergers and Acquisitions." He argues that the literature on cultural issues in M&A errs in treating cultures as coherent substantive elements that are founded as a collectivity of views in each organization. Kleppestø rather argues that each organization consists of numerous individuals with individual self-identities that are socially and contextually produced and that help create meaning on both an individual and collective level. He proposes that sociocultural integration may not necessarily imply creating a unified cultural whole but perhaps is manifested by allowing space for different identities to emerge and coalesce.

The final chapter in this part by Ingmar Björkman, Janne Tienari, and Eero Vaara ("A Learning Perspective on Sociocultural Integration in Cross-National Mergers") provides insight into how and what managers take away from their various merger experiences, the performance effects of applying these learnings across various merger situations, and what factors influence the way in which the common features of the sociocultural aspects of mergers are dealt with.

Throughout these chapters, numerous ways in which the field's understanding of sociocultural processes in integrating M&A are advanced via a greater integration of extant models, application of new models, deeper exploration of recognized factors such as culture, enhanced appreciation of factors we have previously considered such as learning, and a realization of taken-for-granted factors such as the importance of trust.

Each chapter in this part, and in subsequent parts, is followed by an "Executive Commentary." We felt it important to listen to executives who have lived on the firing line of M&A and to seek out their perception regarding the intricacies of the sociocultural processes that occurred during their experience with M&A. Each executive was asked not necessarily to critique or respond to the chapter assigned to them, but to briefly share the insights that they have gained from their experience regarding the topic that the chapter treated. Each executive approached this task a bit differently, and we believe that their comments, observations, and insights add a balancing spice to the academic perspective of the scholars' writings in this book. Delightfully and a bit unexpectedly, the value of the work academic researchers do in this area is clearly affirmed by those on the front lines of M&A strategizing and implementation.

Part III. The Management of Sociocultural Integration in Mergers and Acquisitions

Current theories inclusive of both acquirer and acquiree influences on acquisition performance take into account not only those factors that indicate the *potential* for value creation, but also the processes through which value is *actually* created as synergistic benefits come to be realized. As Hitt, Harrison, and Ireland (2001) note with respect to achieving synergy in postacquisition integration, managerial actions are an essential foundation of the creation process. In this part, the chapters again reflect a diversity of levels of analysis and perspectives. Among these are leadership theories, valuation theories, communication processes, and a delineation of the ways managers can address issues of cultural fit or misfit in M&A processes.

In this part's first chapter, "Synergy Realization in Mergers and Acquisitions: A Co-Competence and Motivational Approach," Rikard Larsson uses a comparative case study approach to discover factors that distinguish between those M&A that achieve high synergy realization and those where synergy realization is low. Interestingly, it is the combination of strategic, organizational, and HR factors that result in low employee resistance that is so essential for synergy achievement. The "co-competence and motivational approach" to acculturation, communication, and career development proposed by Larsson provides a means of reducing employee resistance in M&A.

In "The Neglected Importance of Leadership in Mergers and Acquisitions," Sim Sitkin and Amy Pablo reflect on the fact that despite a general acknowledgment of how important leadership is to the M&A processes and performance, there remains a lack of serious scholarly or practitioner focused work that dissects what M&A leadership really is, and there is little clarity as to the ways leadership truly makes a difference. This chapter presents a model that proposes to provide a foundation for filling this gap in the M&A literature.

In Angelo DeNisi and Shung Jae Shin's chapter ("Psychological Communication Interventions in Mergers and Acquisitions"), the authors examine specific aspects of the management of sociocultural integration that can enhance the functioning of employees in their jobs *and* in their relationships with their new coworkers. They suggest that specific types of communication interventions are essential to the development of a psychological readiness for the new identity that is built in the postmerger organization.

In the concluding chapter of this part ("Developing a Framework for Cultural Due Diligence in Mergers and Acquisitions: Issues and Ideas"), Susan Cartwright and Simon McCarthy shift the reader's perspective on culture in M&A from the employee level (the focus of Part I) to the management level. From this perspective, cultural fit and compatibility are deemed to be desirable to avoid major obstacles due to the risk and severity of potential problems arising from cultural differences. "Gap analysis" is suggested as a means to assess how cultural fit affects the management of the integration process and M&A performance.

Throughout this part of the book, we are led to consider an approach to management of sociocultural integration in M&A that moves us beyond the traditional command and control focus of earlier researchers. Kitching (1967), for example, stressed the importance of change management in M&A to ensure adequate focus on gaining control in the postacquisition situation, specifically highlighting attentive management direction as fundamental to achieving strategic and operating fit in M&A. Further, integration has been conceptualized as a varying degree of boundary disruption initiated by the acquiring organization to create mechanisms within the acquired company that facilitate the achievement of parent company goals. This perspective on acquisition integration is one of administrative control, which focuses on integration as the use of formal authority mechanisms to coordinate the goal-directed activities of organizational subunits (March and Simon, 1958). However, the conceptualization of the management of sociocultural integration in M&A presented in this part of the book reflects a mutual adjustment view and suggests the variety of elements that must be attended to in this complex managerial process.

Part IV. Learning from Experience: Case Analyses of Sociocultural Processes in Mergers and Acquisitions

The cases in this part present some valuable, real-world lessons for M&A from a variety of national and industry contexts. The industries represented include high technology, automobile, construction, pharmaceuticals, and consumer products. The geographic coverage of case companies in the above industries is worldwide, reinforcing the global context of the challenges in sociocultural aspects of postcombination integration.

Saikat Chaudhuri presents in his case issues that relate to how companies can best retain, transfer, and apply the human value in an acquired high-technology firm to enable creation, manufacturing, and selling of products from the postacquisition organization. The sociocultural issue being faced here is one of human capital management in the acquisition context. How do we keep the resources that potential synergies motivating the acquisition were based on?

In the CNH Global case presented by Piero Morosini, value creation in global interorganizational relationships is addressed from a "social capabilities" perspective. This paradigm of leveraging social capital to increase success in organizational combinations again reflects the power of bringing a sociocultural focus to bear on understanding the source of value creation when joining companies across borders. Important questions raised here include the how and when of implementing this approach.

René Olie's contribution gives an in-depth look at cross-border mergers and some of the opportunities and challenges associated with them through the three case studies he has prepared. Through analysis of these cases, the importance of a number of key factors can be deduced: the dynamism and unpredictability of the process; the need for favorable initial conditions—including strategic fit; the criticality of effective postmerger integration incorporating attention to key sociocultural features such as national and organizational culture, identities, goals, and resources; competent leadership; and time for the development of trust and good will.

Torsten Kühlmann and Peter Dowling look inside one of the most publicized mergers in recent history, that of Daimler-Benz AG and Chrysler Corporation. As they take the reader on this fascinating ride, they encourage the consideration of questions of HR issues that emerged at different stages of the merger process. How these HR issues were handled and what part the HR function played in the merger process are variables that produce insights both for future research as well as for managers involved in M&A.

In their discussion of the partnering of Renault and Nissan, Harry Korine, Kazuhiro Asakawa, and Pierre-Yves Gomez relate how an effective relationship was ultimately built between these two unlikely partners to the benefit of both. These authors demonstrate how attention to sociocultural elements in a process that emphasizes early coordination and communication resulted in subsequent trust and collaboration for achieving the long-term strategic goals of the companies.

The final case study in this part brings us back to the issue of trust in M&A. Chei Hwee Chua, Hans-Peter Engeli, and Günter K. Stahl detail the story of what happened in the merger of Ciba and Sandoz to form the pharmaceutical giant Novartis. This "marriage made in heaven" got off to a good start but soon foundered on the rocks of various sociocultural issues, including the need to create commitment to a new identity and culture, rebuild employee trust, and establish HR policies and practices that were considered just and fair. This case analyzes what went wrong at various steps along the way, and how the organization was able to right itself through timely leadership and the implementation of suitable selection, reward, and career systems.

All of these cases provide a sense of the reality of the multidimensional issues that must be addressed as challenges that arise in situations of postmerger integration are identified and solutions are formulated. Again, these case examples give a greater understanding of what faces those "at ground zero" in M&A, and provide opportunities to assess how managers might have resolved the issues in more effective ways.

Part V. Lessons for Research and Practice

Although the psychological, social, and cultural issues involved in integrating merging or acquired firms have received considerable research attention in recent years, several important issues related to the postcombination integration process have been left unexplored. Günter Stahl, Mark Mendenhall, and Yaakov Weber discuss inconsistencies and paradoxes that emerged from prior research in this area, and illustrate that the sociocultural implications of M&A discussed in this book provide a rich foundational platform for further research efforts of organizational scholars.

In the last chapter of the book, the importance and role of cultural and HR processes are highlighted and clarified by Paul Evans and Vladimir Pucik, two international management scholars who possess a uniquely deep expertise in this discipline because of their academic and consulting experience, which has provided them with a keen understanding of the implications of M&A for organizations and their employees.

The chapters in this book address the critical issues involved in M&A management processes from rich, novel perspectives. In doing so, this book attempts to act as a catalyst for scholars who work in the field of M&A by providing them with a wider scope of theoretical understanding regarding the complexity of variables that influence long-term productivity and synergies in M&A.

References

Barney, J. B. (1991). Firm resources and sustained competitive advantage. *Journal of Management*, 17: 99–120.

Bastien, D. T. (1987). Common patterns of behavior and communication in corporate mergers and acquisitions. *Human Resource Management*, 26: 17–34.

Birkinshaw, J., Bresman, H., and Hakanson, L. (2000). Managing the post-acquisition integration process: How the human integration and task integration processes interact to foster value creation. *Journal of Management Studies*, 37(3): 395–425.

Bower, J. (2002). *When We Study M&A What Are We Learning?* Keynote address, M&A Summit 2002 Conference, Calgary, Alberta, Canada.

Buono, A. F., and Bowditch, J. L. (1989). *The Human Side of Mergers and Acquisitions*. San Francisco: Jossey-Bass.

Cartwright, S., and Cooper, C. L. (1993). The role of culture compatibility in successful organizational marriage. *Academy of Management Executive*, 7(2): 57–70.

Chatterjee, S. (1992). Sources of value in takeovers: Synergy or restructuring—Implications for target and bidder firms. *Strategic Management Journal*, 13: 267–86.

Datta, D. K., and Puia, G. (1995). Cross-border acquisitions: An examination of the influence of relatedness and cultural fit on shareholder value creation in U.S. acquiring firms. *Management International Review*, 35: 337–59.

Evans, P., Pucik, V., and Barsoux, J.-L. (2002). *The Global Challenge: Frameworks for International Human Resource Management*. New York: McGraw-Hill.

Fuller, R. B. (1975). *Synergetics*. New York: MacMillan.

Ghoshal, S. (1987). Global strategy: An organizing framework. *Strategic Management Journal*, 8: 425–40.

Greenwood, R., Hinings, C. R., and Brown, J. (1994). Merging professional service firms. *Organization Science*, 5: 239–57.

Hambrick, D. C., and Cannella, A. A. (1993). Relative standing: A framework for understanding departures of acquired executives. *Academy of Management Journal*, 36(4): 733–62.

Haspeslagh, P., and Jemison, D. B. (1991). *Managing Acquisitions: Creating Value Through Corporate Renewal*. New York: The Free Press.

Healy, P. M., Palepu, K. G., and Ruback, R. S. (1997). Which takeovers are profitable? Strategic or financial? *Sloan Management Review*, 38(4): 45–57.

Hitt, M. A., Harrison, J. S., and Ireland, R. D. (2001). *Mergers and Acquisitions: A Guide to Creating Value for Stakeholders*. New York: Oxford.

Hitt, M. A., Hoskisson, R. E., Ireland, R. D., and Harrison, J. S. (1991). Effects of acquisitions on R&D inputs and outputs. *Academy of Management Journal*, 34(3): 693–706.

Hunt, J. W. (1990). Changing pattern of acquisition behaviour in takeovers and the consequences for acquisition processes. *Strategic Management Journal*, 11: 69–77.

Jensen, M. (1986). Agency costs of free cash flows, corporate finance and takeovers. *The American Economic Review*, 76: 323–29.

Jensen, M. C. (1988). Takeovers: Their causes and consequences. *Journal of Economic Perspectives*, 2(1): 21–48.

Jick, T. D. (1979). *Process and Impacts of a Merger: Individual and OrganizationalPerspectives*. Unpublished doctoral dissertation, Cornell University.

Kitching, J. (1967). Why do mergers miscarry? *Harvard Business Review*, 45: 84–107.

Larsson, R. (1989). Organizational integration of mergers and acquisitions. In *Lund Studies in Economics and Management 7*. Lund, Sweden: Lund University Press.

Larsson, R., and Finkelstein, S. (1999). Integrating strategic, organizational, and human resource perspectives on mergers and acquisitions: A case survey of synergy realization. *Organization Science*, 10: 1–26.

Lubatkin, M. (1983). Merger and the performance of the acquiring firm. *Academy of Management Review*, 8: 218–25.

Lubatkin, M. (1987). Merger strategies and stockholder value. *Strategic Management Journal*, 8: 39–53.

March, J. G., and Simon, H. A. (1958). *Organizations*. New York: John Wiley & Sons.

Marks, M. L., and Mirvis, P. H. (1983). Situational and personal factors influencing employee response to corporate merger. Paper presented at the annual convention of the American Psychological Association, Anaheim, CA.

Marks, M. L., and Mirvis, P. H. (1998). *Joining Forces: Making One Plus One Equal Three in Mergers, Acquisitions, and Alliances*. San Francisco: Jossey-Bass.

Morosini, P. (1998). *Managing Cultural Differences: Effective Strategy and Execution Across Cultures in Global Corporate Alliances*. New York: Pergamon.

Morosini, P., Shane, S., and Singh, H. (1998). National cultural distance and cross-border acquisition performance. *Journal of International Business Studies*, 29(1): 137–58.

Nahavandi, A., and Malekzadeh, A. (1988). Acculturation in mergers and acquisitions. *Academy of Management Review*, 13: 79–90.

Napier, N. K. (1989). Mergers and acquisitions, human resource issues and outcomes: A review and suggested typology. *Journal of Management Studies*, 26: 271–89.

Pablo, A. L. (1994). Determinants of acquisition integration level: A decision-making perspective. *Academy of Management Journal*, 37: 803–36.

Pablo, A. L., and Javidan, M. (2002). Thinking of a merger...Do you know their risk propensity profile? *Organizational Dynamics*, 30(3): 206–22.

Pablo, A. L., Sitkin, S. B., and Jemison, D. B. (1996). Acquisition decision-making processes: The central role of risk. *Journal of Management*, 22: 723–46.

Porter, M. E. (1985). *Competitive Advantage: Creating and Sustaining Superior Performance*. New York: The Free Press.

Sales, A. L., and Mirvis, P. H. (1984). When cultures collide: Issues in acquisition. In Kimberly and Quinn (eds.), *Managing Organizational Transitions*. Homewood, IL: Richard D. Irwin, Inc.

Schweiger, D. M., and DeNisi, A. S. (1991). Communication with employees following a merger: A longitudinal field experiment. *Academy of Management Journal*, 34: 110–35.

Schweiger, D. M., and Goulet, P. K. (2000). Integrating mergers and acquisitions: An international research review. *Advances in Mergers and Acquisitions*, 1: 61–91.

Schweiger, D. M., and Walsh, J. P. (1990). Mergers and acquisitions: An interdisciplinary view. *Research in Personnel and Human Resource Management*, 8: 41–107.

Seth, A. (1990). Value creation in acquisitions: A re-examination of performance issues. *Strategic Management Journal*, 11: 99–115.

Shanley, M. T., and Correa, M. E. (1992). Agreement between top management teams and expectations for post-acquisition performance. *Strategic Management Journal*, 13(4): 245–67.

Shelton, L. M. (1988). Strategic business fits and corporate acquisition: Empirical evidence. *Strategic Management Journal*, 9: 279–87.

Shrivastava, P. (1986). Postmerger integration. *Journal of Business Strategy*, 7: 65–76.

Singh, H., and Montgomery, C. A. (1987). Corporate acquisition strategies and economic performance. Strategic Management Journal, 8(4): 377–86.

Sirower, M. (1997). *The Synergy Trap*. New York: The Free Press.

Thomson Financial Services (2001). *The World Grows While Europe Slows*. Available at www.tfibcm.com, November 10.

Trautwein, F. (1990). Merger motives and merger prescriptions. *Strategic Management Journal*, 11: 283–95.

Walsh, J. P. (1989). Doing a deal: Merger and acquisition negotiations and their impact upon target company top management turnover. *Strategic Management Journal*, 10: 307–22.

Walter, G. A., and Barney, J. B. (1990). Research notes and communications management objectives in mergers and acquisitions. *Strategic Management Journal*, 11: 79–86.

2   Integration
The Critical Link in M&A Value Creation

DAVID M. SCHWEIGER AND ROBERT L. LIPPERT

Time and time again, the word *synergy* has been used to justify a merger or an acquisition. In their zeal to sell the idea and the price paid to both shareholders and employees, senior leaders often talk about the numerous synergistic benefits that will accrue and how they will create value for all involved. The following example illustrates this point:

> We believe that the merger of Chrysler Corporation and Daimler-Benz AG to form DaimlerChrysler is a historical step that will offer Daimler-Benz shareholders exciting perspectives. In addition to participating in the growth of two very profitable automobile companies, the merger offers the opportunity to benefit from the additional earnings potential that we believe will be generated by the merged activities of the company. We have already identified opportunities to increase sales, to create new markets for DaimlerChrysler, to reduce purchasing costs and to realize economies of scale. We are well positioned to capitalize on these opportunities to increase the earnings power of DaimlerChrysler AG. In the short term, we see synergies of $1.4 billion that we expect to more than double in the medium term. Even beyond that, given the creativity and inventiveness of our teams, we expect to be able to identify substantial additional benefits as the integration process accelerates.[1]
>
> *Jurgen E. Schrempp, Chairman and CEO, Daimler-Benz AG*
> *Robert J. Eaton, Chairman and CEO Chrysler Corporation*

Yet, in spite of such optimistic pronouncements, both practical experience and research evidence clearly demonstrate that most mergers and acquisitions (M&A) have not lived up to the financial expectations of those transacting them.[2] Clearly, they do not add any additional value for the buying company's shareholders. An excellent example of this is the merger between America Online (AOL) and Time Warner. Touted as a marriage made in heaven, this merger was going to be the first to capture the synergies inherent in merging content (Time Warner) with Internet access (AOL).

> The deal has potential synergies that make some observers drool.... At that time what synergy apparently meant was that the gathering of many media properties and distribution platforms was, by definition a source of awesome power. With CNN, Time Inc. magazines like Sports Illustrated, and Looney Tunes characters all "linked" to AOL's millions of subscribers, well something wonderful was bound to result.[3]

The merger has thus far been a disappointment. It has been noted that many synergies were overestimated and others could not be achieved. Questions have also arisen whether there was a real opportunity to cross-sell Time Warner products through the AOL distribution network. Unfortunately, to satisfy the government, Time Warner promised to open its cable lines to competitor's of AOL, thus mitigating exclusive distribution.

Are M&A doomed to fail? Are there actions that executives can take to ensure that they succeed? Many reasons have been advanced to explain the dismal M&A results. They have been documented in a number of authoritative sources. Reasons have included inaccurate valuations, inflated market multiples, poor due diligence, over optimism, exaggerated synergies, overpayment, and failed integration. Although each reason has merit, it is the interrelationship among them that ultimately determines whether value is created or lost. In this vein, it is the purpose of this chapter to illustrate the relationship among valuation, pricing, intended synergies, integration, and thus value creation (see Figure 2.1). Particular focus will be given to integration and human resource (HR) practices in the successful realization of synergies. We begin by discussing what we mean by value.

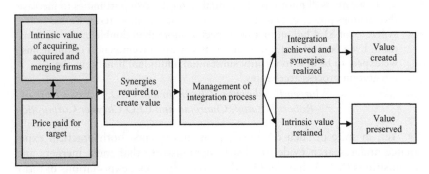

FIGURE **2.1 M&A Value Creation**

Perspectives on Intrinsic Value

Value is a function of cash flow. Whether you are investing in a performance management system, consciously growing inventory in anticipation of increasing market demand, or making an acquisition to expand geographically, successful strategies generate cash flow above and beyond what was invested. For a strategy to truly create value, it must produce more cash flow on a risk-adjusted basis than that which could be achieved by investing in the next best investment alternative of similar risk. Consequently, value is dependent upon the future cash flows generated by the investment and the risk associated with these future cash flows.

Discounted cash flow models are built upon the fundamental belief that the intrinsic value of an investment is the present value of future free cash flows.[4] Present value is determined by estimating cash flows associated with the acquisition strategy over some reasonable period of time (for example, five years), calculating a terminal value, and then discounting these two elements back to the present using a required return consistent with the risk undertaken. The required return, or discount factor, may be the weighted average cost of capital of the acquiring firm, the firm being acquired, a combination of the two, or a higher return if warranted by the risk factors and characteristics of the transaction.

From a financial economist's perspective, value is created when the return on the investment exceeds the required return. As the majority of M&A transactions employ a discounted cash flow model,[5] value creation would be defined as a positive net present value from the investment. Value destruction occurs when the return on the investment is less than the required return, or the net present value is negative. Value is maintained when the return on the investment is equal to the required return. This result would imply a net present value equal to zero and an investment that met the expectations of the investor. These definitions of value and the simplicity of the discounted cash flow approach result in a valuation methodology dependent upon three key factors: (1) the forecasted free cash flow, (2) the estimated terminal value, and (3) the risk-appropriate required return.[6] As there is uncertainty in each of these factors, it is important that multiple valuations be calculated under a series of scenarios and assumptions to arrive at a realistic valuation. This approach also highlights the relative importance of various assumptions surrounding cash flows attributable to specific synergies.

Distinguishing Between Price and Value

The price paid for a target and its intrinsic value to a particular acquirer can be quite different. Pricing of M&A is driven by a number of tangible and intangible factors, and it may or may not be consistent with value as defined above. Perceived synergies, supply and demand, negotiation position, emotions, hubris, market conditions, and other factors influence the price of the transaction. Throughout much of the 1990s, many transactions occurred at prices that were greatly in excess of what discounted cash flow models using reasonable assumptions could justify. Market measures of valuation based on comparable transactions (for example, price-earnings multiples and market-book ratios) reflect what companies have been sold for in the marketplace, not what a particular target may be worth to a specific acquirer.[7] Exorbitant multiples and inflated pricing often result in the acquiring company exaggerating potential synergies.[8] This exaggeration creates unrealistic expectations and essentially commits the integration team to a doomed strategy of trying to capture cash flows that do not exist. Therefore, although realizing synergies in terms of tangible cash savings or cash generation creates value, flawed pricing limits the success of even the most effectively executed integration strategies.

The fundamental driver of value in M&A is the stream of free cash flows that the target and/or combined firms will produce after the combination is completed. Target firms recognize this potential value and attempt to extract a premium from the acquiring firm that approximates the present value of the improved cash flow stream that results from realizing synergies. Consequently, value creation, destruction, and maintenance are driven by the price paid relative to the intrinsic value of the target and the degree to which synergies are realized. Under perfect integration conditions where all identified synergies are realized, value creation, destruction, and maintenance would accrue to the target and acquiring firms as illustrated in the four scenarios below.

1. If the target is successful in negotiating a premium equal to the present value of the cash flow improvements, then value creation would accrue to the target firm but not to the acquiring shareholders.
2. If the target is successful in negotiating a premium greater than the present value of the cash flow improvements, then value creation would accrue to the target firm and the acquiring firm would suffer value destruction.
3. If the target firm negotiates a premium less than the present value of the cash flow improvements, then both the acquiring and target shareholders have an opportunity to benefit from value creation.
4. If the target firm negotiates a price that is less than its stand-alone value, then value creation would accrue to the acquiring firm and the target firm would suffer value destruction.

These four scenarios demonstrate that, from an acquirer's perspective, the execution of a well-designed integration process that captures all forecasted synergies is absolutely critical to ensuring value maintenance (scenario 1), minimizing value destruction (scenario 2), or maximizing value creation (scenarios 3 and 4). Only in the rare instance when a target is acquired at a discount to its intrinsic value (scenario 4) does any deviation from perfect integration result in value creation for the acquiring firm. These scenarios illustrate the importance of understanding the strategic intent of the acquisition, clearly defining the expected synergies, and executing a comprehensive integration process focused on delivering forecasted cash flows.

Identifying the Sources of Synergy

As the majority of the integration execution takes place after the merger or acquisition has been legally completed, the burden of value creation, maintenance, or destruction falls onto the process of realizing the cash flows associated with specific synergies that were identified in the valuation process. The likelihood of capturing the forecasted cash flows is dependent upon the type of synergy. Those synergies that are most easily identified, quantified, and captured are often related to redundancies in personnel, facilities, and distribution channels. Synergies associated with cross-selling new or complementary products and tapping alternative distribution channels are more challenging to capture and measure. This was illustrated in a recent review of the HP–Compaq merger. A *Business Week*[9] article stated that "The cost-cutting looks doable, but other synergies may be more elusive than expected." Although HP and Compaq employees reportedly spent more than 1,000,000 hours on planning the integration of the two companies prior to closing, analysts forecasted revenue losses to be as much as twice as large as the combined company had forecasted only weeks earlier.

Essentially, there are four basic categories of synergy: cost reductions, revenue enhancements, increased market power, and intangibles. Reducing costs is the most reliable way to realize cash flow from synergies. Fixed cost reductions are typically achieved through the elimination of redundant personnel in support areas, sales and administration, headquarters reductions, a reduction in fixed assets, increased utilization of existing assets, distribution optimization, and overall economies of scale. Variable costs can be reduced through increased productivity and increased purchasing power.

Enhancing revenue growth opportunities is one of the most cited but least successful synergies put forth by companies in the midst of an acquisition or merger. These revenue growth initiatives typically surround cross-selling opportunities of new or complementary products and services through sales organizations or distribution channels that call upon different geographic regions and customers. The success of this strategy is inherently dependent upon the degree to which markets demand these diverse products and services.

Market power synergies accrue to firms that survive a market consolidation. This type of synergy is common in industries or markets suffering from long-term overcapacity, deeply deflated margins, and diminishing opportunities for organic growth. Market power may provide opportunities for increasing price, more favorable terms for the seller, or increased negotiating power over suppliers.

Intangible synergies encompass everything else that has not been previously addressed. They typically are difficult to quantify and are even more difficult to realize. Intangibles such as brand name and knowledge management are not only difficult to capture but are difficult to transfer across organization and geographic extensions.

The success of a company realizing multiple synergies lies in the management's ability to define and quantify what the synergies are and devise a concrete strategy to realize the cash flows associated with them. Successful integration plans must prioritize synergies in terms of impact and achievability to ensure that the highest impact synergies with the greatest probability of success receive the most attention. Similarly, negative synergies (for example, defection of key employees and customers, redundant facilities personnel, and assets; unnecessary cannibalization of existing market share with lower margin products; poor morale) must be managed to minimize value leakage and destruction.

Standard Integration Approaches

The amount of synergy available in any merger or acquisition is dependent upon the size and scale of the participating companies as well as the strategic intent of the acquirer. Owing to the nature of the different types of synergies, each one has a varying probability of success, a different level of impact, and necessitates a different level of integration. The integration method will vary with the strategic intent of the acquisition, the synergies to be captured, and the types of assets and personnel involved. The following is a framework that classifies the level of integration into four primary approaches.[10]

1. *Consolidation.* Consolidation is the most invasive approach in terms of integrating the cultures, processes, functions, and activities of separate entities into one fully consolidated organization.

2. *Standardization.* Standardization is less invasive and takes a best-practice approach to organizing operations and processes. Formal plans and procedures ensure that skills, processes, performance management systems, and so on are transferred across acquired or merged operations. This approach may benefit from some immediate cost reductions and long-term

revenue generation synergies, but relies more on transferring knowledge and best practices across the combined entities.

3. *Coordination.* Coordination of functions and activities attempts to blend the existing and acquired methods of business in a noninvasive manner. There is minimal standardization, but a general strategy of consistent and open communication between the two companies is combined with consolidated financial reporting and treasury management. This coordination approach is consistent with a conglomerate or holding company system that achieves synergies mainly through cheap sources of capital, management depth and breadth, and occasionally cost reductions or cross-selling synergies. Berkshire Hathaway and Tyco International employ this integration approach.

4. *Intervention.* Intervention requires immediate changes in systems, management, and/or processes to correct an undesirable or entity-threatening situation. This approach is very invasive and must be managed quickly and carefully to avoid immediate value destruction. It reflects a focused turnaround strategy that has a high potential return.

Linking Strategic Objectives, Synergies, and Integration

M&A represent growth strategies. Just as firms attempt to grow organically through launching new products, executing geographic expansions, deploying new distribution channels, and so on, M&A are undertaken to achieve specific strategic objectives. The more common strategic objectives include consolidating the market within a geographic area; extending or adding products, services, or technologies; entering a new geographic market; vertically integrating; and entering a new line of business. Although there are other strategic objectives that describe individual M&A strategies, most M&A can be categorized in one or more of the above groups, which are described below.

Consolidate the market within a geographic area. The ability to consolidate companies within a geographic area has the potential to increase purchasing power, eliminate redundant overhead expenses, increase utilization of fixed assets, improve pricing power, and lead to other economies of scale. This consolidation often involves rolling up a fragmented market, acquiring competitors, and taking capacity out of the market.[11] These synergies are most fully captured through high levels of organizational consolidation, standardization, and coordination.

The paper industry in the United States has consolidated in large part due to overcapacity. Larger organizations acquired smaller regional facilities with the intent of removing capacity from the marketplace in hopes of improving pricing power. Warren Buffet, a long-time consolidator of businesses that reliably generate cash flow, continues to invest in the electric utility industry. His strategy is to consolidate companies in a deregulating industry, thus taking advantage of increased purchasing power, the opportunity of eliminating redundant overhead expenses, increasing the utilization of fixed assets, and achieving other economies of scale.

Extend or add products, services or technologies. The ability of an organization to increase its capabilities, product base, and service offerings provides critical drivers for growing free cash flow. Increased opportunities often arise from acquiring new skills and technologies that enhance current products. Although this strategy pursues synergies related to purchasing power, higher fixed asset utilization, and the elimination of redundant functions and overhead, the main focus is on increasing market presence and market share through revenue growth. This growth is usually achieved by filling new distribution channels with complementary products and services. Realizing the common synergies associated with extensions usually requires high levels of coordination and a reasonable degree of organizational consolidation and standardization.

IBM provides an excellent example of a company that has extended its service offerings to the point where it is now more of a consulting company than a hardware or software manufacturing concern. It continues to pursue this strategy and is in the midst of acquiring PricewaterhouseCooper Consulting for $3.5 billion that will bring IBM hundreds of new customers, high-margin consulting skills, and the opportunity to cross-sell new and complementary products and services through its soon-to-be combined distribution channels. IBM's clients will benefit from PricewaterhouseCooper's expertise in financial services, consumer products, and government issues to capitalize on existing business opportunities. PricewaterhouseCooper's customers will have access to IBM's research laboratories, financing operations, and outsourcing units. PepsiCo Inc. acquired Tropicana, SoBe, and Quaker Oats to expand its orange juice, new-age drink, and sports drink segments. PepsiCo's acquisition of Quaker Oats reduced cost by $400 million, well above the original estimate of $230; however, the elusive synergy of cross-selling products and tapping into new distribution channels has been disappointing.[12]

Enter a new geographic market. The strategy of extending the reach of a particular firm geographically leads to a number of tangible synergies and has been the approach of many of the roll-ups of fragmented industries (that are free of regulatory constraints) over the last several years. These types of M&A focus on the advantages of being able to serve a customer who has broad geographical reach, increased sales volume from new markets by providing complementary products, achieving improved economies of scale, and improved purchasing power and eliminating redundant costs.[13] Very little consolidation typically occurs in these acquisitions but high levels of standardization and coordination are the norm; however, it is highly dependent upon the extent to which regional differences impact the service or product being delivered.

Tool rental companies, lawn care companies, funeral homes, hospitals, banks, security monitoring companies, and numerous other businesses were once dominated by one- or two-location companies. These industries are now dominated by national companies that have consolidated hundreds or even thousands of companies under one umbrella. The purchasing-power strategy has been strongly emphasized in the tool rental, funeral home, and hospital roll-ups. The suppliers to these firms would likely attest to the purchasing-power pressure they have endured. In a different approach, the security monitoring business has successfully reduced fixed cost per customer to almost zero by consolidating call and monitoring centers, combining support functions, and transferring best practices across a national network of regional centers.

Integrate. Vertical integration involves acquiring up or down the supply chain. This type of M&A is typically undertaken to either guarantee control over critical resources or to acquire an attractive source of growth opportunities. This approach tends to pursue cost reductions and enhanced customer service via better control of the supply chain and increased purchasing power. It attempts to improve profitability by reducing the cost of support functions, improving product development and manufacturing interfaces, and eliminating the costs of maintaining relationships with external vendors and customers. This strategy also attempts to take existing products and services through new channels or customer bases to enhance revenue and profitability. These acquisitions usually result in little consolidation or standardization but capitalize on close coordination. Automobile manufacturers owning car rental companies, Disney owning ABC, and public utilities owning natural gas companies all represent strategies where the intention was to gain control of additional portions of the supply chain.

Royal Dutch Petroleum's subsidiary, Shell Oil, recently acquired Pennzoil-QuakerState, the largest producer of motor oil. This vertical acquisition, which includes over 2000 Jiffy Lube oil-change centers, is consistent with Shell's parent company's strategy to acquire a company that complements its lubricant and oil-products businesses and Shell's gas station chain. There has been significant vertical integration at the other end of this supply chain as well. The Venezuelan oil company PDVSA was uncomfortable with the long-term contracts common in the marketplace, and so it acquired Citgo to gain control of a source for refining and distribution of its heavy crude oil.

Segments of the automobile manufacturing supplier market have implemented the vertical integration strategy as a means of survival in coping with automobile manufacturers' demands for annual price reductions of 5 percent or more. Several tier-one and tier-two suppliers have merged in order to build multicomponent modules for automakers. Lear Corp., which was an automotive seating company in the early 1990s, has since made seventeen acquisitions that have enabled it to provide complete automotive interiors. Lear now produces and delivers higher quality automobile interiors at a lower cost than the automobile manufacturers can. This acquisition strategy has enabled Lear to quadruple revenue, increase profitability, expand supplier relationships, and increase its buying power among its current suppliers.

Enter a new line of business. In the 1960s and 1970s many M&A involved companies entering new lines of business that resulted in large-scale conglomerates. Justifications for entering new lines of business include eliminating redundant staff in support roles, lowering the overall cost of capital for the organization because of the portfolio effect, and occasionally finding cross-selling opportunities via diverse distribution channels. Most of these acquisitions rely on strong and efficient holding company that provides cheap capital and deep bench strengths of management talent. In achieving the synergies associated with this acquisition strategy, virtually no consolidation or standardization will take place except possibly in the treasury and finance areas. Based on a strict definition of "new line of business," it is also unlikely that much coordination will occur across businesses because of the different operations, customer base, and distribution channels.

Berkshire Hathaway has relied on inexpensive capital and excellent management. It has recently further enhanced its ability to provide inexpensive capital to its portfolio of companies through its recent insurance acquisitions. Similarly, GE has been able to leverage the power of its financial arm to provide other businesses with a cheap source of capital while simultaneously developing a deep bench of capable managers that can be inserted in almost any line of business to implement the GE model of business management. Formerly powerful conglomerates, like ITT and Tyco International, relied on inexpensive financing as well. However, these conglomerates also attempted to capitalize on additional synergies (cost reductions, revenue enhancements, increased market power, and intangibles) to extract additional free cash flow from their acquisitions. It is difficult to determine whether the lack of execution on these other synergies contributed to the eventual downfall of these firms or whether their excessive risk-taking, use of too much debt, and aggressive accounting policies were to blame.

Pursuing multiple strategic objectives. Most of the mega-mergers of the late 1990s pursued multiple strategic objectives in their M&A strategies, adding both opportunity and complexity to the integration process and a company's ability to capturing specific synergies. Consequently, the integration plan must be even more defined and focused on the most critical synergies that must be realized to generate the cash flows forecast in the valuation process. Therefore, it is critical that the integration plan rank and prioritize activities designed to capture synergies with the greatest cash flow impact while paying particular attention to minimizing negative synergies that result in value destruction.

Many M&A continue to struggle. It is difficult (as an external party) to determine whether the original synergies were exaggerated or nonexistent, the execution plan was deficient, the price paid to value was too high, the strategic intent was misguided, or the integration was poorly executed; it is obvious that significant value was destroyed. By internally investigating the link between strategic objectives, price paid, synergies required, integration achieved, and synergies realized, we can determine where the value creation, destruction, and maintenance occurred. This process would not be an exercise in futility. It would represent a positive evolution in maximizing the probabilities of creating value in future M&A.

The Role of Integration and HR Practices in Value Creation[14]

Thus far, our discussion has focused on the importance of strategic objectives, synergies, and cash flow in value creation. Two issues are paramount in this discussion. First, efforts must be made to avoid the leakage of sources of cash flow (for example, customer defection loss of key technical people, unanticipated liabilities) that would not have occurred if the M&A had not taken place; that is, at a minimum the stand-alone value of each firm must be preserved. Second, the additional cash flows due to the synergies that were hoped for during the valuation, pricing, and negotiation process must be realized. It is our contention and that of others that the management of the integration process and HR practices play a critical role in value preservation and realization.[15]

To better understand the role of integration and human resource practices, it is useful to define the stages of the M&A process and illustrate how various integration and HR activities can play a valuable role during each stage. The M&A process can be characterized as three overlapping stages: transaction, transition, and integration. It is important to note that the stages are somewhat fluid and that due to information availability and access, some activities that should occur during an earlier stage may be deferred to a later stage. In the next section we will more specifically define each stage, with the objectives of and the integration and HR practices required for value preservation and realization during each stage.

Transaction Stage

Transaction characterizes the period where valuations, synergy estimations, pricing, due diligence, and negotiations take place. During this stage, the buyer or merging partners attempt to gather enough information on the other firm to decide whether to do the deal and the terms under which the deal will be consummated. It is a time where the presence of synergies and the organization and integration issues that will have to be managed to achieve them should begin to be assessed. It is a challenging time because a great deal of information is needed to make the assessments. It is also a time, however, where secrecy considerations, antitrust regulations, issues of trust, need for speed, and negotiation strategies may preclude access to such information. In a perfect world, access and cooperation would be complete. In practice, it varies greatly. Thus, a buyer or merger partner may have to rely on a combination of indirect sources of information (for example, public sources, consultants, customers, suppliers) and direct access to the company itself.

Objectives

During the transaction stage, there are four objectives that an acquirer or merger partner should focus on. These are

1. Gather and analyze information (that is, due diligence) to learn as much as possible about a target. In particular, the acquirer must decide whether the target and the deal make sense from four perspectives:
   a. *Strategic.* Will the deal allow the company to achieve some or all of its strategic objectives? Can enough synergies be documented to support the strategic objectives and justify the price being paid?
   b. *Financial.* Will the deal likely deliver the financial results expected? Are the cash flow and earnings forecasts accurate? Is the valuation model correct? Do we have an accurate assessment of the assets and liabilities?
   c. *Legal.* Do we understand all of the target's off-balance sheet liabilities and their impact? Have we complied with all laws and regulations?
   d. *Organizational.* Do we have an accurate assessment of the people and organizational cultures? Do the two organizations fit together enough to ensure that the deal can be integrated and synergies can be captured?
2. Negotiate the right price. Based on all the information gathered, the acquirer must not pay a price beyond what a target is worth. This requires accurate valuation and objectivity during the negotiation process.
3. Ensure that the behaviors of all acquirer personnel who come in contact with the target and the activities conducted during this stage create a constructive environment for successful integration and preserve the value of both the acquirer and the target.
4. Anticipate roadblocks that need to be managed for effective integration. These may include technical, political, or cultural issues.

Clearly, HR has a significant role to play in achieving these objectives. Below we will discuss key activities that contribute to their achievement.

Integration and HR Activities

There are four key activities that need to be managed during the transaction stage. These activities can have a direct impact on value preservation and realization. First, they provide insights on the value of a target firm or merger partner. Second, they lead to an understanding of the source of that value and its sustainability. Third, they identify those issues that must be managed for value to be preserved and synergies to be realized. These are as follows.

Detailing, Understanding, and Comparing HR Practices of the Buyer and the Target.[16] To the extent possible, HR organizations need to gather as much information as possible concerning the HR practices and employees of the combining companies. These include head counts and staffing, salaries, compensation and benefits, pension systems, training and development, labor relations, performance management systems, organizational cultures, and other HR functions. Such comparisons are typical for major acquirers such as GE and Cisco Systems.

The objective of this information is to understand any cost and liabilities associated with the merger or acquisition (for example, underfunded defined benefits plans) and any practices that might create integration roadblocks. Undetected liabilities may lead to unanticipated decrements in future cash flows and thus value leakage. Unanticipated roadblocks may either slow or prevent successful integration. The earlier such information can be collected the better. They may be severe enough that a deal should be killed, especially in cases where synergies are critical to its success.[17]

Differences in how HR activities are managed between combining firms give insights into challenges that will be faced during the integration. For example, differences in HR philosophies in compensation, training and development, benefits and the like may be a major source of conflict, especially in the case when one company's programs are obviously inferior (in the eyes of employees) to the other. To correct the problem may require additional expenses and investments such as when an acquirer must bring compensation and benefits of a target up to its standards or to fund an underfunded defined benefits plan. Such comparisons of practices may also provide an opportunity to identify a best practice that can be employed in the combined firm and the costs associated with implementing that practice. It may also provide the merging companies with an opportunity to innovate and redesign a practice to a new standard.

Assessing the Culture of the Target. It is increasingly becoming common knowledge that differences in culture between merging firms are a major source of conflict in M&A. As such, it is necessary that an acquirer assess the cultures of both a target and itself to determine whether culture is important to a deal, differences are so severe that a deal should be killed, or interventions can be employed that can ensure that differences become a source of value rather than destructive conflict.

The importance of such assessments is reflected in the following examples. Abitibi Consolidated Sales Corporation, the U.S. subsidiary of Abitibi-Price of Canada, understands the importance of cultural analysis during the transaction and transition stages. The largest producer of newsprint in the world attempts to gather cultural information from a target as soon as it can when making an acquisition. At the early stages of an acquisition, they will simply attempt to observe a target from afar, observing cultural artifacts such as how they dress and answer the phone. As they progress into due diligence, they will attempt a full cultural assessment including interviews with and surveys of target employees. In their merger with Stone-Consolidated, they got the twenty people in both companies considered critical to the success of the merger together in an off-site meeting to analyze and discuss their cultures and aspirations for the new organization. A similar approach was used in the Chevron/Texaco merger.

Before Compaq acquired both Digital Equipment and Tandem corporations, their HR teams analyzed the cultures of both companies from afar. This gave them key insights into the challenges they would face and the interventions to employ to successfully merge the combined companies. It also allowed them to move quickly once the deals closed. Southwest Airlines undertook a comprehensive cultural due diligence prior to its acquisition of Morris Air, a smaller entrepreneurial firm. Using cultural information, Southwest Airlines carefully managed the integration, which resulted in a profitable outcome. In contrast, USAir's lack of cultural assessment and awareness and autocratic methods in its acquisition of Piedmont Aviation caused years of cultural warfare.

In spite of these examples of cultural due diligence, the cultural fit between an acquirer and a target is one of the most neglected areas of analysis prior to the closing of a deal. Often culture is considered too soft and fuzzy. It does not have the precision of financial analyses or the excitement of potential synergies.

Although many definitions of culture exist, most experts agree that it characterizes the basic values, beliefs, and assumptions that members of an organization hold.[18] In many organizations, especially small and successful ones, culture can be very powerful in shaping how people think and behave and has been shown to have a direct impact on an organization's growth and profitability.[19]

The primary responsibility for assessing culture should lie with an HR or organizational development expert or an outside consultant knowledgeable of this area. This person should become a member of the due diligence team. With input from others, this person conducts the assessments, interprets the results, and determines the implications of the results.

There are several important questions to address in assessing the impact of culture on a merger or an acquisition. These include

1. How important culture is to a particular acquisition?
2. How similar and different are the acquirer's and target's cultures?
3. What is the impact that similarities and differences are likely to have on the success of integration and synergy realization?
4. What interventions should be employed during integration to capitalize on similarities and deal with differences?

Cultural assessment is rather complex. There are direct and indirect methods requiring differing levels of contact and access to information with a target firm. These include secondary sources of information (that is, little or no contact with a target) and primary sources (that is, direct contact with a target). For direct assessment, there are numerous commercially available instruments that can be employed. For indirect assessment, a variety of information sources to piece together a profile are needed. This may be easier for a publicly traded company.

As an example, Catholic Healthcare West, a healthcare system in California, was interested in selling a hospital to Columbia HCA (CHCA), a publicly traded hospital management company. The hospital in question no longer fit within the geographic scope of the seller's system. Before doing so, they wanted to understand CHCA culture and what would likely happen to their hospital after the deal was closed.

CHCA had grown rapidly over ten years by aggressively making acquisitions and engaging in joint ventures. The Catholic system's management had serious concerns, however, about whether the values and ethics of their hospital would be compromised once it was sold to CHCA. In anticipation of negotiations, they decided to quietly conduct an assessment of CHCA. They did not want CHCA to know about it.

Through the use of an Internet search (based on information, which included SEC documents, trade journals, newspapers, and the like) and select interviews with other hospitals that had dealt with CHCA, the assessment was conducted. As CHCA was fairly high profile, such information was relatively easy to gather and a solid story pieced together. Based on this assessment, the Catholic system's management decided not to undertake the sale and looked for another alternative.

Assessing Key Target People. Identifying and assessing people in both an acquirer and a target who might be important to either the success of the transition or the long-term viability of the combined organization are essential. Without qualified people an organization cannot function effectively. It is critical that such efforts focus on retaining people who are critical to the future success of the combined company.

Moreover, the sooner that selection decisions be made the better. Until people are named to key positions, the "me" question will preoccupy them. Good people are likely to update their resumes and start looking for new jobs. The net result is not likely to be positive, resulting in possible value leakage. Although it would be desirable to assess everyone in a target or merging organization, at this stage it is not possible. It would require too much time, access, and resources. Focusing on key people at this point is sufficient. Experience has shown that an orderly and fair process of selection focused on performance and competence is far superior to one in which a balance in numbers of employees retained between the two companies are sought.

There are several key activities required in the assessment process. First, a rough pro forma of the consolidated postclosing organization needs to be developed to determine the basic organization structure, key positions, and number of positions; roles and responsibilities for each position; talent, skills, competencies, style, and motivation needed for each position; and target staffing costs (salaries and benefits) the acquirer is willing to sustain. Second, the staffing capability of both the target and the acquirer need to be assessed.

Third, it must be determined for how long key people are needed. Some people (for example, information technology) will be needed only for the duration of the transition but will have no future with the company, whereas others will be retained as "long-term" employees. This distinction is important because many companies fail to consider transitional needs.

Fourth, the individual assessment process must be conducted. There are four major questions that are useful in assessing people:

1. Have the key people performed effectively in the past?
2. Do the key people have the talent, skills, competencies, style, and motivation to manage in the new organization?
3. What is the likelihood the key people will fit and succeed in this new environment?
4. What actions, if any, can be taken to ensure that key people will succeed?

Finally, based on the assessments above, a strategy needs to be developed to retain key target people; identify possible successors in the target; identify the acquirer's replacements; prepare to recruit replacements in the marketplace, or if critical people cannot be retained or replaced, terminate the deal.

Guide Behaviors and Attitudes of Negotiators and Due Diligence Teams. As noted above, the integration process begins the minute that people from an acquirer and a target come in contact with each other. Thus negotiators, due diligence team members, and relevant others should be trained on how to properly interact with the target and create a context for cooperation.

Transition Stage

The transition stage begins when the acquirer or merger partners announce a deal or sign a merger or an acquisition agreement. This marks the point at which both parties are serious about doing the deal and detailing how they will put it together. It is also a point where the integration of combining firms can be considered and planned for. During transition, secrecy will become somewhat difficult, as more people are likely to become involved in the deal. There is likely to be speculation among employees, customers, and other key stakeholders over the likelihood of the deal taking place and its implications for them. There will also be greater and broader interaction among people from the involved firms. It is a time when value preservation plans need to be implemented and a process for ensuring an orderly integration process begins.

Objectives

There are four objectives during the transition stage:

1. Ensure that the activities conducted during this phase continue to create a constructive environment for successful integration.
2. Ensure that the value of both the acquirer and the target or merger partners are preserved.
3. Ensure that any preliminary integration analyses and assessments begun during the transaction stage are either completed or conducted in more depth.
4. Conduct the integration planning process.

Below we will discuss key activities that are instrumental in achieving these objectives.

Integration and HR Activities

Creation of an Integration Transition Structure. A transition structure to manage the process of taking two independent companies and creating one can help create an orderly and effective integration. The objectives of this approach are to ensure that critical knowledge from the combining organizations is captured and utilized, decisions to ensure that a more competitive company emerges from the integration are captured, people needed in the new organization are retained and motivated, necessary changes to one or both organizations are made, value is preserved, and synergies are captured.

Such an approach has been used effectively in the integration of Exxon and Mobil, International Paper and Union Camp, UBS Warburg and Paine Weber, GTE and Bell Atlantic, Smithkline and Beecham, among others. Although the structures varied in each case, they shared some important common elements. Typically, a merger integration office (MIO), composed of senior executives, was created to lead the integration effort. A series of cascading teams were then created. These included transition and integration teams, often led by members of the buyer and target or merger partners. The teams were responsible for making recommendations to the MIO or champion concerning the integration of strategy, functions, support areas such as HR and technology, business and product lines, and geographic areas. Several companies created stability/audit teams to independently monitor key business indicators during the transition. These included employee and customer retention, service, productivity, and other indicators that denote the stability of the business. This team typically reported to the MIO or champion. Another independent team, the synergy capture team, was responsible for identifying and tracking synergies. Specifically, these included costs, revenues, net working capital and investments, all components of cash flow, and earnings. They worked closely with transition and integration teams and the MIO or champion.

The selection of members to participate in these various teams and the development of the team to work in an efficient and effective manner was an essential activity. Also critical was the assignment of a facilitator to each team to help it develop and work through an agenda. Often such facilitators were outsiders who helped the team manage numerous activities ranging from agenda development to intergroup conflict management.

Articulation of Integration Guiding Principles. There are numerous activities that are performed during the transition stage. There are also many people involved. Thus, it is impossible to control everything tightly. Guiding principles should be developed by the MIO to ensure that basic philosophy underlying the integration is understood and that the decisions and behaviors of those involved are in concert. Moreover, those participating in the integration process should be held accountable for the behaviors underlying these principles. For example, when Baxter acquired American Hospital Supply they utilized the following principles:

1. The organization will be based on doing what is best for the business.
2. The best people will be retained regardless of company affiliation.
3. The merger will proceed in an orderly fashion, but it must achieve early and visible benefits.
4. We will seek decentralization to the extent that it serves our customers.

5. The need to do it right will be balanced with the need to do it expeditiously.
6. The integration will include participation from executives of both companies at every step.
7. Management intends to conduct the merger integration in an unprecedented, model way.
8. Employees of both companies will be treated in an open and honest fashion, and will be kept informed about the progress of the integration through constant communication.[20]

After examining the principles of numerous integration efforts, we found that they all tended to address the following issues:

1. The involvement of people from both organizations in the integration process.
2. How people will be treated in selection and retention decisions and communications.
3. How the merger or acquisition integration processes will be managed.
4. The focus of the integration effort.
5. The focus on customers and strategic priorities during the integration

Deciding What to Integrate and How to Do It. Those areas of the business to integrate and how best to integrate them needs to be defined by each integration team. This includes such issues as using best practices or innovating new practices. Preparing for the integration decision requires that two activities be performed:

1. The current state (that is, baseline) of each area should be examined and compared. This includes the area's vision, objectives and strategies; culture; human resource practices; activities performed; systems; business processes; operating/business models; organization structure; positions, descriptions and head count; and operating and capital budgets.
2. Strategic objectives for each area should also be developed. This provides a basis for understanding any gaps between what each organization is currently doing and what the new organization needs to be doing in each area.

There are multiple integration approaches that can be used to combine firms, including

1. using an integration template or best practice that the acquirer has already developed and can apply to new acquisitions,
2. using a best practice developed by a target and applying it to the acquirer and subsequent acquisitions,

3. using a best practice developed by one of the merger partners and can be used in the combined organization, or

4. working in collaboration with the target or merger partner to develop a new best practice.

The decision of which approach to use depends on the availability of a best practice by one or both firms and how that practice contributes to the development of competitive advantage and synergies.

Developing an Integration Project Plan to Drive Implementation. Project planning methodologies can be of great help in managing the numerous complex activities involved in integration. These were used in a number of mergers including Bank of America/Nations Bank and Chevron/Texaco. Such plans were coordinated by the MIO and managed by transition and integration teams. In a number of cases we have found that the MIO created a support staff that included a dedicated project management group. Their purpose was to ensure that the overall integration effort proceeded smoothly and provided integration and transition teams with needed support.

Managing Communications with All Stakeholders. Communication is one of the more critical activities to be managed during the integration process and may have a tremendous bearing on value preservation. From the point at which rumors begin to circulate about a possible merger or acquisition, communication with stakeholders (employees, customers, investors) will be critical, especially if the changes being created impact them. In general, stakeholders do not like uncertainty, and the longer it lasts the more likely they will experience adverse reactions. We have found the following eight elements to be critical in establishing an effective communication process:

1. *Establish a communication philosophy.* The philosophy represents the core values driving the plan and guides management in executing it. Such values include honesty. Research has found that honesty does indeed pay[21]. As someone once said, "the truth happens whether it comes from your lips or not." If leaders make commitments they cannot keep or speculate about something that will happen and it does not, they will also be measured against it. The greater the gap between communication and the reality, the lower the credibility of the leadership. Such credibility is critical in the retention of key people (value preservation) and in gaining commitment to execute complex changes (value realization).

2. *Be timely and relevant.* Communications should be made as soon as possible and focused on what people want to hear. Clearly, needs for secrecy and legal restrictions must be balanced against people's need to know.

3. *Understand what people want to hear.* In general, most employees involved in a merger, or any change for that matter, want to hear about the impact it will have on them. Although they care about the company and strategic issues, they are more concerned about jobs, roles compensation, and the like. Although timing of decisions and needs for secrecy play a critical role in the availability of pertinent information, people will remain unsettled until such information is communicated.

4. *Choose effective communication media.* Once the communication philosophy and the message are established, the media need to be determined. The most effective way to communicate daily with employees is through face-to-face communications with supervisors and managers.[22] The best way to communicate major changes is through *dialogue* with senior managers in town-hall-type meetings. This means two-way communications! The same approach often works with key stakeholders. They would like to have dialogue with key managers and executives concerning changes that will significantly impact them. Examples of other media that can be used to communicate include rumor mill; videotapes, phone mail, memos, Intranet sites or e-mail for hard to reach groups; normal company newsletter; transition/integration newsletter; bulletin boards; telephone hotlines; internal publications of press releases; brochures; training sessions; and employee assistance program representatives.

5. *Develop and execute a communication plan.* Regardless of the stakeholders, an organized communication plan is extremely helpful. It ensures that the right communications are provided to the right stakeholders at the right time. The plan must identify the objective behind the communication, the message to be communicated, the target audience (stakeholder) that the message is targeted to, the most effective media (including people) to employ in influencing the stakeholder, and the timing of the communication.

Integration Stage

The integration stage begins after closing and continues until after the target or merger partners are integrated. The stage lasts until the firms have achieved the level of cooperation needed to achieve the hoped-for synergies. It is important to note that the level of cooperation and time frame needed to achieve it may vary depending upon the level of synergy sought. Achieving cost synergies through consolidation and reduction of staff may require far less time to capture than revenue enhancements from cross-selling product across sales organizations or distribution channels, or intangible synergies such as knowledge exchange and joint new product development. This stage, however, is "where the rubber hits the road." It is the point where change in control has taken place and promised improvements in cash flow must occur.

Objectives

There are three objectives during integration. These include the following:

1. Complete any analytical activities that were not completed prior to the closing.
2. Execute actions to physically integrate the target or merger partner.
3. Rebuild the organization into a stronger, more competitive entity capable of realizing financial and strategic objectives.

Below we will discuss key activities that contribute to the achievement of these activities.

Integration and HR Activities

Managing the Speed of the Integration Process. A key issue facing executives is how fast they should push the integration process. Speed can best be defined as the time it takes to make changes in the buyer, seller, or both and thus integrate the firms. Some argue that you should move quickly and integrate as fast as possible because people are expecting change and delays prolong the uncertainty. As Sandy Weill, Citigroup's Chairman and CEO, notes, "Make decisions faster than you normally might, rather than slower... it will help you hold onto the good people and send the right message to everyone."[23]

Speed avoids periods of uncertainty in direction, both in the organization and in the marketplace. It also sets an early expectation that changes will be made and mitigates the buildup of political resistance to change.

Others argue, however, that integration should move more slowly whereby careful assessments of how the organizations should be put together can be made. Moving slowly allows for a well-thought-out and planned integration. This argument is probably due to the incompleteness of the due diligence or preclosing acquisition integration planning process.

There are a number of studies that have been conducted on this topic.[24] In general, the research suggests that integration should move purposefully and as quickly as possible. More importantly, speed considerations should be weighed against commitments to delivering earnings and cash flows.

Premiums paid for an acquisition and commitments made to achieving synergies within a specified time frame should have a great bearing on speed.

However, one should be realistic as to how long it might take to implement change. Some synergies (for example, revenue, intangibles) may take longer to capture than others (for example, overhead costs). Some functions (for example, information systems) may require significant time to integrate, even after integration changes have been agreed to. Experience suggests that fully integrating organizations (for example, many areas, cultures) can take anywhere from one to five years, depending upon the relative size of the target and the extent of the integration.

Demonstrating a Committed and Open-Minded Leadership. As integration involves change, it often requires a strong leader to drive the effort. In fact, strong and committed leadership is often cited as a key element in any change effort.[25] An excellent example of this is the role that Carlos Ghosn has played in the acquisition of Nissan by Renault. Ghosn is a highly successful executive who has had great success leading a number of companies and in turning around Renault. He was made President and CEO of Nissan in 1999 and was charged with turning it around while successfully integrating it with Renault. Ghosn faced a radically different culture in Japan where many of the decisions to transform Nissan would not be embraced. He would have to work within a different culture to win support for his ideas and motivate a new organization to take on and successfully implement the challenges. He would have to do this when most people felt that he faced an impossible challenge. He skillfully got the organization and Japanese industry to focus on the issues facing Nissan and the need to turn the company around. He was tenacious in his focus on business objectives and built consensus among those around him why these were critical for the acquisition and the companies to succeed.

Building Teams and Work Units. There are a number of key activities that can and should be performed to ensure that the people work together and are aligned around the same financial and strategic objectives. Clearly, the alignment process must begin at the senior management level, otherwise it is not likely that managers throughout the organization will fall into alignment. If executives do not set an example for acceptable behaviors, it is not likely that those throughout the organization will consistently do so. Asking people from integrating organizations to cooperate while the senior management team battles is not likely to have the desired effect. One only needs to examine the problems that ensued at Citigroup after the merger. Senior management battled and so did everyone else. This led to the departure of many good people who felt they did not fit in the new organization.

The senior team must first address or revisit and then communicate the following:

1. The vision and financial and strategic objectives of the merger or acquisition and the firm in general, and how that translates into organizational priorities and objectives throughout the organization.
2. How the organization will be designed to support these objectives including culture; activities performed; systems; business processes; operating/business models; organization structure; measurements and rewards; positions, descriptions, and head count; and operating and capital budgets?
3. How the integration and change process will be managed?
4. What areas are to be affected?
5. What are the priorities, especially with respect to the financial and strategic objectives?

A critical component in the alignment process is the formation of work units and teams of people who have never worked together. Creating a cooperative context in which this can happen can help facilitate the ease and speed of the integration. The building process must begin with the senior management team and then cascade down through the organization. For each unit created HR can employ a host of team-building exercises. This has been done extensively in a number of mergers including Chevron/Texaco. Such exercises may be built around task activities (for example, setting vision, goals, and strategies of work units) or team process activities (for example, defining roles and responsibilities, decision-making process, team norms). It is our experience that most executives prefer to work on task activities during M&A, perhaps because of the heavy workload that integration creates. With that said, team process activities can play an extremely valuable role in facilitating work and in building a cohesive unit. The approach to lead with depends very heavily on the executives in charge and the organizational cultures. For example, in the Chevron/Texaco merger, Chevron was much more process-oriented than Texaco. As Chevron was really the acquirer in this deal, a process orientation prevailed.

Developing Capable and Motivated People. It is a mistake to assume that people will be able to step into new positions and perform well after a merger or an acquisition has closed. It is essential that executives put into place elements that help people develop the proper capabilities and motivation. The following are a number of elements that can be employed to achieve this.

1. Once people assume positions in the new work unit, their roles and responsibilities must be clarified. Even the most motivated persons will fail if they are unsure where they need to focus their energies.
2. Care must be taken to ensure that people are placed in the right positions. This requires matching the right person to the right job.
3. Training and development are pivotal. Highly qualified people will need training and development to meet the needs of new positions that are created, technologies that are employed, and systems and work processes that are introduced. If done properly, integration teams should identify such needs as part of their work.
4. It is important that a performance and developmental feedback process be established. Without feedback people will not know whether they are meeting expectations.
5. Measurement and reward systems may be among the most powerful elements in shaping behavior. What is measured and rewarded is what people will focus on.
6. Many people in a merger or an acquisition want to succeed in the new organization. Care must be taken that they are properly assimilated and are provided proper coaching and information on how they can succeed.

Cisco Systems is a prime example of a company that has successfully assimilated acquired employees. Cisco, which had acquired more than fifty companies in a seven-year period, created a SWAT team of thirty-six full-time employees who were responsible for the assimilation of acquired firms.[26] They relied on a swift and systematic process to ensure that new employees were shepherded into the new organization. Key to Cisco's process is the philosophy that people are the primary asset in their acquisitions, people must get integrated first and not products, employee retention and continued motivation is the key to success.

Other companies, such as Ameritech, that have developed assimilation and orientation programs for new hires have used them during acquisitions. These can easily be adapted to an integration situation. Such programs range from providing simple job training to explaining benefits programs and to showing how to access the e-mail. Again, the purpose of such programs is to ensure that employees are quickly integrated into the new work and environment and given every opportunity to succeed.

Achieving Cultural Integration. As new units and teams are created with people from different organizations, the opportunities for culture clash are significant. Rather than wait for a clash, there are approaches that executives and managers can employ to ensure cultural learning and cooperation. These can greatly improve the speed of and the impact of the integration effort on the financial and strategic considerations.

Although culture clash is a common by-product of integration, it can be successfully managed. Rather than conflict, cultural synergy can be created. However, it takes sound leadership as in the case of Carlos Ghosn and a well-managed process to do so. The process begins with a managed flow of information between acquiring and acquired or merging employees. The objective is to provide a constructive forum whereby the parties get "accurate" information about each other. Through such information inaccurate perceptions are eliminated and real differences are brought to light. Rather than differences being seen as a problem, cross-fertilization is encouraged and the best features of both cultures are highlighted. The opportunity for cultural synergy and best cultural practices is created. At this point a well-managed process for working through differences is necessary. Recent research in a Fortune 500 company found that through such a process, cultural distance between combining firms can be bridged through deep cultural learning interventions that develop constructive employee perceptions necessary to facilitate integration and enhance acquisition performance.[27]

Managing Staffing, Retention, and Redundancy. In general, decisions concerning the fate of people in a merger or an acquisition are not easy to make, can be quite political, and can have a dramatic impact on everyone in an organization. There are three sets of interrelated "people" decisions that must be managed during the integration process: selecting people, retaining key people, and severing people from the organization.

Many executives agree that these tough decisions should be made, but properly executed. Failure to do so may result in missed cost synergies or the retention of people who will not or cannot execute changes that are needed to make the combined company more competitive. The net result is a failure to realize synergies. But many executives also agree that such a process should be managed fairly and compassionately. People should be treated with fairness and respect. Failure to do so may lead to the premature departure of key people, poor morale, and attitudes that can affect customer service, safety, and productivity. Well-organized approaches for managing these processes were employed in the SBC/Ameritech, Chevron/Texaco, Baxter-Travenol Laboratories/American Hospital mergers. This is an area where the HR organization can play a critical role.

Final Comment

Creating value in M&A is quite complex and elusive. Witness the dismal results that have been achieved. It was our intent in this chapter to illustrate the complex interrelationship among the many elements in the M&A process and the need for them to be managed in an integrated and coherent way. It was also our intent to illustrate the importance of the integration effort and HR practices in the value creation process. The evidence to date clearly suggests that a well-managed integration effort is critical to the achievement of synergies and thus value creation, especially in cases where a purchase price was premised on the former. We hope that the ideas expressed in this chapter will indeed increase the awareness and improve the execution of the integration process among executives and spawn additional scientific research.

Notes

1. Information regarding the merger of Daimler-Benz and Chrysler, Daimler-Benz AG, Investor Relations, 7056 Stuttgart, Germany.

2. See Robert F. Bruner (2002). Does M&A pay? A survey of evidence for the decision maker. *Journal of Applied Finance Theory, Practice and Education*, 12(1): 48–88, for an excellent review of the research to date.

3. Rob Walker (2002). Creating synergy out of thin air. *Wall Street Journal*.

4. Free cash flow is defined as revenue – cost – investment.

5. R. F. Bruner, K. M. Eades, R. S. Harris, and R. C. Higgins (1998). Best practices in estimating the cost of capital: Survey and synthesis. *Financial Practice and Education*, 8: 13–28.

6. The terminal value often represents the majority of an entity's value. The appropriate use of a terminal value is greatly debated because it is extremely sensitive to even minor changes in cash flow forecasts and required return assumptions that are inherently uncertain.

7. In the midst of bidding wars, executives may forget that a target is worth more to some than others.

8. M. L. Sirower in *The Synergy Trap*, 1997, New York: The Free Press, proposes that this is typically a result of the synergies being exaggerated by the buyer, the synergies not being present to begin with, or the synergies not being fully realized during the integration process.

9. Cliff Edwards and Andrew Park (2002). HP and Compaq: It's showtime. *Business Week*, p. 76.

10. The framework was originally developed in David M. Schweiger (2002). *M&A Integration: A Framework for Executives and Managers*. New York: McGraw-Hill.

11. In a recent study of bank mergers [G. DeLong (2001). Stockholder gains from focusing versus diversifying bank mergers. *Journal of Financial Economics*, 59(2): 221–52] it was reported that mergers that focus on competitors in close geographic proximity enhance the buyer's share value by significantly more than other types of mergers.

12. Combining the Gatorade and Tropicana sales forces resulted in a poorly executed sales promotion and price increase on the juice product line that contributed to a drop in division sales of 2 percent.

13. A recent study by Mercer Management Consultants found that 54 percent of European companies acquiring U.S. businesses or vice versa outperformed their rivals. This finding is significantly stronger than research on domestic acquisitions in either the United States or intra-Europe. Lead author Michael L. Lovdal suggests that trans-Atlantic buyers beat the odds "because many such deals were designed to expand geographic reach."

14. This section of the chapter is based on David M. Schweiger (2002). *M&A Integration: A Framework for Executives and Managers*. New York: McGraw-Hill.

15. A continuing stream of research by practitioners and academics points to the importance of integration in M&A value creation. These include several studies by major consulting firms such as Coopers and Lybrand, Mercer Management Consulting, A. T. Kearney, and Hewitt Associates that are reported in J. R. Carleton (1997). Cultural due diligence. *Training*, pp. 67–75, and J. S. Lublin and B. O'Brien (1997). When disparate firms merge, cultures often collide. *Wall Street Journal*. A study of Forbes 500 executives on the top ten reasons why synergies are not realized cites five organizational issues as among the top ten (Schmidt, Forbes, 1999). Comprehensive review of academic research identifying integration as an important element in M&A value creation are presented in D. M. Schweiger and J. P. Walsh (1990). Mergers and acquisitions: An interdisciplinary view. In Rowland and Ferris (eds.), *Research in Personnel and Human Resource Management*, Vol. 8. Greenwich, CT: JAI Press, pp. 41–107, and D. M. Schweiger and P. Goulet (2000). Integrating acquisitions: An international research review. In Cooper and Gregory (eds.), *Advances in Mergers and Acquisitions*, Vol. I. Greenwich, CT: JAI/Elsevier Press, pp. 61–91. Also see S. Chatterjee, M. Lubatkin, D. M. Schweiger, and Y. Weber (1992). Cultural differences and shareholder value: Explaining the variability in the performance of related merger. *Strategic Management Journal*, 13: 319–34.

16. Although we focus on the HR function, the same arguments can be made for all major functions and support activities (e.g., information technology, operations, finance) in an organization.

17. See P. Very and D. M. Schweiger (2001). Creating value through mergers and acquisitions: Key challenges and solution in domestic and international deals. *Journal of World Business*, 36: 11–31.

18. For an excellent discussion of culture, see E. Schein (1985). *Organizational Culture and Leadership: A Dynamic View*. San Francisco: Jossey-Bass.

19. See J. P. Kotter and J. L. Heskett (1992). *Corporate Culture and Performance*. New York: Free Press.

20. This material is presented in Robert J. Kramer, *Post-Merger Organization Handbook*, The Conference Board, Research Report 1241-99-RR.

21. See David M. Schweiger and Angelo S. DeNisi (1991). Communication with employees following a merger: A longitudinal field experiment. *Academy of Management Journal*, 34(1): 110–35.

22. For an excellent discussion of this issue see T. J. Larkin and S. Larkin (1994). *Communicating Change: Winning Employee Support for New Business Goals*. New York: McGraw-Hill.

23. M. Murray and P. Beckett (1999). Recipe for a deal: Do it fast. *The Wall Street Journal*, pp. B1 and B4.

24. For an overview of this research see D. M. Schweiger and P. Goulet (2000). Integrating acquisitions: An international research review. In Cooper and Gregory (eds.), *Advances in Mergers and Acquisitions*, Vol. I. Greenwich, CT: JAI/Elsevier Press, pp. 61–91.

25. See, e.g., J. P. Kotter (1996). *Leading Change*. Boston: Harvard Business School Press.

26. This discussion is drawn from the work of D. Bunnell (2000). *Making the Cisco Connection*. New York: John Wiley & Sons, and S. Thurm (2000). Under Cisco's system, mergers usually work: That defies the odds. *The Wall Street Journal*, pp. A1 and A13.

27. David M. Schweiger and Philip Goulet (2002). Explaining acquisition integration effectiveness through cultural learning: A longitudinal field experiment. In *Best Paper Proceedings*, Academy of Management National Meeting, Denver, CO.

Executive Commentary on Chapter 2

TAE-GYUN SHIN

Many global and domestic companies are using mergers and acquisitions (M&A) as an aggressive strategy to obtain core competencies or to strengthen their own competitiveness. Some have intended to use M&A for early market penetration or for successful entry into a mature industry, whereas others deploy M&A for industry restructuring purposes or to enter a new international market. As noted by Schweiger and Lippert, in spite of these efforts, most companies fail in their M&A activities.

In my experience, a common flaw that exists in M&A efforts is the lack of sophisticated techniques and "know-how" in the areas of human resources and cultural integration on the part of the acquiring and acquired companies. I am not talking solely about "microscopic" techniques, such as team building and communication; rather, I have seen in my experience that the "macroscopic" dimensions of M&A in the human resources context, such as having the "right philosophy," proper strategy, and multidimensional integration tactics, are almost completely overlooked by companies when engaging in M&A efforts. M&A in the twenty-first century seem to be still a frontier area in my view, and the lack of success of most M&A efforts over the past two decades bears this out.

For example, in the 1980s, Korean companies began to start M&A activities, and in the 1990s major Korean companies focused on M&A activity in order to strengthen their business power in global markets and facilitate rapid economic growth. In 1997, the Korean economy faced an economic crisis, and the government became directly involved in M&A among Korean conglomerate companies for industrial restructuring, the so called "Big Deal." These M&A cases in Korea can be categorized into three different types:

1. M&A among domestic companies
2. Large companies merging with a foreign company for globalization or mega-competition purposes
3. M&A that is done for industrial restructuring purposes between conglomerates, the "Chabeol"

Across the three different types of M&A, many companies in Korea have experienced unsuccessful post-combination outcomes, and have tolerated "pain without gain" for several years. The main reasons why they failed, in my view, are as follows:

- All the parties associated with the mergers tended to ignore the difficulty of what true integration entailed, and tended to view the entire process with too much optimism. Processes and procedures of integration were downplayed in terms of being relevant to success, and when integration was attempted, the companies were not ready for the business and management complexities that they faced.
- The management cadres in the companies lacked experience and knowledge about how to successfully integrate two or more companies.
- The management of the combining companies, or of at least one of the companies involved, had poor cultural sensitivity; that is, they exhibited a general lack of acceptance toward different corporate cultures. This flaw seemed to emerge out a lack of intrinsic interest and respect on the part of top management groups for how other companies run their internal operations.

Wisdom from Two Metaphors for Successful M&A

What is the key, then, to enter "the gate of success" of M&A? I would like to use some historical examples to illustrate my opinions. In antiquity, several empires attempted to merge with each other, and some of these empires achieved great success in their global M&A efforts while others did not. The "global M&A champions" of history are easy to isolate; for example, the Roman Empire, Persia, and the Mongols of Genghis Khan are but a few. On the other hand, in spite of their strength and capacity, some countries ended up in failure with their efforts to merge with other nations. What are the major reasons that caused these differing outcomes?

From a human resource and cultural point of view, the successful regimes used an open policy with, and possessed a high capacity of tolerance for, the people they conquered. In other words, they accepted the culture of those they defeated, and respected and allowed each other's different value systems to coexist after acquiring their countries.

Let's look at it from yet another perspective: Before marrying, an engaged couple often takes the view that love can overcome all possible difficulties in a marriage, and they dream of a happy and wonderful married life before the wedding day. However, some time after the honeymoon, this couple will be faced with problems ranging from trivial matters like time differences in getting up in the morning and going to bed at night to important differences in how money should be spent or saved. These differences result from each spouse's unique family background and culture. Unfortunately, these predictable differences often result in divorce—a failed marriage. The cause of divorce is often not due to large, serious issues, but rather to the cumulative effect of many small, trivial disagreements. Additionally, many causes of divorce are related to "value discrepancies" between the spouses. When values are not shared and understood by partners, it is difficult to blend two lives together.

To summarize, then, what we learn from history and marriage is that a successful integration both at the micro and macro levels requires the respect of one's partner, a full understanding of the existing differences in the cultural background of the two partners, the engagement of mutual, fair-minded efforts toward assimilation, and a need to share, understand, and respect the other's values. All these factors are similarly required for an M&A to be successful.

Recommendations for Successful M&A from the HR Perspective

What kind of conditions are necessary to firmly establish an M&A? A clear M&A philosophy should be created and communicated and internalized throughout all of the participating companies. "My perspective" must be changed to "our perspective," because now we are on the same boat, not in different boats. Deep understanding and full acceptance toward partners from the heart will be one of the most important factors for better value creation through desirable integration.

Difference or heterogeneity is natural, and can be used effectively to build synergies by merging complementary skills. However, the merging of complementarities has a danger of being a double-edged sword. Conflict can be useful or destructive in nature, depending on how it is handled. When attempting synergies, conflict is inevitable, but the key to success is how conflict is resolved or managed in the M&A. Sometimes managers want to solve the problem of conflict by attacking it, avoiding it, or compromising around it, but effective problem solving and conflict resolution almost always depends on collaboration.

The ability of M&As to produce effective synergies is proportionate to the degree to which managers in the M&A possess collaboration skills.

Successful integration requires the accurate comparison of two companies in terms of their human resource control system: rules and guidelines around such issues as salary, work schedules, business trips, and holidays. After studying all the rules and regulations, truly collaborative efforts must be deployed to generate new guidelines for the new company—the new control system should be transparent and easily accessed by all members of the new firm.

Finally, deep consideration and interest must be taken in key people who reside in the acquired firm. Core people often tend to move to another company if deep consideration is not taken for their future in the new firm. As a human being, it is natural to judge a new situation as to whether it will have a positive or negative effect on one's career and power. The effective management of core people is another major issue for M&A post-combination management. The importance of how to keep the core people in the new firm cannot be overemphasized, and it is one of the most crucial roles of a human resource department in the M&A process.

Conclusion

The twenty-first century is an era of change and integration. Various kinds of convergence are emerging in all areas of life, including industries, products, organizations, and even scientific fields. The number of M&As in the global business environment—regardless of whether they are big or small, domestic or global, within or between industries—will increase. Unfortunately, on the basis of past experience, I forecast a continuance in the tendency of M&As to fail or to not live up to their premerger/acquisition expectations. Stockholders will be disappointed, executive careers will be derailed, and many employees will suffer.

To counter this, we need to study M&A not only in systematic ways but also in practical ways. The concrete planning of how to deal with soft processes, and not just easily measurable financial criteria, will be crucial in the managing of successful M&A. An attempted M&A that is not carefully supported by a program for management of change associated with post-combination integration is likely to end in failure. In particular, it is important to pay attention to how the ongoing M&A will look to outsiders; otherwise, there is the likelihood of undesirable results due to external factors. M&A are processes of creating a new cultural DNA through the assimilation of two or more heterogeneous entities into one. Those carrying out an M&A will have to continue to ask themselves why they are doing it and what their ultimate target is throughout the entire process.

PART II   *The Process of Sociocultural Integration in*
Mergers and Acquisitions

3 Organizational Learning in Cross-Border Mergers and Acquisitions

DANNA N. GREENBERG, HENRY W. LANE,
AND KEITH BAHDE

Introduction

We live in a time of significant economic change. Increasing interdependence of markets for goods and services is a reality. Trade liberalization has opened borders, and regional economic integration continues to take place. Deregulation and privatization have also contributed to increased international investment. Companies find themselves competing against foreign competition in their home markets while simultaneously looking for new markets in other countries. Many companies are coping with this phenomenon of "globalization" by expanding their geographic reach and "globalizing" as well. This often means that more capital and greater size are necessary to operate in the global marketplace. This growth frequently comes from domestic and cross-border acquisitions.

Some visible examples of cross-border acquisitions include Pharmacia-Upjohn followed by Pharmacia-Monsanto, and then Pfizer-Pharmacia, DaimlerChrysler, and Lycos-Terra Networks, which is majority-owned by Telefonica S.A. of Spain and BP–Amoco just to name a few.[1] There are scores of smaller deals that don't make the headlines. The 2000 UN World Investment Report provides the following snapshot of this phenomenon (World Investment Report, 2000):

- In the decade of the 1990s, most of the growth in international production took place through cross-border mergers and acquisitions (M&A) rather than through greenfield investment.
- The value of completed cross-border M&A rose from less than 100 billion in 1987 to 720 billion in 1999.

– The total number of all M&A (domestic and cross-border) increased by 42 percent annually between 1980 and 1999.

This increase in M&A activity is driven by corporations' need to gain access to highly skilled knowledge workers, R&D capabilities, and new products and processes, and also to gain access quickly for competitive reasons. M&A are a useful tactic for speeding entry to market and/or quickly obtaining a larger percentage of the market share a firm currently serves (Hitt et al., 1991).

As strategically justified as a merger or acquisition may be, most companies may not recognize the challenges associated with these change processes and the infinite barriers to success. Finance and industrial organization researchers have found that between 50 and 80 percent of M&A "fail," meaning that they do not increase shareholder value or profitability, or generate the anticipated strategic and financial goals (Ashkenas and Francis, 2000; Hitt et al., 1991; Ravenscraft and Scherer, 1987; Sirower, 1998). Of the 107 largest cross-border M&A completed between 1996 and 1998, 83 percent of the acquisitions did not lead to any increases in shareholder value (AT Kearney, 1999). A study by *Business Week* in 2002 found that 61 percent of buyers destroyed their shareholders' wealth (Henry, 2002).

Choosing the "right" partner or target for strategic fit is not the end of the M&A process—it is only the beginning. Executing the deal is the challenge. The real problems often come from overestimating the benefits and underestimating the costs of an M&A and from not understanding the difficulties associated with integrating employees or merging different organizational cultures (Lane, Greenberg, and Berdrow, 2004).

Research by AT Kearney (1999) supports this view, as it was found that the primary reasons for failures among bank mergers in the United States were as follows:

– Cultural differences, 35 percent
– Poor planning and execution, 20 percent
– Unrealistic targets, 13 percent
– Inadequate due diligence, 11 percent
– Demotivating employees, 10 percent
– Defection, 8 percent

The individual experiences of industry leaders who have had extensive M&A experience further reinforces the perspective that insufficient attention is given to the organizational issues associated with integration management. When Helmut Maucher was Chairperson of Nestlé S. A., a company with substantial M&A experience, he wrote:

If implemented properly, M&As are an important and efficient strategic instrument for enhancing the competitiveness of a company... M&As do not automatically generate success. Management should give its undivided attention to aspects of the actual integration process itself during the period when all contractual and financial aspects have been taken care of. These aspects include, *inter alia*, motivating the new employees, ensuring equal opportunity for all, and achieving a two-way transfer of knowledge – all aspects that are much more difficult to deal with than, for example, handling a property transfer. (Maucher, 1998)

As the number of cross-border M&A has increased, problems related to differences in organizational cultures have been further compounded by national cultural differences. A report by Towers Perrin states:

The global nature of business today has increased vastly the level of complexity of people-related problems. As more and more companies make acquisitions outside their headquarters countries, differences in company cultures are now compounded by differences in country cultures—in languages and customs...

Research has shown that national culture affects the practice of management and that many management concepts, techniques, and systems (that is, planning and staffing, performance evaluation and compensation, structures, and job design) are culturally influenced (Lane, DiStefano, and Maznevski, 2000; Laurent, 1986; Schneider, 1988). Therefore, cross-border mergers are more likely to encounter differences than a domestic-only situation, and hence an even greater potential for culture clash. National difference in organizational culture, language, and organizational practices significantly increase the difficulties of succeeding in cross-border acquisitions (Lane, Greenberg, and Berdrow, 2004; Madura, Vasconcellos, and Kish, 1991). These cultural differences may cause organizational members to become even more resistant to the changes that occur following a cross-border M&A.

In this chapter, we suggest that learning and the two-way transfer of knowledge, or the lack thereof, may be a key factor contributing to the high failure rate among M&A, in general, and cross-border M&A specifically. In most discussions of learning and M&A, researchers have primarily referred to either:

- *knowledge transfer* that occurs during the post acquisition phase as the newly formed company attempts to create new products, processes, and services that propel the new organization to achieving anticipated synergies, or
- *lessons learned* from previous M&A activities and a firm's ability to apply this learning to improve its management of future M&A.

In addition, prior research has been very *outcome-driven*, focusing on the knowledge necessary for new product and service development or synergy realization rather than as a basic *process* that is itself an important component of M&A activity. We believe, however, that learning in M&A is also fundamentally about the exchange that must occur between individuals, groups, and organizations as the acquisition process unfolds. If the merging organizations are not designed to support learning in the early phases of the acquisition process, particularly in the due diligence and integration phases, then the strategic learning that supports value creation in the later phases is not likely to occur nor is it likely that organizational members will be able to learn from this specific M&A experience.

Thus, to understand the role that learning plays in the success of an M&A, we present a model that focuses on the learning process as a critical part of acquisitions. Our intention is not to add another perspective to the already numerous perspectives of M&A or to challenge the already existing learning or knowledge transfer perspective. Instead, in our reconceptualization we focus on investigating the question "Why don't organizations seem to learn throughout the M&A process?" To address this question, we believe that identifying the potential barriers and bonds to learning in the M&A process offers significant value in helping to understand why information is not obtained, learning does not occur, and anticipated M&A synergies are not achieved. We conclude with the presentation of a simple heuristic derived from *barriers and bonds theory* that should increase the information and knowledge flows in M&A and the learning that occurs throughout the M&A process.

M&A from a Process Perspective

Although research on acquisitions has been conducted from many perspectives such as financial, strategic, and organizational, in this chapter we rely on the process perspective to the study of M&A.[2] The process perspective combines elements of the strategic and organizational behavioral perspectives that frame acquisitions as a series of linked phases each of which has an impact on the subsequent phases and on the final outcome of the M&A. This perspective posits that to fully understand acquisition value creation, one must study the actions that lead up to the acquisition decision along with the integration and management activities that follow the decision (Jemison and Sitkin, 1986). Although there may be a well-identified strategic and organizational fit underlying an acquisition, organizational members play an important role in the realization of the potential value following the acquisition. Hence, integration process management will strongly influence value realization (Haspeslagh and Jemison, 1991).

In the next sections we discuss the three phases of the acquisition process, precombination, combination, and postcombination (Marks and Mirvis, 1998), in more detail as they provide the basis for later exploration of the barriers and bonds to the M&A learning process.

Precombination Phase

In larger firms, M&A are usually planned, initiated, and evaluated by a specialized business development group with the training, background, and experience needed (Bentley, 1996) for these tasks. The business development team reviews M&A opportunities that are brought to it, proactively seeks out opportunities, and does a review of the candidates for strategic fit, synergy potential, and financial performance (Lane, Greenberg, and Berdrow, 2004).

Once an M&A target is identified, due diligence and the process of identifying key liabilities begins in order to avoid an "acquisition disaster" (Begley and Yount, 1994). Many merger problems can be traced directly to a lack of sufficient information about the acquired company and to potential integration problems that were ignored or minimized until after the deal closed (Boland, 1970).

During the due diligence period, financial and legal specialists examine accounting data and potential legal liabilities associated with environmental, employee benefits, and other issues. A range of financial analysis tools are also employed to establish the economic value of the target firm based on the existing assets, future investment requirements, and the future earnings potential, all of which may be heavily influenced by synergies expected from the combination of firms (Bielinski, 1992, 1993; Shrallow, 1985). The challenge during the due diligence process is to find a way to collect and analyze a vast amount of data pertaining to complex operational and financial issues under highly confidential conditions and accelerated timetables.

The evaluation of a target firm is a complex process which, when done comprehensively, should encompass the entire spectrum of firm functions. Many authors have called for a more comprehensive due diligence process that places greater emphasis on some of the less quantifiable, intangible aspects of a firm (Harvey and Lusch, 1995; Lane, Greenberg, and Berdrow, 2004).) and includes such things as human resources, employee benefits, information technology, and customer relationships or even an assessment of cultural issues (for example, Ignatius, 1995; Marks, 1999). The goal according to Marks (1999) is not to exclude firms that have somewhat disparate cultures from consideration as M&A targets, but to understand the differences and to begin developing plans to bridge them. There is no doubt that cultural differences might exist between combining firms, especially in cross-border transactions and that these issues need to be considered during the due diligence process (Lane, Greenberg, and Berdrow, 2004).

Combination Phase

The combination phase begins after the negotiations are complete and the acquisition has been announced. The business development team must now pass on responsibility to the integration teams that will plan and execute the integration strategy. Often important information gathered during due diligence that could affect the integration is not shared with the teams that will be overseeing the combination phase. Furthermore, there may be added problems if the operations personnel fail to buy into the strategy that underlies the acquisition.

Despite these issues, the integration teams will need to establish a comprehensive plan for the integration activities (Bower, 2001). Depending upon the strategic justification for the merger as well as the specific integration approach being utilized (for example, typology of preservation, symbiosis, absorption of Haspeslagh and Jemison (1991)), the integration plans will need to be tailored accordingly. With any of these integration approaches, some of the key issues that will need to be addressed include integration of information systems, manufacturing processes, human resource practices, and organizational structures.

Execution during the combination phase is the most difficult part of the acquisition process (Lane, Greenberg, and Berdrow, 2004). Disruptive turnover of key employees, uncertainty and insecurity that afflicts employees of firms involved in M&A, the disruption of identity and work processes, and the potential for cultural conflicts all make it difficult for the integrated organization to move forward during this phase. This situation is further exacerbated in cross-border mergers because there is likely to be greater uncertainty regarding the differences between the firms and how these differences will affect the new organization. The uncertainty, suspicion, and fear in employees, if not managed properly, can prevent information flow between the two organizations and can hinder the achievement of anticipated synergies (Lane, Greenberg, and Berdrow, 2004).

Postcombination Phase

There is no definitive time frame on when an acquisition moves into the postcombination phase as it is dependent on how successful and quickly the combination occurs. In best-case scenarios, the postcombination phase begins a few months after the acquisition announcement and in worst-case scenarios this phase begins a few years after the acquisition announcement.

In the postcombination phase, the new organization is expected to move forward and begin to find ways to capitalize on the synergies that were identified during the precombination or combination phase. The newly combined organization should now be focused on becoming more than a "the sum of its parts." Unfortunately, problems that arose in earlier phases often are carried forward, delaying or preventing successful integration and anticipated value creation opportunities. Thus, from a process perspective each of these phases along with the organizational, strategic, and financial issues must be managed to influence ultimate value creation.

The learning and knowledge transfer process and the attendant challenges facing executives responsible for implementation can be seen in the three phases. Multiple groups of specialists with different backgrounds, foci, and responsibilities are interacting across organizational boundaries, national boundaries, cultures, and languages and, hopefully, are engaged in the full and accurate two-way transfer of information and knowledge. This is not an easy or straightforward process and one, which we believe, should be understood in finer detail.

Learning and Knowledge Transfer in M&A

Most discussions of learning and knowledge transfer in M&A have primarily involved outcomes as they relate to knowledge transfer in the postcombination phase or to lessons learned from past M&A experiences. Researchers have focused on knowledge transfer following an acquisition as knowledge transfer is critical to synergy realization. We believe there are significant theoretical and practical differences between knowledge transfer and learning, but we reference the knowledge transfer literature as there is limited existing research that is directly relevant to M&A as a learning *process* that is distinct from knowledge transfer. In a second stream of research, researchers have focused more on learning; however, this research focuses on lessons learned from prior M&A activities in order to improve management of future M&A dealings. Both of these streams of research are discussed in more detail below.

Knowledge Transfer

As the earlier quote from Helmut Maucher, former chairperson of Nestlé S.A. indicated, to realize synergy from an M&A there has to be the two-way transfer of knowledge between combining firms. Knowledge transfer has increased in importance, as a growing number of firms have been using M&A as a strategy for gaining access to innovative technology and processes. In many industries, technological change is occurring so rapidly that no single firm has been able to develop the required knowledge or technology in-house. Rather, firms such as Cisco have made M&A a core competency and have pursued a strategy of purchasing and integrating technology (Carey, 2000) as opposed to pursuing a strategy of strategic alliances, joint ventures, and other forms of collaborative learning partnerships. Vermeulen and Barkema (2001) suggest that a combination of internal technology development and acquisition is preferred, as "acquisitions may broaden a firm's knowledge base and decrease inertia" (p. 457).

While acquisitions may broaden a firm's knowledge base in theory, in practice achieving this objective is much more challenging. One of the key challenges that prevents organizations from achieving this objective following an acquisition relates to the *type* of knowledge being transferred. The strategic knowledge that needs to be transferred following an acquisition often relates to strategic processes such as new product development. Unfortunately, this type of knowledge is defined as tacit knowledge and as such it is not documented but rather resides in the shared understandings of organizational members (Singh and Zollo, 1998). These characteristics make tacit knowledge difficult to transfer following an acquisition (Ranft and Lord, 2002). Even if this knowledge can be transferred, it may lose its value because the knowledge may be dependent upon the culture in which it was developed (Hakanson, 1995). This point is echoed by Leroy and Ramanantsoa (1997), who note that M&A provide both opportunities for and barriers to organizational learning. We will explore the barriers and facilitators to learning in more depth in the next section.

The second key challenge to knowledge transfer relates to the *nature* of the acquisition process itself. Organizational members are more likely to engage in knowledge transfer activities when they feel connected to organizational members from the merging firm. *Connected* is defined as occurring when these two groups of organizational members trust each other, share similar belief structures, and feel they are supporting shared objectives. In short, the development of social capital between the two firms will facilitate the emergence of knowledge transfer activities (Greenberg and Guinan, 2004). This, however, is inherently difficult to achieve following an M&A. Following an acquisition, employees often feel a sense of insecurity and alienation, which leads them to engage in disruptive, noncompliant behaviors (Nahavandi and Malekzadeh, 1994). Fear of change and the unknown and differences between cultures can prevent the integrated organization from ever creating a new cooperative relationship. The challenge of creating a social community in cross-border M&A is further complicated by the fact that organizational members differ in their languages, national cultures, and institutional and social contexts.

Following an M&A, some organizations try to build social capital between the merging organizations by engaging the support of boundary-spanning managers who can create connections between the organizations. In most organizational context, boundary-spanning managers are critical to the knowledge transfer process (Tushman and Scanlan, 1981). A boundary-spanning manager is a manager who connects individuals and groups who are separated by geographic, departmental, and other organizational boundaries and in connecting these groups, boundary spanners are able to facilitate knowledge transfer. Following an M&A, organizations can encourage boundary-spanning activity through a resource redeployment process in which organizational members from the acquirer are reassigned to the target and vice versa. This transferring of staff forces boundary spanning to occur and as such helps build bridges and community across the target and acquirer. While this activity can be a very valuable tool for facilitating knowledge transfer in an M&A, it may not be enough if other barriers exist as well.

Lessons Learned

In addition to focusing on knowledge transfer as it relates to synergy realization via new product/service development, researchers have also examined the issue of learning but with a focus on how organizations learn from past M&A experiences in order to improve their management of and success with future M&A endeavors. Acquisition performance and synergy realization has been tied directly to an organization's experience level with M&A. Organizations that engage in an extensive number of M&A are more likely to be successful in managing acquisitions because they have developed a core competence around acquisition management. This core competence develops as the firm learns from its past failures and successes and applies this learning to future M&A activity. This learning does not develop simply from the accumulation of experience, rather it is through the investment of time and effort in activities that enable the firm to learn directly via processes of interpreting and institutionalizing the lessons learned from previous M&A dealings. Thus, it is not enough that a firm establishes a separate department to oversee M&A activity but that department must also establish processes that facilitate its learning from prior experiences. For example, GE Capital has built a core competency around M&A activity by creating an M&A department that is responsible for identifying and managing acquisitions and for conducting post-M&A appraisals that enable GE to learn from past mistakes and successes and build its core competency in M&A management (Ashkenas, DeMonaco, and Francis, 1998). Although these activities do relate to learning following the M&A and to some extent during the M&A, they do not relate to the learning process that must occur between the two organizations.

In summary, discussions of knowledge transfer and learning relative to M&A have primarily focused on knowledge transfer that needs to occur during the postcombination phase in order to fuel synergy realization via new products/services and on learning that occurs after the M&A process is complete that leads to better management of future M&A activities. Most researchers have only hinted at the role of learning throughout the M&A process. For example, it has been suggested that the learning process needs to begin during the precombination phase when members of the combining firms gather information about the physical assets, financial issues, and process factors that will need to be managed during the integration process (Begley and Yount, 1994). However, this research does not create a conceptual framework for a learning process in acquisitions, nor does it provide insight into the organizational factors that inhibit or facilitate learning during the M&A process or during knowledge transfer once the merger or acquisition has been completed.

Recasting M&A as a Learning Process

Our basic premise in the reconceptualization of the M&A process as a learning process is that the knowledge transfer and learning that must occur following an acquisition in order to achieve synergy realization will only occur if learning has been a fundamental consideration in the earlier stages of the M&A process. In other words, a newly merged organization probably will not learn during the postcombination phase of the M&A process if it has not been engaged in a learning process throughout the prior phases.

When M&A are used strategically to gain access to proprietary knowledge, sharing information and knowledge across organizations seems to be an obvious activity. However, understanding the combined capabilities of the two organizations' people, products, processes, and competitive advantages means executives have to obtain and share this information and knowledge. This means these executives have to be able to work in both organizations, which may have two very different cultures and be organized and managed by different logics of action (Lane, Beddows, and Lawrence, 1981a, 1981b). They then must leverage this understanding of the two organizations to motivate people in a common direction. This movement of knowledge is a dynamic process and should be more than just a one-way transfer from the acquirer to the target (Lane, Greenberg, and Berdrow, 2004).

We believe that the 4I theory of organizational learning can help in understanding this dynamic process (Crossan, Lane, and White, 1999; Lane, Beddows, and Lawrence, 1981a, 1981b). Organizational learning takes place through the four processes of intuiting, interpreting, integrating, and institutionalizing, and these processes link three levels: individuals, groups, and the organization. Simply, the 4I model says that individuals' ideas are shared with others, actions are taken, and shared meaning is developed by groups, which becomes institutionalized in organizational systems, processes, and routines.

Previous lessons learned by the organization become codified into systems, routines, procedures, and responses that over time form the organizational logic of a company (the way things should be done) and contribute to the development of a distinctive corporate culture. This "feedback" from the organization to the group level and to individuals influences and may even dictate how employees think and act. How do new information, knowledge, and lessons from another organization penetrate such a system? The potential barrier between assimilating new learning (feed-forward) and exploiting, or using, previous lessons (feedback) is the fundamental problem facing executives in knowledge transfer and learning in M&A. The tension between the feed-forward processes that facilitate change and innovation and the feedback processes that facilitate structure and routine must be managed explicitly and carefully (Lane, Greenberg, and Berdrow, 2004).

Learning requires communicating across different personal cognitive maps and organizational cultures, and integrating these maps with others in a way that develops a shared, collective understanding. This is not always easy or successful. Within firms there are barriers to communication as people try to communicate between groups and functional entities and communication choke points can develop which block the flow of information and knowledge.

While the 4I model has largely been used to explore intraorganizational learning, more recently this model has been extended to examine interorganizational learning among high-technology firms (Meyer, 2001). Meyer (2001) argues that the same processes of intuiting, interpretation, integrating, and institutionalizing that are the foundation to intraorganizational learning also underlie interorganizational learning. The question that still remains, however, is what gets in the way of learning that derails the learning process.

Following an M&A there are an infinite number of challenges to learning and developing a shared view of the new organizational reality. Because so many aspects of our understanding are tacit, communicating them requires making these tacit ideas explicit. Even if organizational members are able to do this, a new shared understanding may not develop. The language that underlies the organization culture and the resulting investment in assets may present a formidable fortress of physical and cognitive barriers to change, agreement, and the realization of synergies. While these barriers can exist within a firm, they are even greater when one is examining interfirm dynamics. Furthermore, additional complications arise in cross-border deals, where the barriers are more complex and the tension may be between

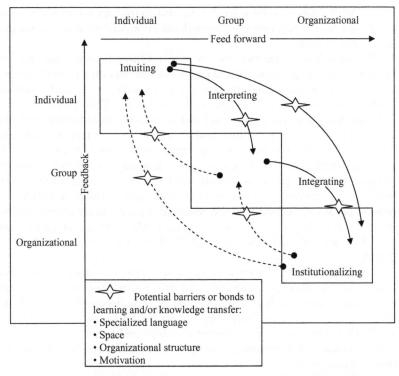

FIGURE **3.1** Barriers and Bonds in the M&A Learning Process. Adapted from Crossan, Lane, and White (1999, p. 532)

exploration and the possible creation of synergies or the imposition of the ways of the purchaser. This process is depicted and summarized in Figure 3.1. We now explain barriers and bonds theory in more detail.

Barriers and Bonds in the M&A Learning Process

Communication is essential for knowledge development and learning to take place. Therefore, it is appropriate to explore some of the key factors that help or hinder the flow of information across boundaries as we examine the inhibitors and enablers to learning during the acquisition process. In particular, we adapt Morton's identification (Morton, 1967) of four factors, specialized language, space, organizational structure, and motivation, which are central to the type of communication that is needed to stimulate learning and innovation. Morton argues that these factors can be used by an organization to facilitate the flow of information as "... we can deliberately build into the system certain bonds and barriers that will either inhibit or encourage the flow of information. These barriers and bonds are used in complementary fashion; whenever we have a spatial barrier we try to have an organizational bond and vice versa. Two barriers never exist together lest information flow be impeded and two bonds never exist together lest one specialist group dominate the other" (Morton, 1967).

In the following sections, we describe in more detail these four factors and how they can affect learning during the acquisition process.

Language

Without shared language, organizational members cannot share ideas, debate differences, and learn from each other. In cross-border acquisitions, language differences can create misunderstandings, confusion, and frustrations that can hinder learning and the development of a social community that supports learning (Schoenberg, 2001). The language gap may be a result of differences in national languages, specialist languages (for example, law, accounting, or engineering), or industry languages. For example, in the merger between Merita and Nordbanken (see Chapter 7 in this volume) the choice of a corporate language became an important issue symbolizing the dominance of one group over another. Similarly, when the Bank of Nova Scotia from Canada bought Grupo Financiero Inverlat in Mexico it also signaled the dominance of one group, culture, and language over another. Language differences created operational and managerial difficulties for the English-speaking expatriates assigned to Mexico City who had to manage Spanish-speaking employees and interfered with the smooth integration of the banks (Lane, Slaughter, Campbell, 1996).

Language differences can occur even when a merger or acquisition involves companies from the same culture that share the same national language but are from different industries or business, such as a clothing retailer acquiring a real estate firm and a financial services firm (for example, Sears Roebuck's acquisition of Coldwell Banker and Dean Witter). These language differences arise because different businesses rely on different logics (Prahalad and Bettis, 1986). Language barriers may also emerge from differences in organizational culture or differences in types of scientific or technical backgrounds and experience (Lane, Greenberg, and Berdrow, 2004).

Two other language differences can hinder communication. The first is in the actual words used to communicate an idea (Lane, Greenberg, and Berdrow, 2004). When IBM acquired Lotus, one of the challenges to learning and joint development was building a shared language between software and hardware programers who were likely to use slightly different terminologies. With regards to national language, German executives speaking English may use words differently to convey an idea than an American or an

English executive. The second challenge relates to how feelings or thoughts are conveyed using the words. This is a more difficult barrier to overcome because it relates to tacit knowledge. Organizational members may not be aware of the differences in how they are communicating and if aware they may not be able to explain the subtlety of these differences if asked. This issue is particularly prominent if one of the merging firms is from a high context culture in which communication is often subtle and indirect and the other firm is from a low context culture in which communication is explicit and direct (Lane, Greenberg, and Berdrow, 2004).

These language barriers can prevent the transfer of information between the merging partners at all stages of the acquisition process. At the earliest stages, language may be a barrier to learning during the due diligence phase in which the acquirer conducts an extensive legal and financial investigation of the target. This process is inherently complex as the acquirer tries to juggle competing pressures of secrecy and the need for exhaustive information gathering. These competing pressures have lead to an inherently flawed process that has been highlighted by numerous researchers (for example, Boland, 1970; Haspeslagh and Jemison, 1991; Marks and Mirvis, 1998).

Language barriers may be one of the primary barriers to learning during the due diligence phase of the acquisition process. Some of the problems discussed earlier regarding due diligence include an overemphasis on legal and financial information and a lack of emphasis on critical factors such as human resources, operational strategies, infrastructure, and external relationships with customers and suppliers. Specialists conducting due diligence may not understand the language being used by the target's human resource or financial staff as they try to evaluate the resources of the target (Marks and Mirvis, 1998). Additionally, the technical experts from the acquirer may not understand the language being used by the technical experts from the target. Consequently, the acquirer cannot fully learn and evaluate the value creation potential of the target (Lane, Greenberg, and Berdrow, 2004).

During the integration phase, language barriers may also hinder the organizations' ability to gather basic information about one another's structures, systems, and operating procedures. Without this information, it is difficult for the merging organizations to create a realistic plan for integrating the two organizations and (Lane, Greenberg, and Berdrow, 2004). Even if the two organizations are able to create a realistic plan, language differences may hinder the implementation of the integration plan. Members of one of the merging organizations, typically the target, may respond quite negatively if the language that is used in carrying out the integration process is substantively different from the language that they are familiar with. This hostility will further hinder the merging organizations' ability to learn from one another (Lane, Greenberg, and Berdrow, 2004).

Space

Physical space can hinder or facilitate the effective flow of information and learning (Lane, Greenberg, and Berdrow, 2004). Research tells us that geographic proximity is an important factor to consider when assessing the potential success of an M&A (Lane, Greenberg, and Berdrow, 2004). Cisco uses it to identify potential acquisition targets—whether the target company is located in Silicon Valley or near one of Cisco's remote sites (Tempest, 1999a). Physical proximity enables informal relationships to develop between staff in the merging organizations, which should facilitate the flow of information. Although e-mail, meetings, and conference calls may be used to communicate basic information, these mechanisms are not as useful for building interpersonal relationships which are the foundation for the new integrated community (Lane, Greenberg, and Berdrow, 2004). When Genzyme purchased BioMatrix in 2000, one of the issues in the integration process was how to integrate researchers who were located in Massachusetts with those who were located in New Jersey. Scientists ended up traveling extensively between the two locations in order to build more personal relationships between the two groups. As a result the two research groups were able to share more sensitive and complex information and learn more about how to combine their capabilities.

Research into the performance of virtual global teams has shown that as message complexity and ambiguity rise and as task interdependence increases, the communication medium chosen for interaction must fit the characteristics of the message (Maznevski and Chudoba, 2000). Additionally, as the number of boundaries (functional, organizational, or cultural) spanned increases, the richness of the communication medium should increase as well. We believe that the task of integrating organizations in a cross-border merger or acquisition can be characterized as being high in complexity and ambiguity, with multiple boundaries being spanned. This generally means face-to-face meetings would be the preferred communication vehicle, which would be facilitated by close physical proximity and frequent meetings. If subunits of the merging organizations can be expected to have high task interdependence, then organizations need to consider extended secondments, formal boundary spanners, and possibly colocation (Lane, Greenberg, and Berdrow, 2004).

When employees in the merging firms are colocated in one physical location and not simply in close proximity, connections between employees in the firms develop quicker and as a result more learning opportunities are generated. For example, when EMC acquired Data General, each located thirty miles west of Boston, MA, their close geographic proximity was expected to facilitate the integration process. Yet, the cultural differences between the firms were so great that geographic proximity was not sufficient to overcome the barrier to learning and information flow that these differences posed. It was only after EMC relocated staff such that employees from the two firms were colocated in one building that organizational members began to share information and learn what the companies could accomplish together with regards to new product development.

Organizational Structure

The third factor that has the potential to permit or prevent learning during the acquisition process is the organizational structure. Organizational structure refers to the (1) established subunits, such as departments or divisions of the organization, (2) the management hierarchy that delineates authority, and (3) linking mechanisms such as committees and task forces that ensure that the groups work together. All three of these factors work together to create an organization's structure (Greenberg, 2002; Lane, Greenberg, and Berdrow, 2004). Following an acquisition, a new organizational structure needs to be established that facilitates integration between the firms and value creation (Marks and Mirvis, 1998). Yet, it is difficult to establish such a structure when existing organizational structures along with the integration management structure do not facilitate the learning that will contribute to the establishment of a new arrangement. Below we explain in more detail how organizational structure can impede such learning.

Organizational structure impacts learning in an M&A from the start of the due diligence process. One of the central goals of the due diligence phase is to assess the "fit" between the target and the acquirer. Fit encompasses two areas: strategic fit and organizational fit. Strategic fit references the extent to which the merging firms' resources and strategy are aligned. Organizational fit examines the degree to which the merging firms' structures, cultures, and management processes are aligned (Marks and Mirvis, 1998). Differences in organizational structure can impede the acquirer from accurately assessing both strategic and organizational fit during the due diligence process (Lane, Greenberg, and Berdrow, 2004).

Many researchers have suggested that companies whose strategy is to use frequent acquisitions to grow and gain a competitive advantage should form a separate subunit to oversee preacquisition decision making and due diligence (Ashkenas, DeMonaco, and Francis, 1998), which is what Cisco does. Cisco's permanent new business development department identifies and assesses the fit of acquisition targets (Tempest, 1999b). This department is comprised of organizational members who have experience evaluating and managing the acquisition process. These experts take their key learnings from these experiences and use them to evaluate and manage future M&A activity. In addition to having organizational memory, an important strength is that the department remains well connected with the other departments at Cisco (Lane, Greenberg, and Berdrow, 2004).

As due diligence begins, the project manager from the new business development group will develop cross-functional due diligence teams that include members from marketing, engineering, and manufacturing who are chartered with assessing the strategic and organizational fit of the acquisition candidate. The functional expertise of these individuals positions them to understand and learn about the target's respective functional areas in order to make an accurate assessment. Cisco's organizational structure that relies on a permanent subunit that is well connected to the remainder of the organization is instrumental to its ability to learn about the strategic and organizational fit between itself and its target. Presumably, if the acquisition was a cross-border deal, the business development group could augment its team with experts who possess the appropriate language and cross-cultural skills.

Even if the acquirer's due diligence team is structured to facilitate learning, the target organization may have barriers that prevent it. A highly centralized firm may have formal or informal policies that inhibit lower level employees from sharing information, which may hinder learning during due diligence. If the areas or departments within the target have not had a history of sharing information, then representatives from the target may not be able to provide the information that will enable the due diligence team to accurately assess strategic fit, as was the case when AT&T acquired NCR and misjudged NCR's capabilities. Although there were many factors that influenced this poor assessment, part of the issue was that representatives from NCR could not provide the due diligence team with information necessary to accurately assess the technological fit of the two organizations (Lane, Greenberg, and Berdrow, 2004).

Finally, during due diligence it may be difficult for organizations to assess strategic and organizational fit when they have significantly different structures. When organizations have different product development processes, it may be more difficult for each acquisition partner to assess the potential complementarities and value creation potential of a merger (Lane, Greenberg, and Berdrow, 2004).

Structure may also affect the learning that needs to occur during the combination phase as a new organization is established that will capitalize on anticipated and unanticipated synergies. The most important component of structure relative to learning during this phase involves the structuring of the integration team. The goal of the integration team is to manage the integration process, not the new business (Ashkenas, DeMonaco, and Francis, 1998). To do this effectively the integration team must first learn about both the target and the acquirer as they create a new organizational structure that may create changes regarding financial and legal reporting processes, human resource policies, job responsibilities, and even organizational structure. The integration team must then help executives and employees learn about these changes. Hence, the integration team must first gather enough information to design an effective integration process but more importantly, then, it must facilitate organizational learning in order to execute this integration process (Lane, Greenberg, and Berdrow, 2004).

As the integration team is assembled, it needs to coordinate with the due diligence team, which may now be disbanded or partially disbanded. If due diligence is conducted well, the due diligence team not only learns about the target's financial and legal position but it also gathers information about its strategy, culture, and structure. Yet, this information is often not shared with the integration team, which results in a more costly and slower integration phase (Ashkenas, DeMonaco, and Francis, 1998). In these mergers, the failure results from the integration team not learning from and benefiting from the knowledge the due diligence team gained. In order to prevent the loss of this information, the due diligence team needs to be linked with the acquisition integration team. This linkage may be the carryover of a person from the due diligence team to the integration team or it may be a formal debriefing process that enables the due diligence team to pass on information that is of value to the integration process. Creating these structural linkages will ensure that the integration team learns and benefits from previously acquired knowledge.

The structure and composition of the integration team can also affect learning (Lane, Greenberg, and Berdrow, 2004). Following Compaq's acquisition of Digital in 1998, an integration team within the services group was created that included members from the services division at Compaq, Digital, and Tandem, a previous acquisition. This structure avoided at least one double barrier (space and organizational structure). These individuals were best positioned to share their knowledge regarding current organizational structures, processes, and expertise. They created an integration process and a new organizational structure that best fit with the three organizations' capabilities. Also, because of their familiarity with their own organizational cultures and human resource systems, team members were better prepared to educate their organizations on the changes (Lane, Greenberg, and Berdrow, 2004).

Finally, an integration team needs to find structural ways to engage other organizational members in the integration process. While the integration team may create the general structure for the newly integrated organizations, the rest of the organizational members actually execute the integration process. Consequently, it is not only important to gain "buy-in" from these lower level employees but the integration team also needs to find ways to encourage employees from the merging companies to take joint actions that will support integration and future knowledge transfer. Participation in the integration process is one way to begin to create buy-in and support the development of this behavior. Creating linking mechanisms that enable other organizational members to undertake joint actions that lead to quick results can show the potential of the integrated companies. This approach was used by GE Capital when they acquired a Japanese services firm (Ashkenas, DeMonaco, and Francis, 1998). Short-term projects (100 days) provided a common motivational goal that facilitated the employees to work together and avoid the double barrier of structure and space. Organizational members quickly experienced the value of postacquisition integration which in turn led to more learning opportunities (Lane, Greenberg, and Berdrow, 2004).

Motivation

To fully understand motivation, one must examine the relationships that exist between organizational members as well as between organizational members and the larger context. One must assess the personal and organizational objectives that exist and the relationship between the two as one evaluates how and why learning occurs following an acquisition. Morton (1967) suggests that when motivation is positive and strong among organizational members, a climate is created in which organizational members want to communicate to support organizational goals. A culture of trust and social community will contribute to this increased flow of knowledge.

Unfortunately, most acquisitions do not fuel a desire among organizational members to learn about each other in order to integrate their organizations. Employees are often demotivated as they worry about job security and their changing roles and they are motivated to look out for their own best interests. This territorial reaction to uncertainty and change inhibits sharing knowledge with their colleagues and may create resistance that often leads to the "NIH Syndrome" (Not Invented Here). Performance appraisal and compensation systems can be used to encourage or discourage the motivation to share and to learn.

Domestically, differences in organizational culture complicate the integration process and the achievement of anticipated synergies but in cross-border M&A national culture may magnify the complications. Hofstede (1980) defined culture as "the software of the mind that distinguishes one group from another." It is a shared body of beliefs and values that define the *shoulds* and the *oughts* of life for those who hold them and, thus, influence peoples' actions (Lane, DiStefano, and Maznevski, 2000).

A key issue that must be addressed during the acquisition process is culture clash (Buono, Bowditch, and Lewis, 1985; Shrivastava, 1986). When SmithKline and Beecham merged, the integration process was complicated by the vast differences between the U.S. and European company cultures.

As Jan Leschley, former CEO of SmithKline Beecham, stated, "The British and American (management) philosophies are so far apart on those subjects (pay, centralization, and management of a global firm) that they were almost impossible to reconcile" (Carey, 2000, p. 151). Out of culture clash, an antagonistic environment can develop in which organizational members become enamored with the positive features of their culture and protective of that culture (Buono, Bowditch, and Lewis, 1985; Marks and Mirvis, 1998). Culture clash at either the organizational or national level may demotivate organizational members from learning from each other. They may become ethnocentric—seeing their culture as superior to that of their merging partner (Hambrick and Cannella, 1993). In this situation, organizational members will be demotivated from learning from their merging partner as they see the knowledge, processes, and norms of their partner as inferior (Lane, Greenberg, and Berdrow, 2004).

As a counter-balance to the forces that may demotivate organizational members from engaging in knowledge sharing following an M&A, organizations need to purposefully encourage a different type of behavior and to motivate people to see the value in sharing their knowledge and learning from their new colleagues. Part of this motivation toward knowledge sharing comes from organizational members reframing their views of their prior organizational culture and their potential fears of changes that may be made to this culture as a new integrated organization is created. To help this reframing, major changes regarding job responsibilities, new organizational structures and systems, and layoffs should be made as quickly as possible so that a new stable order can be created. Stability will allow organizational members to concentrate on the real work of integrating the organizations (Ashkenas, DeMonaco, and Francis, 1998). They will worry less about the changes and will see the value in sharing their knowledge and learning from their merging partner as they work toward the vision of the new organization (Lane, Greenberg, and Berdrow, 2004).

Another tactic organizations can use to motivate organizational members toward knowledge sharing and learning is to make sure the incentive systems support this learning. Existing systems that may demotivate learning about the other organization need to be altered. After acquiring Data General, EMC put in place a sales incentive system that had the reverse effect and actually "disincented" the sales team from selling DG products. Consequently, EMC sales staff did not learn about the DG product line nor did they try to learn new selling strategies that would support this line. EMC sales staff began to learn about DG products when the system was changed. Secondly, new performance appraisal systems and compensation systems must be created that reward behavior that supports integration between the two organizations. When IBM acquired Lotus, one of the sales departments created a new financial incentive for sales people, the Green award. The Green award was given when IBM and Lotus sales people successfully teamed to close an account. The name for the award was chosen to symbolize the merging of blue, IBM's corporate color, and yellow, Lotus' color. Not only did this incentive directly motivate knowledge sharing and learning but the symbolic name further reinforced employees' support of the newly merged organization.

Conclusion

Value creation and synergy realization following an acquisition is based on learning and the effective transfer of knowledge—preferably a two-way transfer. To achieve these outcomes of learning, learning must also occur throughout the acquisition process. Managers who are involved in the various phases of the acquisition process must evaluate the barriers and bonds that can affect learning throughout all the stages of this process (Lane, Greenberg, and Berdrow, 2004). By identifying these barriers and bonds and managing them so that double barriers or double bonds do not coexist, firms may be able to avoid the creation of chasms across which information cannot flow. By increasing information flow and learning throughout the acquisition process, managers increase the likelihood of creating a new integrated organization that will support knowledge transfer and achieve its value creation proposition.

Notes

1. For a list of the top (value) fifty cross-border M&A deals during 1987–99, see World Investment Report, 2000, pp. 110–11.

2. For more detailed discussions of these different perspectives, see Bahde, 2001; Haspeslagh and Jemison, 1991; Larsson, 1989.

References

Ashkenas, R. N., DeMonaco, L. J., and Francis, S. C. (1998). Making the deal real: How GE capital integrates acquisitions. *Harvard Business Review*, 76(1): 165–78.

Ashkenas, R. N., and Francis, S. C. (2000). Integration managers: Special leaders for special times. *Harvard Business Review*, 78(6): 130–45.

Bahde, K. P. (2001). Synergy Is Created, Not Imagined: Towards Theoretical Progress in the Integration of Mergers and Acquisitions. Unpublished 2nd qualifying exam at Benedictine University.

Begley, T. M., and Yount, B. A. (1994). Enlisting personnel of the target to combat resentment. *Mergers and Acquisitions*, 29(2): 27–32.

Bentley, T. (1996). Putting the right people on in-house M&A teams. *Mergers and Acquisitions*, 30(6): 30–6.

Bielinski, D. W. (1992). Putting a realistic dollar value on acquisition synergies. *Mergers and Acquisitions*, 27(3): 9–12.

Bielinski, D. W. (1993). How to sort out the premium drivers of post-deal value. *Mergers and Acquisitions*, 28(1): 33–7.

Boland, R. J. (1970). Merger planning: How much weight do personnel factors carry? *Personnel*, March/April: 8–13.

Bower, J. L. (2001). Not all M&As are alike—and that matters. *Harvard Business Review*, 79(3): 92–101.

Buono, A. F., Bowditch, J. L., and Lewis, J. W. (1985). When cultures collide: The anatomy of a merger. *Human Relations*, 38(5): 477–500.

Carey, D. (2000). A CEO roundtable on making mergers succeed. *Harvard Business Review*, 78(3): 145–54.

Crossan, M. M., Lane, H. W., and White, R. E. (1999). An organizational learning framework: From intuition to institution. *Academy of Management Review*, 24(3): 522–37.

Greenberg, D. N. (2002). Designing effective organizations. In Cohen (ed.), *The Portable MBA*. New York: JohnWiley & Sons,pp. 243–76.

Greenberg, D. N., and Guinan, P. J. (2004). Trusting relationships: Uncovering the role of social capital in post-acquisition knowledge transfer. Paper presented at the Academy of Management Meeting, New Orleans, LA.

Hakanson, L. (1995). Learning through acquisitions: Management and integration of foreign R&D laboratories. *International Studies of Management & Organization*, 25(1/2): 121–57.

Hambrick, D.C., Cannella, A. A., Jr. (1993). Relative standing: A framework for understanding departures of acquired executives. *Academy of Management Journal*, 36: 733–62.

Harvey, M. G., and Lusch, R. F. (1995). Expanding the nature and scope of due diligence. *Journal of Business Venturing*, 10(1): 5–21.

Haspeslagh, P. C., and Jemison, D. B. (1991). *Managing acquisitions: Creating value through corporate renewal*. New York: Free Press.

Henry, D. (2002). Mergers: Why Most Big Deals Don't Pay Off. *Business Week*, October: 60–70.

Hitt, M. A., Hoskisson, R. E., Ireland, R. D., and Harrison, J. S. (1991). Are acquisitions a poison pill for innovation? *Academy of Management Executive*, 5(4): 22–34.

Hofstede, G. (1980). Motivation, leadership and organization: Do American theories apply abroad? *Organizational Dynamics*, Summer: 42–63.

Ignatius, B. (1995). Cultural Due Diligence: Managing The Human Integration in Mergers and Acquisitions. Unpublished master's thesis, University of San Francisco.

Jemison, D. B., and Sitkin, S. B. (1986). Corporate acquisitions: A process perspective. *Academy of Management Review*, 11(1): 145–63.

AT Kearney (1998). White Paper on Post-Merger Integration. KPMG report.

Lane, H. W., Beddows, R. G., and Lawrence, P. R. (1981a). *Managing Large Research and Development Programs*. Albany, NY: State University of New York Press.

Lane, H. W., Beddows, R. G., and Lawrence, P. R. (1981b). The technical logic of research and development. *R&D Management*, 11(1): 1–24.

Lane, H. W., DiStefano, J. J., and Maznevski, M. L. (2000). *International Management Behavior*, 4th edn. Oxford: Blackwell Publishers Ltd.

Lane, H. W., Greenberg, D., and Berdrow, I. (2004). Barriers and bonds to knowledge transfer in global alliances and mergers. In Lane, Maznevski, Mendenhall, and McNett (eds.), *Blackwell Handbook of Global Management: A Guide to Managing Complexity*. Oxford: Blackwell Publishers Ltd., pp. 342–61.

Lane, H. W., Slaughter, K. E., Campbell, D. D. (1996). Grupo Financiero Inverlat. Ivey case 9–97-L001. Richard Ivey School of Business, London, ON, Canada.

Larsson R. (1989). *Organizational Integration of Mergers and Acquisitions: A Case Survey of Realization of Synergy Potentials*. Lund, Sweden: Lund University Press.

Laurent, A. (1986). The cross-cultural puzzle of international human resource management. *International Studies of Management and Organization*, 13(1/2): 5–96.

Leroy, F., and Ramanantsoa, B. (1997). The cognitive and behavioural dimensions of organizational learning in a merger: An empirical study. *Journal of Management Studies*, 34(6): 871–94.

Madura, J., Vasconcellos, G. M., and Kish, R. J. (1991). A valuation model for international acquisitions. *Management Decision*, 29(4): 31–8.

Marks, M. L. (1999). Adding cultural fit to your diligence checklist. *Mergers and Acquisitions*, 34(3): 14–20.

Marks, M. L., and Mirvis, P. H. (1998). *Joining Forces: Making One Plus One Equal Three in Mergers, Acquisitions, and Alliances*. New York: Jossey-Bass.

Maucher, H. O. (1998). Mergers and Acquisitions as a Means of Restructuring and Repositioning in the Global Market—Business, Macroeconomic and Political Aspects. Transnational Corporations, 7(3). United Nations Conference on Trade and Development, Division on Investment, Technology and Enterprise Development.

Maznevski, M. L., and Chudoba, K. M. (2000). Bridging space over time: Global virtual-team dynamics and effectiveness. *Organization Science*, 11: 473–92.

Meyer, J. P. (2001). Embrace and extend: A case of inter-organizational learning. Paper presented at the Eastern Academy of Management, New York.

Morton, J. A. (1967). A systems approach to the innovation process. *Business Horizons*, 10(2): 27–36.

Nahavandi, A., and Malekzadeh, A. R. (1988). Acculturation in mergers and acquisitions. *Academy of Management Review*, 13: 79–90.

Prahalad, C. K., and Bettis, R. A. (1986). The dominant logic: A new linkage between diversity and performance. *Strategic Management Journal*, 7: 485–501.

Ranft, A. L., and Lord, M. D. (2002). Acquiring new technologies and capabilities: A grounded model of acquisition implementation. *Organization Science*, 13(4): 420–42.

Ravenscraft, D. J., and Scherer, F. M. (1987). *Mergers, sell-offs and economic efficiency*. Brookings Institutions: Washington, DC.

Schneider, S. C. (1988). National vs. corporate culture: Implications for human resource management. *Human Resource Management*, 27(2): 231–47.

Schoenberg. R. (2001). Knowledge transfer and resource sharing as value creation mechanisms in inbound continental European acquisitions. *Journal of Euromarketing*, 10(1): 99–114.

Shrallow, D. A. (1985). Managing the integration of acquired operations. *Journal of Business Strategy*, 6(1): 30–6.

Shrivastava, P. (1986). Postmerger integration. *Journal of Business Strategy*, 7(1): 65–76.

Singh H., and Zollo, M. (1998). *The Impact of Knowledge Codification, Experience Trajectories, and Integration Strategies on the Performance of Corporate Acquisitions*. Fontainebleau, France: INSEAD.

Sirower, M. L. (1998). *The Synergy Trap: How Companies Lose the Acquisition Game*. New York: The Free Press.

Tempest, N. (1999a). *Cisco Systems, Inc.: Acquisition Integration for Manufacturing*. Palo Alto, CA: Harvard Business School California Research Center.

Tempest, N. (1999b). *Cisco Systems, Inc.: Acquisition Integration for Manufacturing (A)*. Cambridge, MA: Harvard Business School Publishing.

Towers Perrin, Seven Steps to a Successful Merger or Acquisition. Towers Perrin Company Report.

Tushman, M. L., and Scanlan, T. J. (1981). Boundary spanning individuals: Their role in information transfer and their antecedents. *Academy of Management Journal*, 24(2): 289–305.

Vermeulen, F., and Barkema, H. (2001). Learning through acquisitions. *Academy of Management Journal*, 44(3): 457–76.

World Investment Report: Cross-Border Mergers and Acquisitions (2000). United Nations Conference on Trade and Development, New York and Geneva, pp. 110–11.

Executive Commentary on Chapter 3

JEAN LUC SCALABRE

Cross-border mergers and acquisitions (M&A) have surged in the last thirty years, led by the global expansion of U.S. companies followed by European companies trying to challenge U.S. economic leadership. More recently, a few Asian companies have attempted to become global players by making selective overseas acquisitions or investments. Cultural factors have always been a key issue for the success of all these cross-border transactions. Although differences between business cultures have greatly diminished in the last twenty years between the United States, Europe, and Asia, they still remain the main reasons for many failed attempts on all sides. A few spectacular cases reported in the chapter confirm that in spite of an abundant literature covering the subject, and many examples of poorly executed M&A, companies seem not to have learned from each other's experience and continue to make the same mistakes. My own experience at a more modest level seems to corroborate these observations: companies do not learn well from each other and must improve their internal learning process through their own experiences.

My experience of M&A in the United States, Western Europe, and particularly in Northern Asia confirms that differences in business culture are the main reasons for failed projects and add a tremendous level of difficulty to an already complex business situation. As soon as cultural factors become an issue, the success rate of M&A dramatically drops below 50 percent. Hence, the need to find exceptional managers to run them and to rely on well-trained and experienced teams to support the acquisition process is critical. In their reach for global expansion, Northern Asia is the new frontier for multinational companies to make strategic and meaningful acquisitions creating shareholder value and global competitive advantage. The business culture of this part of the world is radically different from our Western standards, and is not known to many managers involved in M&A activities. Carlos Ghosn, the emblematic Renault/Nissan CEO, is rather the exception than the rule in terms of leadership, management skills, and capability to turn around a difficult acquisition.

The comments that follow are drawn mainly from my experience of M&A in Asia and will focus on this part of the world where M&A are notoriously more difficult to implement than anywhere else. Completing and running a successful M&A is both "an art and a science," requiring pragmatism and implementation of well-established management principles. One can learn from the business literature, which extensively covers the subject, but nothing replaces the experience of seasoned managers and acquisition teams with appropriate cultural sensitivity, having learned from previous similar experiences. The authors are right in suggesting that companies should have dedicated acquisition managers and teams, and that the three-phase acquisition process (precombination, combination, postcombination) should be carefully planned.

However, in today's fast changing corporate management structures, which are characterized by obsession with synergies and efficiency, few companies are able to capitalize on their past experience and maintain a pool of specialized managers that can be sent on short notice anywhere in the world to implement an M&A project. When M&A opportunities arise, mid-size companies often resort to "ad hoc" acquisition teams comprising senior managers available for the task, who are temporarily assisted by specialized consultants. This lack of appropriate and permanent structure is a clear barrier to knowledge transfer between merging partners during the M&A process and accounts for a large share of failures.

As pointed out in the chapter, bidirectional knowledge transfer is essential for the success of M&A, as the "acquired company" has to successfully integrate into the new organization and embrace the new management culture, while the acquiring company must work diligently to fully understand the local business conditions and culture. This is especially difficult when business cultures are very different from each other, which is the case in Asia.

Owing to the uniqueness of the Northern Asian business culture, my previous experience of M&A in the United States and Western Europe did not build the necessary experience or expertise to address "cultural factors" in this part of the world. The urgency and challenges of the business environment, and the lack of postacquisition support did not give me either the time or the resources to properly focus on acquisition and integration processes, which later created a few serious problems which I will mention later.

The authors suggest that a newly created organization will not learn during the postacquisition phase of the M&A process if it had not been engaged in a learning process during the prior phases. This is probably true, but how often is it possible for companies being merged or acquired to orderly follow the three-stage acquisition process given the constraints set by regulatory bodies and the need to quickly implement a new business strategy? Many M&A these days are driven by cost reduction factors rather than strategic issues, and they set very ambitious short-term financial goals. Very few companies find themselves in ideal conditions where they can apply M&A theory and most, in fact, execute their integration plans under pressures of all kinds of time constraints and financial challenges.

The authors have identified four types of barriers that hinder the flow of information across boundaries: language, space, organization structure, and motivation. They suggest that language was an issue during the acquisition of Rover by BMW. One can imagine the issues created by differences of language when a European or an American company acquires a Korean, Japanese, or Chinese company. In these scenarios, language becomes the biggest barrier to successful information collection and knowledge transfer, and this is often totally underestimated and not anticipated by top management. Communication between top managers speaking a common language is not good enough: a direct communication link with all management levels of the acquired company must be established to insure the proper dissemination of information and to give all employees a vehicle for expressing their views or concerns. It is a common mistake of many change efforts to underestimate communication challenges.

Regarding organization structure, the authors rightly stress the need to have an "integration team to manage the integration process, and not the new business," and to be involved during the combination phase. This continuity is absolutely essential, especially for acquisitions involving companies of significantly different business cultures, which is the case in Asia. Unfortunately, very often the "combination team" is different from the "precombination team" and the transfer of knowledge and information acquired during the due diligence process is not efficient, making it more difficult for the "combination team" to achieve the expected results or to prevent serious integration issues. Thus, the barriers are not removed and the bonds are not created which are necessary to pave the way for a smooth integration process.

Experience shows that management teams are often so busy running the newly merged company in the new business environment that they have very little time for handling and leading personnel integration matters. These matters should be detected and handled early in the M&A process in order to prevent further problems and to properly motivate and lead employees. A full-time "Human Resources Integration Manager" or even an HR integration team for large M&A, which handle only HR integration matters, is probably the best solution when top management is too busy "putting out fires."

Knowledge will not transfer automatically by just putting people under the same roof, or by sending memos, e-mails, or calling frequent meetings. Every possible communication vehicle should be used to insure proper communication between the new partners in order to broadcast the new vision and strategies and to receive feedback from all employees.

In mergers between companies of significantly different business cultures it is imperative to create bonds between people, to establish mutual trust, and to put in place a representative management team to lead the new company and to communicate the new vision. Only a powerful and inspiring coalition will create the conditions for people to communicate, to learn from each other, and ultimately to embrace and promote the values of the new company. In the Asian business culture, relations between employer and employees are driven by emotional and psychological factors: implicit social rules, trust, dependence, and interpersonal respect affect employee behavior. By contrast, in the Western business culture, employee/employer relations are very formal and based on visible and documented rules and contracts.

Another important factor is the pace of change, especially in Asia, where the pace of change imposed by headquarters or by the financial objectives of the M&A are often not compatible with the capacity of local teams to adjust to the new situation and to quickly assimilate the new corporate culture. In this case, reactions can be brutal, as they proved to be in the M&A I was implementing in Northern Asia: A ninety-day strike erupted after many staff found that the pace of change was too fast and driving them too quickly out of their comfort zone. The Asian business culture is not used to drastic and quick changes unless forced by major economic events.

Too often in large corporations managers compete for cash, and financial targets are the main criteria used to award resources among several competing projects (acquisition, production, or R&D investment). Short-term financial returns play a more important role than long-term strategic moves, and financial objectives are often set that are beyond realistic achievement.

This competition for resources and their necessary financial justification often push the precombination teams to be overly optimistic in their financial forecasts, creating unrealistic challenges for the postcombination teams. One way to reduce the risk of setting unattainable financial targets would be to assign the precombination team or some of its senior managers to the management of the acquisition. Financial forecasts would suddenly become much more realistic, probably leading to the cancelation of many M&A projects. To prevent this early elimination, a positive discount factor could be applied to take into account the complexity of the projected acquisition and its strategic importance.

Top management plays an important role in M&A by insuring proper leadership and leading by example. Successful M&A in Asia have top management executives who spend a large portion of their time communicating with people, listening to them, and showing empathy to create the conditions for all employees to engage in "knowledge and learning transfer." Without the genuine involvement of the company leaders, other employees are likely to refrain from fully engaging themselves in necessary integration activities, and thus maintaining barriers between merging teams.

Keeping employees motivated is obviously a key factor for the success of any new company created by an M&A. Again, differences in cultural values and business cultures should be taken into account when building a motivational plan. In one of the mergers I was involved in, I noticed a significant difference in employee salaries between the two companies being merged. One of my first decisions was to raise salaries across the acquired company by an average of 15 percent, which at that time was significantly higher than the inflation rate. I thought it would create the initial necessary motivation, and show to the acquired company our desire to treat all employees equally. To my surprise, it failed to create the desired effects as many employees attached more importance to other traditional "values" that were typical of Asian business culture. In our case, the local management of the acquired company had failed to convey the expectations and concerns of the staff, and the foreign management, isolated from the field, made the wrong assumption that significant salary differences would create serious concerns in the acquired company staff. In fact, employees were more concerned with layoffs, changes of management culture, and the new HR policy than with salary increases.

The acquisition of local companies in Northeast Asia (Japan, Korea, China) by European or American companies is probably an extreme scenario, where differences in business culture create significant integration challenges and are the main reasons for unsuccessful acquisitions. Approaching M&A in this part of the world by drawing on Western-style concepts could be misleading and counterproductive. It is not because Chinese, Japanese, or Koreans drink Coca Cola, eat hamburgers or pizza, wear Louis Vuiton accessories, and drive Mercedes Benz automobiles that they have joined the ranks of "westernized societies." Downtown Tokyo, Seoul, and Shanghai look very much like Manhattan these days—on the surface at least. The apparent change toward a "consumer society and a convergence of consumer tastes" has not yet impacted some of the traditional and fundamental behavior of people and the values of local business cultures. This issue remains by far the most critical factor in any M&A in this important economic part of the world and often prevents the necessary removal of barriers and creation of bonds between individuals involved in cross-border M&A.

4 Trust in Mergers and Acquisitions

GÜNTER K. STAHL AND SIM B. SITKIN

Imagine commuting to work one day and hearing over the radio that your employer had agreed to merge with a competitor and that substantial workforce reductions were expected. Ciba Geigy employees experienced this scenario in March 1996, when employees and financial analysts alike were surprised by the merger announcement between Ciba Geigy and Sandoz (Whitener et al., 1998). No information was provided in the days following the announcement about how the merger would affect employees—only that the combined company, named Novartis, would probably employ at least 10 percent fewer workers.

> Employees arrived at work anxious and bewildered. If management couldn't trust them with such vital information, how could employees trust management to look out for their interests once the merger occurred? . . . Change was underway and employees didn't know who or what to believe. In a perfect world, this would never happen. Good news or bad, employees could trust management to give it to them straight, to mean what it said, and always to follow through on promises. (Caudron, 1996, p. 20)

In the weeks and months following the merger, Novartis suffered from what has been described as the "merger syndrome" (Cartwright and Cooper, 1996; Marks and Mirvis, 1998), an organizational response to crisis that can be observed at three levels. At the *personal level*, people go through a state of culture shock, including reduced job performance and resistance to change, rumor mills of possible layoffs or reassignments drain energy and productivity, and feelings of fear, betrayal, and anger prevail, particularly among employees in the acquired company. At the *organizational level*, executives adopt a crisis-management mode; the quality and quantity of communication decreases; and decision making becomes centralized. At the *cultural level*, there are dysfunctional culture clashes; in-group out-group bias increases (the "we vs. they" syndrome); and stereotypes and chauvinistic biases become a source of hostility and distrust.

In the case of Novartis, senior executives realized soon after the merger that there was a trust problem, and started to take corrective action (see Chapter 17 in this volume). Perhaps the most telling statement on the detrimental effects that the merger had on employee trust, and the challenges that top management confronted in the months following the merger, is that of Daniel Vasella, Chairman of the Board and CEO of Novartis:

> Trust is the most important of our values.... Only in a climate of trust are people willing to strive for the slightly impossible, to make decisions on their own, to take initiative, to feel accountable; trust is a prerequisite for working together effectively; trust is also an ally to fight bureaucracy.... Among all the corporate values, trust was the one that suffered most from the merger.... We must fill this vacuum as fast as we can, we must restore confidence. We must earn it by "walking the talk", with candour, integrity, openness, fairness... We need to create a culture based on trust. (cited in Engeli, 1999, p. 5)

Why did trust in management suffer as a result of the merger? What are the factors influencing the development of trust following mergers and acquisitions (M&A)? And how can management restore trust? In this chapter, we build on our earlier work on M&A trust to discuss the previously neglected, but potentially critical, role that trust plays in the integration process following M&A.

Why Is Trust Important to the Success of M&A?

Theoretical frameworks for explaining M&A success and failure have traditionally focused on financial and strategic factors, for example, the degree of "strategic fit" or industry relatedness between the acquiring and the target firm. Only recently, research endeavors have begun to analyze the "softer," less tangible social, cultural, and psychological issues involved in integrating merging or acquired firms. Factors such as cultural fit, the pattern of dominance between merging firms, management style similarity, combining firms' preferred mode of acculturation, and the social climate surrounding a merger or an acquisition have increasingly been recognized to be of critical importance to M&A success and failure (see Cartwright and Cooper, 1996; Schweiger and Walsh, 1990; Stahl et al., 2004, for reviews).

Recently, we have suggested that trust may play a key role in the integration process following a merger or an acquisition (Stahl and Sitkin, 2001). Evidence about the critical importance of trust to M&A success and failure can be drawn from a large body of research on intra- and interorganizational trust. This research has shown that trust is important in a number of ways: it can improve the quality of employee work performance, problem solving, and communication, and can enhance employee commitment and citizenship behavior. Trust can also improve manager–subordinate relationships, implementation of self-managed work groups, and the firm's ability to adapt to complexity and change. Further, trust can decrease agency and transaction costs by limiting the need for monitoring and control and, ultimately, can provide firms with a competitive advantage (for reviews, see Dirks and Ferrin, 2001; Jones and George, 1998; Kramer, 1999; Rousseau et al., 1998).

Further, a large body of research on interorganizational trust has shown that trust is of critical importance to the formation and implementation of cooperative alliances between firms, such as joint ventures, R&D collaborations, and marketing partnerships (Das and Teng, 1998; Ring and Van de Ven, 1992; Zaheer et al., 1998). As alliances and M&A share many characteristics, it seems reasonable to assume that trust plays an important role in the M&A process as well. In fact, a large number of M&A case studies (for example, Buono, Bowditch, and Lewis, 1985; Cartwright and Cooper, 1996; Olie, 1994) as well as interviews with managers and employees of acquired organizations (for example, Krug and Nigh, 2001; Napier et al., 1989; Schweiger, Ivancevich, and Power, 1987) suggest that trust is of critical importance to the success of M&A.

But what is the process by which trust affects M&A outcomes? Before answering this question, it is important to understand the nature and dynamics of trust within and between organizations.

Central to most definitions of trust are the notions of risk and vulnerability (Stickel, 1999). Risk means that a party could experience negative outcomes if the other party is untrustworthy. The risk of negative outcomes must be present for trust to operate, and the trustor must be willing to be vulnerable. In the absence of risk, trust is irrelevant because there is no vulnerability (Mayer et al., 1995; Rousseau et al., 1998). Rousseau et al. (1998, p. 395) define *trust* as "a psychological state comprising the intention to accept vulnerability based upon positive expectations of the intentions or behavior of another." Conversely, *distrust* can be defined as negative expectations of another's intentions or behavior (Lewicki et al., 1998; Sitkin and Roth, 1993).

This conceptualization of trust has been applied to strategic alliances (for example, Currall and Judge, 1995; Inkpen and Currall, 1997), and it can also be applied to M&A. In the context of M&A, there are numerous sources of risk and forms of risk-taking involved for the members of both organizations. For employees of the acquired firm (or, in the case of a merger, the subordinate partner), the period following the announcement of the takeover is one of intense personal risk analysis, in which the individual decides whether s/he will leave the organization or stay. During this period, employees have to rely on statements of top management concerning their future employment status and roles in the organization. Another type of risk concerns the efforts of managers devoted to building cooperative relationships, dispelling rumors, and reducing employee anxiety—efforts that may prove futile if the acquirer decides to lay off significant parts of the workforce. The top management of the acquiring firm, on the other hand, may run the risk of opportunistic behavior if it allows the members of the acquired firm a high degree of autonomy. It also has to rely on employee willingness to focus attention on the organization's best interest as opposed to self-interest. These examples illustrate that the sources of risk vary considerably for the different parties involved in a merger or an acquisition. But for all parties, trust-related concerns are critical because of the high degree of risk involved.

One approach to understanding why a given party will have a greater or lesser amount of trust for another party is to consider attributes of the trustee (Gabarro, 1978; Mayer et al., 1995; Whitener et al., 1998). The organizational trust literature suggests that five characteristics of a trustee appear to be particularly critical for the development of trust in a relationship:

1. Competence
2. Integrity
3. Benevolence
4. Openness
5. Value congruence

For example, in the context of acquisitions, failure of a project team to meet performance expectations may be judged by the acquirer to be typical of the in *competence* of the target firm as a whole. Inconsistent information about the extent of job losses provided by the acquirer may adversely affect target firm members' perceptions of the acquiring firm management's *integrity*. Resistance to the changes that inevitably follow an acquisition may create distrust among acquiring managers by reinforcing fears concerning target firm members' lack of loyalty or *benevolence*. Failure of the acquirer to share critical information with employees of the target firm may detrimentally affect perceptions of *openness*. And differences in organizational culture (for example, different problem-solving styles, and risk propensities) may be seen as indicators of distrust-creating *value incongruence*. We

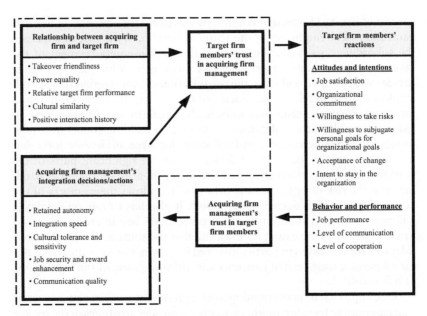

FIGURE **4.1** Model of Trust in the Postacquisition Integration Process (Stahl and Sitkin, 2001). Dotted lines denote the part of the model that has been empirically tested

propose that in M&A, these five dimensions form the basis for a generalized perception of the trustworthiness of the other party (Stahl and Sitkin, 2001).

Factors Influencing the Development of Trust in M&A

Our model of trust in the postacquisition integration process (see Figure 4.1) draws on prior research on intra- and interorganizational trust as well as M&A integration. It focuses on the two main parties involved in an acquisition: the members of the target firm and the top management of the acquiring firm. Although the model deals with acquisitions only, it is conceptualized to be applicable to any merger in which power is asymmetrical. As M&A researchers have noted, the actual occurrence of "mergers of equals" is rare, although many acquisitions may be described as mergers to avoid the appearance of dominance by one firm (Cartwright and Cooper, 1996; Hogan and Overmyer-Day, 1994; Jemison and Sitkin, 1986).

Proceeding from left to right, the model suggests that certain characteristics of the initial takeover situation—in particular the nature of the relationship between the acquiring firm and the target firm—as well as the acquirer's integration decisions and actions will affect target firm members' trust in the acquiring firm management. It is evident that the two sets of antecedents are not independent of each other. For example, the mode of takeover will likely have an impact on the amount of control that is imposed on the target, because in hostile bids the acquirer is usually inclined to adopt a more "hands-on" integration strategy than in amicable bids (Hunt, 1990; Jemison and Sitkin, 1986). Also, within each of the two sets of antecedents, the variables cannot be assumed to be independent of each other. For example, the amount of control exerted by the acquiring firm management will likely have an impact on the quality of communication between the acquiring firm and the target firm (Bastien, 1987; Schweiger and Walsh, 1990).

An important feature of the model is its reciprocal and dynamic nature. The model suggests that the degree to which the target firm members trust the acquiring firm management will affect both target firm members' attitudes and intentions, as well as their postacquisition behavior and performance. Further, it suggests that target firm members' reactions to a takeover will affect the acquirer's integration decisions and actions through perceptions of the target's trustworthiness, thus possibly leading to a cycle of escalating distrust between the members of the two organizations.

Next, we will examine how the characteristics of the initial takeover situation and the integration process affect target firm members' trust in the acquiring firm management.

Characteristics of the Initial Takeover Situation Affecting Target Firm Members' Trust

Five aspects of the relationship between the two firms are proposed as determinants of trust: takeover friendliness, power equality, relative firm performance, cultural similarity, and positive interaction history.

Takeover Friendliness

The most extreme and probably most devastating form of hostility in M&A is the unwanted takeover attempt, occurring when a company either overtly or covertly acquires another firm against its will. The purchasing company, driven by financial interests, usually seeks domination of the acquired firm rather than a cooperative mode of integration. Prior research on M&A has shown that hostile takeover tactics can result in sharp interorganizational conflict and major difficulties integrating the acquired company (Buono and Bowditch, 1989; Hambrick and Cannella, 1993; Hunt, 1990). In a hostile takeover, target and acquiring firm executives battle each other in a public forum, each being suspicious of the other's intentions, and claiming the other party's lack of credibility. Compared to friendly acquisitions, in hostile takeovers the acquirer is more likely to replace the management of the target firm and impose rigorous controls on the target (Hambrick and Cannella, 1993; Krug and Nigh, 2001). Executives of acquired firms have likened the unwanted takeover to a rape and described the acquiring firm's managers as attackers or barbarians—people not to be trusted (Marks and Mirvis, 2001).

Power Equality

Although there are various sources of power in and between organizations, the capability and tendency of the acquiring firm for exercising power to enforce its preferences upon the target is particularly strong when the acquirer is significantly larger than the target firm (Pablo, 1994). In this case, target firm members' needs tend to get overlooked or trivialized by the acquiring firm management (Chatterjee et al., 1992; Datta and Grant, 1990). The impact of a power differential between the two organizations involved in an acquisition "is not simply the overwhelming and domination of the smaller entity through sheer magnitude, but also the intensification of beliefs about superiority and inferiority" (Pablo, 1994, p. 810). The mere existence of a power differential may lead to distrust through anticipation of an acquirer's future actions. As power asymmetry increases, the weaker party usually becomes distrustful because the more powerful firm has no need to be trusting, as it can use its relative power to obtain cooperation (Anderson and Weitz, 1989; Kumar, 1996).

Relative Target Firm Performance

The impact of a takeover on employee morale and productivity is not always negative. Being liberated from weak and ineffective management may actually enhance employee satisfaction, commitment, and job performance (Hunt, 1990; Larsson, 1990; Schweiger and Walsh, 1990). For example, Bastien (1987) found that the overall mood of employees was celebratory and optimistic after a "white knight" acquisition by a healthy buyer. If a poorly managed, underperforming firm is acquired by a healthy one, target firm employees may see this as a chance for greater job satisfaction, more job security, and increased prospects for promotion and compensation. At the same time, poor target firm performance in the past may increase an acquirer's tendencies toward arrogance and domination. As the poor performance of a company is commonly attributed to its top managers, the prospect of being acquired by a more successful company will be particularly threatening to the target firm's executives. As Hambrick and Cannella (1993) have noted, even if executives of a poorly performing firm are not fired outright after their acquisition, they may feel inferior or depart voluntarily because they are anticipating the dominating behaviors of their "conquerors." Relative firm performance may thus have a positive or negative effect on target firm members' trust in the acquiring firm management, depending on their hierarchical level in the organization.

Cultural Similarity

It has often been argued that culture barriers can pose major obstacles to fully reaping envisaged integration benefits in M&A (Cartwright and Cooper, 1996; Nahavandi and Malekzadeh, 1988; Very and Schweiger, 2001). The "cultural distance hypothesis," in its most general form, holds that the difficulties, costs, or risks associated with cross-cultural contact increase with growing cultural divergence between two individuals, groups, or organizations (Kogut and Singh, 1988). Cross-border acquisitions seem to be particularly difficult to integrate because they require "double-layered acculturation" (Barkema et al., 1996), whereby not only different corporate cultures, but different national cultures also have to be combined. Thus, although studies on the impact of cultural differences on M&A performance have yielded mixed results (see Stahl and Voigt, 2005, for a review), extant theory predicts that cultural differences are negatively related to trust. Prior research on intra- and interorganizational trust has suggested how shared values or other sources of cultural similarity can facilitate the development of trust (Gabarro, 1978; Sitkin and Roth, 1993). In contrast, culture barriers, stereotypes, and chauvinistic biases are frequently cited as a source of hostility and distrust between members of merging organizations (Elsass and Veiga, 1994; Malekzadeh and Nahavandi, 1998).

Positive Interaction History

Indirect evidence for the importance of the combining firms' interaction history to the postcombination integration process comes from a large body of research on the role that trust plays in workgroups, strategic alliances, and socially embedded partnerships. This research has shown that trust evolves over time through repeated interactions between partners (Gulati, 1995; Zaheer et al., 1998). Like romantic relationships, interfirm relationships mature with interaction frequency, duration, and the diversity of challenges that partners encounter and face together (Lewicki et al., 1998; Sitkin and Roth, 1993). As Rousseau et al. (1998, p. 399) have noted, "[r]epeated cycles of exchange, risk taking, and successful fulfillment of expectations strengthen the willingness of trusting parties to rely upon each other and expand the resources brought into the exchange." However, trust can be expected to emerge between members of organizations only when they have *successfully* completed transactions in the past and they perceive one another as complying with norms of equity (Ring and Van de Ven, 1992). Thus, the nature of the relationship may be more important than its duration. If members of the combining organizations had a conflict-rich or inequitable exchange prior to the merger or acquisition, this may limit the potential for trust to emerge.

Integration Process Variables Affecting Target Firm Members' Trust

Five aspects of the acquiring firm management's integration-related decisions and actions are proposed as determinants of trust: retained autonomy, integration speed, cultural tolerance and sensitivity, job security and reward enhancement, and communication quality.

Retained Autonomy

Although, theoretically, integration can result in a balanced merging of two organizations, cultures, and workforces, this balance rarely occurs in practice. Instead, the acquirer typically imposes control onto the target firm, and where changes occur in policies, systems, and culture, they affect the members of the target firm more strongly than those of the acquirer (Hambrick and Cannella, 1993; Marks and Mirvis, 2001). Autonomy removal can be devastating from the perspective of the members of the target firm (Buono and Bowditch, 1989). Senior managers are likely to suffer most from a loss of autonomy and control following an acquisition because they were accustomed to doing things their own way and must now look to the acquiring firm management for approval (Hambrick and Cannella, 1993)— a situation that Datta and Grant (1990) have termed the "conquering army syndrome." Autonomy removal and being put under close monitoring will likely lead to feelings of helplessness, hostility, and distrust on the part of the target firm members. Because controls tend to signal the absence of trust, their use typically hampers the emergence of trust (Rousseau et al., 1998; Sitkin, 1995).

Speed of Integration

In the M&A literature, there is considerable disagreement about the nature of the relationship between speed of integration and integration outcomes. Many authors have suggested a "window of opportunity" (for example, Buono and Bowditch, 1989) occurring during the first 100 days following an acquisition, when employees expect organizational change. This line of reasoning suggests that changes should be implemented quickly so as to minimize the amount of uncertainty and trauma that employees must face. In contrast, others have cited the tendency to consummate M&A too hastily as a major contributor to the high failure rates (for example, Jemison and Sitkin, 1986). Robino and DeMeuse (1985) found that both a fast-paced and a slow-paced rate of change resulted in undesirable integration outcomes and concluded that a moderate speed of integration is advisable—fast enough to reduce anxiety, and slow enough to provide thorough communication among all parties involved. Paradoxically, though, as members of the target firm usually expect significant change following a takeover, hesitation in approaching integration and telling employees that little will change can generate suspicion. As Mitchell (1989, p. 44) has noted, "if the acquirer does not act quickly to harness the expectations of the target firm and take advantage of the new loyalties, the chances are these expectations and loyalties will rapidly disappear into a miasma of disillusionment and mistrust."

Cultural Tolerance and Sensitivity

The extent to which a takeover has a negative effect on target firm members' morale and productivity will likely depend on the acquirer's degree of multiculturalism and cultural sensitivity (Chatterjee et al., 1992; Pablo, 1994). The term *multiculturalism* refers to the degree to which an organization values cultural diversity and is willing to tolerate and encourage it. A multicultural organization considers diversity an asset, and is therefore likely to allow an acquired firm to retain its own values and practices. In contrast, a unicultural acquirer emphasizes conformity and adherence to a unique organizational ideology, and is therefore likely to impose its culture on the target firm (Nahavandi and Malekzadeh, 1988). A related variable that will likely affect target firm members' reactions to a takeover is the acquirer's cultural sensitivity. Research on trust in alliances suggests that cultural sensitivity, defined as a firm's capability to deal sympathetically with cultural differences, can enhance partner trust and increase the likelihood of successful strategic integration (Johnson et al., 1997). In contrast, where key symbols that provide continuity and meaning for the members of the target firm are cast aside by the acquirer, the cultural arrogance of the acquiring firm can detrimentally affect the level of trust in the relationship (Jemison and Sitkin, 1986).

Reward and Job Security Enhancement

Several authors have stressed the importance of the quality of postcombination reward and job security changes in determining organizational members' reactions to a takeover (see Chapter 8 in this volume). If members of the target firm see the takeover as a chance for greater job satisfaction, more job security, and increased prospects for compensation and promotion, this will reduce the potential for conflict in the postacquisition integration period. In a study of British takeovers conducted by Hunt (1990), the degree to which the target firm members' career opportunities were expanded in the postacquisition implementation phase was directly related to acquisition success. Graves (1981), in a study on the effects of a merger involving two brokerage firms in the reinsurance industry, found that employee reactions depended on personal benefits and losses attributed to the merger. In a similar vein, Larsson's study of Swedish acquisitions (Larsson, 1990) revealed that increased job security, rewards, and opportunities for future career advancement reduced target firm members' resistance to a takeover. The strategic alliance literature also addresses this issue. Research on alliance trust has shown that the perceived benefits derived from an alliance have a positive effect on the mutual trust and commitment of the parties involved (Anderson and Weitz, 1989; Sarkar et al., 1997).

Communication Quality

The quality and quantity of information provided by top management has been proposed to be a key factor in the postcombination integration process. M&A are usually associated with high degrees of ambiguity and uncertainty, and communication can reduce this ambiguity and decrease employee anxiety and stress (Bastien, 1987; Davy et al., 1988). Providing employees with credible and relevant information has been shown to mitigate the traumatic effect that M&A have on employee well-being, satisfaction, and trust in the top management (Schweiger and DeNisi, 1991). A lack of credible and open communication, on the other hand, is believed to adversely affect such outcomes as employee commitment, productivity, and trust (Napier et al., 1989). While the credibility of the information provided by top management can be considered a sine qua non for trust to emerge, the optimal amount and timing of communication will likely depend on contingencies such as level of attempted integration and stage in the integration process. For example, Hogan and Overmyer-Day (1994) found that too much information disseminated to employees in mergers characterized by high levels of integration exacerbated undesirable attitudes and behaviors because it increased anxiety in a situation where employees already felt uncertain about their jobs. Therefore, it may be the quality, rather than the absolute amount and promptness, of the information provided that will determine how organizational members respond to a merger or takeover.

Target Firm Members' Reactions to the Perceived
Trustworthiness of an Acquirer

To this point, our focus has been on the various antecedents of target firm members' trust in the acquiring firm management. We now turn to the next part of the model, in which we examine the effects of trust on target firm members' reactions to the takeover (see Figure 4.1).

Prior research on intra- and interorganizational trust (for example, Dirks and Ferrin, 2001; Jones and George, 1998; Mayer et al., 1995) has suggested that trust is important in a number of ways that are manifest in specific organizational member reactions. For example, trust can enhance employee job satisfaction, organizational commitment, willingness to take risks, and willingness to subjugate personal goals for organizational goals. It can also enhance the willingness to accept change and the intent to stay in the organization. Further, trust can improve employee job performance and the level of communication and cooperation within and between organizations.

The attitudinal, behavioral, and performance effects of trust are the very variables that have been observed to be suffering significantly during postacquisition integration. Some of the typical employee reactions following a takeover include a decrease in productivity, low job satisfaction, high rates of turnover, resistance to change, a focus on personal security rather than organizational goals, a tendency to not pass information up or down, and lack of cooperation (for example, Buono and Bowditch, 1989; Cartwright and Cooper, 1996). Together, these two different streams of research suggest that target firm members' trust in the acquiring firm management will have a positive effect on a variety of individual, group, and organizational outcomes.

Acquiring Firm Management's Trust and Subsequent
Integration Decisions and Actions

The model presented in Figure 4.1 depicts how the target firm members' reactions to a takeover can influence the acquiring firm managers' trust in the target firm, and that this trust, in turn, can affect the acquiring firm management's subsequent integration decisions and actions.

On the basis of prior research on M&A, we expect that the target firm members' reactions to a takeover will affect all five dimensions of trust, namely, perceived competence, integrity, benevolence, openness, and value congruence. Trust may be undermined, for example, when performance expectations are not met and the lack of performance is attributed to a lack of competence on the part of the target firm's management. The massive departure of key employees after an acquisition may violate expectations about the target firm members' commitment or integrity and be generally applied to remaining employees who are now viewed with suspicion. Even normal levels of resistance to the changes that inevitably follow an acquisition may create distrust by reinforcing fears concerning target firm members' lack of loyalty to their new parent firm. Trust can also be undermined when there is a concern among managers that their employees are not being forthright about problems. Thus, failure to pass critical information up the acquirer's management, if discovered or even falsely assumed, may adversely affect the perceived openness of employees and, thus, managers' trust in them. Finally, disagreements may be seen as indicators of distrust-creating value incongruence.

Further, we propose that the acquiring firm managers' trust in the target firm is a critical variable that affects integration-related decisions and actions. A large body of research has shown that the level of trust in a relationship affects the amount of risk a person is willing to take (for example, Mayer et al., 1995; Rousseau et al., 1998). Integration decisions require a willingness on the part of the acquiring firm management to take various forms of risk. For example, the acquiring firm management may take a risk by allowing the target firm a high degree of autonomy, but the willingness to grant such autonomy is likely to be higher to the extent that the acquirer trusts the target firm members. Similarly, we propose that other key acquisition integration features rest on a willingness on the part of the acquiring firm management to tolerate risk and trust the target firm. Management is thus more likely to reduce the speed of integration, tolerate and encourage cultural diversity, and guarantee job security and rewards to the extent that the target firm members have built a basis for trust. Finally, open communication can be quite risky when handling highly sensitive and delicate issues like those that surround acquisitions. Acquirer openness is much more likely to occur when a relationship of trust has been established or is emerging.

This analysis suggests that target employee behavior and performance is critically important as an influence on how acquiring firm managers take decisions and actions as the firms are integrated. However, we propose that this influence is not direct. Instead, we argue that this influence is mediated by the degree to which target firm members' behaviors and performance engender trust, for even the most stellar target outcomes are insufficient if they have not effectively created a willingness to trust on the part of the acquiring firm management. Conversely, if the acquirer distrusts the members of the target firm, the opposite effect is likely to occur (that is, tighter control, a tendency to complete the integration process quickly, intolerance of cultural diversity, reduced communication quality, and, in general, less benign integration decisions).

The Critical Role of Trust in M&A: Empirical Evidence

In the first of a series of studies planned to test our model of trust in the postacquisition integration process, we used a policy-capturing approach (a decision-making simulation) to examine a subset of the hypothesized relationships. Specifically, we examined how certain characteristics of the initial takeover situation and the integration process affect target firm members' trust in the acquiring firm management. In doing so, our research focused on the first part of the model only (the part denoted by dotted lines in Figure 4.1).

Through the policy-capturing technique, individuals' decisions in certain domains (for example, trust decisions) can be modeled by presenting them with a number of experimentally designed scenarios (Pablo, 1994). We used five of the proposed antecedents of target firm members' trust in the acquiring firm management as decision criteria around which we constructed a set of hypothetical takeover scenarios to simulate trust decisions. These antecedents were mode of takeover, cultural distance, extent of imposed control, interaction history, and attractiveness of the acquirer's HR and reward system. Next, we presented these experimentally designed takeover scenarios in the form of a questionnaire to a sample of employees. Each questionnaire contained sixteen randomly varied takeover scenarios, and after reviewing each takeover scenario, respondents were asked to indicate on a rating scale the extent to which they would trust the acquiring firm management if they were a member of the target firm. This research design allowed us to study individuals' trust decisions in a variety of takeover scenarios.

Figure 4.2 summarizes the hypothesized relationships and the findings of the first (Stahl and Chua, 2002) of a series of policy-capturing studies in which we used samples of employees of different nationalities to test our model (Stahl, Chua, and Pablo, 2003; Stahl and Wagner, 2002). The sample in this study consisted of 213 Singaporean employees, a broad group of respondents who varied in their age, gender, level of education, prior experience with M&A, and the positions they held in their companies.

The findings show that four out of the five decision criteria were significant influences on respondents' trust decisions. The effects were all in the hypothesized direction. Only cultural distance was not significant in influencing respondents' trust decisions, suggesting that the extent of cultural differences between the acquiring and target firm (whether it is a cross-border acquisition or a domestic one) does not affect target firm members' trust in the acquiring firm management. This finding, albeit unexpected, is consistent with the results of studies that have shown that cultural differences do not always have a negative effect on M&A outcomes (for example, Larsson and Risberg, 1998; Morosini, Shane, and Singh, 1998). However,

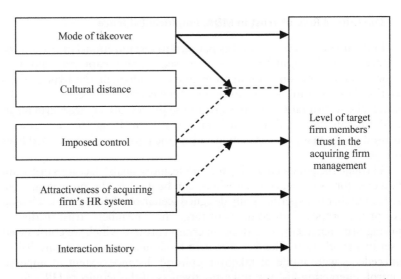

FIGURE **4.2** Hypothesized Relationships and Findings of a Policy-Capturing Study (Stahl and Chua, 2002). Solid arrows indicate significant relationships ($p < .01$); dotted arrows indicate nonsignificant relationships

we found a significant interaction effect between mode of takeover and cultural distance (see Figure 4.2), indicating that the detrimental effects of a hostile mode of takeover on target firm members' trust in the acquiring firm management are more pronounced in cross-border acquisitions than in domestic ones. Thus, cultural distance does matter in certain takeover situations.

In addition, we examined whether the five decision criteria were equally important in influencing respondents' trust decisions. Our findings suggest that the characteristics of the takeover situation and postacquisition integration process are not equally important in affecting trust. In the decision-making simulation employed in this study, the attractiveness of the acquiring firm's HR policies and reward system was by far the most important factor influencing respondents' trust decisions. This finding is consistent with the results of prior studies (for example, Graves, 1981; Larsson, 1990) that have shown that the employee reactions to a merger or an acquisition depend primarily on the personal benefits and losses attributed to this event.

Interaction history was the second most important factor influencing respondents' trust decisions, suggesting that this sample of Singaporean respondents was influenced in their trust decisions by the strength and quality of prior relationships with members of the acquiring firm. As comparative management scholars have noted (for example, Hofstede, 1980; Redding,

1990), Asian cultures are in general characterized by a strong relationship orientation—much importance is placed on building trust through personal contact and collaborations over time.

Somewhat surprisingly, demographic variables (such as age, gender, position level, and prior experience with M&A) only had a minor influence on respondents' trust decisions. Thus, the reactions to a takeover seem to be remarkably consistent across a broad group of individuals—including both male and female, all age groups, managers and nonmanagers, diverse functional, diverse industries, and those with or without prior personal experience with M&A.

The Critical Role of Trust in M&A: Implications for Practice

In M&A, special emphasis is usually put on the strategic and financial goals of the transaction, while the "human factors" do not receive much attention (Cartwright and Cooper, 1996; Nahavandi and Malekzadeh, 1988). Our model of trust in the postacquisition integration process, as well as the findings of a series of policy-capturing studies of employees' trust decisions following takeovers, suggest that the "softer," less tangible psychological, social, and cultural factors play a key role in the postacquisition integration process. Characteristics of the initial takeover situation such as hostile takeover tactics or lack of prior personal contact between the members of the combining organizations can be major obstacles to achieving integration benefits because they can undermine target firm members' trust in the acquiring firm management. Therefore, the sociocultural implications have to be considered at an early stage in the acquisition process, in the evaluation and selection of a suitable target, and in the planning of the integration process.

Further, consistent with a "process perspective" on acquisitions (Haspeslagh and Jemison, 1991; Jemison and Sitkin, 1986), the findings of this study suggest that the outcome of an acquisition depends heavily on the management of the postacquisition integration process. While characteristics of the initial takeover situation may form the upper bound on the degree of success that an acquisition can achieve, top management's integration decisions and actions will determine the degree to which that potential is realized (Pablo et al., 1996). Being aware of (and appropriately tempering) the tendency to remove more autonomy from the target firm than might be necessary in order to achieve the projected synergies can go a long way toward building a relationship that is based on trust. Carefully setting the appropriate tone in and after the negotiations, providing opportunities for interaction between members of the target and the acquiring firm, and improving incentive and reward systems will also have a positive impact on trust, and increase the chances for successful integration.

Our proposed cyclical model of trust in the postacquisition integration process suggests that trust (or distrust) between the members of the two organizations involved in a merger or an acquisition can be contagious. If unaddressed, mutual distrust between the members of the combining organizations may grow in intensity until relationships are irreparably damaged and integration fails. Symbolic or tangible acts of trust can help to reverse this negative spiral and aid in creating a climate of trust. This chapter delineated a number of interventions that can be taken by the top management in order to prevent the occurrence of distrust and to create a culture based on trust following M&A.

References

Anderson, E., and Weitz, B. (1989). Determinants of continuity in conventional industrial channel dyads. *Marketing Science*, 8: 310–23.

Barkema, H. G., Bell, J. H., and Pennings, J. M. (1996). Foreign entry, cultural barriers, and learning. *Strategic Management Journal*, 17: 151–66.

Bastien, D. T. (1987). Common patterns of behavior and communication in corporate mergers and acquisitions. *Human Resource Management*, 26: 17–34.

Buono, A. F., and Bowditch, J. L. (1989). *The Human Side of Mergers and Acquisitions: Managing Collisions Between People, Cultures, and Organizations*. San Francisco: Jossey-Bass.

Buono, A. F., Bowditch, J. L., and Lewis, J. W. (1985). When cultures collide: The anatomy of a merger. *Human Relations*, 38: 477–500.

Cartwright, S., and Cooper, C. L. (1996). *Managing Mergers, Acquisitions, and Strategic Alliances: Integrating People and Cultures*, 2nd edn. Oxford: Butterworth & Heinemann.

Caudron, S. (1996). Rebuilding employee trust. *Training & Development*, 50: 19–21.

Chatterjee, S., Lubatkin, M. H., Schweiger, D. M., and Weber, Y. (1992). Cultural differences and shareholder value in related mergers: Linking equity and human capital. *Strategic Management Journal*, 13: 319–34.

Currall, S. C., and Judge, T. A. (1995). Measuring trust between organizational boundary role persons. *Organizational Behavior and Human Decision Processes*, 64: 151–70.

Das, T. K., and Teng, B.-S. (1998). Between trust and control: Developing confidence in partner cooperation in alliances. *Academy of Management Review*, 23: 491–512.

Datta, D. K., and Grant, J. H. (1990). Relationships between type of acquisition, the autonomy given to the acquired firm, and acquisition success: An empirical analysis. *Journal of Management*, 16: 29–44.

Davy, J. A., Kinicki, A., Kilroy, J., and Scheck, C. (1988). After the merger: Dealing with people's uncertainty. *Training and Development Journal*, 42: 57–61.

Dirks, K. T., and Ferrin, D. L. (2001). The role of trust in organizational settings. *Organization Science*, 12: 450–67.

Elsass, P. M., and Veiga, J. F. (1994): Acculturation in acquired organizations: A force-field perspective. *Human Relations*, 47: 431–53.

Engeli, H.-P. (1999). Klippen einer Fusion—Novartis International AG. Paper presented at the Conference, *Den Erfolg der Internationalisierung gestalten, Deutsche Gesellschaft für Personalführung (DGFP)*, Offenbach/Main, February 8–9, 1999.

Gabarro, J. J. (1978). The development of trust, influence and expectations. In Athos and Gabarro (eds.), *Interpersonal Behavior: Communication and Understanding in Relationships*. Englewood Cliffs, NJ: Prentice-Hall, pp. 290–303.

Graves, D. (1981). Individual reactions to a merger of two small firms of brokers in the reinsurance industry: A total population survey. *Journal of Management Studies*, 18: 89–113.

Gulati, R. (1995). Does familiarity breed trust? The implications of repeated ties for contractual choice in alliances. *Academy of Management Journal*, 38: 85–112.

Hambrick, D. C., and Cannella, A. A. (1993). Relative standing: A framework for understanding departures of acquired executives. *Academy of Management Journal*, 36: 733–62.

Haspeslagh, P., and Jemison, D. B. (1991). *Managing Acquisitions: Creating Value Through Corporate Renewal*. New York: The Free Press.

Hofstede, G. (1980). *Culture's Consequences: International Differences in Work-Related Values*. Beverly Hills, CA: Sage.

Hogan, E. A., and Overmyer-Day, L. (1994). The psychology of mergers and acquisitions. *International Review of Industrial and Organizational Psychology*, 9: 247–81.

Hunt, J. W. (1990). Changing pattern of acquisition behaviour in takeovers and the consequences for acquisition processes. *Strategic Management Journal*, 11: 69–77.

Inkpen, A. C., and Currall, S. C. (1997). International joint venture trust: An empirical examination. In Beamish and Killing (eds.), *Cooperative Strategies: North American Perspectives*. San Francisco: New Lexington, pp. 308–334.

Jemison, D. B., and Sitkin, S. B. (1986). Corporate acquisitions: A process perspective. *Academy of Management Review*, 11: 145–63.

Johnson, J. L., Cullen, J. B., Sakano, T., and Takenouchi, H. (1997). Setting the stage for trust and strategic integration in Japanese–U.S. cooperative alliances. In Beamish and Killing (eds.), *Cooperative Strategies: North American Perspectives*. San Francisco: New Lexington, pp. 227–254.

Jones, G. R., and George, J. M. (1998). The experience and evolution of trust: Implications for cooperation and teamwork. *Academy of Management Review*, 23: 531–46.

Kogut, B., and Singh, H. (1988). The effect of national culture on the choice of entry mode. *Journal of International Business Studies*, 19: 411–32.

Kramer, R. M. (1999). Trust and distrust in organizations: Emerging perspectives, enduring questions. *Annual Review of Psychology*, 50: 569–98.

Krug, J. A., and Nigh, D. (2001). Executive perceptions in foreign and domestic acquisitions, *Journal of World Business*, 36: 85–105.

Kumar, N. (1996). The power of trust in manufacturer–retailer relationships. *Harvard Business Review*, 74: 92–106.

Larsson, R. (1990). *Coordination of Action in Mergers and Acquisitions: Interpretive and Systems Approaches Towards Synergy*. Lund, Sweden: Lund University Press.

Larsson, R., and Risberg, A. (1998). Cultural awareness and national versus corporate barriers to acculturation. In Gertsen, Søderberg, and Torp (eds.), *Cultural Dimensions of International Mergers and Acquisitions*. Berlin: De Gruyter, pp. 39–56.

Lewicki, R. J., McAllister, D. J., and Bies, R. J. (1998). Trust and distrust: New relationships and realities. *Academy of Management Review*, 23: 438–58.

Malekzadeh, A. R., and Nahavandi, A. (1998). Leadership and culture in transnational strategic alliances. In Gertsen, Søderberg, and Torp (eds.), *Cultural Dimensions of International Mergers and Acquisitions*. Berlin: De Gruyter, pp. 111–27.

Marks, M. L., and Mirvis, P. H. (1998). *Joining Forces: Making One Plus One Equal Three in Mergers, Acquisitions, and Alliances*. San Francisco: Jossey-Bass.

Marks, M. L., and Mirvis, P. H. (2001). Making mergers and acquisitions work: Strategic and psychological preparation. *Academy of Management Executive*, 15: 80–92.

Mayer, R. C., Davis, J. H., and Schoorman, F. D. (1995). An integrative model of organizational trust. *The Academy of Management Review*, 20: 709–34.

Mitchell, D. (1989). The importance of speed in post-merger reorganization. *Mergers and Acquisitions Europe*, 1: 44–8.

Morosini, P., Shane, S., and Singh, H. (1998). National cultural distance and cross-border acquisition performance. *Journal of International Business Studies*, 29: 137–58.

Nahavandi, A., and Malekzadeh, A. R. (1988). Acculturation in mergers and acquisitions. *Academy of Management Review*, 13: 79–90.

Napier, N. K., Simmons, G., and Stratton, K. (1989). Communication during a merger: The experience of two banks. *Human Resource Planning*, 12: 105–22.

Olie, R. (1994). Shades of culture and institutions in international mergers. *Organization Studies*, 15: 381–405.

Pablo, A. L. (1994). Determinants of acquisition integration level: A decision making perspective. *Academy of Management Journal*, 37: 803–36.

Pablo, A. L., Sitkin, S. B., and Jemison, D. B. (1996). Acquisition decision-making processes: The central role of risk. *Journal of Management*, 22: 723–46.

Redding, G. (1990). *The Spirit of Chinese Capitalism*. Berlin: de Gruyter.

Ring, P. S., and Van de Ven, A. H. (1992). Structuring cooperative relationships between organizations. *Strategic Management Journal*, 13: 483–98.

Robino, D., and DeMeuse, K. (1985). Corporate mergers and acquisitions: Their impact on HRM. *Personnel Administrator*, 30: 33–44.

Rousseau, D. M., Sitkin, S. B., Burt, R. S., and Camerer, C. (1998). Not so different after all: A cross-discipline view of trust. *Academy of Management Review*, 23: 393–404.

Sarkar, M., Cavusgil, T., and Evirgen, C. (1997). A commitment-trust mediated framework of international collaborative venture performance. In Beamish and Killing (eds.), *Cooperative Strategies: North American Perspectives*. San Francisco: New Lexington, pp. 255–85.

Schweiger, D. M., and DeNisi, A. S. (1991). Communication with employees following a merger: A longitudinal field experiment. *Academy of Management Journal*, 34: 110–35.

Schweiger, D. M., Ivancevich, J. M., and Power, F. R. (1987). Executive actions for managing human resources before and after acquisition. *Academy of Management Executive*, 1: 127–38.

Schweiger, D. M., and Walsh, J. P. (1990). Mergers and acquisitions: An interdisciplinary view. *Research in Personnel and Human Resources Management*, 8: 41–107.

Sitkin, S. B. (1995). On the positive effect of legalization on trust. *Research on Negotiation in Organizations*, 5: 185–217.

Sitkin, S. B., and Roth, N. L. (1993). Explaining the limited effectiveness of legalistic "remedies" for trust/distrust. *Organization Science*, 4: 367–92.

Stahl, G. K., and Chua, C. H. (2002). A decision-making approach to modeling individuals' reactions to a takeover: Findings of a study of Singaporean employees. In *Proceedings of the 7th Asia-Pacific Decision Sciences Institute Conference*, Bangkok, Thailand, p. 5.

Stahl, G. K., Chua, C. H., and Pablo, A. (2003). Trust following acquisitions: A three-country comparative study of employee reactions to takeovers. *Best Paper Proceedings*, Annual Meeting of the Academy of Management, Seattle, p. 5.

Stahl, G. K., Pucik, V., Evans, P., and Mendenhall, M. (2004). Human resource management in cross-border mergers and acquisitions. In Harzing and van Ruysseveldt (eds.), *International Human Resource Management: An Integrated Approach*, 2nd edn. London: Sage, pp. 89–113.

Stahl, G. K., and Voigt, A. (2005). The performance impact of cultural differences in mergers and acquisitions: A critical research review and an integrative model. In C. L. Cooper & S. Finkelstein (Eds.) *Advances in Mergers and Acquisitions*, Vol. 4. New York: JAI Press.

Stahl, G. K., and Sitkin, S. B. (2001). *Trust in Mergers and Acquisitions*. Presented at the annual meeting of the Academy of Management, Washington, DC.

Stahl, G. K., and Wagner, A. (2002). Antecedents and consequences of trust in mergers and acquisitions. In *Proceedings of the Carnegie Bosch Institute's 5th International Conference on Growing the International Firm: Success in Mergers, Acquisitions, Networks and Alliances*, Berlin, Germany.

Stickel, D. (1999). *Building Trust in the Face of Hostility*. Unpublished doctoral dissertation, Duke University, Durham, NC.

Very, P., and Schweiger, D. M. (2001). The acquisition process as a learning process: Evidence from a study of critical problems and solutions in domestic and cross-border deals. *Journal of World Business*, 36: 11–31.

Whitener, E. M., Brodt, S. E., Korsgaard, M. A., and Werner, J. M. (1998). Managers as initiators of trust: An exchange relationship framework for understanding managerial trustworthy behavior. *Academy of Management Review*, 23: 513–39.

Zaheer, A., McEvily, B., and Perrone, V. (1998). Does trust matter? Exploring the effects of interorganizational and interpersonal trust on performance. *Organization Science*, 9: 141–59.

Executive Commentary on Chapter 4

HANS-PETER ENGELI

Employee loyalty is out! The merged company no longer expects employees to be loyal in the future, but it still needs to keep as many key managers and professionals on board as possible. In their chapter on "Trust in Mergers and Acquisitions," Stahl and Sitkin defined trust as "a psychological state . . . based upon positive expectations of the intentions or behaviors of another." This shows that trust is closely linked to looking into the future. Employees' expectations about their future at their companies are molded as their careers progress. However, with a merger or acquisition, there is suddenly a new player in the picture, threatening their value to their companies before the merger or acquisition. Hence, a merger or acquisition is like a knife cutting into the lives of employees, drastically changing what they can expect of their future at their companies overnight. The merged company no longer expects loyalty from employees and employees can no longer expect job security from the merged company. Thus, employees experience a very high degree of risk during a merger or acquisition. Under the menace of risk, employees inevitably find it difficult to perform their tasks and duties at expected and acceptable levels. This is the time when they start developing all kinds of manoeuvres around the central question of "to leave or not?" If the acquirer firm's management does not pay enough attention to the shift in these employees' minds, the acquiring firm is likely to lose many key target firm employees whom it had originally identified and labeled as "worthy to retain." In this case, retention bonuses will not help in the short- or mid-term. Speedy action is required as other players will appear on the scene quickly. Personnel recruiters and head hunters are very quick in getting to know about the new situation of the target firm. There is strong evidence that M&A are often initiated during a rather positive economic cycle with optimistic outlook. That is reflected on the labor market with a large supply of promising positions targeting at those employees with excellent professional records. These target employees are usually amongst the best performers and exactly the ones the merged or acquiring company has earmarked to be retained. Hence, speedy action in making personnel decisions is crucial in this situation of uncertainty.

In the merger that I had experienced, although it was labeled as a "merger of equals" right from the beginning, it soon became obvious that "some were more equal than others." This is not a big surprise because power situations are often asymmetrical in the end, no matter how hard one tries. Hence, my experience can possibly be applicable to the situation of an acquisition where power is asymmetrical right from the start.

After going through the merger process, there is no doubt to me that although the initial takeover situation can affect acquired employees' trust in the acquiring firm management, the most critical phase where trust may be maintained, built, or destroyed is during the integration process. During the initial takeover situation, nothing is really being decided yet and employees still have their hopes about how things would turn out. They are still in the process of learning and appraising the situation, and seeing how things develop. One of the strengths of human beings is their ability not to lose hope too quickly. In my case, the two premerged companies had a positive "interaction history"—one of the determinants of trust proposed by Stahl and Sitkin—at least on the operational level. At the top management and board levels, their interaction prior to the merger negotiations can be described as "an absence of interaction." Therefore, it can be said that there were no existing negative feelings on either side. From the perspective of the top management, "takeover friendliness"—another determinant of trust—was seen as courageous, enlightening, and promising for the future. The merger clearly made both strategic and economic sense. "National cultural similarity" was certainly very high in this case—same nationality, same language, same geographical location (both headquarters were only about one kilometer apart). However, both companies' corporate cultures were quite different, especially their management styles, and to a lesser degree, their corporate values. Also, from a corporate strategy perspective, the two companies were not on the same track. So, they could either have a bigger portfolio of businesses through the combination or sell off parts of their businesses and focus on the businesses that they both had in common to become a stronger global player. "Relative target firm performance," as Stahl and Sitkin have rightly noted, may produce either positive or negative results. On the one hand, target firm employees may hope for improved financial performance of the new company, resulting hopefully in higher compensation, and on the other hand, target firm's executives may feel threatened. In any case, I feel that its impact on trust on the majority of employees does not seem to be very direct.

Factors associated with the integration process certainly affect acquired employees' trust in the acquiring firm management much more directly. Barely ten months lay between the official merger announcement and the day of the legal merger that I went through. Both boards of directors and the designated executive committee of the merged company were determined to integrate all operations quickly. The global personnel announcements were made within the first 100 days and thousands of managers had to wear two hats: perform the old job in the premerged company and play an important role in one or several global integration teams. Top management believed that an extremely high-speed integration process was necessary to fulfil the optimistic expectations the financial world, the media, and the public at large had for the merger.

Although a "high-speed approach" is good to get things going, such an approach meant a tough top–down decision-making style for all business and personnel issues. However, doing this brought along some unwanted repercussions. First, empowerment happened to be one of the main shared values espoused by the merged company. This contradictory situation confused and frustrated many managers and professionals because they did not know what to make out of empowerment in a top-down style of management. So, they did not know what to do and what to believe. The merged company had an ambition to standardize and roll out new operational processes and procedures globally based on a strictly top-down approach and this inevitably suffered many setbacks during implementation and afterwards. Second, a noticeable degree of delegation in decision making is necessary to generate trust, but this opportunity was traded off so that speed would not be lost. This sent out yet another signal that autonomy was to remain with only a very few people. This brings to mind "retained autonomy," which Stahl and Sitkin had pointed out in their chapter as an important determinant of target firm members' trust in the acquiring firm management. I feel that managing the issue of autonomy and control well is critical. Very often, the acquirer tends to impose control onto the target firm and show its true colours. However, this has negative effects. Loss of autonomy will eventually destroy acquired employees' loyalty as they feel a loss in their status and that it was no longer fun to work at the company. Moreover, employees may question the point of working extra hard during the integration period. As the removal of autonomy would mean an introduction of tight controls, and controls tend to signal the absence of trust, removal of autonomy would mean a negative impact on trust in the acquiring firm management. An interesting point to note is that the degree of loss of autonomy and the burden of control suffered by the target firm's management is a good indicator for all employees to speculate on the new power balance and their own chances to survive decently in the merged or acquired company.

In the merger I experienced, the command and control style of management adopted led to the exodus of many valuable and well-performing managers. They felt that important company values that they firmly believed in, such as empowerment, were sacrificed to ensure speedy integration and doubted that these values would ever be restored. Of course, the top management knew that a very large number of managers and professionals would have to be made redundant anyway. However, what happened during integration was a "negative selection."

In the initial phase of the merger, "cultural tolerance and sensitivity" was not given much attention. It was when the merged company became a global company in reality that top management realized the need for cultural tolerance and sensitivity. Initially, some of the "global positions" had to be filled with top managers from outside, poached from direct competitors or from a third industry, such as the consumer goods industry, for global marketing positions. Such moves would not have been feasible in the premerged companies that prided themselves as "research-based" firms. This new approach inevitably caused some cultural disturbances. In the premerger days, top managers used public transport to go to work. But at the merged company, they were provided with chauffeur-driven limos and corporate jets. In addition, traditional business lunches have almost been completely abandoned. As integration started, business lunches among colleagues meant sandwiches hastily eaten during a meeting's break. In fact, this is still the case today! Such changes are strong formal signals of a new corporate culture, highlighting a sharp break from the past.

The strong empirical evidence shown by Stahl and Sitkin that "HR policies and reward systems" play a crucial role in determining target firm members' trust in the acquiring firm management comes as no surprise. An M&A is the time when employees reassess their professional development and remuneration situation, and their actions will be guided by their appraisal of the personal benefits that they can realistically gain from the new situation, such as job security and higher rewards. In the merger I went through, the employees who knew that they would be losing their jobs soon could not see any benefits of the merger for themselves. In addition, every employee who knew personally one or several colleagues who would be losing their jobs were also plagued with a sense of job insecurity, even though their jobs were not in danger. Further, this negative impact is reinforced by the fact that the "survivors" will feel bad for those hit by redundancy. In terms of rewards, the "explosion of rewards"—as might have been hoped for by many employees—did not realize, except for the very few senior executives worldwide whose total compensation packages had been increased by a factor of 40–50 (in cash, deferred pay, and stock options). Those who thought that this was excessive were reminded that this was the price to pay for the "global labor market" and essential to attract and keep high performers.

Timing and an optimum amount of communication are clearly the keys to maintaining trust. I would stress the importance of the "communication quality," and add adequate language and a clever segmentation of the audience as essential elements. In the merger that I went through, communication was excellent in timing but lacked the necessary segmentation of the audience. What was communicated in the beginning was overwhelming for some recipients and too little for others. The language was very professional and it caused some distrust among employees who were not so familiar with the economic and financial background of such a huge transaction. It seemed that the communication professionals did not consider much about the almost unbearable stress that their audience was exposed to. On the day of the announcement, plain confusion dominated the scene. And on top of this, an approximately forty-page document was distributed at each workplace. After this initial effort of in-depth communication, there was a (too) long period of absence of further substantial news. This was probably because almost all that could be told had been told on the very first day! The main "bodies carrying the news on progress made" were the integration teams. But they were not allowed to leak out anything as long as the legal merger was not finalized. I feel that communication is crucial in any change process and has to be given a high priority as the top management is critically judged by all stakeholders based on what is told, when and to whom it is told, as well as on what is not being told.

In conclusion, I feel that the degree to which the potential for sustainable growth and synergies of the merged company that can be achieved certainly depends heavily on top management's integration decisions and actions, and during this critical phase of the merger process, it is crucial for the top management to foster relationships based on trust as this will increase the chances for a successful integration. The top management can earn employee trust by showing them how much they care and how strongly they are identifying themselves with the new company and proving this by their actions that go beyond the short-term range. However, this is not an easy process, especially if—as happened in the merger that I experienced—trust was almost completely destroyed in the beginning. It took a lot of effort and time for the top management to rebuild employee trust. Building trust is difficult. Rebuilding trust is even more difficult. There is no easy way to establish a corporate culture based on trust, but without trust, there is no way to sustain the success of the merged company.

5   The Role of Corporate Cultural Diversity in Integrating Mergers and Acquisitions

GEORG SCHREYÖGG

Culture Matters

Corporate culture has been conceived as a coherent system of symbols, values, and basic assumptions. The emphasis is on cultural artefacts and values of one specific system. The same holds true for the notion of national culture. The major concern is the framework of one national culture or possibly a comparison between two distinct cultures. Recently, cultural studies have started to stress differentiation and to reveal inconsistencies in action, symbols, and ideology in organizational cultures (for example, Kunda, 1991; Martin, 2001). These studies doubtlessly picture organizational cultures in a more multifaceted way (although to varying degrees); the major focus, however, remains the same, the organizational culture of *one* particular organization.

Studying the role of corporate culture in mergers and acquisitions (M&A) confronts us with a structurally different perspective. The focus shifts from a single system to at least two different corporate cultures that have been brought about in separate systems reflecting their specific history. Although these cultures often are totally different by their very nature, they are expected to merge. Whatever the direction taken, cultural boundaries are supposed to blur. The traditional internal view of cultural studies has to be replaced. The focus is on two (or more) different corporate cultures and their interaction, which is more or less enforced by the merger process.

The confrontation of different corporate cultures in the context of merger and acquisition raises a series of questions: Do the cultures mix? Will there be a cultural clash? And, if so what are the consequences in terms of motivation, productivity, profitability, and so on? Can we actually merge corporate cultures? Are there cultural winners and losers and how are the firms' stakeholders affected? How does the power structure react on cultural changes (in whatever direction)? and various other questions. All these questions point to the relevance of the cultural issue. We know by now that the answers given to those questions are critical for the success or the failure of mergers and/or acquisitions (see, for example, Deal and Kennedy, 1999).

What are the major cultural challenges in a merger from a managerial point of view? There are many of them: reassuring organizational members, foster interest in cultural differences, mastering cultural change, surfacing cultural assumptions, and so on. The first and most important challenge in our view, however, is to develop a convincing conception on how the two (or three) corporate cultures should relate to each other in the time after the merger has taken place. That means to elaborate on the cultural framework and to reach a decision on the preferred cultural relationship or to put it more precisely, the overall *cultural gestalt*. Accounting for their far-reaching consequences and the high importance M&A processes usually have, it seems imperative to address the gestalt question from a strategic point of view.

What are the basic options and what criteria can provide orientation in determining the best solution?

Consistency and Cultural Issues

When the question on how to handle the cultural issue in the merger process is considered, the dimensions to be addressed are a major concern. Alternatives in getting a handle on the cultural issue in M&A processes can be considered along various dimensions:

1. *Consistency*: What degree of cultural consistency, that is, homogeneity of norms, values, symbols, and so on, is required across the two corporate cultures to make the merger a success?
2. *Diversity*: What degree of cultural diversity is preferred? In case of high cultural diversity, how can cultural diversity be managed effectively?
3. *Realization*: Up to what degree can long-standing cultures be made subject of a transformative change at all?
4. *Dominance*: Is one of the two or more cultures in question intended to become the dominant one? Or is it supposed to be a cultural merger of equals resulting in a new amalgamated "melting pot culture"?

To find an answer to all these questions is clearly beyond the scope of a single chapter. One dimension, however, seems to be of salient importance because it clearly *precedes* the others. It is the dimension of *consistency*. Our discussion therefore focuses on this dimension.

In M&A literature, consistency in most cases is considered a major aim. If we look at the rhetoric in many corporations, it becomes obvious that "management of postmerger integration" is actually used as a synonym for creating consistency across the corporations involved. Generally spoken, consistency is considered being the basic prerequisite for making the merger success happen. In this chapter we call this conception into question and suggest instead making consistency *a matter of degree*. The thesis is that it depends on the overarching strategic framework whether or not a high degree of cultural consistency is needed.

How to determine the *degree of cultural consistency* needed between different corporate cultures in the merging process? Obviously, we need a template to start this discussion systematically. The suggestion is to discuss the question of cultural consistency on the basis of two generic types of cultural integration, the two antipoles on the dimension of consistency. There is on the one hand the high consistency type, we call it "universal corporate culture," and there is on the other hand the low consistency type, in this chapter called "pluralist corporate culture."

Generic Types of Overall Corporate Cultures

The Pluralist Corporate Culture

The first alternative favors a policy of unassimilated diversity. Corporate subsystems are supposed to fully reflect their original cultural milieu so that a specific corporate subculture is likely to exist in each subsidiary. By implication, within this type of corporate culture the former autonomous cultural systems are not expected to change a lot after the merger. The creation of such plurality does not require any particular effort; it simply develops by itself. As a result, the merged company is likely to become a multicultural company; it builds the arena for various corporate subcultures and has only a limited set of commonly shared values and beliefs throughout the organization (Rose, 1988). To put it differently, it represents a conglomerate corporate culture with well-defined coexisting subcultures and weak overarching ties.

In terms of cultural strength, a pluralist culture builds a corporate culture with strong subcultures and only weak overall strength. Companies that seem to pursue this type of diverse corporate culture are, for instance, ITT, Philips, and Dr. Oetker. The orientation system, the beliefs, norms, and so on do not necessarily span the whole corporation, rather the opposite holds true. The pluralist perspective expects corporations to largely preserve and practice their cultures of the premerger stage.

The policy of the pluralist corporate culture inevitably leads to strong internal differentiation. It stresses diversity and allows for rival beliefs and even competing practices of sense making (Martin, 1992, 2001). The sub-cultures might fit in with each other or they might not. Subcultures can clash over beliefs, rituals, or meanings; in these cases, conflicting views are likely to become a salient feature of those organizations. But subcultures can also exist side by side neutrally without many conflicting areas. And finally, differ-ent subcultures can complement each other. Drawing on the fit idea, Meffert (1990) suggests differentiating between synergetic (fitting) and polycentric (nonfitting) pluralist cultures. The latter include conflict and contradiction, power and political processes inevitably come to the foreground (Trice and Morand, 1991). Whatever the perspective, the major emphasis in this type of corporate culture is on the interaction and the relationship among diverse subcultures.

There are a number of advantages of such highly differentiated cultures. Among possible advantages stand out flexibility, adaptability, and encour-agement of creativity (see Cox and Blake, 1991; Fernandez and Barr, 1993; Billings-Harris, 1998; Begley and Boyd, 2003). Differing orientation pat-terns and images are likely to call continuously locked views and practices into perspective and to stimulate curiosity—and as is well known, these are prerequisites for innovation and creativity in organizations. Further-more, highly differentiated subsystems leave scope for becoming specialized in fairly different ways and areas that hence allows earning *economies of specialization*.

Also, the pluralist culture approach is, as a rule, much more welcome in acquired firms and makes it easier hence to get the merger or the acquisition accepted. This cultural approach signals tolerance and respect to former competences and skills, and may thereby help to overcome suspiciousness and resistance ("we against them") in the acquired organizations.

The advantages of the pluralist option are obvious and convincing; how-ever, they must stand out against the advantages of the opposite universal alternative.

The Universal Corporate Culture

By way of contrast the second generic alternative of cultural architecture after a merger places the internal consistency into the foreground. The focus is on cultural homogeneity. There are different ways to realize this option. One way is—and it is the most frequent one—to simply absorb the newly acquired company deliberately into the existing corporate culture of the ac-quiring company—a culture that may have been developed over years. An-other way is to literally merge the existing cultures in order to bring about a new amalgamated corporate culture. Whatever the way chosen—the scope of choice here is also a question of economic power and the negotiated conditions of the underlying contract—the result is a similar one: The universal solution does not favor a policy of heterogeneity; the major feature rather is *homogeneity*. This implies an overarching culture that gives the whole corporation its own distinctive character, which is expressed in common patterns of beliefs, joint practices, and consistent symbolic forms. Common perception and standardized selection patterns are in the foreground; they ensure a coherent frame of reference in corporate interactions. Organizational behavior is imprinted by assumptions, patterns, and symbols that are shared in all parts of the corporation, whatever their history is.

The universal type of corporate culture stresses coherence and draws at the same time a clear distinction to other adjoined systems; in a multinational context by implication it often sets a counterpoint to national cultures as well (Begley and Boyd, 2003). In sum, organizational members share a common view of the world and the way their organization exists in that world. However, a caveat is due here. This type of corporate culture represents a general tendency in values and orientation patterns, but does not mean a system of total consistency. Large systems cannot survive without any differentiation (Lawrence and Lorsch, 1967). And also, corporate cultures do never fully imprint the behavior of organizational members; it is secondary socialization and therefore of partial influence only (Hofstede et al., 1990). We should refrain from exaggerating this perspective; a culture is not an iron cage. Furthermore, the inner logic of culture is based on compliance, and that means at the same time mindful deviation is always possible and actually occurs (Van Maanen, 1991). When deviation becomes a universal attitude, a culture dissolves (Martin, 1992).

From a process point of view, the different companies in M&A integration are not intended to build subcultures that are "exotic" to one another; they are rather expected to become integral parts of the universal corporate culture. The management wants the systems to go for creating and reproducing a specific cultural profile. This kind of corporate culture is called "universal" because it shapes cognitions and values in the same way across the various departments within and outside a national culture. IKEA, Hewlett-Packard, Apple and Siemens could be quoted as examples for practicing this type of corporate culture policy.

As opposed to the pluralist culture, which stresses the cultural differentiation of a system and the advantages of specialization, the universal culture clearly emphasizes conformity and efficiency. A universal corporate culture standardizes perception and orientation patterns, thereby eliminating redundancy. At the prelanguage level, the use of shared signs and symbols creates a common identity and promotes global system motivation ("clan"). In sum, it enhances the mutual understanding and compatibility of actions, thereby raising significantly the level of connectivity among organizational members.

Obviously, it is much more difficult and precarious to bring about a universal corporate culture than a pluralist one. A cultural orientation cannot be transferred mechanically from one system to another, cultures grow (Schein, 1997). Furthermore, the request to absorb the culture of another corporation is often seen as a humiliation or a submersion (Deal and Kennedy, 1999). The most likely initial reaction therefore is tacit reluctance or even overt rejection. Those problems are likely to become even more delicate in case of a *transnational merger* or acquisition; *national cultures* constitute a second possibly conflicting cultural dimension with its own logic of consistency and diversity (Schneider, 1992; Schreyögg, 1998). In an international context, a unified corporate culture is often perceived as an imposed culture ignoring host countries' values. Concurrently, those feelings and perceptions can convey an aura of ethnocentrism or colonialism (Begley and Boyd, 2003).

As it is much more difficult and precarious to realize a universal type of corporate culture than a pluralist one, the question whether or not a universal corporate culture should be pursued in postmerger integration cannot only be answered by checking its benefits and by weighing them against losses of specialization or the missed advantages from the pluralist culture. Rather, "creation and maintenance costs" and possibly social costs would have also been accounted for.

It is a difficult task to set up such common frameworks of orientation (cf. Nahavandi and Malekzadeh, 1988). This is all the more true in a postmerger setting that is usually characterized by a flurry of excitement and ambivalence (Pritchett et al., 1997). It is too naïve an assumption that patterns of meaning prevalent in the acquiring firm can simply be transferred by order or by "hard selling" to the acquired firm. To incorporate the culture of a new firm or to merge two existing cultures requires more than to sell a unified vision and to produce beautifully designed brochures on what the new culture is. Whatever the attempts, culture by its very nature comes only into being through continuous reproduction by its members. Culture brochures, guidelines, culture integration teams, and so on are doomed to failure if corporate culture does not become the actual basis of daily acting.

Up to now, very little is known in management theory about the transfer of an existing corporate culture to other systems. Some lessons can, however, be learnt from successful transfers (Garsten, 1994; Gerpott, 1995; Haspeslagh and Jemison, 1991; Jaeger, 1983; Simonin, 1999).

First of all, surprisingly enough, among corporate policies, human resources policy is likely to play a (or even *the*) critical role. It is surprising because M&A are mostly discussed in the context of strategic management, which is an area in which human resource management notoriously plays a minor role. A second general principle is that cultural integration because of its organic character takes time; it cannot be realized "overnight."

Of particular importance for transferring cultural issues seem to be uniform screening and hiring procedures to select qualified people who are likely to fit into the overall corporate culture. IKEA, as one salient representative of a universal corporate culture approach, prefers, for instance, hiring young people not yet assimilated to any other company culture. The same is true for McKinsey and Apple (see the instructive description of Apple's transfer practices provided by Garsten (1994)).

In addition to this, promotion from within also appears to play a key role, that is, people already socialized in the cultural milieu become managers. Also, management development seems to be of critical importance (Jaeger, 1983). The latter does not only include the well-known job rotation programs (Edström and Galbraith, 1977; Gupta and Govindarajan, 1991) or "boot camps" to build up networks dispersed across all subsidiaries, but also, and more importantly, the company-wide standardization of in-house training programs (Kuin, 1972; Schneider, 1992).

Along with these indirect forms via human resource practices, the *direct transfer* of symbols and rituals is also of considerable importance including the creation of a company-wide language, company uniforms, annual parties, or architecture. A well-known example is the legendary Apple-T-shirt, then worn and desired in all parts of the corporation throughout the world.

According to the *fit-model* (for example, Donaldson, 2001; Miles and Snow, 1994), transfers can be recommended only in those cases where the culture of the acquired firm roughly fits in the corporate culture of the acquiring firm. There are, however, many problems with this solution. One problem is that there is simply no cultural theory that could specify in any sound way what exactly "harmony" or congruency means in terms of cultural fit and how those fittings could be identified. A second problem is that "fit" approaches are prone to conceive the problem too statically and too mechanically; they grossly underrate the importance of the process. Transfers do not simply occur, in most cases it means hard work to make them happen. Thirdly, there are successful transfers of corporate culture in cases where the acquiring firm's culture had quite different orientation patterns. Even in cases of seemingly cultural misfits, marriages work. A prominent example here is the Volkswagen culture, which obviously has been transferred successfully to the Czech motor company Skoda. Or let us take another example from the multinational area. Hewlett-Packard came in the 1960s to Germany and brought with it the egalitarian addressing of employees by first names, regardless of hierarchy and age, something which was (and is) for Germans completely unusual—and even taboo. But it worked—many Germans actually enjoyed the cultural difference and even became keen on working in such "misfitting" American type of corporate culture.

The issue of cultural transfer therefore should not be formulated as a static fit problem. From the long-standing debate on contingency theory of organizational design we have learnt the lesson that fit-models aiming to determine an optimal congruent constellation between context and structure inevitably run into insurmountable difficulties because of their static logic and their circular thinking (cf. Child, 1972; Donaldson, 1982, 2001; Schreyögg, 1982). We should call to mind that cultures shape behavior but they do not determine it. As mentioned above, cultures are always open for both mindful and intuitive deviation; the cultural influence is a plastic one by its very nature. A conceptualization of cultural absorption should reflect this essentially dynamic character; it is not a problem of fitting, it rather is a problem of successful learning and becoming.

Ethics of Corporate Culture Transfer

Along with these conceptual features of plasticity and reproducibility, the idea of a universal corporate culture also raises ethically motivated questions. This holds particularly true if the transfer is attempted in an international context, that is, the merger includes companies from different countries. The reproach of ethnocentricity can often be heard here (Begley and Boyd, 2003). It has been discussed in the theory of international management for a long time (cf. Perlmutter, 1969). In Perlmutter's typology, the universal "corporate culture" in most cases would have to be called ethnocentric. From his point of view the concept of a universal corporate culture would have to be considered as basically ignorant or even arrogant against other cultural traditions and values (see also Boyacigiller and Adler, 1991). This reproach applies in its core not only to the case of transferring an existing corporate culture but also to the case in which the uniform culture represents an amalgam emerging out from different cultures.

In our view, this is too sweeping an argument. This general suspicion against universality and cultural consistency tends to obscure the actual ethical question at stake. In this perspective the traditional culture, whatever its content, is regarded generally as good; influences from foreign corporate cultures are generally accused of being illegitimate. This may be adequate emotionally, but cannot be accepted as an ethical argument. From an ethical point of view, the question rather is whether or not the values represented in the cultures at stake are legitimate ones (Lorenzen, 1991). Ethics focus on justifiable values and norms irrespective of who brought them in.

An example may prove the significance of this differentiation. For instance, in a "developmental policy" view, a universal corporate culture can have positive and/or negative effects; it can promote or hinder development—as it is true for a pluralistically adjusted corporate culture. We may recall the Bhopal tragedy here (Shrivastava, 1986). The American company Union Carbide was accused of applying different safety standards in its plants, and of not carrying out in India the safety regulations and trainings they used to have in the United States. In our frame of reference this means that the company was accused of not having developed a milieu (corporate culture) that would guarantee safety to the same extent as in the United States. Nobody thought of taking into consideration the particular attitudes and cultural patterns in Bhopal, arguing that Bhopal culture simply did not fit into the Western safety procedures. At least as far as "safety culture" was concerned a universal cultural orientation was generally expected from Union Carbide. From an ethical point of view, the universal and not the pluralist corporate culture was preferable then.

By implication, it is recommendable to refrain from sweeping preferences for one or the other cultural alternative given above; the ethical situation is likely to be different from situation to situation.

Modeling the Choice

The pluralist and the universal corporate culture represent two alternatives with very different cost–benefit profiles. Any comparison should also take into account that the distinctive advantages of a universal corporate culture are not only to be juxtaposed with the advantages of the pluralist culture but also with the considerably higher efforts that are required to realize this alternative. Whatever the best way to compare costs and benefits, it seems quite obvious that there is no *general* superiority of one alternative over the other. A simple comparison of pros and cons without considering the context does not yield any convincing result. By implication, the choice cannot be separated from the context of the merger. Rather, it has to be embedded into the overall merger policy and the question of internal complexity. This chapter suggests taking *coordination requirements* as a point of reference, that is, the demand and the importance of cultural consistency in postmerger integration.

Our basic proposition is: *The more salient the need for coordination, the more critical become the advantages of a universal corporate culture.* The importance given to coordination covaries with the overarching merger policy and the complexity of the focal organization. The argument is as follows.

Merger Policy and Multidimensional Differentiation

At the core of any merger policy is a decision on the nature of the integration process. As mentioned above, the required and attempted degree of integration is at variance. Some acquisitions require only a minimal amount of integration, for instance in case of a conglomerate diversification (see Haspeslagh and Jemison, 1991, p. 106). Other acquisitions badly need complete integration, for instance to fully exploit economies of scale in production, marketing, and logistics or in case of mergers among former competitors in order to cumulate market share. The overwhelming majority of acquisitions do, however, not allow for a clear-cut "yes" or "no" decision upon the integration issue. In most cases mergers ask for a mixed strategy, that is, the acquiring or the merging corporations aim at drawing on economies of integration and diversity at the same time. The result is a complex mix of autonomy and coherence. Haspeslagh and Jemison (1991, p. 106) quote as an example the case of ICI, the British chemical corporation, which, having acquired Beatrice Chemicals, on the one hand intended to preserve the entrepreneurial structure of the acquired firm while on the other hand leveraging ICI R&D into it. To put it more generally, in pursuing a mixed merger strategy, corporate functions (marketing, R&D, production, distribution, and so on) and corporate projects become integrated to highly varying degrees, for example, separate R&D, fully integrated distribution, and multiplant operations. This kind of multifaceted variation also holds for the management functions, for example, integrated planning, decentralized human resources management, dispersed control systems, and common codes of conduct.

There is a striking similarity between the mixed merger strategy and Porter's conception of multidimensional globalization in multinational corporations that advocates a differentiated optimization of the corporate wide value chain in order create maximal value (Porter, 1986). This broad concept of corporate globalization includes all value chain activities (see also Kogut, 1985). Globalization—as it is the case for integration in the mixed strategy—becomes a matter of degree on the corporate, the business unit, and the functional level. As a major implication, the optimal degree of globalization is to be determined for each level and function/project separately. Each level and corporate function is to be treated as a separate optimization problem. As a consequence the corporate functions and projects can become globalized in largely different ways so that across the corporation, varying globalization patterns and policies may coexist. Many multinational companies have redesigned their value activities in exactly this way. As a result, multinational corporations become complex multidimensional entities; a worldwide network with differentiated units and marked interdependence evolves. Corporations are also used to differentiate into many centers of different kinds. Some functions are centralized in one division, some in another; still other functions are essentially decentralized among the geographically dispersed operations (Bartlett and Ghoshal, 1986, 1989; Frost, 2001; Gupta and Govindarajan, 1991, 2000; Medcof, 2001).

Any multidimensional mixed design of corporate activities, that is, varying degrees of functional integration and unit diversity, inevitably raises the complexity of the whole system. Lawrence and Lorsch (1967) pioneered in clarifying this wicked nexus. Complexity in this more sophisticated understanding does not simply refer to a high number of positions and levels in a hierarchy (Daft, 2001); it rather points to the differences and to the diversity within a system. Organizational complexity essentially reflects differences in use.

High internal complexity (highly differentiated units across the organization) is a functional prerequisite for many modern firms, but poses at the same time a management problem; it basically threatens the system's total coordination and effectiveness (Lawrence and Lorsch, 1967). If subunits differ largely in terms of products, structures, skills, knowledge, degrees of autonomy, and so forth, the problem of ensuring the *connectivity* of actions among all these individualized subsystems is likely to become a most critical problem of the management process. Coordination efforts gain salience importance to ensure efficiency. The management has to guarantee the continuous coupling of at least three "resource flows" throughout the system (Bartlett and Ghoshal, 1989): (1) flow of prefabricated parts, components, software; (2) flow of personnel, services; (3) flow of know-how, knowledge, and ideas. Among these flows, the flow of know-how and knowledge nowadays has perhaps the greatest importance. It serves as a source of differentiation and hence of competitive advantages (Barney, 1991).

Because of the multidimensional design and diversity of relationships in mixed merger settings, activities are prone to become dispersed and difficult to foresee for organizational members. As a consequence, the coordination of the entire system is threatened. Traditional coordination mechanisms, such as hierarchy, organizational formalization, or conditional programming soon become overloaded and fall short of fulfilling their function (Lawrence and Lorsch, 1967). As is well known by now, such complex constellations are beyond the logic and the capacity of those traditional problem-solving mechanisms, they are simply lacking the absorptive capacity to master high degrees of internal complexity (Luhmann, 1994). In most cases those internal constellations concur in addition with a dynamic external environment and the demand for more flexible forms of organizations (Daft and Lewin, 1993). Organizations therefore are prone to suffer from serious troubles such as "control loss," decoupling of units, and entropy if no additional and more appropriate coordination efforts are undertaken. Diverse systems, such as multidimensional merger designs or differentiated globalization, need multiple channels of communication and arenas for decision making to master the growing complexity. Additional and new forms of coordination efforts are imperative.

What type of measures can keep these systems coordinated nevertheless? The lesson to be learnt from studies of how organizations master a high degree of internal complexity (Daft and Lewin, 1993; Luhmann, 1994) is that *informal self-coordination* among the broadly scattered subsystems seems to provide the best solution. Successful coordination in those systems largely depends on spontaneous communication, horizontal overlaps, and lateral communication patterns.

Informal self-coordination, however, only works if subunits are *connective* to each other, that is, subunits can receive, understand, and transform information from others and can communicate directly and spontaneously with each other. In other words, *connectivity* of the diverse functions and actions of the individual subsystems is likely to amount to the critical success factor in sophisticated integration processes.

To make connectivity happen, a common frame of reference and shared patterns of cognitions and values are required—and that means in terms of our initial discussion, a *universal corporate culture* is needed. The shared values and assumptions can become the anchors to stabilize the differentiated network resulting from a multidimensional merger policy.

It is exactly this point where the specific strength of a universal corporate culture applies and is likely to play a key role. Complex network-like organizations badly need coordination efforts beyond formal organizational measures; it requires a common platform to facilitate interaction and to make joint efforts of highly diverse units effective. Sensible communication and informal relationships across departments and borders gain utmost significance. The reason for this requirement seems to be quite obvious. If people relying on totally different orientations and beliefs are supposed to interact informally and spontaneously, troubles in sending and lacking understanding of information are likely to occur. This is all the more true if the merger takes place in an international context. Faulty attributions about the meanings of others' reactions and decisions are likely because attributions flow from the attributor's own cultural patterns that may grossly differ from the one of the sender (Black and Mendenhall, 1990, p. 120). All these arguments highlight the central importance of a universal corporate culture for mergers operating on a multidimensional and varying design of internal resource flow. A common framework is required to build the platform needed to interweave effectively the multiple arrays of ties and to speed up coordination to meet the market challenges.

The former chief executive of Hewlett-Packard, Germany, once hit the nail on the head when stating "When I take a bird's eye view of Hewlett-Packard today I can see two things: on the surface there is a tremendously varied multidimensional structure but the core consists of a unit with marked uniformities in orientation and a strong feeling of togetherness." (Knoblauch, 1988, p. 75).

Knowledge Flows

As mentioned, the flow of know-how and knowledge has emerged as a most critical factor in many organizations and mergers. Let us look at this resource flow in a multidimensional merger setting in more detail in order to demonstrate the validity of the argument advocated above. Through acquisition specific knowledge and know-how of one firm is often merged with knowledge assets of another to create additional value through combined knowledge assets. It may exactly be the firm-specific knowledge and know-how of why the merger was pursued. The ability to access new knowledge from the acquired firm, to recombine it, and hence to redistribute it across the differentiated units amounts to a competitive concern (Rosenkopf and Nerkar, 2001). The combination of the acquired firm's and the acquiring firm's knowledge and know-how potentially expands the synergetic competence and increases, for instance, innovation output or product market scope (Ahuja and Katila, 2001; Lubatkin et al., 2001). Those postmerger effects only occur if the transfer of knowledge works. Knowledge is primarily transferred through interactions and transmissions that are rich enough to capture the subtle character of knowledge and know-how (Gupta and Govindarajan, 2000; Subramaniam and Venkatraman, 2001).

The bulk of firm specific knowledge is not codified and the know-how mostly exists in a narrative form only. If the communication process does not account for this specific character of skills, know-how, and semicodified knowledge, the transfer is likely to fail. Organizations are not able to make sense of signs and signals. Knowledge and know-how research has observed that transfer occurs primarily on informal transmission channels; more often than not the most effective media are unconventional in nature: storytelling, chats, spontaneous conversation, and so on (Brown and Duguid, 2001; Orr, 1996; Schreyögg and Geiger, 2003). Orr's observation of the way repair people keep themselves informed and exchange their experiences shed light on the criticality of the technicians' discourse. He demonstrated that technical knowledge (with Rank Xerox) is a distributed resource retained and diffused through a narrative process. In other words, common symbols, shared languages, similar orientation patterns, and values are required to enable communication and transfer ill-structured knowledge and know-how. This conclusion refers back to our proposition on the criticality of a universal corporate culture for mixed merger strategies and multidimensional resource flows in complex organizational settings.

Conclusion and Discussion

In conclusion, the relative importance of cultural consistency varies with the extent and depth of multidimensional operations aimed at in M&A. In all those cases where—for whatever strategic reason—the postmerger strategy implies a high degree of differentiation (diversity, complexity) and stresses the importance of knowledge flows, the capacity of traditional coordination measures, such as hierarchy and conditional programming, is limited, and more sophisticated coordination approaches come to the fore and gain competitive concern. The critical challenge is to retain connectivity among the dispersed and highly differentiated organizational units. Considering its distinctive strengths, a universal corporate culture is likely to match this critical challenge. In other words, the more complex a merger is in terms of manifold functional differentiation and resource flows, the more pressing becomes the integration issue and the more critical is the problem-solving capacity of a shared system of meanings (universal corporate culture).

In all these constellations specified above, the additional efforts to create in a postmerger integration process a universal, highly consistent corporate culture are likely to pay. In all other cases, however, the pluralist mode seems to be preferable.

This proposition stresses the importance of informal coordination and the criticality of common orientations in complex merger designs. This conclusion must, however, not be exaggerated. The criticality of informal coordination measures does not mean that in all those cases organizations can or should refrain from any formalization at all. Organizations need some rules, routines, and decision programs to guarantee stability. Traditional coordination measures therefore cannot be completely neglected. They build the all-encompassing and enabling frame. There is no informality without formality.

The problem, however, is that in those complex settings, tasks are less and less predictable and repetitive in nature. That means the prerequisite for developing formal rules are diminishing. If tasks and decisions are uncertain, tough standardization simply does not make much sense. Routinization is not only less useful, it can do harm to the effectiveness of the entire system. In those settings a common frame of reference is capable to create a (more) reliable basis for sensible communication and interaction than routines and programs (Luhmann, 1984, p. 434). Shared patterns of orientation are assumed to replace other organizational measures in stabilizing the network of actions on a broader scale soon.

On the other hand, one should not forget that common frames of reference do not develop within a couple of days, it takes time and there are no time compression economies possible. In some cases this process takes perhaps too much time. And also, acquiring firms are usually impatient. More often than not, they are keen on demonstrating as soon as possible that the merger is a success in order to impress shareholders or other stakeholders. These intentions challenge the suggestion advanced in this chapter. In those cases other efforts to manage complexity, such as radical change or charismatic leadership, come into the foreground and may be preferred. They are faster, doubtlessly, but do they work better in the longer run? Hard to believe.

References

Ahuja, G., and Katila, R. (2001). Technological acquisitions and the innovation performance of acquiring firms: A longitudinal study. *Strategic Management Journal*, 22: 197–220.

Barney, J. B. (1991). Firm resources and competitive advantage. *Journal of Management*, 17: 99–120.

Bartlett, C. A., and Ghoshal, S. (1986). Tap your subsidiaries for global reach. *Harvard Business Review*, 64(6): 87–94.

Bartlett, C. A., and Ghoshal, S. (1989). *Managing Across Borders*. Boston: Harvard University Press.

Begley, T. M., and Boyd, D. P. (2003). Why don't they like us overseas? Organizing U.S. business practices to manage culture clash. *Organizational Dynamics*, 15(4): 357–71.

Billings-Harris, L. (1998). *The Diversity Advantage: A Guide to Making Diversity Work*. Winchester: Oak Hill Press.

Black, J. S., and Mendenhall, M. (1990). Cross-cultural training effectiveness: A review and a theoretical framework for future research. *Academy of Management Review*, 15: 113–36.

Boyacigiller, N., and Adler, N. (1991). The parochial dinosaur: The organizational sciences in a global context. *Academy of Management Review*, 16: 262–90.

Brown, J. S., and Duguid, P. (2001). Knowledge and organization: A social practise perspective. *Organization Science*, 12: 198–213.

Child, J. (1972). Organizational structure, environment and performance: The role of strategic choice. *Sociology*, 6: 1–22.

Cox, T., Jr., and Blake, G. (1991). Managing cultural diversity: Implications for organizational competitiveness. *Academy of Management Executive*, 5(3): 45–56.

Daft, R. L. (2001). *Organization Theory and Design*, 7th edn. Cincinnati, OH: South-Western.

Daft, R. L., and Lewin, A. Y. (1993). Where are the theories for the "new" organizational forms? An editorial essay. *Organisation Science*, 4: I–VI.

Deal, T. E., and Kennedy, A. A. (1999). *The New Corporate Cultures*. Cambridge, MA: Lexington.

Donaldson, L. (1982). Comments on "Contingency and choice in organization theory", G. Schreyögg. *Organization Studies*, 3: 65–72.

Donaldson, L. (2001). *The Contingency Theory of Organizations*. Thousand Oaks, CA: Sage.

Edström, A., and Galbraith, J. R. (1977). Transfer of managers as a coordination and control strategy in multinational organizations. *Administrative Science Quarterly*, 22: 248–63.

Fernandez, J. P., and Barr, M. (1993). *The Diversity Advantage*. New York: Lexington.

Frost, T. S. (2001). The geographic sources of foreign subsidiaries' innovations. *Strategic Management Journal*, 22: 101–24.

Garsten, C. (1994). *Apple World*. Stockholm: Stockholm University Press.

Gerpott, T. (1995). Successful integration of R&D functions after acquisitions: An exploratory empirical study. *R&D Management*, 25: 161–78.

Gupta, A. K., and Govindarajan, V. (1991). Knowledge flows and the structure of control within multinational corporations. *Academy of Management Review*, 16: 768–92.

Gupta, A. K., and Govindarajan, V. (2000). Knowledge flows within multinational corporations. *Strategic Management Journal*, 21: 473–96.

Haspeslagh, P. C., and Jemison, D. B. (1991). *Managing Acquisitions: Creating Value Through Corporate Renewal*. New York: Free Press.

Hofstede, G., Neuijen, B., Ohayv, D. D., and Sanders, G. (1990). Measuring organizational cultures: A qualitative and quantitative study across twenty cases. *Administrative Science Quarterly*, 35: 286–316.

Jaeger, A. M. (1983). The transfer of organizational culture overseas: An approach to control in the multinational corporation. *Journal of International Business Studies*, 14(2): 91–114.

Knoblauch, E. (1988). Ist Unternehmenskultur international übertragbar?. In Demuth (ed.), In *Imageprofile '90', 3rd year*. Düsseldorf: Econ, pp. 75–83.

Kogut, B. (1985). Designing global strategies: Profiting from operational flexibility. *Sloan Management Review*, 26: 27–38.

Kuin, P. (1972). The magic of multinational management. *Harvard Business Review*, 50(6): 89–97.

Kunda, G. (1991). *Engineering Culture: Control and Commitment in a High-Tech Corporation*. Philadelphia: Temple University Press.

Lawrence, P. R., and Lorsch, J. W. (1967). *Organization and Environment. Managing Differentiation and Integration*. Cambridge, MA: Harvard University Press.

Lorenzen, P. (1991). Philosophische Fundierungsprobleme einer Wirtschafts-und Unternehmensethik. In Steinmann and Löhr (eds.), *Unternehmensethik*, 2nd edn. Stuttgart: Poeschel, pp. 35–68.

Lubatkin, M., Schulze, W. S., Mainkar, A., and Cotterill, R. W. (2001). Ecological investigation of firm-effects in horizontal mergers. *Strategic Management Journal*, 22: 335–57.

Luhmann, N. (1984). *Soziale Systeme. Grundriss einer allgemeinen Theorie*. Frankfurt a.M: Suhrkamp.

Luhmann, N. (1994). *Funktionen und Folgen sozialer Organisation*, 4th edn. Berlin: Duncker & Humblot.

Martin, J. (1992). *Cultures in Organizations: Three Perspectives*. New York: Oxford University Press.

Martin, J. (2001). *Organizational Culture: Mapping the Terrain*. Thousand Oaks, CA: Sage.

McKendrick, D. G. (2001). Global strategy and population level learning: The case of hard disk drives. *Strategic Management Journal*, 22(4): 307–34.

Medcof, J. W. (2001). Resource-based strategy and managerial power in networks of internationally dispersed technology units. *Strategic Management Journal*, 22: 999–1012.

Meffert, H. (1990). Implementierungsprobleme globaler Strategien. In Welge (ed.), *Globales Management*. Stuttgart: Poeschel, pp. 93–115.

Miles, R. E., and Snow, C. C. (1994). *Fit, Failure and the Hall of Fame*. New York: Free Press.

Nahavandi, A., and Malekzadeh, A. R. (1988). Acculturation in mergers and acquisitions. *Academy of Management Review*, 13: 79–90.

Orr, J. E. (1996). *Talking About Machines*. Ithaca, NY: Cornell University Press.

Perlmutter, H. V. (1969). The tortuous evolution of the multinational corporation. *Columbia Journal of World Business*, 4(1): 9–18.

Porter, M. E. (1986). Competition in global industries: A conceptual framework. In Porter (ed.), *Competition in Global Industries*. Boston: Harvard University Press, pp. 15–60.

Pritchett, P., Robinson, D., and Clarkson, R. (1997). *After the Merger: The Authoritative Guide for Integration Success* (Revised Edition). New York: McGraw-Hill Trade.

Rose, R. A. (1988). Organizations as multiple cultures: A rules theory analysis. *Human Relations*, 41(2): 139–70

Rosenkopf, L., and Nerkar, A. (2001). Beyond local search: Boundary-spanning, exploration, and impact in the optical disc industry. *Strategic Management Journal*, 22: 287–306.

Schein, E. H. (1997). *Organizational Culture and Leadership*, 2nd edn. San Francisco: Jossey-Bass.

Schneider, S. C. (1992). National versus corporate culture: Implications for human resource management. In Pucik, Tichy, and Barnett (eds.), *Globalizing Management*. New York: Wiley.

Schreyögg, G. (1982). Some comments about comments: A reply to Donaldson (Comments on "Contingency and choice in organization theory," Schreyögg, G.).*Organization Studies*, 3: 73–78.

Schreyögg, G. (1998). Die Bedeutung der Unternehmenskultur für die Integration multinationaler Unternehmen. In Kutschker (ed.), *Integration in der internationalen Unternehmung*. Wiesbaden: Gabler, pp. 27–50.

Schreyögg, G., and Geiger, D. (2003). Wenn alles Wissen ist, ist Wissen am Ende nichts?!—Vorschläge zur Neuorientierung des Wissensmanagement. In *Die Betriebswirtschaft 2003*.

Shrivastava, P. (1986). *Bhopal*. New York: Paul Chapman Pub.

Simonin, B. L. (1999). Ambiguity and the process of knowledge transfer in strategic alliances. *Strategic Management Journal*, 20: 595–624.

Subramaniam, M., and Venkatraman, N. (2001). Determinants of transnational new product development capability: Testing the influence of transferring and deploying tacit overseas knowledge. *Strategic Management Journal*, 22: 335–58.

Trice, H. M., and Morand, D. (1991). Cultural diversity: Organizational subcultures and countercultures. In Miller (ed.), *Studies in Organizational Sociology*. Greenwich, CT.: JAI Press, pp. 69–105.

Van Maanen, J. (1991). The smile factory. In Frost, Moore, Louis, Lundberg, and Martin (eds.), *Reframing Organizational Culture*. Newbury Park, CA: Sage, pp. 58–76.

Executive Commentary on Chapter 5

ALBERT YOUNG

In this chapter, Georg Schreyögg addresses the fundamental issue of a successful cultural integration after a merger or acquisition, which is a key factor for the overall success of the new entity.

When he argues that the emerging entity's corporate culture is less the result of an initial and possibly predetermined quick fit than that of a longer process of learning and becoming, I can relate to it very well. I have witnessed this process of the transfer of corporate culture. This can especially be true in the case where both parties have a strong and successful past behind them and both exude a sense of pride in their respective corporate cultures. The transfer becomes challenging in the case of a cooperation between equals, bringing complementary resources and skills. The new entity would and should benefit from taking the best from each existing entity. But how to determine what is the best and how to choose when there is a conflict and when both entities have very different and equally strong corporate cultures? I saw one instance where security and safety were debated among the parties in a joint venture. They had difficulty understanding each other's point of view. One party was arguing that protecting and saving human lives in the case of incidents should be the paramount guiding principle. The other believed that the protection of assets and property was equally important and that stories of staff risking their lives for the company should be widely publicized and encouraged. The discussions were passionate and were going nowhere. They had to be adjourned until an opportunity was given to organize a workshop. The same viewpoint came out at the beginning of the workshop. Both parties started to work on a case study, and had to role-play the crisis team trying to resolve a robbery escalating to a hostage taking. It was only when one hostage involved was portrayed as a family member related to the crisis team, that the working teams suddenly started to see things from a common point of view. This did not mean that the discussion was over, but both parties made a big step toward each other. It was really a process of learning and becoming, and this has to start even prior to the formation of the new entity.

Georg Schreyögg proposes two extreme archetypes of corporate cultures, the universal type (highly standardized and uniform) as opposed to the pluralist type (highly diverse and inclusive). When I use those archetypes and try to categorize the large companies, from what I know, into them, I tend to find more in the universal type. Those are typically large and multinational corporations, successful today in a global market. And many of them have grown through mergers and acquisitions (M&A). However, at the same time, I see many of them undergoing a transformation to become more diverse and inclusive. An example is the emphasis put in place by many large companies to accelerate the development of female and non-Anglo-Saxon staff. One obvious beneficiary is the Asian staff, as the large companies realize that the Asian market is their fastest growing and potentially largest market. But beyond gender and race, there is also a genuine realization of the need to take in people who are different, who can generate different ideas and act differently in a given situation, to ultimately provide more resilience to the organization, through flexibility and creativity, which are the hallmarks of the pluralist type. But where will this transformation lead to? For many of the corporations, the journey has just begun, and it will be interesting to see in a few years time where it takes them to.

Georg Schreyögg models the choice for the emerging entity between the two extremes of universal and pluralist cultures on the coordination requirements and argues that the choice is key to the success of the integration. However in real life, do the parties actually take the time and effort to address this choice, and more generally design the future corporate culture prior to the formation of the new entity? Many M&A are opportunistic, others are by necessity, and in most cases time is of essence. Once the decision to form the new entity has been taken by the respective headquarters for strategic reasons, it is left to the companies at the local level to expedite. The avoidance of conflicting issues before the actual formation of the new entity can be another barrier. A discussion on the choice of corporate culture, although fundamental and beneficial, before the actual formation of the new entity, in the context of other difficult or critical issues at hand and taking into account the time pressure to conclude, is often neglected or postponed by the parties. The focus is often on the financial and commercial issues that are more seen as making or breaking the deal. Once the new entity is formed, the task of the cultural design and integration becomes more difficult and even impossible. This was the case in a venture formed by a large partner and a small silent partner, which had in essence the corporate culture of the larger partner. The venture operated quite well until the day it had to take on a new larger partner who bought out the existing smaller partner who wanted to quit and move on. Pressed by time, the parties focused only on the financial and commercial issues, and overlooked completely the future cultural integration. The new partner, once in the venture, was in total dissent with the way the venture was originally operated and wanted to bring in its own culture, and exercise influence on many essential aspects of the venture. Many changes had to be brought in; the original operating model was put under question. The disruptions to the operations of the venture were such that the only solution was to break up, and to have one party buy out completely the other one.

The centerpiece of the chapter argues the necessity and the effectiveness of an informal self-coordination in large and complex corporations. This self-coordination is in turn facilitated by the connectivity between the different functions in a universal type of corporate culture. I have seen this in action in a large organization. This was particularly obvious when members, coming from different parts of this organization and from different regions of the world, meeting for the first time in a workshop, could in a matter of minutes get off to work, and tackle together very effectively different subjects. They shared a common language, coded with acronyms totally incomprehensible to outsiders, and a common way of working, with a set of common tools, which are parts of the connectivity described by the author. But what was also most important, and as the first point of connectivity, was that the members could immediately relate to each other through common acquaintances or colleagues in the organization. They were part of a network and the workshop was another opportunity to expand this network for its members and to reinforce their connectivity. I would see this networking as an essential prerequisite to self-coordination.

The chapter logically concludes on the advantage of the universal culture in the case of M&A involving complex organizations. But how can such a corporate culture be created from the outset? The task is even more challenging in the case of the merger of two universal corporate cultures. In this case, the integration team, if it only comprises members from the original entities, may not have the ability to resolve the potentially strong conflicts, partly because they would lack objectivity and neutrality. I would suggest here the use of a third party. A neutral third party, with a previous experience of merger, respected by the preexisting entities, can be of help to this process. The third party, to be selected jointly, can bring in examples of successes and failures, be the vent for conflicts and reduce passion in the debates, and facilitate a genuine creation. He or she would work very closely with the future management team of the new entity and see it through during the whole initial stage of the formation. I would be glad to see this put to test.

Georg Schreyögg sets out in this piece of research a useful framework for corporations to decide on and design the cultural integration after a merger or acquisition. I could not agree more that corporations would benefit from taking the time and effort to negotiate and resolve the issues of cultural integration prior to the merger or acquisition and give them the same importance as to the financial and commercial considerations.

6   The Construction of Social Identities in Mergers and Acquisitions

STEIN KLEPPESTØ

Introduction

It is probably not necessary to present the many general findings and manifestations of the problems related to mergers and acquisitions (M&A). The publications of these are numerous. Countless studies have shown that M&A, almost by default, lead to conflicts between the two organizations, conflicts that severely hamper the performance of the new organization (cf. Buono and Bowditch, 1989; Larsson, 1993; Lubatkin, 1983; Pritchett, 1985). The dominating explanation for these culture clashes is basically that the organizations carry with them a preset structure of norms and values. In as much as these structures or organizational cultures are different, conflict is to be expected (cf. Altendorf, 1986; Cartwright and Cooper, 1993; Nahavandi and Malekzadeh, 1988). As an example, Cartwright and Cooper (1993) found, in a survey of a large number of managers, that "the existing pre-combination cultures of the partnering organizations played a major and fundamental role in determining merger and acquisition outcomes" (p. 61). The earlier studies on culture clashes are largely based on Berry's theories of acculturation (Berry, 1980, 1983). The foundation is that, as the merger or acquisition is developing, the organizations will go through different stages of polarization, creation of monolithic structures, and ethnocentrism, that is, the two organizational cultures will each be increasingly more coherent and distinguishable, and people will put a stronger emphasis on the norms and values of their organization. This understanding of cultural clashes is based on a predominantly functionalist and realist understanding of culture, seeing it as a static structure, coherent and unambiguous, very much in line with the popular teachings of Schein (1985).

From a radically different understanding of culture, I have elsewhere (Kleppestø, 1993, 1998) argued that cultural clashes should not be understood as clashes between preset structures of norms and values, but as conflicts over definitions of the situation at hand. On the basis of empirical findings, it was suggested that we are better off focusing on what goes on in such a conflict by studying processes rather than structures, and ambiguity rather than coherence. Culture was perceived as an ongoing narrative aiming at the creation of meaning. It could also be said that the important thing is not how different the two organizations are, in terms of historically founded cultural traits, but what is made of these differences.

The foundation of the two opposing views are perhaps well known to the readers as they resemble ongoing discussions within anthropology and other social sciences. Historically, anthropologists have, axiomatically, assumed that the cultural core of any group is relatively fixed and coherent through time and space. This gave the phenomenon of culture a life of its own, separate from the bearers of that particular culture. Since the 1970s, certainly beginning with Geertz (1973), but perhaps gaining speed in the mid eighties with Marcus and Fischer (1986) and Clifford and Marcus (1986), this has been put under debate, and the traditional (rationalist) understanding of culture is being replaced by an understanding of culture as being ambiguous and incoherent. Culture is no longer seen as a structure but as a process, that is, as a highly contextual creation of (narrated) meaning (Clifford, 1988; Marcus, 1992). Similar lines of reasoning have, of course, been applied to the study of organizations and organizational culture (Czarniawska-Joerges, 1992; Martin and Meyerson, 1988; Meyerson, 1991; Schultz, 1995).

Barth (1993) adequately summarizes the discussion by saying that we "should give up the pipe dream of coherence" (p. 5). He goes on to say that "[m]ost of our experience of social life should lead us to accept as plausible [a] view of disorder, multiplicity, and underdeterminedness" (ibid.). He succinctly points out the need to look beyond how preestablished cultures clash, to how culture is contextually produced. To do this, we must focus on processes rather than structures—that is, on the construction of a verb not a noun, to use Barth's (ibid., p. 7) formulation. One of Barth's main ideas is to understand variation rather than coherence. There are a number of good reasons to expect the cultural knowledge, in any community, to be diverse. Barth (ibid., p. 5) points out several; there are variations in the level of "expertise in the population; there is diversity in received traditions; there is a varied particularism of local history, contention, and context; there are all the differences between people in positioning and experience; and there are finally, the pragmatics of purpose and interest" (ibid.). We should therefore expect divergence in cultural expression and life. This is not to say that there are no shared premises, shared understandings, or norms and values. Barth points out that there are plenty of them, "far too many to be put together in one cohering structure or one person's practice, and too many to be universally and equally shared" (ibid.). The cultural life of any individual is constructed (or narrated) and varied, not given and coherent. This does not mean that we are free to come up with any story. Our narratives are constantly being checked by other narratives. The stories are, furthermore, constructed from the cultural material at hand, from the "surfeit of cultural materials and ideational possibilities" (ibid., p. 4).

Culture is perhaps best understood as man's collection of thoughts and images, material available for individuals and groups of individuals to create an understanding of any situation or event. This thought suggests that our understanding of an event—an integration process following a merger—must be understood not primarily from this cultural material, but from how this material is used in the situation. Accordingly, I argue that we should focus on how individuals (and groups of individuals) in any event, on the basis of the cultural material at hand, create a cultural identity, that is, an understanding of themselves in that situation.

From a social constructivist frame of reference (Berger and Luckmann, 1966), I am arguing for the need to focus on the local and temporal creation of self-concepts and meanings on both an individual and a collective (group) level. To do this, I will rely heavily on the recent debate on identity as outlined by Bruner (1990) and others (Blumer, 1969; Czarniawska, 1997; Deetz, 1994; Lash and Friedman, 1992; Luhmann, 1990; Shotter and Gergen, 1989), and on the concept of social identity as developed by Tajfel (1978a, 1978b, 1982) and others (cf. Hewstone and Jaspers, 1982; Hinkle and Brown, 1990; Hogg and McGarty, 1990; Turner, 1978, 1982; Turner and Brown, 1978). From a practical point of view, this implies that cultural clashes in mergers and acquisitions need to be understood in terms of the process by which the involved organizations try to establish separate identities and through that establish themselves as being unique, and worthy of respect. Very often, this will produce a strong focus on cultural differences and hence create clashes.

Identity or Self

The term *identity* (on an individual as well as collective level) has traditionally brought to mind "a bounded, unique, more or less integrated motivational and cognitive universe, a dynamic center of awareness, emotion, judgment, and action, organized into a distinctive whole and set contrastively against such other wholes and against a social and natural background" (Geertz, 1979, p. 229). Groups and their identities are, following the same reasoning, usually understood to be associations of members sharing some important common traits; showing consistency through time and space; sharing common perceptions and common cognitive structures (Albert and Whetten, 1985; Alvesson and Björkman, 1992; Dutton and Dukerich, 1991). As actors and outside observers, we do, for practical purposes, tend to assume clear boundaries between different organizations or different groups. We also tend to understand groups and group identities as objects in and of themselves.

This understanding of identity and self is under heavy debate (Bruner, 1990; Czarniawska-Joerges, 1994; Czarniawska, 1997; Deetz, 1994; Lash and Friedman, 1992; Shotter and Gergen, 1989). In a simplified manner, it seems reasonable to state that the argument is one of "essentialists" vs. "constructivists" (or "conceptualists" or "narrativists"). The essentialist perspective assumes that groups, as well as individuals, are owners or bearers of a unique character coherent through time and space. This essentialism is to be understood "as if Self were a substance or an essence that preexisted our effort to describe it, as if all one had to do was to inspect it in order to discover its nature" (Bruner, 1990, p. 99). It might be well concealed and hard to find (as in "finding one self"), but it is there and it is of importance. In such a case, it would be natural to assume that in situations of stress and insecurity, individuals as well as groups, would, in a form of regression, fall back on their essential selves. The constructivists, on the other hand, claim that introspection is at best an early retrospection and is as such subject to the same kind of selectivity and construction as any other construct from memory. Self is a concept created by reflection, "a concept constructed much as we construct other concepts" (ibid., p. 100). The notion of "self" grows not from "inner essence independent of the social world, but from experience in a world of meaning, images, and social bonds, in which all persons are inevitably involved" (Rosaldo, 1984, p. 139). It might be suggested that we are a "colony of Possible Selves, including some that are feared and some hoped for, all crowding to take possession of a Now Self" (Markus and Nurius, 1986, p. 954).

Gergen (1982) argues that our self-concept varies according to the context of people within which we find ourselves. These conceptions are not necessarily coherent or continuous. They do, however, reflect our general capacity to reinterpret the past, and our capacity to envision alternatives. In a certain social situation, the only relevant self (identity) is the one we conceptualize there and then. As situations to a large extent are repetitious, we are, however, able to see patterns. Self is "both a guardian of permanence and a barometer responding to the local weather" (Bruner, 1990, p. 110). How an individual or a group would depict themselves in a particular situation is therefore a product of the situation at hand. At the same time no situation is created out of nothing. A more accurate description of the processes of identification is therefore that of a *rewriting* of identities in a new context.

Polonoff (1987), speaking of self-deception, claims that this self-narrative should not be understood as a reference to a real or true self, a hidden thing. The object of the narrative is to achieve a "coherent, livable and adequate" (and why not plausible) telling. Schafer (1981, p. 31) took an even more radical stance claiming that we are our stories; we have no other understanding of ourselves but the stories we tell. In this context it is important to see that we have to tell a story about the other to be able to tell our self-story, that is, we cannot just tell any story to just any other person.

The Social Creation of Groups

In a given situation and for a relatively short period, groups might easily give the impression of having clear-cut, coherent, and well-founded identities. These can be experienced by outside observers, as well as by members of that particular organization. Organizations, at times, convey a sense of unity, shared frame of reference for guiding action, shared history, and other things that seem to tie members of an organization or a group together. Seeing an organization in such an objectified way is actually seeing it as identifiable, that is, as something that is distinct from what it is not. We should, however, remember that organizations must be assumed and must be created by all significant actors as they go along.

In a sense, groups and their boundaries are figments of our imagination. Groups exist only when someone talks about them; or think in terms of them; or assume them in their discourse or actions. Furthermore, they (that is, the groups and their identities) exist only in the forms that the actors, at that particular time, assume (or attribute) them. Obviously groups can be identified and defined in terms of their members, structures, and boundaries. They can of course also be institutionalized, and so can their identities. Nevertheless, groups are meaningful only if they are considered relevant and are given an identity by significant actors. Put in the words of phenomenologists, the world exists only in our tails of it and is therefore "inherently precarious [...], because [its] continuation relies upon the willingness of human beings to subscribe to, account for, and (re)enact [its] existence" (Willmott, 1996, p. 927).

As actors seek to make sense of their world, organizations, in particular large and complex ones, can only be grasped through simplification. In order to work as an emotional and rational element of meaning, organizations have to appear as relatively coherent and stable. They also have to fit in, meaning they must be connected to other relevant elements in the construction of meaning. One such element is of course history, other elements might be norms and values; organizational aims or objectives; professional status; and so on. Therefore, it is not surprising to find that organizational identity brings to mind a sense of coherence, continuity, and predictability.

This understanding of the concept of identity has relevance from a pragmatic everyday perspective. It is an intuitive and integrated part of our way of thinking and talking. It can, however, be carried too far. We need to be aware of the shallowness of this coherency. Boland and Schultze (1996, p. 69) point to one reason a narrative identity is shallow by saying that any account of oneself " 'falsify' the world by portraying it in very particular ways." They go on to say that, "the beginning-middle-end structure which story-telling imposes on events, gives them a sense of wholeness, completeness and closure" (ibid.). "Seemingly unrelated incidences are given significance with respect to one another and the plot when they are brought into a chrono-logical relationship" (ibid.).

Stressing the social construction perspective means seeing groups as contextually bounded categories or labels. These categories are given emotional, cognitive, and political meaning. This is important both in an understanding of self-definition of in-groups and definition of out-groups. Groups and group identities should be understood as social categories used by actors in a specific situation to understand that situation. Thereby groups and identities become phenomena created by the actors in an ongoing narration. The fact that some categories (that is, groups) seem to exist permanently is not "evidence" of their basic or intrinsic nature—it is a call for research into their emotional, cognitive, and political history, that is, for a closer look at the forces that created them and keep them alive.

We should assume that organizations are fields of action (Czarniawska-Joerges, 1994) where people constantly account (Boland and Schultze, 1996; Willmott, 1996) for their actions, hence create meaning for these actions and thereby create the world they live in and the organizations in it. This highlights the public effort in which we create the world around us, and thereby create ourselves in a relationship with significant others (Bateson, 1972; Hora, 1959; Watzlawick, Bavelas, and Jackson, 1967).

Social Identity and Social Categories

A group's identity and boundary are created in a relationship with the group's social surrounding, that is, other groups. One example of this is given by Edheim (1969, p. 40). He talks about how a small ethnic minority group within a Norwegian local community was very visible and salient in spite of a long-lasting contact with the surrounding community and a "conspicuous lack of contrasting cultural traits." The explanation given was that groups and group identities should be seen as "categories of ascription and identification [created] by the actors themselves" (Barth, 1969, p. 10), and that empirical experience of group characteristics or essence is a product or outcome of ongoing rhetoric rather than "a primary and definitional characteristic of ethnic group organization" (ibid., p. 11). The two ethnic groups are better understood as categories used to maintain a given political order, a given definition of the community, and a given understanding of the dominant group. The rhetoric emphasized the small but publicly accepted differences rather than similarities; it even created contrasts beyond "visible" differences by linking them to larger, "invisible" differences such as norms and values.

In line with this thinking, it can be said that all human beings need to classify themselves and others into various social categories. Our world and our place in it are incomprehensibly complex and multifaceted. We cannot deal with this unless we are able to simplify by ascribing to graspable categories. Introducing oneself to others is often a matter of a positioning in terms of claimed group membership—in my case, male, Norwegian, university teacher (Tajfel, 1978b; Turner, 1982). This might be a result of one's need (emotionally) to belong to a certain category, but it is also a result of the need to simplify and ascribe to understandable or meaningful phenomena. One cannot (in a given context) understand oneself without reference to one's gender, nationality, or some other meaningful category, and one assumes that the social groups and identities one refers to are equally understandable and meaningful to others. In the same way one understands oneself through group identities, one also tries to understand others through identifying them as members of groups and hence as carrying a characterizing identity. Some of these groups are, of course, omnipresent in society, some are "obvious" in a given situation, and some are unexpectedly (and temporarily) created to make sense of the situation at hand (Brown and Ross, 1982; Turner, 1978).

Where, then, do the groups come from; how are the categories created; how do people end up as members of a particular group; and how are groups given an identity? Tajfel (1978a, 1978b, 1982) has experimented with "minimal groups," that is, groups based on matters of marginal or no relevance to the members. (Often these experiments start with assigning the experimentees to different groups by tossing a coin.) Obviously, such spontaneous groups have no history, no norm structure, or other cultural traits. The group as such can give no guidance as to behavior. There are no cultural rules to be learned. Nevertheless, Tajfel can demonstrate that membership effects the participants' understanding of the experiment's situation. Tajfel's experiments show that the subject matter of membership and group identity is created out of the situation. This does not mean that all groups are short-lived and unstable. The situation that created the groups and their identities can, of course, last and hence the groups remain. One should, however, avoid the mistake of confusing label with content. As groups are not objects in and of themselves, but social creations, they are constantly reshaped. A given group label (category), let us say "the department faculty," might remain but eventually refer to a totally different socially created idea and identity. In everyday rhetoric, this might be forgotten and the "the department faculty" of today might be seen as an unbroken continuation of the faculty of yesterday and hence create a sense of stability. I would, in line with Tajfel, suggest that all groups for analytical purposes should be seen as spontaneous and created (and recreated) in the situation at hand, bearing in mind that these creations are made of the extensive cultural material accessible to the actors.

Creation of groups and group identity is a question of the construction of meaning. We do this partly by defining ourselves through membership (I am like these individuals) and by exclusion (I am not like these individuals). Identity is a mixture of similarity and difference. This is, for obvious reasons, a question of proving uniqueness vis-à-vis other groups. It is equally important, of course, to demonstrate the value or status of that uniqueness. Whenever a group approaches another group, it is to be expected that it might want to "fight" for the establishment of a unique and valuable identity (Ashforth and Mael, 1989; Deschamps, 1982; Hewstone and Jaspers, 1982; Turner, 1982). Similar thoughts are introduced by Moscovici and Paicheler (1978) when talking about *social comparison* and *social recognition*. The argument is that groups react to other groups the same way individuals do, by constantly comparing themselves with relevant others and thereby seeking recognition of identity (Bateson, 1972; Hora, 1959). As long as recognition is received and the recognized identity is acceptable by both parties, nothing happens. In all other cases, intensified communication takes place in order to ensure recognition of desired identities.

"Tajfel's law" states that whenever, for some reason, an out-group becomes more visible, the in-group responds by increasing efforts to define their boundaries. If both groups are in agreement as to the norms and values applicable to the situation or encounter, things will go smoothly. If not, an intensified interaction will take place in order to establish a clear understanding of group identities and thereby give meaning to the situation at hand. This interaction or conflict tends to follow certain patterns such as stereotyping of both groups, reduced possibilities for exchange of membership, and an increased need for marginal members to choose a side (Tajfel, 1978b, 1982; Turner, 1982). This process resembles the common description of cultural clashes in mergers. How strong the conflict will be depends on the importance of the situation. If the in-group feels that their identity and status are under debate, it will increase its efforts to establish its identity and status. Again, this resembles findings in studies of mergers (Nahavandi and Malekzadeh, 1988). According to Tajfel and others, these efforts can follow one of several patterns (ibid.; Turner and Brown, 1978). There might be an increased *social mobility*, that is, a migration of members from one group to another. This requires that there are no sanctions from the abandoned group and that the receiving group accepts immigration. Furthermore, there might be an increase in *social creativity*, either by the threatened group trying to identify new dimensions in order to compare the groups with (that is, dimensions that would resolve the conflict by reestablishing identity and status), or by trying to establish new values in existing dimensions, or by finding other groups to compare with. Finally, there might be an increase in *social competition* in the form of arguments to the effect that the in-group's identity and status are established in the larger society and therefore legitimate.

The development of identities and their constituting uniqueness depends on which out-group it is important to distance the in-group from. Identifying topics presented in one situation might therefore differ from the topics in another situation. Construction and reconstruction of the group's identity are a part of an on-going narration, aiming at creating meaning and legitimacy, possibly following some basic rules or patterns. Albert and Whetten (1985) suggest that when the question of identity triggers a search for content, the organizational identity will be built on (a) features that are seen as the *essence* of the organization—which is a claim of central character; (b) features that *distinguish* the organization from others by which it may be compared—which is a claim for distinction; and (c) features that exhibit *continuity* over time—which is a claim for temporal continuity.

In a similar way, Kavolis (1984) suggests that the credibility of an identity requires elements of coherence, continuity, and commitment. There must be coherence between experience and the way this experience is expressed. The expressed identity must have a memorable continuity, that is, must be seen as in line with what we remember. Finally, there must be a committed relationship between the expressions in act and speech. The creation of groups and group identities are based on the material at hand in the specific situation and will supposedly adhere to these syntaxes or grammars. The assumption is that credibility and legitimacy are established by the rhetoric, typically following Albert and Whetten's and Kavolis's requirements. Groups following these rules seek to establish a coherent and consistent identity through time and space, an identity that might easily be mistaken for an inherent or essential quality of the group, rather than a highly contextual and temporal construction. The coherency and consistency thus created is as such a product of rhetorical strategies.

Interpretation of Some Empirical Observations

In one particularly investigated acquisition, an international corporation bought a smaller, but still fairly large, international manufacturer of high-quality food. In several published case studies, this acquisition was described as being very difficult because the two corporations allegedly had very different cultures. They had operated in very different ways, particularly because the acquired company was basically a single business corporation, whereas the acquirer was operating in many businesses (although mostly food-related). As a part of this acquisition, several minor integration processes started all over the world as local (national) headquarters of the two corporations were supposed to integrate their operations. These processes largely followed the same patterns and mirrored alleged culture clashes at the top management level. This also applied for the integration of operations in Sweden. Here, however, a traditional interpretation faced some difficulties. The acquired company had just recently established its own marketing and sales office in Sweden. This organization included some twenty employees who had been recruited from several local companies. The top manager in Sweden had previously handled the acquired company's products being the key account manager for a national wholesaler, and only one employee had worked in the parent company for a short period. It is consequently hard to see how these people could be seen as socialized into a culture aligned with the worldwide organization. Nevertheless, the first year followed the general pattern of culture clashes. The actors had, of course, some knowledge of their parent company and its assumed culture as it was read into routines, manuals, company slogans, and so on. Interviews with employees did however disclose a very thin or shallow knowledge of the former parent company.

One major conflict between the two local companies concerned the marketing strategy and the budget. This conflict was frequently used to represent the cultural differences. It turned out, however, that the office had had more or less the same conflict with the parent company prior to the acquisition. Although it is hard to see how the conflict with the new parent (and the whole integration process) had anything to do with culture, it is easy to see how it related to attempts to reduce anxiety and conflicts over social identity. The tentative, but still anxious, reaction of the employees was to assume that the acquisition was favorable because their new parent company (that is, the local headquarters of the acquiring company) had long experience with operating in Sweden and would understand local rules of the game better than their former parent. This quickly changed and instead the fear of losing jobs or having to move to another city took over. What tied the employees together was, of course, their common fear. They regarded themselves as a group and as such needed an identity. Following closely the requisites of Albert and Whetten (1985) and Kavolis (1984), their identity was created to establish legitimacy. They claimed to be unique (small and flexible) and to be a part of the history of its successful parent company (which is a paradox because their former parent was quite large and not flexible). They also engaged in a fight over identity and status as suggested by Tajfel, that is, they strengthened the boundaries, and they tried to establish the presence of qualities that demanded respect (knowledge of their products and markets, and their flexibility). When it became evident that this did not work, the group disintegrated and started to break down into smaller groups. One delineation was "young–old" which, at least partly, coincided with people's willingness to join their new parent some 500 kilometers away.

In a merger between two Swedish CPA firms, one large and one medium-sized, the problems experienced were generally attributed to their different cultures. One major clash was displayed in a conflict concerning the selection of one of their two computer systems. The larger firm had a DOS/PC-based system, the smaller Apple Macintosh. Both firms had a computer department located in Stockholm. An early dominant assumption was that the new firm would need only one computer department and that a number of computer support staff therefore soon would be without jobs. Particularly on the part of the smaller firm, this conflict was used as a symbol of the differences between the two organizations. People saw the fact that the smaller firm used Macintosh as explaining important cultural traits. Macintosh was seen as a user-friendly computer, a nonexpert interface, and as a technology one can master after only a few hours trial. This was pointed out to be a parallel to the basic norms and values guiding the business in their firm. Their way of dealing with clients was one of acting as teachers rather than police, helping rather than supervising, aiming at eliminating the need for their services. The knowledge they possessed was shared openly with their clients. They also claimed to use a language understandable to everyone, not the expert lingo of the other firm. The DOS/PC, on the other hand, represented the very opposite of the Mac, and the larger firm was described as the smaller firm's opposite in almost every aspect of their way of doing business. The larger firm of course disputed this. The allegations were, on the other hand, used to show the lack of seriousness in the smaller firm. They seemed, it was said, interested only in surviving as an entity, and not in developing the business of the new organization.

It was later discovered that prior to the decision to purchase the Apple computers, a large majority of the consultants were opposed to the idea. The decision was made in spite of this, largely because the head of the computer department was in favor. The decision created a conflict leading up to the time of the merger. It is accordingly hard to see that the description made by the actors reflected an uncontested, widely shared, historically correct cultural trait. This is not to say that it did not have any support in the ideational world of the firm. As a matter of fact, the ideas of what CPA is all about, or should be all about, were present in most CPA firms in Sweden. The notions were consequently not taken out of thin air. The conflict did function as a medium for displaying belongingness to a group, creating and strengthening identity, and claiming legitimacy. A mixture of forces drove the process. Political issues played an important part, as did the need to establish social identities and the need to make sense of all the turmoil the situation contained. The conflict described here was, of course, interwoven with a lot of other conflicts. To the actors, the situation was therefore considerably more complex than this exposition suggests (that is, one conflict at a time). The stories told and the introspections made by the actors seemed coherent, historically correct, and believable to them. The lack of social recognition received (or felt) made it even more important to engage in a social competition in line with Tajfel's suggestions. Every conflict seemed to verify their identity and that of the other (firm), and the two groups found themselves engaged in a game mutually strengthening each other's understanding of self, of the other, and of the situation.

Another case concerned the two major manufacturers of arms in Sweden—AB Bofors and FFV Ordnance—that merged into Swedish Ordnance. This merger also followed the general pattern connected to culture clashes. FFV Ordnance, the smaller and less known company, soon after the merger, displayed dissatisfaction with the development of the integration process. After only a few weeks, the dominant explanation for the nature of the difficulties was related to the allegedly different cultures. FFV Ordnance was a company owned by the government, containing several small companies producing rifles, ammunitions, torpedoes, and so on. Each company had been managed separately for many years but reorganizations, around ten years prior to the merger, had brought them somewhat closer together. The CEO of FFV Ordnance had worked to "modernize" and "market orient" the company and to bring the various parts of the company closer together. Particularly during the last year or so prior to the merger, this was at the top of his agenda. In FFV Ordnance's internal newspaper, in letters to various managers, and elsewhere, he complained that the speed and commitment for this change was disappointingly low. In light of this, it is perhaps surprising that a central part of the identity displayed by employees in FFV Ordnance after the merger was a sense of familiarity, their modern management style, and a strong market orientation. The claim was also made that AB Bofors very much represented the opposite. This is even more surprising because AB Bofors had always been a privately owned company and had had stunning success internationally for more than a century.

An isolated theme in the story told by people from FFV Ordnance can be helpful to explain my interpretation. As "proof" of the familiarity within FFV Ordnance, the annual sports day was mentioned. This event was said to bring people from all over FFV Ordnance to one of its sites for a weekend of sports and fun. The general understanding was that AB Bofors did not arrange anything similar and that this was evidence of the cold, impersonal culture of AB Bofors. This theme was supported by numerous stories from the games about how fun they were. Investigation showed that these games did not have a long history, and drew very little attention from people in

FFV Ordnance. Not even 5 percent of the employees joined and most of the participators were people active in the labor unions. Moreover, it turned out that AB Bofors in fact had similar activities and with a larger turnout.

I am not suggesting that the stories of FFV Ordnance were pure invention or explicit lies. For many valid reasons (political, financial, emotional, and others), people in FFV Ordnance felt threatened. The integration process was not managed in a particularly sensitive or understanding manner. Furthermore, people in AB Bofors did not realize the need to approach their new colleagues in light of their insecurity. To FFV Ordnance, AB Bofors did indeed appear large, threatening, and unfriendly. This provided them with an angle; hence the security and familiarity of their home organization were highlighted. The narrative of their identity was readily available and needed only little elaboration. Nothing people from AB Bofors did could alter the situation. In fact, the relationship followed a logic of its own in which most statements and actions were used as proofs of the correctness of the initial understanding. As Czarniawska (1997, p. 56) points out, "[o]nce you are 'labeled' you can easily become 'stigmatized'."

As a part of the merger mentioned above, a separate division—Industrial Services—was established to provide technical service to all parts of the new company, Swedish Ordnance. Their services included maintenance of buildings and other facilities; providing electricity, steam, and water; transportation; mail; and telecommunication. The division contained parts from AB Bofors and from Nobel Industries (the previous owner of AB Bofors). A top management team of ten managers—four from Nobel maintenance, three from the headquarters of Nobel Industries, and three from AB Bofors maintenance—managed the division.

The two most important and omnipresent but elusive groups in this situation were referred to as *Bofors* and *Björkborn*. The alleged cultural differences of these two entities were used to explain almost all the problems in the integration process. A short presentation is necessary to explain the context: Bofors is the name of an old iron mill (est. 1646), an institution historically dominating the small community of Karlskoga. Bofors is also the name of an old manufacturer of large guns sold all over the world (est. 1880). Furthermore, Bofors is also the name of a part of Karlskoga where the gun factory is located. Björkborn is situated three miles outside of Bofors. In Björkborn, Mr. Alfred Nobel started production of gunpowder in 1894, after having acquired AB Bofors (the company that produced guns and iron). Since then, the chemical industry in Björkborn (under the name of Nobel Chemicals and owned by Nobel Industries) has developed into a large facility for production of explosives as well as less dangerous chemical products. To make a long story short, it suffices to say that the new division was made up of organizational units with motley backgrounds and organizational ties, in fact so motley that most actors today couldn't keep track of them.

As can be seen, the name *Bofors* is used for many different purposes. Bofors AB is the name of what, initially, was called Swedish Ordnance. AB Bofors used to be the name of the part of Nobel Industries that produced guns and ammunition, and at one point in time, AB Bofors also owned Bofors Explosives, later sold to Nobel Industries and renamed Nobel Explosives. *Bofors* is the trademark of all of Bofors AB's products. When actors use the label *Bofors*, they might refer to all these entities and also to the place called Bofors. *Bofors* can be seen as a label for the idea of the historically dominating company AB Bofors and its reminiscences in various parts of Bofors AB. In the same way, *Björkborn* can be seen as a label for the idea of the chemical industry complex (including explosives), whether or not it might actually be located in Björkborn. *Bofors* and *Björkborn* are both very much a part of the same history, situated in the same town and sharing many resources. For many years, they were in the same corporation (Nobel Industries) and were integrated in many different ways (they shared, for instance, career tracks).

I was told stories that were meant to project identities, characters, cultural traits, and essences of these groups. In conversations about almost everything happening in the division, in Bofors AB and in Karlskoga, we would eventually end up talking about the differences—the opposite sides of E18 (a main freeway dividing Bofors and Björkborn, that is, the places but not the formal organizations). For instance, the ammunition factory was, and had always been, a part of AB Bofors and Bofors AB, but was still seen as being on the side of *Björkborn*. The main part of their facilities was located on the Björkborn side of the freeway. To a large extent, these descriptions were basically uncontested by everyone. If asked, most actors were able to give credible explanations for the present identities of the two groups. Observed from a distance, these stories made sense. They constituted reasonably coherent patterns and they seemed to connect geographically and historically. Especially when people were talking about the other group (that is, the out-group), descriptions were illustrated or demonstrated by reference to visible symbols and events. Very often, these were concrete things like buildings, products, technology, furniture, and clothing.

Obviously, the maintenance and transportation units in Bofors and Björkborn had much in common. Some parts were close to identical in their way of working, their aims, their competence, their technology, and so on. Still, they did not choose to identify with each other. Because the integration, for obvious reasons, was a threat to individual actors as well as groups of actors, it was politically and emotionally important to establish identities. To make the in-group credible, it was necessary to create boundaries and identities. This was done by focusing on the differences relative to the out-group. In the beginning, people working in the former Bofors units brought along an understanding of themselves and their group much colored by the larger *Bofors*. Within AB Bofors, the units dealing with maintenance were seen as a low-status group, but facing *Björkborn*, this changed. Bofors maintenance units no longer saw themselves as underdogs but as representatives of the larger group they earlier might have disliked and actually might have fought. The traits identified with the larger group (that is, *Bofors*) were transferred to themselves. This made them more visible vis-à-vis *Björkborn* and it gave them a desirable identity and a foundation for the production of meaning.

From the beginning, people from *Bofors* probably did not feel that they were under any threat. They were confident, even though they realized some of the political consequences and risks connected to the reorganization. People from *Björkborn*, on the other hand, were somewhat worried that they would be run over by *Bofors*. Soon after the establishment of the Industrial Services division, things changed. To everybody's surprise, the new CEO of Swedish Ordnance (recruited externally) appointed a manager from *Björkborn* as Head of the division and decided to locate the headquarters in Björkborn.

This and other events threatened the identity and status of people in former *Bofors* units and made it more important to establish group identities. It also encouraged people from *Björkborn* in their attempts to seek recognition as a group. Rapidly the two groups got involved in the kind of processes Tajfel (1978b, 1982) describes. Social mobility was hampered, the social sanctions for migration increased, and boundaries were increasingly more important. At the same time, the two groups, particularly on the top management board, engaged in fights to decide relevant dimensions of description (that is, social creativity) and to claim legitimate status (that is, social competition).

None of the groups seriously questioned the historical high status – low status ranking. Even people from *Björkborn* generally agreed that *Bofors* had had a higher status. However, the situation was about to change. The things that had contributed to *Bofors'* success were, according to *Björkborn*, exactly the same that would prevent *Bofors* from surviving in the future. There had been times when the technical excellence, the large bureaucracy, the extravagance of *Bofors* contributed to its business. Now, this had to change because the prerequisites for doing business in the markets of tomorrow would change. *Björkborn* was already there. They claimed to have the lean and mean operation needed for exactly these conditions. This, of course, was an attempt to create new dimensions for social comparison. While establishing new dimensions, *Björkborn* also needed to secure credibility for their claims to be better prepared for the future. This was basically done by reference to history and required a simplification of the descriptions of the in-group and the out-group. Seen through the eyes of *Björkborn*, "nothing" in the history of *Bofors* indicated that *Bofors* would be prepared for the future, and "everything" in *Björkborn's* history indicated that *Björkborn* was prepared. As the process of social comparison continued, the groups and their claimed identities became more and more important, until it totally dominated the situation.

Discussion

The situations described in these cases all contain complexity, anxiety, confusion, and uncertainty, and because of that require structuring and creation of meaning by the actors. Let us therefore focus on the actors as they try to make sense of the situation and their position in it, thereby making their actions rational and legitimate. They do this by looking for locally credible narratives and engaging in locally credible rhetorics. Ultimately, they try to establish in-group identities and seek social recognition from the out-group. As this is not granted them a social identity conflict arises, and the need for a more persuasive group identity and clearer boundaries grow stronger.

These groups should not be understood as groups carrying socially inherited or otherwise a priori given characters, but as social categories created out of the situation. This is not to say that the groups entered the situation without cultural material in the form of norms, values, or worldviews. This material, however, is not coherent and unambiguous and therefore needs clarification in any given context in order to form an identity. In a situation where one's identity is contested, the need to clarify and therefore *restructure* one's self-concept is enhanced. This creation, though made from the material at hand, is very free. So free that we cannot in any meaningful way say that it is a product of the culture, but must in fact be seen as a creation of and for the moment.

The groups' understanding of each other were less relevant prior to the reorganization, because they related to each other in a limited or marginal way. The groups can of course have been part of each other's history prior to the merger. The categories could be established long before the conflict over identity appeared. The distance would in most cases, however, have been large enough not to require sharp and coherent identities and boundaries. It would have been possible to let the boundaries drift and for people to move in and out of the groups without problems. Theoretically, any number and sort of categories could have appeared and could have been filled with any content. However, the new situation was not totally new, there did in fact exist a number of narratives to cling to. The already socially constructed manuscript has its limitations. In this sense, one could say that the two categories—for instance *Björkborn* and *Bofors*—were obvious. As they already were part of a long history, the creation of group identities was also partly predetermined. Going back to Albert and Whetten's three criteria for the creation of identity (Albert and Whetten, 1985), the actors could not just tell any story; the story or stories had to sound *true* to themselves and to others.

Using the pronouns "we" and "them" (or other expressions to the same effect) has a certain magic. They can be used—consciously or unconsciously—to create communities. By saying "we" or "our," a statement is made about common notions, norms, and values, and the speaker claims a right to speak on behalf of that community. Herbert Spiegelberg said, in his article "On the right to say we" (Spiegelberg, 1973), that using the pronoun "we" is a sort of annexation. One claims the right to divide people into different groups and give them certain traits. Saying "we at ACEM Corporation," although relatively harmless in certain situations, can be extremely important in other situations. It implies that this group called "we" exists outside the mind of the speaker, that its membership is equal to employment in ACEM, and that this is understood and accepted by all alleged members. It is also dangerous because it can be hard to see the content of such a group. Referring to a group, such as ACEM, might mean different things to different actors (inside and outside the group), but that might not be evident to all actors in a specific situation. Furthermore, the identification might be "correct" to the extent that actors acknowledge this membership in certain situations, whereas they refrain from doing so in others. This is to say that the actors consider themselves members of many different groups and will choose the relevant membership from context to context. So, although the attribution (made by the speaker) to a certain group might be correct (as they all de facto are employed by ACEM), the individual actors might want to avoid it in this particular instance.

Put differently, one can say that the use of the pronoun "we" creates a category or actually two, because the group "not-we" is also created. This could easily become a falsification, because it might come to include actors that do not accept this membership or do not find it relevant in the present situation. Also, it is a falsification because it might allude to a historical continuity or omnipresence (in time and place) far beyond the temporality of the construction it was based upon. Furthermore, it is a falsification in as much as it implies a monolithic belief structure, shared by all members. For emotional, ideational, and political reasons one might accept (or ascribe oneself to) a certain group in a certain situation without sharing all fellow members' notions of what this group is all about. Although this might be partly evident to the members, it is far more difficult for outsiders to see or acknowledge.

In the type of situations I have described, it is easy to see the strong need to clarify things by creating groups and giving them identities. Both actors and observers might be led to believe that there is only one possible "we" and "they" in the situation. In as much as these groups have historical, ideological, or political connotations, they might be very seductive. In cases where they are created according to the rules suggested by Albert and Whetten (1985) and Kavolis (1984), they can develop into draconian monsters and be given (by actors and observers alike) an explanatory power far beyond their foundation in shared belief systems. This is, of course, not to say that the actors lack a universe of ideas guiding their actions (and emotions for that matter). With Barth (1993), I claim the exact opposite: Our understanding of the world we live in is far too complicated to be reduced to some relatively uncomplicated, coherent, and stable membership of communities of thought. We live lives far too complex and ambiguous for us to be able to develop a concept of self-formed in a coherent, essential self. Accordingly, we cannot assume that the categories taking center stage in a given context have valid existence outside of that context. No matter the amount of culturally inherited material that these groups rely on, in their fabrication of an identity, it is still a creation of and for the moment.

As such, the categories seem rooted in time and space and therefore obvious to the actors. The rhetoric, connected as it is by cultural narratives, gives an illusion of continuity, stability, and coherence. The group conflict seems obvious and unavoidable. As the actors lose their sense of (self-) irony, as Kunda (1992) might have said, the group identities and boundaries take the form of a a priori given character or essence. We should realize that, as a frame of reference for guiding action and creating meaning, identity is a language game and therefore best understood as a figment of imagination.

The suggestion that the problems of integration are less a question of culture clashes than they are a creation of identities brings with it a different set of suggestions for practitioners and researchers. First of all, it questions the wisdom of the search for cultural similarity. A lack of contrasting cultural traits is no guarantee for the absence of group conflicts. Group identification and group preference does not presuppose a shared history or culture. An argument can be made that integration can be facilitated by difference. As long as the actors will rely on in-group – out-group games, they might as well be based on differences visible and acceptable to everyone. The key issue is to what extent the groups will accept or recognize each other's definitions of the situation and the identities and relationships in it. Some empirical observations support such an idea. There is a general agreement that M&A between organizations with clearly different roles (as in mergers between corporations with clearly different and not competing technologies or products), the integration goes much smoother. Traditionally, this has been explained by the lower degree of integration. In one of my earlier studies (Kleppestø, 1998), a different interpretation was made. In an acquisition, the roles (based on products) were very different but the degree of integration was very high; in spite of this, the integration went smoothly. In fact, a number of surprisingly strong (and insensitive) interventions were made by the acquirer, with no corresponding reaction from the acquired part.

Another implication is that efforts to resocialize people to accomplish a new unified whole might easily backfire as employees become deprived of the preferred identity. They need to feel secure and to be recognized on terms acceptable to them. To create a new "we" it is necessary to allow space for several smaller "we." The way to facilitate integration is therefore to recognize the unavoidable, that the actors need to create an understanding of the situation, and that this unavoidably means the creation of groups (or categories) with sharp boundaries. Interaction across these boundaries is in fact possible, as long as we acknowledge the basis for them.

References

Albert, S., and Whetten, D. A. (1985). Organizational identity. In Cummings and Staw (eds.), *Research in Organizational Behavior*, Greenwich, CT: JAI Press, pp. 263–95.

Altendorf, D. M. (1986). *When Cultures Clash: A Case Study of the Texaco Takeover of Getty Oil and the Impact on Acculturation on the Acquired Firm*. Dissertation, University of Southern California, Los Angeles.

Alvesson, M., and Björkman, I. (1992). *Organisationsidentitet och organisationsbyggande – En studie av ett industriföretag*. Lund: Studentlitteratur.

Ashforth, B., and Mael, F. (1989). Social identity theory and the organization. *Academy of Management Review*, 14: 20–39.

Barth, F. (1969). Introduction. In Barth (ed.), *Ethnic Groups and Boundaries*. Oslo-Bergen: Universitetsforlaget.

Barth, F. (1993). *Balinese Worlds*. Chicago: The University of Chicago Press.

Bateson, G. (1972). *Steps to an Ecology of Mind*. New York: Ballantine.

Berger, P., and Luckmann, T. (1966). *The Social Construction of Reality*. New York: Doubleday.

Berry, J. W. (1980). Acculturation as varieties of adaptation. In Padilla (ed.), *Acculturation*. Boulder, CO: Westview Press.

Berry, J. W. (1983). Acculturation: A comparative analysis of alternative forms. In Samuda and Woods (eds.), *Perspectives in Immigrant and Minority Education*. Lanham, MD: University Press of America.

Blumer, H. (1969). Society as symbolic interaction. In Rose (ed.), *Human Behavior and Social Processes*. Boston: Houghton Mifflin.

Boland, R. J., and Schultze, U. (1996). Narrating accountability: Cognition and the production of the accountable self. In Munro and Mouritsen (eds.), *Accountability: Power, Ethos and the Technologies of Meaning*. London: International Thomson Business Press.

Brown, R. J., and Ross, G. F. (1982). The battle for acceptance: An investigation into the dynamics of intergroup behaviour. In Tajfel (ed.),

Social Identity and Intergroup Relations. Cambridge, UK: Cambridge University Press.

Bruner, J. (1990). *Acts of Meaning.* Cambridge, MA: Harvard University Press.

Buono, A. F., and Bowditch, J. L. (1989). *The Human Side of Mergers and Acquisitions.* San Francisco: Jossey-Bass.

Cartwright, S., and Cooper, C. (1993). The role of culture compatibility in successful organizational marriage. *Academy of Management Executive,* 7(2): 57–70.

Clifford, J. (1988). *The Predicament of Culture: Twentieth-Century Ethnography, Literature, and Art.* Cambridge, MA: Harvard University Press.

Clifford, J., and Marcus, G. E. (1986). *Writing Culture: The Poetics and Politics of Ethnography.* Berkeley: University of Berkeley Press.

Czarniawska-Joerges, B. (1992). *Exploring Complex Organizations—A Cultural Perspective.* Newbury Park, CA: Sage.

Czarniawska-Joerges, B. (1994). Narratives of individual and organizational identities. In Deetz (ed.), *Communication Yearbook 17.* Newbury Park, CA: Sage, pp. 193–21.

Czarniawska, B. (1997). *Narrating the Organization: Dramas of Institutional Identity.* Chicago: The University of Chicago Press.

Deetz, S. A. (1994). The micro-politics of identity formation in the workplace: The case of a knowledge intensive firm. *Human Studies,* 17: 23–44.

Deschamps, J. (1982). Social identity and relations of power between groups. In Tajfel (ed.), *Social Identity and Intergroup Relations.* Cambridge, UK: Cambridge University Press.

Dutton, J. E., and Dukerich, J. M. (1991). Keeping an eye on the mirror: Image and identity in organizational adaptation. *Academy of Management Journal,* 34(3): 517–54.

Edheim, H. (1969). When ethnic identity is a social stigma. In Barth (ed.), *Ethnic Groups and Boundaries.* Bergen-Oslo: Universitetsforlaget.

Geertz, C. (1973) *The Interpretation of Culture.* New York: Basic Books.

Geertz, C. (1979). From the Native's Point of View: On the Nature of Anthropological Understanding. In Rabinow and Sullivan (eds.), *Interpretive Social Science.* Berkeley: University of California Press, pp. 225–41.

Gergen, K. (1982). *Toward Transformation in Social Knowledge.* New York: Springer-Verlag.

Hewstone, M., and Jaspers, J. M. F. (1982). Intergroup relations and attribution processes. In Tajfel (ed.), *Social Identity and Intergroup Relations.* Cambridge, UK: Cambridge University Press.

Hinkle, S., and Brown, R. J. (1990). Intergroup comparisons and social identity: Some links and lacunae. In Abrams and Hogg (eds.), *Social Identity Theory: Constructive and Critical Advances.* New York: Springer-Verlag.

Hogg, M. A., and McGarty, C. (1990). Self-categorization and social identity. In Abrams and Hogg (eds.), *Social Identity Theory: Constructive and Critical Advances*. New York: Springer-Verlag.

Hora, T. (1959). Tao, Zen, and existential psychotherapy. *Psychologia*, (2): 236–42.

Kavolis, V. (ed.) (1984). *Designs of Self-Hood*. Rutherford, NJ: Fairleigh Dickinson University Press.

Kickert, W. J. M. (1993). Autopoesis and the science of (public) administration: Essence, sense and non-sense. *Organization Studies*, 14(2): 261–78.

Kleppestø, S. (1993). *Kultur och identitet vid företagsuppköp och fusioner* (Culture and identity in mergers and acquisitions). Stockholm: Nerenius & Santérus.

Kleppestø, S. (1998). A quest for social identity: The pragmatics of communication in mergers and acquisitions. In Gertsen, Söderberg, and Torp (eds.), *Cultural Dimensions of International Mergers and Acquisitions*. Berlin: Walter de Gruyter.

Kunda, G. (1992). *Engineering Culture*. Philadelphia: Temple University Press.

Larsson, R. (1993). Barriers to acculturation in mergers and acquisitions: Strategic human resource implications. *Journal of European Business Education*, 2(2): 1–17.

Lash, S., and Friedman, J. (1992). *Modernity and Identity*. Oxford: Basil Blackwell.

Lubatkin, M. (1983). Mergers and the performance of the acquiring firm.*Academy of Management Review*, 8(2): 218–25.

Luhmann, N. (1990). *Essays on Self-Reference*. New York: Columbia University Press.

Marcus, G. E. (1992). Past, present and emergent identities: Requirements for ethnographies of late twentieth-century modernity worldwide. In Lash and Friedman (eds.), *Modernity and Identity*. Oxford: Blackwell.

Marcus, G. E., and Fischer, M. M. (1986). *Anthropology as Cultural Critique: An Experimental Moment in Human Sciences*. Chicago: The University of Chicago Press.

Markus, H., and Nurius, P. (1986). Possible selves. *American Psychologist*, 41: 954–69.

Martin, J., and Meyerson, D. (1988). Organizational cultures and the denial, channeling, and acknowledgment of ambiguity. In Pondy, Boland, Jr., and Thomas (eds.), *Managing Ambiguity and Change*. New York: John Wiley & Sons, pp. 93–125.

Meyerson, D. E. (1991). Acknowledging and uncovering ambiguities in cultures. InFrost, Moore, Louis, Lundberg, and Martin (eds.), *Reframing Organizational Culture*. Newbury Park, CA: Sage.

Moscovici, S., and Paicheler, G. (1978). Social comparison and social recognition: Two complementary processes of identification. In Tajfel (ed.), *Differentiation Between Social Groups*. London: Academic Press.

Nahavandi, A., and Malekzadeh, A. R. (1988). Acculturation in mergers and acquisitions. *Academy of Management Review*, 13: 79–90.

Polonoff, D. (1987). Self-deception. *Social Research*, 54(1): 45–53.

Pritchett, P. (1985) *After the Merger: Managing the Shockwaves*. Homewood, IL: Dow Jones-Irwin.

Rosaldo, M. (1984). Toward an anthropology of self and feeling. In Shweder and Levine (eds.), *Culture Theory: Essays on Mind, Self and Emotion*. Cambridge, UK: Cambridge University Press, pp. 137–57.

Sales, A. L., and Mirvis, P. H. (1984). When cultures collide: Issues in acquisitions. In Kimberly and Quinn (eds.), *New Futures: The Challenge of Managing Corporate Transitions*. Homewood, IL: Dow Jones-Irwin.

Schein, E. (1985). *Organizational Cultures and Leadership: A Dynamic View*. San Francisco: Jossey-Bass.

Schafer, R. (1981). Narration in the psychological dialog. In Mitchell (ed.), *On Narrative*. Chicago: The University of Chicago Press.

Schultz, M. (1995). On Studying Organizational Cultures. Berlin: Walter de Gruyter.

Shotter, J., and Gergen K. (1989). *Texts of Identity*. London: Sage.

Spiegelberg, H. (1973). On the right to say "we": A linguistic and phenomenological analysis. In Psathas (ed.), *Phenomenological Sociology*. New York: John Wiley & Sons.

Tajfel, H. (1978a). Interindividual behaviour and intergroup behaviour. In Tajfel (ed.), *Differentiation Between Social Groups*. London: Academic Press.

—— (1978b). Social categorization, social identity and social comparison. In Tajfel (ed.), *Differentiation Between Social Groups*. London: Academic Press.

—— (1982). Instrumentality, identity and social comparisons. In Tajfel (ed.), *Social Identity and Intergroup Relations*. Cambridge, UK: Cambridge University Press.

Turner, J. C. (1978). Social comparison, similarity and ingroup favouritism. In Tajfel (ed.), *Differentiation Between Social Groups*. London: Academic Press.

—— (1982). Towards a cognitive redefinition of the social group. In Tajfel (ed.), *Social Identity and Intergroup Relations*. Cambridge, UK: Cambridge University Press.

Turner, J. C., and Brown, R. J. (1978). Social status, cognitive alternatives and intergroup relations. In Tajfel (ed.), *Differentiation Between Social Groups*. London: Academic Press.

Watzlawick, P., Bavelas, J. B., and Jackson, D. D. (1967). *Pragmatics of Human Communication*. New York: W. W. Northon & Company.

Willmott, H. (1996). Thinking accountability: Accounting for the disciplined production of self. In Munro and Mouritsen (eds.), *Accountability: Power, Ethos and the Technologies of Meaning*. London: International Thomson Business Press.

Executive Commentary on Chapter 6

BJØRN Z. EKELUND AND AINA ASKE

Stein Kleppestø writes in the chapter on "The Construction of Social Identities in Mergers and Acquisitions" on how stories being told among employees are important during major transitions in organisations. The chapter highlights the elements during M&A that are rarely presented in books around these processes. It also demonstrates the application of a "constructivistic" perspective in organizational understanding, a challenge in relation to a more general "positivistic" position in science. For practitioners, these perspectives bring out new possibilities on how to work in organizations generally, and especially during M&A.

In his chapter, Stein Kleppestø starts with stating that cultural clashes have been looked upon as important hindrances for successful M&A. He proposes to focus more on the processes of cultural change, on how people tell stories during the process and then create meaning through shared understanding of important conflicts, positions, and identities. From a social constructivist position, he focuses on how people locally, and in a special situation, pick out elements in the cultural material at hand to create self-identities and meaning. Culture is not looked upon as a clear identified and fixed core, but as different stories told with both coherence and ambiguity in relation to the main organizational culture. Important dynamic elements in this process are understanding oneself and the group in the situation keeping up uniqueness, self-respect, and worthiness. The traditional dilemma in science between what is real, and what is a description, is introduced in order to clearly focus on the describers' possibility of creating a world in a dynamic interaction with the real world. Stories being told are looked upon as valid if they capture the essence in the organization, distinguish the organization from others, and feature elements that represent continuity over time.

In line with this understanding, Stein Kleppestø presents different M&A cases with different stories being told by employees during the different stages. A main element in the stories presented is how people in organizations have created stories in defense of the crisis. Stories with consequences for identity are illustrated functionally as a defense mechanism in groups in order to keep up a positive individual and collective self-image. He illustrates further how stories being told to define relationships to an outer organization, often the acquiring company, are stories similar to earlier stories being told in the organization, a form of replication and repetition of significant culturally recognized good/bad stories, positions, and actors. In this way, the intruding organization is understood by already established concepts in the own organization, representing a continuity of collective culture, but unprecise in description of the other. This prescription is often a consequence of uncertainty and anxiety, often materialized as a fear of losing jobs and social belongingness in work situation.

In this chapter, Stein Kleppestø focuses most on a descriptive process, showing how social identities and collective understanding through storytelling influences actions in organizations through M&A. From a practitioner's point of view, it is important to understand the possibilities and limitations of this perspective when M&A is being handled in proactive and planned process.

First of all, we think it is important to not talk about either—or in these perspectives between real and positivistic versus constructivistic and local understanding. As practitioners, we experience that some stories can be told because they interact with reality in a way that functions for creating common understanding enough for joint planning and action. The dynamic aspect of anxiety and positive identity for people involved are good guiding principles for what qualities to look for in stories searched for.

Another aspect of application of this way of thinking is in the creation of a futuristic story, the collective vision created by all members in the M&A process. We see that conflicts here and now could be defocused by future-oriented perspective. The joint creation of a vision functions as a guidance for individual actions. These future-oriented stories will also have a function of creating new joint identities, reducing anxiety and creating positive identities. In a merger, we invited people to draw a vision for their collective processes by asking people to describe "What stories would you like to tell your own children in five years about how you have taken part in the M&A process today?"

In our experience we run jointly processes that build upon central value elements that individual people bring into the process. Cultural values, not only related to "how things are" but more explicit in relation to "how things should be" are elements that together can produce a description of future with a higher probability of success in a merged organization. Such kind of process might create better motivation among workforce than a debate of here-and-now differences.

In cross-cultural mergers we also experience that humble and respectful communication from dominant organizations and their leaders are important elements that reduce defensive group identity processes. This might be more unusual for organizations belonging to a high power distance culture.

In cross-national mergers the national political systems and nationalistic press often constitute an added complication in taking a position that avoids competition—who are the winners and the losers. The national political systems and a nationalistic press are also two communication and legitimization areas that often stimulate negative attributions toward the other company, and in that way create identity and communication challenges among natural reference groups for those leaders who are involved in the process.

In this process of creating a joint positive identity, we have to take into consideration what Kleppestø wisely writes at the end of the chapter, "... efforts to re-socialize people to accomplish a new unified whole might easily backfire as people are deprived of preferred identity. People need to feel secure and to be recognized on terms acceptable for them." We experience that there are possibilities to look upon history from a new perspective, looking, finding, and seeing elements in the organizational history that can be brought forward positively to a new understanding in the collective process of creating tomorrow, creating a new uniqueness but a continuity of essence. This is an active standpoint accepting the constructive process of understanding history and using it as an element in a feed-forwarding process to differentiate real actions in future. This creative freedom, inside the limitation for valid and functional storytelling, is an important proactive stimulating action point for practitioners in Stein Kleppestø's chapter.

7 A Learning Perspective on Sociocultural Integration in Cross-National Mergers

INGMAR BJÖRKMAN, JANNE TIENARI, AND EERO VAARA

Introduction

What do managers learn from their previous experience of integrating merging organizations? How does this learning influence the implementation and success of subsequent mergers? There is today wide agreement that the ability to manage the integration of workforces and cultures is an important factor in the success of mergers and acquisitions (M&A). To the extent that sociocultural integration processes are unsuccessful, they may lead to loss of key personnel, decrease in employee productivity and reduced job satisfaction, communication breakdowns, and resistance to change (see, for example, Buono and Bowditch, 1989; Cartwright and Cooper, 1993b). Cross-national mergers are particularly challenging as "national" identification as well as delineation from other nationalities influence how employees make sense of the integration process following the merger decision (Calori, Lubatkin, and Very, 1994; Gertsen, Søderberg, and Torp, 1998; Olie, 1994). Ultimately, lack of sociocultural integration may result in failures to reach the intended synergy benefits and growth potential of the merger. It is therefore of crucial importance for firms, and top decision makers within them, to develop their integration capabilities.

In this chapter, we present a learning perspective on sociocultural integration. Key actors in firms with merger experience learn from their earlier integration efforts, and the lessons learnt are likely to guide integration decisions in subsequent mergers. To the extent that key actors in firms adequately learn from previous merger processes, experience may offer the potential for firms to improve their performance in subsequent mergers. However, research has failed to establish a direct positive relationship between merger experience and performance. Although it has been demonstrated that previous experience tends to influence subsequent M&A (Haleblian and Finkelstein, 1999; Hayward, 2002; Finkelstein and Haleblian, 2002), it has also been shown that experience does not necessarily lead to improvements in performance. For instance, the insights gained from one merger may be applied in a subsequent merger that appears superficially similar but where the differences are big enough to make the lessons from the first merger wrong or even dangerous (Finkelstein and Haleblian, 2002). Surprisingly, there is a lack of research on perceptions of the actual learning that takes place in firms as they increase their experience of M&A (cf. Greenberg, Lane, and Bahde, •••; Leroy and Ramanantsoa, 1997; Zollo and Singh, 2001).

A learning perspective on sociocultural integration offers several potential contributions to the literature on M&A. First, a learning perspective may enhance our understanding of why decision makers in firms undertake specific approaches to sociocultural integration. Second, an augmented understanding of the key features of the process of learning in the M&A context may help managers to better understand these processes in their own organization, thereby contributing to improved sociocultural integration in the future. Third, a learning perspective may provide insights into when learning from one merger context can be transferred to another with positive performance effects, and when the use of previous experiences have negative impacts on the success of a subsequent merger.

In this chapter, we focus on learning around sociocultural integration when firms move from one cross-border merger or acquisition to another. We concentrate on the problems and challenges related to making sense and use of previous experiences when dealing with sociocultural integration. Our insights are based on an in-depth analysis of the making of the financial services group Nordea, which has been built through a series of domestic and cross-border M&A in the Nordic and Baltic region in Europe. The core of Nordea now comprises leading financial institutions in Denmark, Finland, Norway, and Sweden. We focus the analysis on four ideas concerning sociocultural integration that seems to have played a major role in the merger processes: (1) the development of shared corporate visions to create top management commitment, (2) the idea of "virtual headquarters" as a sign of balance of power, (3) the need to outline a corporate language policy, and (4) the need for cultural awareness programs. We analyze top managers' recollections of learning experiences in the series of mergers. On the basis of our analysis, we draw attention to three points: learning is inherently context-specific, it often involves ambiguity, and the significance attributed to specific learning experiences depends on the dominant coalition of actors. We end this chapter by offering suggestions on how decision makers in firms can avoid becoming trapped in their learning from the past and instead foster effective exploitation of their previous experiences in cross-national M&A.

Sociocultural Integration

Much of the research on sociocultural integration in M&A has started from the assumption that *cultural differences* are major causes of potential integration problems (for a review of this literature, see Vaara, 1999). Both the distance between the organizational cultures (for example, Chatterjee et al., 1992; Datta, 1991) and the home countries of the two organizations (for example, Lubatkin et al., 1998; Olie, 1994) have been pointed to as potentially problematic in merger implementation.

However, there are several problems attached with the focus on cultural differences. First, cultural differences are not stable objects of analysis but rather something that tend to be constructed in merger processes. Cultural identification is highly context-specific, and the sociocultural integration among the merging organizations is the outcome of idiosyncratic processes of social interaction. These processes are often characterized by the construction of "us" versus "them" settings, where the perceived cultural differences depend, among other things, on the relationship between the merger parties and their representatives (for example, Vaara, Tienari, and Säntti, 2003). Second, most organizational scholars today agree that national and organizational cultures tend not to be monolithic. Although there may be some cultural consistency, organizations are typically characterized by cultural differentiation and ambiguity (see, for example, Martin, 1992). In merger settings involving complex organizations, one can thus expect to see multiple, complex, and ambiguous cultures and views on cultural differences. Third, there is growing agreement that it is not the organizational or national cultural differences per se than rather cultural "fit" or "misfit" that determines the dynamics of sociocultural integration. Consequently, the extent to which the specific cultures in question are compatible is a key issue (see, for example, Cartwright and Cooper, 1993a). Others have gone further and argued that it is not either this fit but how sociocultural issues are dealt with or managed after the merger that matters (for example, Calori, Lubatkin, and Very, 1994). Fourth, some researchers have even questioned the very rationale of associating cultural differences with problems or failures. Specific studies have, in fact, indicated that cultural differences can in specific circumstances also be a source of value (for example, Morosini, Shane, and Singh, 1998).

Organizational researchers have therefore focused increasingly on the processes of sociocultural integration. Inspired by anthropological models, researchers have examined different modes of acculturation (Elsass and Veiga, 1994; Nahavandi and Malekzedeh, 1988). These studies have, among other things, shown how the dynamics of acculturation depend greatly on how the merger parties and their representatives view each other and which kind of relationship is built between them over time. Other researchers have focused more on how organizational members *make sense of and socially construct* the merger process (Gertsen, Søderberg, and Torp, 1998; Kleppestø, 1993; Vaara, 2002; Vaara, Tienari, and Sântti, 2003). These studies have in particular illustrated how complex and ambiguous culture creation and identity-building are and consequently how difficult it is to manage these processes. Although these studies have significantly contributed to our understanding of the complexities of sociocultural integration processes, little in-depth research has been carried out on *why* organizational decision makers in specific situations tend to use certain approaches to sociocultural integration. We propose that a learning perspective can fruitfully be used to augment our understanding of this issue.

Learning in Organizations

Many learning theorists characterize organizations as systems that adapt to interpretations of the relationship between previous action and their effects (Cyert and March, 1963; Levitt and March, 1988). According to this organizational learning perspective, adopted in this chapter, organization members engage in interpretations of the success/failure of actions, routines, procedures, and strategies. If central organization members—sometimes referred to as the "dominant coalition" (Duncan and Weiss, 1979)—interpret a certain historical action as having been successful, these insights are coded in cognitive structures that mirror the causal relationship that has been inferred. Hence, interpretations shared among top managers of what has constituted successful versus unsuccessful actions are likely to influence decision making and to be translated into strategies, processes, procedures, and structures (Crossan, Lane, and White, 1999; Levitt and March, 1988). In this study, we analyze decisions made by top management on how to integrate the merging organizations; hence, in the empirical part of the chapter we focus on examples of the role of individual and collective learning in integration decision making.

Although individuals, groups, and organizations learn from experience, researchers have identified a number of factors influencing the inferences that are drawn from history. First, a range of *socio-psychological factors* influence the inferences that managers make based on history. Managers need to perceive and present the outcome of previous decisions as successful to both themselves and others so as to protect their self-esteem and their own identity as successful professionals (Staw, McKechnie, and Puffer, 1983). The ambiguity about cause–effect relationships that often exist may mean that managers misread information and engage in superstitious learning

(March and Olsen, 1976). It has also been shown that managers often attribute good organizational performance to their own actions, further strengthening existing routines and strategies (Fiske and Taylor, 1991). In fact, within the context of M&A it has been shown that managers often reframe and reinterpret as successes what had previously been considered failures, for example by shifting measures of success from a focus on profitability or synergy to one of sociocultural integration of the two units (Vaara, 2002).

Second, learning depends on the *focus of attention* of the learners (Cyert and March, 1963; Levinthal and March, 1993). Hence, depending on the kind of issues that the top management team focuses on in the organization and its environment, different learning outcomes result. For example, if top managers focus on the competitive environment of the firm, the management group is more likely to develop insightful interpretations of the effects of a merger on the competitive situation of the merged firm than to consider the effects of the sociocultural integration process on organizational performance. In this case, managers are unlikely to critically examine whether or not previous experience from sociocultural integration also might work under other conditions.

Third, the question of *who learns* is central to the learning perspective. Not only do different groups in the firm have access to different information and focus on different issues and, therefore, tend to learn about different things, they may also evaluate the outcome of a certain action differently and have different interpretations of the factors that led to the outcome (Huber, 1991). For example, new managers are more likely to define previous outcomes more negatively than are their predecessors (Hedberg, 1981). Further, the learning that takes place within the management group of one organizational unit does not necessarily impact the activities of others (Levitt and March, 1988).

Fourth, the impact of learning on organizational decision is dependent on the *power* of the individuals, units, and coalitions to implement what has been learnt (Huber, 1991). The vertical and hierarchical structure of the organization, and change within it, influences the implementation of the learning experience (Levitt and March, 1988). Organizational actors who pursue their own interests are also likely to be selective in terms of the learning points that they share with and adopt from others in the organization.

Finally, organizational learning can be said to depend on the *memory* of the organization (Levitt and March, 1988; Walsh and Ungson, 1991). Learning at a certain point in time may not be available for retrieval at a later stage. Although the inferences that managers draw from history may be codified and recorded in written manuals, procedures, and reports, these may not be widely known. Consequently, they are not sought and retrieved by organization members at later moments. Retrieving the outcome of learning tends to be even less likely when the "organizational memory" mainly resides with the memory of individuals. Reorganizations and turnover of personnel may further aggravate the availability of historical insights about what "works" and what does not.

Previous research taking a learning perspective on M&A has mostly examined the statistical relationship between (quantitative measures of) the organization's merger or acquisition experience and the performance of the focal merger or acquisition (Haleblian and Finkelstein, 1999; Hayward, 2002; Finkelstein and Haleblian, 2002). These studies have shown that experience does not necessarily lead to improvements in performance, but in-depth analyses of how firms learn from their acquisition experiences are rare (Leroy and Ramanantsoa, 1997). Of the many areas of postmerger or postacquisition integration, sociocultural integration represents a particularly cumbersome challenge (Shrivastava, 1986). Even the conceptualization of what constitutes sociocultural integration is difficult, and outlining key managerial activities and tasks in this context is not at all straightforward. Furthermore, agreeing upon what are the most appropriate and effective integration strategies is likely to be difficult in organizations where the actors, because of their different backgrounds, positions, roles, and identities, are likely to look at issues in different ways. This means that learning concerning sociocultural integration is likely to involve complicated social processes. To outline some of the characteristics and outcomes of these processes, we now turn to our empirical illustration.

The Nordea Case

Deregulation and radical development of information technology have trigged a wave of M&A in the financial services sector (Canals, 1997). A basic rationale for M&A in this sector lies in the quest for increasing size and the pursuit of synergy benefits through extensive integration of operations. Also, it seems that an important element of recent M&A is to profile the merged company as an attractive partner for future mergers. Increasing sensitivity for shareholder value is an overarching rationale in these actions. All these features are prominent in our case.

Our empirical analysis focuses on the series of mergers that led to the creation of a leading Nordic financial services group called Nordea. In October 1997, Finnish Merita and Swedish Nordbanken joined forces in an unprecedented cross-border merger in the European retail banking sector. Already at this stage, the representatives of the new Merita–Nordbanken group announced their intention to proceed with M&A in the other Nordic countries. In March 2000, it was announced that Merita–Nordbanken was to merge with the Danish Unidanmark, a group created just one year before

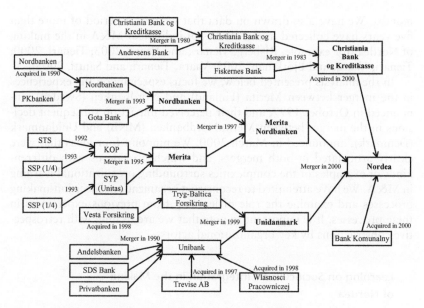

FIGURE **7.1 Mergers and Acquisitions in the Making of Nordea**

by a merger of leading Danish banking and insurance groups. Already before this step, in September 1999, Merita–Nordbanken had made a public offer for the state-owned Norwegian Christiania Bank og Kreditkasse (CBK), which after long negotiations, it was eventually able to acquire in October 2000. The name Nordea was launched at the end of 2000. Figure 7.1 summarizes key M&A leading to the creation of Nordea. It is important to note that the cross-border mergers were preceded by a series of domestic M&A.

The Nordea case is a particularly fruitful setting for analyzing organizational learning as the organization has been created through a series of cross-border M&A within a relatively short time period, allowing us to examine the emerging learning and its impact on subsequent actions. Our empirical material was gathered in a research project involving a group of scholars from Denmark, Finland, Norway, and Sweden.[1] A total of fifty-five interviews were conducted among the top executives in the company in the latter part of 2001 and the beginning of 2002. The idea was to employ a "storytelling" approach with the use of a semistructured interview guide. Most interviews were carried out by a researcher representing the same nationality as the interviewee, using a shared native tongue. The insights presented in this chapter are also based on a detailed study of one of Nordea's business units, carried out longitudinally over a period of eighteen months. We have also drawn on data that we over a period of more than five years have collected in our studies of individual M&A in the making of Nordea (for example, Risberg, Tienari, and Vaara, 2003; Tienari, 2000; Tienari, Vaara, and Björkman, 2003; Vaara, Tienari, and Säntti, 2003).

In the analysis presented below, we focus especially on the experiences in the merger between Merita (Finland) and Nordbanken (Sweden), announced in October 1997, and their perceived impact on subsequent decisions in the merger between MeritaNordbanken (MNB) and Unidanmark (Denmark), announced in March 2000. We pinpoint four ideas that were clearly articulated in both mergers, and which provide us with different kinds of examples of the complexities surrounding organizational learning in M&A. We have attempted to reconstruct organizational decision-making processes and examine the role of learning from previous experiences in these processes. It is important to note that we are dealing with retrospective constructions by key organizational actors.

Learning on Sociocultural Integration in the Making of Nordea

In the following, we present our findings regarding learning in relation to four issues of sociocultural integration: (1) working on shared corporate visions to create commitment, (2) the idea of virtual headquarters as a sign of balance of power, (3) the need to outline a corporate language policy, and (4) the need for cultural awareness programs.

Shared Corporate Vision

One of the challenges in sociocultural integration in a merger is to be able to tackle cultural issues early. However, this is often not on the top of the managerial agenda as planning and negotiation processes tend to be dominated by strategic and financial considerations. Also, the division of responsibilities and activity segmentation often implies that specific cultural projects are not initiated by the people responsible for the strategic plans. Top management seldom pays much attention to sociocultural issues (cf. Jemison and Sitkin, 1986). In this respect, our case is an interesting exception. In fact, creating a shared corporate vision was one of the key issues that the top management focused on both in the Merita–Nordbanken and MNB–Unidanmark mergers.

Apparently, key representatives of Nordbanken (Sweden) had focused on outlining a shared corporate vision already in their previous domestic acquisition of Gota Bank in 1993. In this acquisition, top managers had started negotiations with a focus on a joint vision statement to ensure that the expectations of both parties would fit together. This vision statement later provided the basis for the actual integration of the new organization. A Swedish top manager who played a central role in this process stressed the positive experience of this exercise as follows: "If there is something that I've learnt it is that it is much more important to share a vision for the bank than to mechanistically estimate the synergy savings." It seems that the Finnish managers coming from Merita had similar kinds of ideas concerning the importance of focusing attention on a joint future as a means to avoid cultural confrontation and the politicization of specific questions.

Working on a shared corporate vision became a key managerial objective in the Merita–Nordbanken merger. When the negotiations were initiated, the representatives of Nordbanken and Merita deliberately focused on outlining a positive but realistic vision for the new bank. Only after this endeavor did they turn to those questions that are usually seen as critical in merger negotiations. These include the valuation of the firms and distribution of top management positions in the new firm. This first shared vision provided the preliminary guidelines for future decisions. For the new top management of MeritaNordbanken, working on shared visions served as a method for solving problems in the following organizational change processes. Several top managers saw this idea as a key learning experience. As a Finnish manager put it: "What was important in this process, and what I then learnt and used later, was not at all to discuss critical issues concerning the merger deal itself, but rather, through the business concept, [to discuss] our vision concerning the development of the industry and the business concept of the new, merged bank."

Not particularly surprising in view of the positive experiences of the Swedish and Finnish top managers, they insisted on starting the negotiations between MeritaNordbanken and Unidanmark in a similar way. "We used the same model," as a representative of MeritaNordbanken put it bluntly. Apparently, the Danish representatives had nothing against this, as they had themselves seen the importance of clear-cut corporate messages in their previous domestic merger between Unibank and Tryg-Baltica in 1999.

The discussions between these two parties resulted in a document providing the basis for the operations of the organization after the merger. When the top managers of MeritaNordbanken and Unidanmark announced their decision to merge in March 2000, they presented a revised version of the joint document containing a brief statement of the mission, the vision, and the overall values for the new organization. This corporate statement was presented to the public as well as to the employees of the merging companies. Work on the corporate vision continued after the announcement of the merger. Revised versions of the corporate statement were drafted in the following year. The corporate value programs, orchestrated by the Group Identity and Communication unit and discussed further below, could be seen as a follow-up of this process.

On the whole, the top managers viewed the focus on shared visions as "the right approach" to avoid unnecessary cultural confrontation and organizational politics, which often characterize international merger settings. In fact, the idea of starting any negotiation with a future vision has thereafter been presented as a key learning experience in various internal and external forums by the top managers of Nordea. However, on a more critical note, it has been speculated that this focus on corporate statements made the corporate management rely too much on this particular method as a means of solving problems related to (cultural) confrontation. The limited dialogue between top management and the rest of the organization was criticized. It was seen to undermine the value of the corporate visions. The perceived success with the corporate visions was apparently a reason behind the decision not to engage the organization in specific cultural training programs in the MNB–Unidanmark merger—an issue that we will return to later.

"Virtual Headquarters"

Comparisons between the two merger parties regarding such issues as ownership, distribution of managerial positions, location of headquarters, and—in cross-national settings—choice of the corporate language appear to be inherent parts of sociocultural integration. These questions involve concrete decisions, but it is the symbolic aspects that are crucial in terms of understanding internal divisions and cultural confrontation. The Nordea case illustrates well the challenges related to headquarter location and the choice of corporate language.

In the negotiations concerning the Merita–Nordbanken merger in 1997, it soon became apparent that this would have to be perceived as a "merger of equals"; otherwise it would be very difficult to accept the merger in Finland and Sweden. This posed specific challenges as to the division of ownership and creation of a symbolic balance of power within the postmerger organization (see also Vaara and Tienari, 2003). The location of headquarters was in this sense a sensitive issue. However, the negotiators came up with an innovative decision to place the official domicile of the firm in Helsinki (Finland) but to move the actual corporate management headquarters to Stockholm (Sweden). Instead of concentrating top management work in one location, top managers were to spend time both in Sweden and Finland. This was viewed as symbolically important in the new organization. The extensive travels by executives were also intended at improving personal contacts and relationships between Swedes and Finns. The common interpretation among top management was that the decisions concerning headquarters and mobile managers had been correct.

When MeritaNordbanken and Unidanmark merged in 2000, the issue of headquarters location was again discussed. Apparently strongly influenced by the positive experiences gathered in MeritaNordbanken, it was decided that the new company would have no formal headquarters. Instead, there would be a "virtual headquarters"—a term later frequently used to denote this innovative idea. Top managers would retain their offices in their home country organizations but travel extensively in all the Nordic countries. Group executive meetings were to take place once a week either in Denmark (Copenhagen), Finland (Helsinki), Sweden (Stockholm), or later Norway (Oslo). This was a choice that effectively promoted the idea of equality between the different country organizations and nationalities.

However, after some time had elapsed, the problems of this approach became apparent. The difficulties that had been seen as minor in the Merita–Nordbanken merger grew into severe problems because of the increased size, geographical dispersion, and larger operational scope of the new pan-Nordic organization. The absence of a clear geographical center in the Nordic financial services group led to inflated travel costs and much valuable (and costly) time spent traveling. In addition, the rare colocation of the top managers—with few opportunities for spontaneous informal face-to-face discussions between representatives of different nationalities—was viewed as hampering effective decision making. A senior manager coined the general learning experience as follows: "What has received too little attention here is that the management does not spend enough time together." From an individual perspective, the constant traveling had negative effects on the "life balance." As a result of such experience, without making a big issue out of it, the top executive group agreed during the fall of 2001 to try to spend two days a week in Stockholm, geographically the most centrally located of the Nordic capitals. A senior manager explained this solution as follows:

> This model that we now have (virtual headquarters) was probably chosen to prove ourselves, our colleagues, or the journalists in Helsingin Sanomat (the leading daily newspaper in Finland) that this is a Nordic bank. But it cannot function like that, one has to establish one headquarters, and Stockholm is the only option.

Language Policy

In the negotiations leading to the merger of Merita and Nordbanken in 1997, the question of the language of the top management of the new bank was discussed, though not seen as particularly important at the time. Ironically, it was the Finn Vesa Vainio, the CEO of Merita, who suggested that the new top management would use Swedish. The reasons were pragmatic; the Swedes had Swedish as their mother tongue and the entire Finnish top management team spoke Swedish, some of them fluently. As Swedish is the second official language of Finland (and Swedish is obligatory for everyone at school), all Finnish employees supposedly spoke at least some Swedish. This decision just "happened by accident," as one Finnish negotiator put it. When the decision to introduce Swedish as the working language of the corporate management of MeritaNordbanken was made public, it became a major issue of debate within the new organization. It also attracted considerable media coverage in Finland (see Risberg, Tienari, and Vaara, 2003). As a result, the top managers had to justify the decision made, for example, by referring to pragmatic needs, to the proficiency of the Finns in Swedish, and to the inadequate English skills of Nordbanken (and Merita) staff. Later, it was also specified that this language policy would apply only in areas where it was meaningful, in top management meetings and those business operations where interaction between Finns and Swedes was the liveliest.

The choice of Swedish as corporate language created various internal problems on the Finnish side of the organization. For example, many Finnish managers and members of staff perceived a power imbalance and felt inferior in their social interaction within the bank. The language choice also created a sense of professional incompetence and was psychologically strenuous for some. For example, Finnish experts had frequently considerable difficulty in communicating their views and expertise in meetings where Swedish was used. It was also speculated that the choice of Swedish as the working language was a reason for several key individuals leaving the Finnish part of MeritaNordbanken. At a symbolic level, the choice also involved a reconstruction of a history-laden Finnish–Swedish confrontation. In fact, not only the people within the bank but also the Finnish media framed this issue as (yet another) example of Swedish dominance, linked with the historical colonial relationship between the two nations (see Risberg, Tienari, and Vaara, 2003). Interestingly, it was not an issue frequently discussed in Sweden, being a "nonissue" for many Swedes who were able to continue speaking Swedish as before. For the Swedes, the symbolic aspects of this language choice were not obvious.

Most Finnish and Swedish managers, including members of the top management, saw the initial decision as a mistake, as the following reflections of two key actors illustrate:

> One can see this language issue as a strategic mistake, which was made a bit carelessly at some point in the merger negotiations.
> I'd say it [the choice of Swedish] was a mistake. This might be a bit difficult for the Swedes to admit. For us [Finns], it is perhaps a little easier.

When the merger of MeritaNordbanken and Unidanmark was planned, the top managers had several choices as to how to handle language policy issues. In the Nordic context, "Scandinavian"—a mixture of Swedish, Danish, and Norwegian—is widely used. English has, however, become an increasingly dominating language in most Nordic corporations, not only to be used externally but also internally. In this situation, the previous problematic experiences in MeritaNordbanken had, according to many interviewees, a fundamental impact on the language policy issue—not only on the eventual choice of English but also on the careful formulation of an explicit language policy.[2] Especially the Finnish interviewees could in this context talk about "correcting a mistake." According to the newly formulated language policy, English would become the official corporate language. However, in all locations everyone would be encouraged to use the language preferred by the customers.

Within the merged organization, the explicit choice of English as the corporate language was widely interpreted as the right decision. Among most Finns, the change from Swedish to English as working language was particularly welcomed. Almost all of the internal corporate communication is now carried out in English. Customers continue to be served in their own language in the four countries but most meetings among top management in Nordea are held in English, at least if there is a native Finnish speaker among the participants. This has created a situation where in professional interactions everyone is expected to use a neutral, nonnative language.

This language policy did not, however, turn out to be unproblematic. Although the choice of English solved the apparent question of inequality among the merger parties, it also meant that all organizational members had to communicate in a foreign language, creating problems in terms of clarity of expression as well as impoverished internal communication. Some people also questioned whether this language policy was consistent with the distinctive "Nordic" image of the Nordea organization. In everyday work-related and social interaction in the organization, "Scandinavian" is still widely used. Therefore, in many concrete situations the Finns may still find themselves in inferior positions vis-à-vis native speakers.

Cultural Awareness

The importance of being aware of cultural differences and potential cultural confrontation is frequently stressed in the cross-border merger context. In brief, cultural awareness can reduce unexpected postmerger problems, help map out potential areas of conflict, and help avoid misunderstandings and confusion. Explicit discussions of different cultural legacies may also allow people in merging organizations to raise and deal with issues concerning "us" versus "them" that otherwise would be too contentious to confront directly. However, discussions on cultural differences may also be counterproductive as they may strengthen nationalism and belief in the existence of "fundamental" cultural differences across countries and organizations as obstacles to integration. It has also been suggested that one should focus on the development of a "new corporate culture" instead of concentrating on the initial differences between the merging organizations. Our case provides an interesting illustration of how specific efforts aimed at increasing cultural awareness had a prominent role in managing the Merita–Nordbanken merger, but not in the subsequent merger between MNB and Unidanmark.

On the Finnish side, there was extensive experience with cultural training already before the Merita–Nordbanken merger. The domestic merger between the Union Bank of Finland and Kansallis in 1995 had involved a cultural training program where hundreds of managers and employees were brought together to discuss differences between the merging organizations and challenges in the integration of the banks, referred to in the Finnish tabloids as "Serbs" and "Croats" (Tienari, 2000). In the Merita–Nordbanken merger, based on their previous successful experience, it was the Finns in particular who pushed for cultural training (Säntti, 2001).

In the Merita–Nordbanken merger an important role was played by the Human Resource Development unit, which was responsible for running a series of culture seminars. These intensive events concentrated on cultural differences between Swedes and Finns, and Nordbanken and Merita. Approximately 330 managers and specialists took part in these seminars. The participants were encouraged to identify ways in which to develop cross-national cooperation in the new organization. Within MeritaNordbanken, the seminars were generally viewed as useful and interesting. It was seen as specifically important to acknowledge and openly discuss the historical and cultural background of the merging parties and to develop suggestions concerning how to further develop the new organization. On a more critical note, some experienced the seminars to be somewhat detached from their daily work.

The domestic Danish merger involving Unibank and Tryg-Baltica in 1999 was in many ways different from the MNB case. It was a merger combining a bank and an insurance company. The merger involved very limited integration of the actual operations of the banking and insurance parts of the merged organization. The need for specific sociocultural training programs was thus not obvious. Instead, the top management of Unidanmark (the merged company) relied extensively on communicating the strategy and values of the new organization to internal and external stakeholders.

When MeritaNordbanken and Unidanmark merged in 2000, the top management led by the incoming new Danish CEO decided not to initiate any centrally orchestrated cultural training programs. In fact, top management deliberately downplayed national cultural differences, and few organized efforts were made to address issues related to organizational or national differences. One of the key reasons for this approach was apparently a conviction among Danish members of the corporate management that one should focus on the future and not to spend too much time on "irrelevant" cultural differences. Successful experiences with working on shared vision statement also made other members of the corporate management confident that "things were moving in the right direction" (see the discussion above). It should be noted that the joint corporate statement published when the merger was announced emphasized that the new organization would build on common Nordic values. Dwelling on differences between the Nordic countries could thus be seen as contradicting this message, which was intended to internal and external stakeholders. Of the latter, especially those outside the Nordic countries typically perceive the region as a "cultural block."

Interestingly, the Group Identity and Communication unit led by a Danish top manager was given a prominent role in developing, presenting, and cascading throughout the firm a set of corporate values for Nordea in 2001 (see Björkman and Søderberg, 2003; Søderberg and Björkman, 2003). While much effort was focused on the branding of Nordea, national or organizational cultural differences were not paid attention to in this process. The Human Resources function, which had been responsible for organizing cultural seminars in MeritaNordbanken, only became actively involved late in this process. Neither Finnish nor Swedish executives, who had experience from the cultural seminars in MeritaNordbanken, had any overall responsibility for sociocultural integration projects in Nordea.

Overall, this lack of specific cultural training programs got mixed responses among the top managers in Nordea. Some viewed it as the right choice given other priorities. Many others saw a need to reflect on the differences that were perceived to exist across the countries and organizations. Interestingly, some managers recognized this need only after some time had elapsed since the first integration efforts. As a Danish senior manager in charge of a major unit put it: "I have learnt that one should be more aware of the cultural differences before starting this kind of process." Some individual units in Nordea did in fact at an early stage initiate their own actions to tackle cultural integration in the implementation of the MNB–Unidanmark merger.

Discussion

Our analysis of learning in the multiple M&A leading up to the creation of the financial services group Nordea shows how learning on sociocultural integration is inherently context-specific, that it is characterized by ambiguity, and that the significance attributed to learning from past experiences depends on the dominant coalition of organizational actors. First, owing to the fact that the nature and form of sociocultural integration challenges vary from case to case, the learning experiences tend to be closely linked with specific cases. The Nordea case highlights the *context-specificity* of learning in M&A. Approaches that are found to work in one context do not necessarily produce positive outcomes in others. For instance, the experiences around "the virtual headquarters" illustrate how ideas developed and supported by experience in a specific context may produce unintended consequences in a new situation. However, this does not mean that learning cannot be useful also in changing circumstance as illustrated by the positive experiences in using corporate vision statements in several consecutive M&A.

Second, learning is *ambiguous* in the sense that it is very difficult to evaluate the outcomes of specific sociocultural integration strategies. As our examples illustrate, many actions taken to promote sociocultural integration in a merging organization are, at least to some extent, controversial. For instance, evaluating whether the cultural training program in Merita–Nordbanken was "successful" or not is subject to interpretation. Large-scale, complex mergers involve a multitude of integration efforts and events, planned as well as unplanned. Actions and events that initially are not considered important by top managers may later in the integration process be found to have significant consequences. This means that knowing whether or not certain integration efforts lead to results above or below an aspiration level, that is, a good or bad experience—the cognitive basis of learning—is ambiguous. Although most Merita–Nordbanken managers interpreted that the effects of the cultural training seminars overall had been positive, they had little concrete unambiguous data to back this up with. This ambiguity may have led to a questioning of the learning experiences, especially from people who were not personally involved in deciding on and implementing the cultural seminars.

Third, our analysis illustrates how learning is to a significant extent embedded in specific social groups and even personified, and that the significance of the learning that takes place in the organization depends on the *dominant coalition of actors*. Our examples show how the experiences gathered in MeritaNordbanken influenced several of the sociocultural integration decisions concerning the new group. However, concerning the idea of promoting cultural awareness through specific programs, it was the Unidanmark model that prevailed. The cultural training methods—and learning experiences—of the domestic Finnish (Merita) and Swedish–Finnish (MeritaNordbanken) mergers were not used. The Group Identity and Communication unit, which was given a prominent role in sociocultural integration process in the MeritaNordbanken–Unidanmark merger, did not contain people with first-hand experience from developing cultural awareness programs in MeritaNordbanken. Hence, the experiences in the preceding cross-national case were not exploited in the subsequent one. These observations are important as they point to an inherent problem concerning learning in merger contexts; the experiences of those who are— because of organizational reshuffling or shifts in dominant coalitions across organizational units—no longer in key positions are easily lost.

How to Enhance Learning in Cross-National Mergers

As the Nordea case illustrates, learning concerning sociocultural integration is far from straightforward. It is therefore easy to understand why previous research has shown that an increase in merger experience does not automatically translate into enhanced merger integration capabilities. Nonetheless, organizing always involves learning, whether people are aware of it or not, and previous experiences do have an impact on people's thinking and behavior. We suggest that there exist several challenges for decision makers in firms in terms of how to enhance processes of learning on sociocultural integration:

- *Identify who has learnt what.* The firm should ideally try to make sure that the existing experiences and knowledge are teased out and used—albeit with caution—when new strategies and actions are outlined. The Nordea case illustrates that although extensive sociocultural integration experience had been accumulated in some parts of the organization, this learning was not drawn on in the subsequent merger.
- *Establish who is responsible for learning what.* Learning requires actions, observations of outcomes, and interpretations of the relationships between actions and outcomes. Individuals tend to learn about issues that they pay attention to. Individuals and units with a specific area of responsibility in the merger integration process are therefore more likely to collect data on how well the sociocultural integration process is proceeding. Concrete actions to achieve integration are also more likely to be undertaken if somebody is responsible for the issue in question. In the merger between MeritaNordbanken and Unidanmark, announced in March 2000, no separate integration organization was established (until a new Deputy CEO was appointed in September 2002 with this responsibility) and no unit carried overall responsibility for sociocultural integration. It appears that this may have led to both a lack of utilization of some of the prior merger integration experience residing with units within the merging organizations, and only relatively limited attention to how the sociocultural integration process in general was proceeding.
- *Stimulate processes of experience articulation and codification.* A particular problem in a cross-national merger is to make explicit and codify the

knowledge residing in different parts of the organization. Even though explicit responsibility for different sociocultural integration activities is likely to rest with some units and individuals, it is important to collectively engage in a process of explicitly sharing and then critically discussing and articulating what "worked" and what did not (Zollo and Winter, 2002). A higher level of effort is needed when individuals codify their learning in writing, such as manuals.

– *Ascertain that the contextual nature of learning is critically evaluated.* The actions that are perceived to have led to positive outcomes in one merger process may or may not have positive performance effects in another context. It is therefore of utmost importance to critically scrutinize previous experiences from the point of view of being able to see how new circumstances differ from previous ones as well as to understand links between the two. The end result could be an enhanced understanding of what kind of approach to sociocultural integration works in what kind of situation. For this to materialize, it is crucial for the firm to develop an understanding of why a certain approach works in a specific context. A major challenge may in some situations be active unlearning of earlier successful ways to deal with sociocultural issues. Learning how to better handle sociocultural integration is not likely to be a simple task, but the potential payoffs in terms of improved merger performance are likely to be significant.

Notes

1. In addition to the authors of this paper, the following persons participated in the data collection: *Tore Hundsnes* (Norwegian School of Economics), *Christine B. Meyer* (Norwegian School of Economics), *Annette Risberg* (Copenhagen Business School), and *Anne-Marie Søderberg* (Copenhagen Business School). *Karl-Olof Hammarkvist* (Stockholm School of Economics) was also a member of the research team.

2. English became the language for the board, executive management teams, and some of the wholesale banking units (working in an international setting), whereas local languages remained the primary means of communication for employees in, for example, retail banking.

References

Björkman, I., and Søderberg, A.-M. (2003). Quo vadis HR? An analysis of the roles played by the HR function during the post-merger process. In Søderberg and Vaara (eds.), *Merging Across Borders: People, Cultures and Politics.* Copenhagen: Copenhagen Business School Press.

Buono, A. F., and Bowditch, J. L. (1989). *The Human Side of Mergers and Acquisitions. Managing Collisions Between People, Cultures, and Organizations.* San Francisco: Jossey-Bass.

Calori, R., Lubatkin, M. H., and Very, P. (1994). Control mechanisms in cross-border acquisitions: An international comparison. *Organization Studies*, 15: 361–79.

Canals, J. (1997). *Universal Banking: International Comparisons and Theoretical Perspectives.* Oxford: Clarendon Press.

Cartwright, S., and Cooper, C. L. (1993a). The role of culture compatibility in successful organizational marriage. *Academy of Management Review*, 7(2): 57–70.

Cartwright, S., and Cooper, C. L. (1993b). The psychological impact of merger and acquisition on the individual: A study of building society managers. *Human Relations*, 46: 327–47.

Chatterjee, S., Lubatkin, M. H., Schweiger, D. M., and Weber, Y. (1992). Cultural differences and shareholder value in related mergers: Linking equity and human capital.*Strategic Management Journal*, 13: 319–34.

Crossan, M., Lane, H., and White, R. (1999). An organizational learning framework: From intuition to institution. *Academy of Management Review*, 24: 522–37.

Cyert, R. D., and March, J. G. (1963). *The Behavioral Theory of the Firm.* Englewood Cliffs, NJ: Prentice Hall.

Datta, D. K. (1991). Organizational fit and acquisition performance: Effects of post-acquisition integration. *Strategic Management Journal*, 12: 281–97.

Duncan, R. B., and Weiss, A. (1979). Organizational learning: Implications for organizational design. In Staw (ed.), *Research in Organizational Behavior.* Greewich, CT: JAI Press.

Elsass, P. M., and Veiga, J. F. (1994). Acculturation in acquired organizations: A force-field perspective. *Human Relations*, 47: 431–53.

Finkelstein, S., and Haleblian, J. (2002). Understanding acquisition performance: The role of transfer effects. *Organization Science*, 13: 36–47.

Fiske, S. T., and Taylor, S. E. (1991). *Social Cognition*, 2nd edn. New York: Random House.

Gertsen, M., Søderberg, A.-M., and Torp, J. P. (1998). *Cultural Dimensions of International Mergers and Acquisitions.* Berlin: Walter de Gruyter.

Greenberg, D., Lane, H. W., and Bahde, K. Organizational learning in cross border mergers and acquisitions. In Mendenhall and Stahl (eds.), *Mergers and Acquisitions: Managing Culture and Human Resources.* Palo Alto, CA: Stanford University Press.

Haleblian, J., and Finkelstein, S. (1999). The influence of organizational acquisition performance on acquisition performance: A behavioral learning perspective. *Administrative Science Quarterly*, 44: 29–56.

Hayward, M. L. A. (2002). When do firms learn from their acquisition experience? Evidence from 1990–1995. *Strategic Management Journal*, 23: 21–39.

Hedberg, B. (1981). How organizations learn and unlearn. In Nystrom and Starbuck (eds.), *Handbook of Organizational Design*. New York: Oxford University Press.

Huber, G. (1991). Organizational learning: The contributing processes and the literatures. *Organization Science*, 2: 88–115.

Jemison, D., and Sitkin, S. (1986). Corporate acquisitions: A process perspective. *Academy of Management Review*, 11: 145–63.

Kleppestø, S. (1993). *Kultur och identitet vid företagsuppköp och fusioner*. Stockholm: Nerenius & Santérus forlag.

Leroy, F., and Ramanantsoa, B. (1997). The cognitive and behavioural dimensions of organizational learning in a merger: An empirical study. *Journal of Management Studies*, 34: 871–94.

Levinthal, D. A., and March, J. G. (1993). The myopia of learning. *Strategic Management Journal*, 14: 95–112.

Levitt, B., and March, J. G. (1988). Organizational learning. *Annual Review in Sociology*, 14: 319–40.

Lubatkin, M., Calori, R., Very, P., and Veiga, J. F. (1998). Managing mergers across borders: A two-nation exploration of a nationally bound administrative heritage. *Organization Science*, 9: 670–84.

March, J. G., and Olsen, J. P. (1976). *Ambiguity and Choice in Organizations*. Oslo: Universitetsforlaget.

Martin, J. (1992). *Cultures in Organizations: Three Perspectives*. New York: Oxford University Press.

Morosini, P., Shane, S., and Singh, H. (1998). National cultural difference and cross-border acquisition performance. *Journal of International Business Studies*, 29: 137–58.

Nahavandi, A., and Malekzadeh, A. R. (1988). Acculturation in mergers and acquisitions. *Academy of Management Review*, 13: 79–90.

Olie, R. (1994). Shades of culture and institutions in international mergers. *Organization Studies*, 15: 381–405.

Risberg, A., Tienari, J., and Vaara, E. (2003). Making sense of a transnational merger: Media texts and the (re)construction of power relations. *Culture and Organization*, 9: 121–37.

Säntti, R. (2001). *How Cultures Interact in an International Merger: Case MeritaNordbanken*. Doctoral thesis, University of Tampere.

Shrivastava, P. (1986). Postmerger integration. *The Journal of Business Strategy*, 7: 65–76.

Søderberg, A.-M., and Björkman, I. (2003). From words to action? Socio-cultural integration initiatives in a cross-border merger. In Søderberg

and Vaara (eds.), *Merging Across Borders: People, Cultures and Politics.*
Copenhagen: Copenhagen Business School Press.

Staw, B. M., McKechnie, P. I., and Puffer, S. M. (1983). The justification of
organizational performance. *Administrative Science Quarterly*, 28: 582–600.

Tienari, J. (2000). Gender segregation in the making of a merger. *Scandinavian
Journal of Management*, 16: 111–44.

Tienari, J., Vaara, E., and Björkman, I. (2003). Global capitalism meets national
spirit: Discourses in media texts on a cross-border acquisition. *Journal of
Management Inquiry*, 12: 377–92.

Vaara, E. (1999). *Towards a Rediscovery of Organizational Politics: Essays on
Organizational Integration Following Mergers and Acquisitions.* Helsinki:
Helsinki School of Economics and Business Administration.

Vaara, E. (2002). On the discursive construction of success/failure in narratives
of post-merger integration. *Organization Studies*, 23: 213–50.

Vaara, E., and Tienari, J. (2003). The "balance of power" principle—nationality,
politics and the distribution of organizational positions. In Søderberg and
Vaara (eds.), *Merging Across Borders: People, Cultures and Politics.*
Copenhagen: Copenhagen Business School Press.

Vaara, E., Tienari, J., and Säntti, R. (2003). The international match: Metaphors
as vehicles of social identity building in cross-border mergers. *Human
Relations*, 56: 419–51.

Walsh, J. P., and Ungson, G. R. (1991). Organizational memory. *Academy of
Management Review*, 16: 57–91.

Zollo, M., and Singh, H. (2001). *Post-Acquisition Strategies, Integration
Capability, and the Economic Performance of Corporate Acquisitions.*
Unpublished paper, INSEAD.

Zollo, M., and Winter, S. G. (2002). Deliberate learning and the evolution of
dynamic capabilities. *Organization Science*, 13: 339–51.

Executive Commentary on Chapter 7

BERND RATZKE AND TOM KELLY

In the following commentary, we will look at three aspects of Ingmar Björkman, Janne Tienari, and Eero Vaara's essay. Our experience in this field results from the merger of HYPO-Bank and Vereinsbank in 1997 and from the integration of BPH, Krakow, and Bank Austria, Vienna.

We will first of all look at the issue of resistance to change and examine helpful approaches from a training as opposed to a learning perspective. Secondly, we will look at "Mergers of Equals" and "Mergers of the Best" and show how managers learn about their potential new roles during a structured selection process. Finally, we will examine the role vision plays in the whole merger and integration process.

Resistance to Change

We are living in a world of change, of that there can be no doubt. Some social scientists even speak of chronic change, which might suggest that change is some sort of new virus. One would therefore expect the scientists to develop new medicine or raise antibodies to resist or combat this virus. Ingmar Björkman et al. point out clearly that one of the main reasons mergers fail is resistance to change. The question which then arises is: How do we deal with change?

Viewing change as some sort of corporate virus will not help—the desired state will be one where the systems and the individuals within them can adapt themselves to the changing environment. Creating such a state will allow a new vision to be translated into strategies.

So how do we develop this positive attitude to change? First of all, the reasons for the change have to be clearly communicated; and after the initial decision on a merger has been taken, probably the next most crucial factor determining the success or failure of a merger is the way the change process is communicated. Secondly, the entire executive management team must be actively involved and on board in the change process. Actively involved means sticking closely to the targets, processes, and actions in the new environment. Good managers, not only in merger situations, should be in a position to answer their employees' questions about targets and processes. Not knowing what these targets and processes are or sticking to old modes of behavior will make it extremely difficult to implement new ideas. (See also John Kotter Leading Change.)

Do managers see a difference between the old and the new system or not? Ingmar Björkman et al. ask if it is possible to transfer previous experiences into a new system. The HVB Group was recently faced with the challenge of implementing a new business model in the whole retail banking area. This involved the implementation of a new IT-based interactive customer relationship management process that was an absolute revolution for bank clerks. They had to learn a fundamentally different way of dealing with customers, which involved learning how to sell using the PC screen but without losing the customer's attention. In the process, the bank clerk was no longer free to choose products for his/her customer. His/her consulting role had changed dramatically.

The management leading these clerks also had to go through behavioral changes. They were faced with the challenge of how to support their employees, and new coaching concepts to help them perform this duty were developed. This is a far cry from the exciting talk of visions and missions and charismatic leadership. This is the gruelling and vital task of ensuring that the new business model is implemented in the same way in every part of the business. The new targets and quality standards have to be achieved and new processes put into practice and it is the job of management to ensure that the staff are fully aware of this and work together to accomplish this goal.

What did we learn during this process? We learned that it is extremely important and helpful to train managers in specific and defined situations of change so that they in turn can reach their employees. You have to identify the success factors and coach these. The magnitude of the task becomes clear if you do this for the whole group and not just for a single unit. But it is a worthwhile investment, because as a result every manager can see the difference between the old and the new system. Every manager gets the instruments and behavioral rules they need to support their employees. Every employee gets answers to his or her questions. McDonald's led the way in defining such quality standards and then implementing them simultaneously, with success, worldwide.

In merger cases, the approach is the same as for business model changes. The main difference lies in the fact that you have to pick up the experience and values of the various managers and employees. The training and coaching experience of the HVB Group showed that if you focus on the actual day-to-day work, focus on the content of their job, the cultural, and behavioural aspects will crystallize in a very relevant context. This is far more beneficial than dealing with culture on its own in training sessions where the context is missing and possibly also the opportunity to learn.

Ingmar Björkman et al. say that it is of "crucial importance for firms to develop their integration capabilities." This would mean the integration of content, people, culture, and behavior. Very often, attempts are made to integrate the people, culture, and behavior without the content. Our experience showed that this approach tended to be unbalanced.

Merger of Equals

From our point of view, the "merger of equals" is just a dream. The success of mergers will depend on the ability of the new company to formulate new strategies. Structures follow strategy and new structures call for competent and efficient managers who reach the new targets.

Selecting the right people for the new management positions is not a question of choosing equal members from the companies merging. It is essential to select the best candidate for the respective job. This is not the nicest of tasks but top management who are involved in this selection process must be able to explain why one candidate is more suited to the new job than the other, and this process must be transparent and fair. By this, we mean the selection criteria must be objective and the process structured. In the case of HYPO-Bank and Vereinsbank, this process was awarded top priority. In hindsight, the executives praised the work done here—it was transparent and fair. Everyone had the same chance but it was a "merger of the best" and not a "merger of equals."

Let us now have a brief look at the selection process itself as it represented an example of how to create and live values in the new company. The process started at the top because all the executive levels were needed in the structured interviews. Each interview lasted ninety minutes. There were three interviewers: one from human resources, the candidate's previous boss, as well as the candidate's designated new boss. The goal was to find the best candidate and there were normally two candidates for each management position, both former banks having, for example, one head of accounting. A number of scenarios were envisaged. One was that neither of the candidates was suited to the new job based on previous performance, lack of knowledge, or for age reasons (a number of executives were nearing retirement age). Another scenario was that you had more than two candidates because of high potentials in the existing executive portfolio. Therefore, it became important not to focus too closely on the position alone but to identify the top team for a particular management level. So, in the postin-terview selection panel meetings, the first question was: "Has this candidate got the potential for this management level or not?" If the answer was yes, then the next question was: "What possible positions could they fill and did they have the scope to fill a number of different positions?" Of course, mobility also played a role. In cases where two excellent branch managers were located in one area, it didn't really matter who you offered the job to but it did matter that you had comparisons with candidates in other locations.

As already mentioned, the executives were quite happy with the level of transparency and fairness in the process. But the next stage called for greater commitment. It is quite easy to bring the good news "you've got the job," but it is much more demanding to convey the news "you're an excellent employee but we feel that you do not yet have the management skills for this new, expanded job." Interestingly, many of the executives involved in the interviews asked the human resources interviewer to do this job for them. We feel this is a leadership task and responsibility and should have been done by the potential new leaders.

Sharing One Vision

Ingmar Björkman and his coauthors quoted the former CEO of Nord-banken and Merita–Nordbanken in their chapter, "If there is something that I have learnt it is that it is much more important to share a vision for the bank than to mechanically estimate the synergy savings." We support this view fully and see it "as a useful basis for all integration activities." The HVB Group had such a vision, a story for the new company right from the beginning. It was called "Bank of the Regions." It was a good message for the public and for the analysts and proved very helpful in further integration activities. "Be part of the HVB Group with IT-platform synergies but have separate market access with an individual brand name!", like Vereins- und Westbank in Northern Germany or Bank Austria in Vienna.

In 1997 HYPO-Bank and Vereinsbank each had approximately 13,000 employees. By 2002, the group, together with BPH in Krakow and Bank Austria in Vienna, had become the second largest bank in Germany with a total member of 73,000 employees at its peak.

At the end of 2002, the Group announced that Dieter Rampl would take over the helm at HVB. In his first speech to the employees, Rampl paid tribute to the strategic success of Albrecht Schmidt's "Bank of the Regions," a vision which ensured the group's independence. All eyes are now focused on Rampl in expectation of a new vision, one which will excite the minds of employees and customers in the search to shake off the crises now hitting the whole German banking sector.

PART III *The Management of Sociocultural Integration in Mergers and Acquisitions*

8 Synergy Realization in Mergers and Acquisitions

A Co-Competence and Motivational Approach

RIKARD LARSSON

The secret of merger and acquisition (M&A) success has captivated and eluded many corporations during the last century. Failure rates are still reported as high as 50–75 percent (for example, Marks and Mirvis, 1998), although with typically debatable scientific support. Consultants and researchers provide contradictory advice and fragmented theories (Haspeslagh and Jemison, 1991; Schweiger and Walsh, 1990). Rather than continuing the common debate whether M&A are good or bad in general, we need to recognize that they are probably the most volatile events in corporate life including fantastic synergies as well as value-destroying disasters. Learning systematically how to increase the likelihood of success is therefore more imperative than ever.

In a study that Professor Kathleen Eisenhardt of Stanford University expects "to become a defining paper in M&A research," Larsson and Finkelstein (1999, p. 1) compared sixty-one in-depth cases of synergy realization[1] in M&A and found key answers to what do top-synergy realizing M&A have in common that no M&A were able to succeed without and that no M&A failed to succeed with (see Figure 8.1).

It is not sufficient to merely look at one or more success cases to determine what are the requirements of M&A success. The key to learn about success that is missing in such "in search of excellence" approaches is the comparison with failure. Without such comparison, we do not know if the so-called excellent advice is the distinguishing factor between success and failure. Not surprisingly, success advice based on some success stories tends to fail rather quickly (cf. Aupperle, Acar, and Booth, 1986). Thus, it is important to ask the two complementary questions of what tends to be necessary as well as sufficient requirements that separate M&A with high synergy realization from those with low.

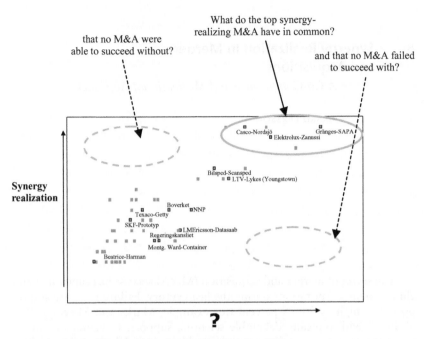

FIGURE **8.1** A Study of Synergy Realization in Sixty-One M&A

There is of course no one single and simple answer to these pertinent questions. Instead, we need to synthesize the fragmented strategic, organizational, human resource, financial, and economic M&A research regarding selection as well as integration issues across different levels. This chapter offers a practical review of this research with the aim to provide as useful answers to these questions as possible.

From Performance Controversy to Synergy Factors

Many researchers have studied the performance of M&A. This has resulted in mainly a controversy between skeptical economic and enthusiastic financial research regarding whether M&A create or destroy value in general. Goldberg (1983; pp. 207, 209) summarizes more than fifty years of mainly economic findings as "shareholders of the acquiring firm tend to lose from mergers ... Earnings of firms in mergers decline after consolidation." (cf. Ravenscraft and Scherer, 1987). In contrast, financial researchers claim that acquiring firms do not lose and earnings do not decline in the years following integration (for example, Jensen, 1984; Weston and Chung, 1983).

This performance controversy is in part explained by the different methods and perspectives of economic and financial M&A research (cf. Datta, Narayanan, and Pinches, 1992) that seem to bias their respective findings. However, continuing this controversy of whether M&A are good or bad in general is of very limited practical use. If one side was to win, then the unreasonable consequence would be that we either should do as many M&A as possible or never do any more.

The more practical view of this controversy is to recognize the great variety in M&A performance that makes generalizations such as M&A are all good or bad untenable. The most useful knowledge is instead what are the factors that determine high versus low M&A performance. Rather than "choosing" sides between economic accounting and financial stock market performance measures and their respective biases, Larsson and Finkelstein (1999) focused on actual *synergy realization* as a useful performance measure of value creation in M&A. The chapter will now review strategic, organizational, and human resource factors that can determine this synergy realization.

Strategic Synergy Factors: Selecting the Right Combination Upfront

Strategic research has focused on mainly *selection* factors as determinants of M&A performance. That is, the initial choice of which firms are to be combined is posited as a key determinant of M&A outcomes. Different types of corporate combinations are suggested to represent different strategic synergy potentials (for example, Bower, 2001; Lubatkin, 1983; Singh and Montgomery, 1987). The more related the joining firms are, the greater their strategic combination potential.

This *relatedness* is typically viewed in terms of strategic similarity of markets, products, and production. The greatest combination potential is often attributed to so-called horizontal M&A that combine competing firms with overlapping operations. Synergies are not limited to such "economies of sameness," though. Larsson (1990) also points toward the "economies of fitness" between different, but complementary, operations, such as vertical combinations between supplier and customer firms and market or product extension combinations where one firm adds either new markets or new products to the other.

It can be relatively easy to distinguish between the high strategic combination potential of overlapping operations versus low potential of completely unrelated operations (that is, pure conglomerate M&A). In contrast, the combination potential of strategic complementarities is likely to vary greatly from high to insignificant and therefore be harder to determine beforehand. Larsson and Finkelstein (1999) found that both strategic similarities and complementarities were the key selection determinant of synergy realization.

Organizational and Human Resource Selection Factors

Many M&A researchers warn against merely considering strategic factors when selecting corporate combinations. So-called cultural clashes are seen as substantial barriers to synergy realization in M&A (for example, Cartwright and Cooper, 1996; Chatterjee et al., 1992). It is therefore commonly recommended to avoid combinations that have different corporate cultures even if they have high strategic combination potential.

This recommendation to more or less sacrifice strategic potential in favor of selecting as culturally similar combinations as possible is questioned by other M&A researchers, such as Kleppestö (1993). Larsson (1990) points out that organizational cultures include strong defense mechanisms that maintain the shared norms and values of the employees. These cultural defense or maintenance mechanisms are mobilized by external threats like M&A. This can be most clearly seen by the *"we versus they"* interpretations that are found in almost all M&A *irrespective* of how similar or different the cultures were beforehand.

Consequently, there is little reason to sacrifice strategic potential in favor of selecting culturally similar combinations, as the cultural defense mechanisms will find enough differences anyway to rally against in defense of us and our ways being better than them and their ways. Larsson and Lubatkin (2001) also found in their award-winning study that cultural clashes and subsequent acculturation between joining firms were primarily determined by what happened during the ensuing integration process and not by initial similarities at the point of combination selection.

Another organizational selection issue is whether to choose so-called good or bad firms to join. A natural "garbage in, garbage out" selection principle would be to choose the quality of high-performing firms. There are several reasons for cautioning the acquisition of peak performance, especially during boom periods. Buying a good company with high profitability in a boom period typically means a much higher price than a poor performer during a recession. At the same time, the risk of damaging employee resistance is greater in the high-priced, high-performing company. The high-performing managers and employees are more likely to consider their own ways as superior and therefore less willing to adjust during the integration process. Furthermore, the boom period offers more external employment opportunities and therefore allows greater employee resistance through exit of especially valuable key persons. Selecting good companies can thus easily become bad M&A.

On the other hand, bad companies can turn into good M&A. Even though there are of course many problem-ridden companies that one should clearly stay away from, some troubled companies may not be as bad as they look. If a company has managed to survive for many years, there are often many values (for example, customer contacts and experience from overcoming start-up problems) that are not included in a poor balance sheet during a recession. It may be only one or two missing pieces in its performance puzzle that the acquirer can add. In addition to lower prices and hidden values, a temporarily troubled company is also less prone toward employee resistance, especially if they are aware of the need for being rescued from bankruptcy threats.

In any event, neither strategic combination nor organizational and human resource selection factors are sufficient by themselves to realize synergies in M&A. The strategic combination potential is a necessary precondition determined by the chosen selection, but the extent to which this potential is actually realized is determined by the subsequent integration process.

Organizational Integration Factors: Doing It
Right Afterwards

M&A are often accused of looking strategically good on paper, but then fail in reality. This has led to serious doubts if synergies can be realized at all (Sirower, 1997). The fears of the nonexistence of synergy are exaggerated, though. While synergy realization is highly volatile and risky, there are still many examples of very high levels of synergies being realized. One important reason for the great variety in M&A performance is different approaches to the organizational integration following the legal combination (cf. Pablo, 1994). There are several different integration typologies (for example, Haspeslagh and Jemison, 1991; Napier, 1989). Larsson (1990, 1993) attempts to synthesize some of these typologies into three major organizational integration types.

The *soft* or *avoiding* integration approach aims at mainly preserving the existing values of the joining firms by minimal intervention. Organizational integration is largely put on hold until it is supposed to slowly develop as the joining firms have learned about each other and gained mutual trust. This approach is geared at minimizing employee resistance, but does so by basically sacrificing integration efforts to placate the acquired employees.

The *hard* or *controlling* integration approach attempts instead to crush possible cultural clashes and employee resistance as fast as possible by immediate, forceful, and one-sided implementation of the acquirer's ways of operating. This approach recognizes that synergy realization requires substantial organizational integration and this should be implemented at once to reduce uncertainties, take charge, and not lose momentum. It often starts with the "worst" changes to "cut off the dog's tail in one swoop, rather than bit-by-bit" to clear the way for subsequently building the joint organization based on the acquirer's superior competence.

These soft and hard approaches make up a classic M&A integration dilemma. There are proponents for both sides that either prioritize the soft preservation of existing values and minimizing employee resistance (for example, Chatterjee et al, 1992) or the hard implementation of the acquirer's control to begin quickly realizing intended synergies and assimilate acquired employees (for example, Searby, 1969).

The major reason for this dilemma not being easily solved is that both sides are right about the other approach being inadequate, but both are wrong about their own approach being the best. Our research clearly shows that neither the soft nor the hard approach is systematically successful in realizing M&A synergies (Larsson, 1990; Larsson and Finkelstein, 1999). While the soft approach sacrifices the necessary organizational integration requirement, the hard approach sacrifices the equally necessary requirement to avoid employee resistance. As long as the integration process is merely viewed in terms of soft versus hard approaches, M&A are caught in a "catch 22" situation that can explain many of the difficulties that so many corporate combinations encounter.

The *co-competence* integration approach has instead proven to be a superior way of accomplishing the required organizational integration. While the hard approach sacrifices all the competence of the acquired firm, an equality approach of so-called "merger of equals" sacrifices some of the competence of the better firm by dividing positions 50-50 based on the equally unrealistic assumption that both firms have equal competence. The co-competence approach avoids the common pitfall of distributing control based on which company one belonged to (that is, hard = 100 percent acquirer and equality = 50 percent both) by focusing on combining the best, complementary competencies from both sides. This is done through starting with positive joint projects to also avoid both the lack of speed of the soft approach and the immediate negativity of the hard approach.

The co-competence approach is of course not without difficulties. It is common to recognize most of one's own competencies while neglecting most of the competencies of the other and thereby risk starting a battle for control in the name of competence. In certain clearly complementary combinations, it may be apparent that both companies contribute unique and valuable competencies that should guide the organizational integration. However, in more overlapping cases, such as one company with 20 percent market share acquiring a smaller competitor with 10 percent market share, it is tempting to attribute most, if not all, competence to the larger acquirer with its superior management, production, and marketing, and thereby resort to the hard approach. From a co-competence point of view, though, this view should be moderated by the acquirer asking how come this competitor with inferior management, production, and marketing has actually been able to win half of our market share. There must consequently be some things that they know better than us.

It is therefore important to mutually identify and respect the competencies of the other joining firm in order to pursue the superior co-competence approach to organizational integration. This requires constructive and learning interaction between the joining firms, which leads us to the human side of M&A. One of the advantages of the co-competence approach is that it is also better at dealing with the third major synergy determinant, namely, employee resistance.

Human Resource Integration Factors: Avoiding Resistance

Most employees tend to react negatively on being acquired, but the strength, duration, and dysfunctional effects of such reactions vary much between different M&A. One major reason for this variation is the different organizational integration approaches discussed above. Other reasons can be found in the again striking differences between perspectives on the human side of M&A.

A common perspective on employee reactions is to view them in terms of *cultural clashes* (for example, Buono and Bowditch, 1989; Cartwright and Cooper, 1996; Chatterjee et al., 1992; Nahavandi and Malekzadeh, 1988). That is, employee resistance is seen as originating from different corporate cultures at the collective level. The researchers and practitioners who adhere to this perspective claim that (in addition to trying to reduce cultural clashes by selecting combinations with similar cultures) it is essential to develop and foster a new, joint corporate culture. However, other research indicates that this is much easier to say than to actually accomplish (Kleppestö, 1993; Larsson, 1990; 1993; Larsson and Lubatkin, 2001).

Another common perspective is to view employee resistance as stemming from *communication* problems (Brousseau, 1989; Driver, Brousseau, and Hunsaker, 1993; Schweiger and DeNisi, 1991; Sinetar, 1981). Here, lack of information, misunderstandings, interpreted threats, and negative rumors are suggested as key sources of employee resistance at the interpersonal level. The communication solutions include more precise, extensive, early, and true information and team building, which is also hard to achieve.

A third and more purely individual perspective is to view employee reactions in terms of *career* implications (for example, Gaertner, 1986; Hirsch, 1987; Walsh, 1989). From this point of view, individual employees can resist

M&A because of anticipated or actual negative effects on their own careers or working lives, such as less job security, reduced benefits, blocked advancement opportunities, greater workloads, upset career planning, and so forth (Larsson et al., 2001). Career solutions typically involve having reward systems that counteract these negative implications and instead support the integration process, even though this is no simple feat either (Larsson, Eneroth, and König, 1996; Schweiger, Ivancevich, and Power, 1987).

Thus, these cultural, communication, and career perspectives span the collective, interpersonal, and individual levels of employee resistance in M&A. While all three perspectives/levels are proven relevant, researchers as well as practitioners tend to focus on only one of them. This is quite unfortunate, as they all represent simultaneous sources of employee resistance, and focusing on only one is likely to result in two negative surprises. For example, trying to reduce cultural clashes through joint socialization efforts at the collective level can still lead to resistance from lacking information and/or negative career implications at the interpersonal and individual levels. If one instead focuses on improving communication, then this still leaves both the risks of cultural clashes and negative career implications at the two other levels.

Employee resistance is also an important determinant of synergy realization. The key to reducing employee resistance is to manage all collective, interpersonal, and individual levels with joint acculturation, communication, and career development efforts (Larsson, 1990). This is possible by combining the co-competence approach for achieving organizational integration with multiple, mainly "co-motivational" human resource considerations at all three levels.

A Co-Competence and Motivational Approach to Acculturation in M&A

Larsson and Lubatkin (2001) tested six alternative determinants of achieved acculturation (that is, the development of a jointly shared, constructive culture and overcoming cultural clashes) in fifty M&A. None of the four selection-based determinants of relatedness, relative size, domestic versus cross-border, and acquirer nationality were found to have statistically significant effects. Nor had the imposition of formal controls through autonomy removal a necessary negative impact. Instead, the only strong determinant for achieving acculturation was "social controls," that is, socialization and coordination efforts like cross-visits, introduction and training programs, joint social events, celebrations, transition teams, job rotation, and other motivational human resource exchanges between the joining firms.

It is important to recognize that achieving acculturation is still a lot easier said than done. Single organizations develop and retain their cultures through socialization and maintenance mechanisms (cf. Berger and Luckmann, 1966). M&A face the dual barriers to acculturation of both having separate maintenance mechanisms that perpetuate we-versus-they interpretations and lacking joint socialization mechanisms to create jointly shared norms and values (Larsson, 1990). Socialization mechanisms are built into the culture and the development of joint socialization mechanisms in M&A is therefore a long-term endeavor that requires overcoming the persistent cultural defenses of the separate maintenance mechanisms. This typically requires, in turn, more immediate integration efforts on the interpersonal and individual levels.

A Co-Competence and Motivational Approach
to Communication in M&A

There are also several barriers to effective communication to manage uncertainty and threat interpretations at the interpersonal level. On the one hand, the acquiring company has initially only limited knowledge about the acquired company and how it is supposed to become integrated. Some of this knowledge may also be viewed as secret. The acquiring company is also located some distance away from the acquired company. Thus, the initial communication from the acquired tends to be minimal and often limited to promises of "no changes" (Austin, 1970).

On the other hand, there is hardly any event that creates more uncertainty among acquired employees than becoming acquired. What will happen? Will we stay or be moved? Who will do what? Will there be lay-offs? Who will be my boss? Will we have to change our name? Will the sales forces be kept separate or integrated? It seems like almost everything is up in the air and the need for detailed information is greater than ever at the same time as the acquirer provides very little. Distrust also undermines whatever information the acquirer offers, especially because very few believe any common promises of "no changes." This great information vacuum tends instead to be filled with negative rumors (for example, Pritchett, 1985).

The resulting suspicious and resisting reactions from the acquired employees can disappoint even the most well-intended acquirer. This disappointment can, in turn, further limit the acquirer's communication and thereby create a vicious communication circle, which represents a strong interpersonal source of employee resistance.

Given that most of the acquired corporate value and synergy potentials are sustained and realized by the acquired employees, a more effective communication approach is an information-wise VIP-treatment that considers and makes the acquired employees feel as very important persons through:

- Voice, that is, not only fast, true, and extensive communication to reduce employee uncertainties, but also listening to their thoughts and feelings to learn how to best integrate the combining companies and make them feel heard;
- Involvement to avoid the feelings of the integration being imposed by the acquirer and instead make use of the collective motivation to sustain as much of the acquired corporate value as possible by the acquirer asking what they can do to help the acquirer to develop through, for example, a suggestion program where employees are systematically encouraged and rewarded to generate and submit their integration and improvement ideas; and
- Precision in the two-way communication and integration to deal with the fact that people process information in different ways, have different career motives, experience threats in different ways, and therefore need different information and solutions.

Driver and Brousseau have developed the Decision Style model as a conceptual, assessment, communication, and team-building tool that can be helpful in avoiding common misunderstandings and increasing the precision of the two-way VIP communication approach in M&A (Brousseau, 1989; Driver, Brousseau, and Hunsaker, 1993). It is based on how people differ when processing information.

The first dimension where people differ significantly is the amount of *information use.* That is, does the individual settle for using only small or moderate amounts of information—satisfice, or does s/he use as much information as possible—maximize. Which is the best way to process information and make decisions? The correct answer is that it depends on the situation that sometimes favors the fast action of satisficing and other times rewards the complex analysis of maximizing. However, a satisficer tends to view a maximizer as slow and prone toward analysis paralysis, whereas a maximizer often sees a satisficer as hasty and irresponsible. Even though their strengths could offset each other's weaknesses, satisficers and maximizers typically consider the other way of processing information as stupid.

The second decision style dimension is *solution focus,* that is, does the person generate one single solution to a problem and stick to it over time—unifocus, or does s/he generate several different solutions that are all entertained and/or changed over time—multifocus. Again, neither unifocus nor multifocus is better than the other is in general. This also depends on the situation, such as stability making unifocus more efficient and multifocus being more able to deal with changing conditions. However, a unifocus person tends to view a multifocus as "wishy-washy" and unreliable, whereas a multifocus individual often sees a unifocus as rigid and narrow-minded. That is, they are more likely to view each other as stupid than as having complementary information processing skills.

The combination of these two dimensions creates a matrix with four major types of decision styles—Decisive, Flexible, Hierarchic, and Integrative (Driver, Brousseau, and Hunsaker, 1993). The *Decisive* decision style is both satisficing and unifocus, that is, fast, action-oriented, persistent, tough, loyal, efficient, bottom-line, and time conscious. The *Flexible* decision style is also satisficing, that is, fast and action-oriented. However, its multifocus is much more open, adaptive, social, conflict avoiding, and humorous. The *Hierarchic* style is maximizing and unifocus, that is, analythic, logical, methodical, planning, and quality-oriented. Finally, the *Integrative* style is also maximizing, but instead multifocus, thereby combining analysis with openness, creativity, being a good listener, tolerant, and team-oriented.

The diagonal relationships between the decision styles represent the worst, most "toxic" style clashes, where two persons can view each other as doubly stupid. For example, a Flexible person can see a Hierarchic as both slow and rigid, whereas the Hierarchic person considers the Flexible as both hasty and unreliable.

The Decision Style model helps interacting persons to understand themselves and others in more constructive ways by pointing out that differences in processing information are complementary rather than stupid and the benefits of mutual accommodation to each others' decision styles. This becomes highlighted in M&A where there are strong tendencies to view "the others" and their ways as stupid (Brousseau, 1989). Learning the Decision Style model and the style profiles of oneself and interacting others can greatly improve communication and teamwork in corporate combinations and other strategic changes (Driver, Brousseau, and Hunsaker, 1993; Driver et al., 1996).

A Co-Competence and Motivational Approach to Career Development in M&A

There are also many negative career implications that can result in employee resistance at the individual level (for example, Gaertner, 1986; Hirsch, 1987). Benefits can be cut to save costs, job security reduced by threatening lay-offs, advancement opportunities thwarted by losing one's boss, and career planning upset by the surprise of the M&A (Larsson et al., 2001). At the same time, most employees are asked to contribute more by having to do additional integration tasks on top of the existing work. Synergies are also typically being realized by having fewer in the joint organization doing the work of the two separate companies. This basically boils down to most employees having to do more for less. That is, the M&A tend to make them double losers career-wise, a quite sufficiently strong motive for resistance.

Motivating employees to contribute additional integration efforts requires additional inducements. This can be done in two major ways. The expensive way is by offering additional extrinsic rewards, that is, basically "bribing" employees with more money to not resist the M&A integration. Unfortunately, such an approach will reward those claiming to need more payoff to not resist doing more. In contrast, the use of intrinsically rewarding integration efforts actually increases the motivation by being allowed to do more.

The difficulty of intrinsically motivating integration efforts is that what one employee feels is a motivating task, another feels to be a demotivating punishment. For example, some appreciate stability and are demotivated by changes, whereas others appreciate change to the extent that will leave an organization merely offering secure stability. We therefore need to better understand individual motivation differences if we are to increase the motivational precision of integration efforts in M&A. The Career Concept model is a suitable framework for doing so (Brousseau et al., 1996; Driver, 1980). It distinguishes between four major career and motivational patterns:

- *Expert* that strives to remain within one occupation and become as good as possible at this during the whole work life. Expert motives include security, being allowed to refine one's expertise, and being recognized for this expertise.
- *Linear* that strives to climb upward on the corporate ladder toward positions of higher authority. Linear motives include power and achievement.
- *Spiral* that periodically (every five to ten years) moves laterally to related occupations where previous experience can be applied in new ways. Spiral motives include creativity and personal growth.
- *Transitory* that frequently (every two to four years) changes to new and unrelated occupations. Transitory motives include variety and independence.

A major contribution of the Career Concept model is that it provides four different perspectives on one's own and others' working lives in general and M&A in particular. Even at the individual career level, there are different reasons or motives to resist M&A. An Expert can resist them because of all the destabilizing changes they tend to bring, whereas a Linear person can resist them if they demote him/her to lower hierarchic levels; Spiral and Transitory persons can resist because they are not being sufficiently involved.

If we only try to manage one type of negative career implications at the individual level, we are likely to get three other negative surprises. However, if we instead try to protect everybody from everything, there will be no integration at all. The more motivationally precise career management of M&A includes protecting an individual from only what is most demotivating to him/her at the same time as offering more such integration work that is intrinsically motivating to the particular person. The Career Concept model can offer an effective basis for precise division of the broad array of needed integration activities according to the individuals' different motivational profiles, as illustrated in Table 8.1 (Larsson et al., 2001).

Requiring the same integration efforts from everybody and offering them all the same rewards produces at best one winner and three losers from a career point of view. Forcing Expert employees to change, demoting or downsizing Linear employees, or neglecting to involve Spiral and Transitory employees are even more imprecise and demotivating integration approaches when almost everybody lose. Unfortunately, this seems not to be uncommon because the two most involved categories appear to be Expert employees being identified with the functions to be integrated and Linear managers having to make the hard decisions to demote, delayer, and downsize redundant employees.

The high-precision career motivational solution to integration is instead to let the individuals with mainly Expert motives take care of "islands of stability" and existing value creation; those with Linear motives focus on growth and achievement opportunities; those with Spiral motives do creative "bridging" between the old and the new; and those with Transitory motives do short-term and novel activities involved in the integration process. This career concept-based co-competence and motivational integration approach builds upon the complementary diversity of career motives to accomplish the wide range of needed integration activities for both maintaining and creating joint value.

It is of course quite unrealistic to do personal career coaching to all employees as an integration tool for large M&A. Time is scarce for most involved in corporate combinations and the cost of bringing in a sufficient host of career coaches would be prohibitive in itself. However, the new era of e-learning enables both time- and cost-efficient solutions where any number of employees can get personalized career e-coaching any time. Internet has already enabled the use of the Career Concept model to assess more than one million persons, mostly through Korn/Ferry International and Sweden's largest white-collar union SIF.

Conclusion: Co-Competence and Motivational Realization of Synergies in M&A

The complete co-competence and motivational approach for realizing M&A synergies is then to combine the three major synergy determinants

TABLE **8.1** Co-Competence and Motivational Division of Integration Work

		Expert	Linear	Spiral	Transitory
Focus		Islands of stability	Opportunities for:	Applying existing competencies in new areas	Network with many new people
		True security	Corporate growth	Integrating new and existing operations	Fast and novel action
		Maintaining existing value creation	Leadership	Strategic renewal	Short-term transition team/projects
		Corporate memory	Efficiency improvements Promotion Achievement/winning	Long-term creative teamwork Personal growth	Travel Quick learning
Avoid		Uncertainty Insecurity Turbulence	Relative demotion Delayering Downsizing	Noninvolvement	Noninvolvement Long-term commitment

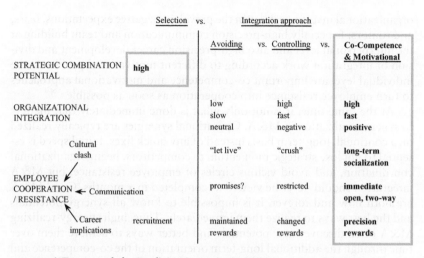

FIGURE **8.2** A Framework for Realizing Synergies in M&A

of selecting high strategic combination potential and managing high organizational integration and low employee resistance during the subsequent postcombination process. Achieving low employee resistance is, in turn, dependent on managing acculturation at the collective level of cultural clashes, communication at the interpersonal level of uncertainties, misunderstandings, and rumors, and career development at the individual level of different negative working life implications such as job insecurity, demotions, and noninvolvement. Figure 8.2 summarizes this integrative framework for synergy realization in M&A that as a whole can account for at least 60–70 percent of the variance in performance.

Timing is an essential aspect of realizing synergies in M&A. Prior to the combination, it is primarily the choice of companies with high strategic combination potential that creates the future opportunities to realize synergies. Mainly anecdotal evidence suggests that corporate combinations made in late recessions have the advantages of lower prices, less organizational integration overload, and less employee resistance compared to those made during boom periods.

Once the combination is made, both speed and long-term orientation become paramount. Integration efforts are necessary for synergy realization and should not be delayed for pacifying purposes. However, it is better to start with positive integration efforts of the co-competence and motivational approach that give resources, influence, and opportunities to the acquired firm rather than taking them away. One of the few easy things in M&A is actually to positively surprise acquired employees with the two-way communication, career development, opportunities to influence, and organizational investments, given the prevalent negative expectations, fears, and rumors. Especially high-precision communication and team building at the interpersonal level and also high-precision career development and division of integration work according to different motivational profiles at the individual level are important co-competence and motivational approaches to turn employee resistance into cooperation as soon as possible.

At the same time, it is not only what is done immediately that matters to synergy realization in M&A. Operational synergies are typically realized on a continual, long-term basis instead of any quick fixes. Initial speed is essential to not lose strategic momentum to competitors, begin organizational coordination, and avoid vicious circles of employee resistance, but M&A integration should never be viewed as completed in x months. Good M&A are both now and forever. It is impossible to know all synergy potentials and the best ways to realize them immediately. Thus, high synergy-realizing M&A often discover new potentials and better ways to achieve them over time through the additional long-term orientation of the co-competence and motivational approach (Larsson, 1990). The achievement of acculturation is also clearly a long-term task to replace persistent "we and our better ways versus they and their worse ways" with a common we with the best of both ways.

As a case in point, Tetra Laval Prepared Food was still suffering from culturally clashing "we versus they" views two years after Tetra Pak's acquisition of Alfa Laval (Larsson et al., 2001). This unit was formed by approximately equal number of employees from each of the combined corporations. Their respective views of themselves and each other were firmly anchored in their different past corporate histories. However, when they through the use of the Career Concept model began adopting a career perspective that was more future-oriented and individualized, the collective defense of their past identities gave way to a more shared view of a joint organization with common goals as well as motivational diversity. By measuring their individual career profiles and organizational career culture, they were able to manage the subsequent integration process with greater precision and mutual understanding.

Notes

1. Synergy realization was measured by two to three raters coding actual cost savings and revenue increases for eleven different synergy sources for each case, such as consolidated purchasing, production, marketing, administration and/or vertical supplier/customer relationship, market power, new market access, cross-selling, transfer of existing know-how, and joint creation of new know-how.

References

Aupperle, K. E., Acar, W., and Booth, D. E. (1986). An empirical critique of in search of excellence: How excellent are the excellent companies? *Journal of Management*, 12(4): 499–512.

Austin, D. V. (1970). Merger myths: We contemplate no changes in personnel. *Mergers and Acquisitions*, 5(5): 20–21.

Berger, P. L., and Luckmann, T. (1966). *The Social Construction of Reality.* New York: Doubleday.

Bower, J. L. (2001). Not all M&As are alike—and that matters. *Harvard Business Review*, March: 93–101.

Brousseau, K. R. (1989). Navigating the merger transition. *Journal of Organizational Change Management*, 2(1): 72–8.

Brousseau, K. R., Driver, M. J., Eneroth, K., and Larsson, R. (1996). Career pandemonium: Realigning organizations and individuals. *Academy of Management Executive*, 10(4): 52–66.

Buono, A. F., and Bowditch, J. L. (1989). *The Human Side of Mergers and Acquisitions.* San Francisco: Jossey-Bass.

Cartwright, S., and Cooper, C. L. (1996). *Managing Mergers, Acquisitions and Alliances: Integrating People and Cultures.* Oxford: Butterworth Heinemann.

Chatterjee, S., Lubatkin, M. H., Schweiger, D. M., and Weber, Y. (1992). Cultural differences and shareholder value. *Strategic Management Journal*, 13: 319–34.

Datta, D. K., Narayanan, V. K., and Pinches, G. E. (1992). Factors influencing wealth creation from mergers and acquisitions: A meta-analysis. *Strategic Management Journal*, 13: 67–84.

Driver, M. J. (1980). Career concepts and organizational change. In Derr (ed.), *Work, Family, and the Career.* New York: Praeger.

Driver, M. J., Brousseau, K. R., and Hunsaker, P. L. (1993). *The Dynamic Decision Maker: Five Decision Styles for Executive and Business Success.* San Francisco: Jossey-Bass.

Driver, M. J., Svensson, K., Amato, R. P., and Pate, L. E. (1996). A human information processing approach to strategic change: Altering managerial decision styles. *International Studies of Management and Organization*, 26(1): 41–58.

Gaertner, K. N. (1986). Colliding cultures: The implications of a merger for managers' careers. Paper presented at Academy of Management Annual Meeting, Chicago.

Goldberg, W. H. (1983). *Mergers: Motives, Modes, Methods.* Aldershot, UK: Gower.

Haspeslagh, P. C., and Jemison, D. B. (1991). *Managing Acquisitions: Creating Value Through Acquisition Activity.* New York: Free Press.

Hirsch, P. M. (1987). *Pack Your Own Parachute: How to Survive Mergers, Takeovers, and Other Corporate Disasters.* Reading, MA: Addison-Wesley.

Jensen, M. C. (1984). Takeovers: Folklore and Science. *Harvard Business Review*, 60(6): 109–21.

Kleppestö, S. (1993). *Kultur och identitet vid företagsuppköp och fusioner.* Stockholm: Nerenius & Santerus.

Larsson, R. (1990). *Coordination of Action in Mergers and Acquisitions: Interpretive and Systems Approaches Towards Synergy.* Lund, Sweden: Lund University Press.

Larsson, R. (1993). Barriers to acculturation in mergers and acquisitions: Strategic human resource implications. *Journal of European Business Education*, 2(2): 1–18.

Larsson, R., Driver, M. J., Holmqvist, M., and Sweet, P. L. (2001). Career disintegration and reintegration in mergers and acquisitions: Managing the competence and motivational intangibles. *European Management Journal*, 19(6): 609–18.

Larsson, R., Eneroth, K., and König, I. (1996). On the folly of rewarding domestic stability while hoping for international expansion. *International Studies of Management and Organization*, 26(1): 105–33.

Larsson, R., and Finkelstein, S. (1999). Integrating strategic, organizational, and human resource perspectives on mergers and acquisitions: A case survey of synergy realization. *Organization Science*, 10(1): 1–26.

Larsson, R., and Lubatkin, M. (2001). Achieving acculturation in mergers and acquisitions: An international case survey study. *Human Relations*, 54(12): 1573–607.

Lubatkin, M. (1983). Mergers and the performance of the acquiring firm. *Academy of Management Review*, 8: 218–25.

Marks, M. L., and Mirvis, P. M. (1998). *Joining Forces: Making One Plus One Equal Three in Mergers, Acquisitions, and Alliances.* San Francisco: Jossey-Bass.

Nahavandi, A., and Malekzadeh, A. R. (1988). Acculturation in mergers and acquisitions. *Academy of Management Review*, 13: 79–90.

Napier, N. K. (1989). Mergers and acquisitions, human resource issues and outcomes: A review and suggested typology. *Journal of Management Studies*, 26: 271–89.

Pablo, A. L. (1994). Determinants of acquisition integration level: A decision-making perspective. *Academy of Management Journal*, 37: 803–36.

Pritchett, P. (1985). *After the Merger: Managing the Shockwaves.* Dallas, TX: Dow Jones-Irwin.

Ravenscraft, D. J., and Scherer, F. M. (1987). *Mergers, Sell-Offs, and Economic Efficiency.* Washington, DC: Brookings Institution.

Schweiger, D. M., and DeNisi, A. S. (1991). Communication with employees following a merger: A longitudinal field experiment. *Academy of Management Journal*, 34: 110–35.

Schweiger, D. M., Ivancevich, J. M., and Power, F. R. (1987). Executive actions for managing human resources before and after acquisition. *Academy of Management Executive*, 12: 127–38.

Schweiger, D. M., and Walsh, J. P. (1990). Mergers and acquisitions: An interdisciplinary view. *Research in Personnel and Human Resource Management*, Vol. 8. Greenwich, CT: JAI Press, pp. 41–107.

Searby, F. W. (1969). Control postmerger change. *Harvard Business Press*, 47(5), 4–12 and 154–55.

Sinetar, M. (1981). Mergers, morale, and productivity. *Personnel Journal*, 60(11): 863–67.

Singh, H., and Montgomery, C. A. (1987). Corporate acquisition strategies and economic performance. *Strategic Management Journal*, 8: 377–86.

Sirower, M. L. (1997). *The Synergy Trap: How Companies Lose the Acquisition Game*. New York: Free Press.

Walsh, J. P. (1989). Doing a deal: Merger and acquisition negotiations and their impact upon target company top management turnover. *Strategic Management Journal*, 10: 307–22.

Weston, J. F., and Chung, K. S. (1983). Do mergers make money: A research summary. *Mergers and Acquisitions*, 18(3): 40–8.

Executive Commentary on Chapter 8

SHLOMO BEN-HUR AND L. TODD THOMAS

The Role of the Corporate Academy in Mergers and Acquisitions: Facilitating Synergy Realization

As Professor Rikard Larsson writes in his chapter, strategic, financial, organizational, and human resource factors are all important for M&A performance, but it is the human side that tends to be the hardest to manage successfully. Progressive HR departments are beginning to play an extensive role in M&A through active work in both the due diligence and integration phase (Corporate Leadership Council, 1999). HR departments are traditionally involved in the integration of compensation plans, benefits, and other personnel issues during the postmerger phase. However, it is our experience that the learning and development areas of HR can add unique and specific value to the premerger, planning, and integration processes.

The HR area involved in "Learning and Development" activities within an organization will be referred to as the Corporate Academy (CA). We assume that the CA is responsible within the organization for traditional training activities, organizational development activities, and executive coaching and consulting. Although this model varies by organization, the thesis should apply to most large- and mid-sized companies involved in merger or acquisition activity who provide not only training but organizational development activity as well.

In examining the activities of each phase of an M&A, it would appear that the CA may have a number of unique characteristics that make it an appropriate tool in facilitating successful M&A projects: (1) focus on the "big picture"; (2) change management coaching and training; (3) assessment experience; (4) career development and succession; (5) relationships with key leaders; and (6) e-learning and e-communication technologies. The foundation for each of these characteristics will be discussed below with the application of each characteristic to a merger or acquisition.

Focus on the Big Picture

If HR is represented at the due diligence phase of an M&A activity, it is most often in examining benefits programs, compensation programs, and other employee relations issues. A representative from the CA of the investigating organization can examine the likelihood of a successful integration in terms of *overall* factors, for example, attitudes of executives and employees, cultural attributes, and the path the new company will have to follow from a human capital perspective in order to achieve the merger objectives.

In working with the executives of the organization to identify development needs and create learning solutions, consultants with the CA have the possibility of understanding the overall operational direction, without being focused on any specific operational area within the organization. This approach to business is clearly a unique attribute to the M&A team.

Change Management Coaching and Training

Organizational training and coaching in change management is a primary responsibility of CAs. In a cross-industry study of organizations with "value-added" organizational development functions, all profiled companies characterized change management as an important issue that the Academy addresses (Corporate Leadership Council, 1997).

Customized to the M&A process would be just-in-time (JIT) modules focused more on application than theory and designed as a "refresher" for leaders who are actively involved in mergers. Another application of this JIT training is for integration teams during the postmerger phases as members of both organizations come together to plan the strategy and actions of the newly formed company.

As a final area of expertise in change management, CA consultants can work with executives from both sides to effectively and efficiently manage the change process in action. Owing to the sheer speed of most planning around M&A activity, executives are challenged to engage in strategic thinking about how to achieve the change necessary to make the new organization work. With this in mind, the internal consultancy or organizational development area within the CA can focus on working with the senior executives to (1) position the effort within the communicated objectives of the company; (2) identify the most high-impact levers for mobilizing positive action in the organization; (3) set up transition and integration teams that represent the most involved stakeholders in the future organization; (4) clarify the new leadership roles and organizational infrastructure; (5) create strategies and conditions to accelerate the integration process; and (6) maintain a realistic expectation as to the pace of change.

As stated earlier, most members of an M&A team have very specific responsibilities to ensure the soundness and feasibility of the deal. With the CA participant monitoring the change process, the predictable barriers associated with change can be better minimized.

Experience in Assessment

The needs analysis process related to training and the employee opinion/corporate culture assessments created by organizational development departments are easily applied to an M&A situation. Especially as it relates to the avoidance or mitigation of "culture clash," the survey and assessment techniques used as tools in the CA are invaluable, especially in the pre- and postmerger phases.

Surveys are difficult to administer before the approval of the acquisition and openness of the acquired company to employee access both for legal access reasons and also because there is insufficient time for a comprehensive cultural survey (Marks and Mirvis, 1998). However, targeted interviews and observations by CA personnel throughout the process can lead to discovery of potential cultural obstacles. In debriefing sessions or strategy discussions as early as the due diligence phase, the CA representative can listen, observe, and share observations about where he or she thinks there may be issues. Once these issues are stated, other members can validate or invalidate the concern on the basis of additional experiences within the soon-to-be acquired organization or, if a cross-organization M&A team, from experiences with each other. Once the merger is announced, the CA can administer a fully organizational cultural and/or employee opinion survey. It is frequently reported that failure to assess a targeted organizational culture can be a major contributor to M&A underperformance (Marks and Mirvis, 1998). Although traditionally the involvement of HR, and especially the CA function, has been at times an afterthought, this one aspect of cultural assessment can well pay off in either a better prepared integration scheme or, in some cases, the recognition that the M&A deal may not be as good as it seems.

Of course it is difficult to identify what aspects of "culture" are best assessed at the beginning of an M&A process. While there are some M&A failures due to poor strategic fit, most costly postmerger issues seem to result from organizational and human factors (Haspeslagh and Jemison, 1991; Larsson, 2003; Marks and Mirvis, 1998). Unless a company is purchasing another company solely for acquisition of "hard" assets, the resistance of employees inhibits the success of the overall approach (Cartwright and Cooper, 1996). Such cultural issues as communication styles, leadership approaches, and overall satisfaction with each of the separate companies can be solid indicators of the ease (or difficulty) in which a merger will produce fairly rapid benefits (Schweiger and DeNisi, 1991).

Career Development and Succession

Larsson et al. (2001) states that when two organizations integrate, the careers of individual employees disintegrate. The employee body "mass" may become more focused on individual survival than on the objectives of the newly formed organization (Bogdandy, 2000).

Although an M&A team may consider the employee body of an organization as one of the elements of the acquisition, the CA team member should be more accustomed to recognizing each individual as a holistic representation *of* the organization. The involvement of CAs in the ongoing succession, development, and identification of high-potential employees within the acquiring organization can be utilized as an assessment of the newly merged members as well. In this case, the concern for individual career can greatly affect the overall impact of the M&A on future success of the organization. Larsson et al. (2001) suggest that it is important to temper the traditional view of M&A from an organizational perspective with the point of view of an M&A impact on individual careers.

Established Relationships with Leaders

The CA must not only leverage the relationships already established within the "home" company, but must also establish the trust and relationships of the senior leadership in the acquired organization. These relationships are much harder to establish if the M&A process has proceeded into the premerger or merger implementation stages. The insights gained by the CA consultant will provide the basis for training, coaching, and consulting throughout the integration.

Scott and Hascall (2001) compare the internal consultant with external consultants and point out that one of the primary strengths that make the internal facilitator valuable is that he or she develops their leadership out of position and character, as opposed to the external provider who is often seen as able to move on to other clients if the specific project does not work out. Adams (2001) points out that the skill in developing relationships with senior executives is a cornerstone to a successful CA and is transferable between various projects and situations.

Although some researchers have surmised that HR and training departments attempting to be involved in the planning stage of an M&A provide relatively feeble influence (Corporate Leadership Council, 1999), the establishment of the relationships alone are well worth the investment in early involvement. Fully leveraging relationships with senior leaders, building partnerships for influence, and coaching leaders to model what they espouse are all relationship skills positioning the CA as a leading management resource (Adams, 2001).

Established E-learning and E-communication Infrastructure

When an M&A takes place, it is often difficult to organize a simple meeting within the new organization, not to mention some critical training or communication event. The CA within an organization often has technologies available that can quickly be focused on the support and development of the new organization. Although the technology to conduct video conferences, tele-conferences, and e-mail are today common among organizations, the more sophisticated aspects of Internet conferencing, Web-based technologies, and electronic forum and meeting infrastructure are often the purview of the CA.

Although these technologies may not be the most effective for the establishment of new personal relationships, they can augment the initial face-to-face time spent between the leadership and employee body of a newly merged organization. Such common CA practices as the establishment of online forums, libraries, and chat rooms can be successfully utilized in the high-paced activity of an M&A. Even e-technologies that have less of an infrastructure demand (servers, intranets, and so on), such as compact disc production, can be utilized to share information, provide orientation, or simply communicate with a large number of employees and/or leaders.

Discussion

Corporate academies can clearly support Professor Larsson's "co-competence and motivational integration approach" that he found to be the common denominator among the most successful M&A. CA can facilitate the organizational integration as well as all three levels of the human side of M&A. By addressing threats and opportunities regarding career issues at the individual level, communication issues at the interpersonal level, and cultural issues at the collective level, CAs play an important role for actual synergy realization in M&A.

This opportunity also creates an enormous challenge for the CA of any organization that pursues M&A activity. It is impossible to put in place the support mechanisms that are necessary and to do so on an ad hoc basis. If the CA is truly to support M&A activity, there must be a commitment made to provide the necessary resources and focus. Further is the need for the CA organization to recognize this innovative involvement and allow the CA consultants access to the activities of M&A as they are being conceived and implemented. Many companies have long traditions of a fairly closed team when M&A is being conducted. The change in philosophy necessary to facilitate the success of CA involvement in M&A is perhaps the largest obstacle to overcome.

References

Adams, B. (2001). OD: The next 10 years—It's still about relationships. In *Proceedings of the 2001 OD Network Annual Conference*.

Bogdandy, C. (2000). Optimizing merger value. Paper presented at the *Annual Organizational Network Conference*, Vancouver, British Columbia, Canada.

Cartwright, S., and Cooper, C. L. (1996). *Managing Mergers, Acquisitions and Alliances: Integrating People and Cultures*. Oxford, UK: Butterworth Heinemann.

Corporate Leadership Council (1997). Fact Brief: Creating a Value-Added Organizational Development Function [Online], *Fact Brief*, Available at: http://www.clcinteractive.com [August, 2001].

Corporate Leadership Council (1999). Executive Inquiry: The Role of HR in Mergers and Acquisitions [Online], *Executive Inquiry*, Available at: http://www.clcinteractive.com [August 2001].

Haspeslagh, P. C., and Jemison, D. B. (1991). *Managing Acquisitions: Creating Value Through Corporate Renewal*. New York: Free Press.

Larsson, R. (2003). Determinants of synergy realization in mergers and acquisitions. In Stahl and Mendenhall (eds.), *Managing Culture and Human Resources in Mergers and Acquisitions*. Palo Alto, CA: Stanford University Press.

Larsson, R., Driver, M., Holmqvist, M., and Sweet, P. (2001). Career dis-integration and re-integration in mergers and acquisitions: Managing competence and motivational intangibles. *European Management Journal*, 19(6): 609–18.

Marks, M. L., and Mirvis, P. H. (1998). *Joining Forces: Making One Plus One Equal Three in Mergers, Acquisitions and Alliances*. San Francisco: Jossey-Bass.

9 The Neglected Importance of Leadership in Mergers and Acquisitions

SIM B. SITKIN AND AMY L. PABLO

Although theorists and practitioners recognize that acquisitions frequently fail to live up to their potential (Larsson and Finkelstein, 1999), the role of leadership and its effect on M&A performance have not been well articulated or studied. In fact, it would be only a slight exaggeration to suggest that the role of leadership in M&A success and failure has been ignored by scholars and practitioners alike.

By applying a recently developed general model of leadership (Sitkin, Lind, and Long, 2001), this chapter offers a framework for understanding how leaders can make a difference in M&A outcomes. Specifically, we identify key attributes of effective leadership that are especially applicable to different M&A circumstances.

This chapter is motivated by two observations. First, a review of scholarly and practitioner-focused writing on M&A suggests that others have referred to the critical importance of leadership in M&A performance, noting that successful M&A require more than just the effective management of M&A tactics and activities. Second, despite a very general acknowledgment of leadership's importance, past work on M&A has not examined or proposed any details concerning what constitutes M&A leadership, nor has it specified how it might make a difference.

The Importance of Leadership in Organizations

Selznick (1957) noted that leadership is fundamental as an organizational mechanism for achieving efficiency and control and for building commitment, understanding, and determination. These leadership functions reflect a continuum of organizational requirements, ranging from the production function (focused on the effective design and implementation of strong output controls and dependent on building and operating functional networks) (for example, Kotter, 1996) to the institutional function (focused on the infusion of perceived value by meeting institutional expectations concerning strong leadership) (for example, Meyer and Rowan, 1977). Drucker (1954, pp. 158, 159) underscores this thinking: "Leadership is of utmost importance. Indeed there is no substitute for it."

Some scholars have challenged assumptions about leadership, suggesting instead that leadership is primarily symbolic (Pfeffer, 1981) or attributed (Calder, 1982). Some have even proposed that leadership is irrelevant, such as Meindl, Ehrlich, and Dukerich's (1985) argument that leaders do not matter and that observers' attributions of organizational performance to leadership are merely the result of a romanticized view that allows these observers to avoid the need to develop and understand more complex or indirect explanations for organizational outcomes (Meindl, Ehrlich, and Dukerich, 1985).

However, we believe leadership *can* matter for organizations. When we look beyond attributing explanations for an event or outcome to looking at how a process is guided, we can identify that some persons or entities in organizations have particular sets of value and knowledge-based capabilities that make them more effective in the leadership role. A context where leadership plays a central part and that has received particular attention in recent years is that of organizational change and renewal. It is with this in mind that we examine how leadership can make a difference in M&A.

M&A as Change

Organizational reorganization, including most mergers or acquisitions, represents a major transformative event for organizations and the people in them. In one of the most well-known and influential works on achieving strategic or operational fit during M&A implementation, Kitching (1967) stresses the importance of attentive management to direct this kind of change. In his study of the underlying causes for variations in acquisition performance, Kitching suggested the importance of installing "managers of change" to handle the critical areas needing change to accomplish the tasks of the acquisition. He also stressed the need to quickly establish effective management relationships between the acquiring and acquired companies, including the appointment of an executive to "ride herd."

While Kitching's work generally emphasizes the importance of focusing change management efforts on control in the postacquisition period, more recent M&A research takes into account not only control-based value creation, but also a variety of integration processes through which those synergistic benefits come to be realized (Hitt, Harrison, and Ireland, 2001, p. 97).

As is traditional in acquisition literature, integration is largely defined by the degree of intrusion of the acquiring company into the acquired organization (for example, Buono and Bowditch, 1989; Finkelstein, 1986; Howell, 1970; Larsson, 1989; Sales and Mirvis, 1984; Shanley, 1987; Walsh, 1987; Yunker, 1983). Although the acquiring organization may also experience change as a result of the acquisition, the traditional focus on integration reflects a concern with the extent to which the acquiring organization creates changes in the acquired organization. In this sense, integration is conceptualized as a boundary disruption initiated by the acquiring organization to create mechanisms within the acquired company that facilitate the achievement of parent company goals. As such, the traditional perspective on acquisition integration as enforced administrative control focuses on integration as the use of formal authority mechanisms to coordinate the goal-directed activities of organizational subunits (March and Simon, 1958).

More recent conceptualizations view integration as a more complex and interactive mutual adjustment process between two organizations (Pablo, 1994), more of a facilitated dialogue (Isaacs, 1999) than a linear, unilaterally directed change process initiated by the acquiring organization to gain administrative control. From this perspective, integration requires significant change on the part of the acquiring organization as well as by the acquired organization (Haspeslagh and Jemison, 1991). Furthermore, the mutual adjustment conceptualization of integration takes into account the relative difficulties of managing a range of degrees of boundary disruption. This may be managerially more difficult to implement than either a largely hands-off or an all-encompassing approach, because it implies the need for selectivity and restraint on the part of the acquirer (Bastien and Van de Ven, 1986; Haspeslagh and Farquhar, 1987; Haspeslagh and Jemison, 1991; Nahavandi and Malekzadeh, 1988).

Leadership in the M&A Literature

An analysis of past work on leadership in M&A has led us to the following five summary conclusions about the M&A literature:

1. The role of leadership in M&A has been neglected or even denied.
2. The denial of leadership can be traced to a disciplinary bias that has led analysts to discuss only what M&A-related advice is quantifiable or lends itself to specifiable recommendations.
3. Yet authors and practitioners know that leadership is important and therefore must be discussed.

4. Thus, it is discussed, but only in the most general terms.
5. The discussion has remained general because analysts have lacked an actionable framework for thinking about the range of leadership dimensions relevant to M&A success and failure.

In this section, we explore each of these explanations for the treatment of leadership in M&A writing to date. In the next section, we propose a specific framework that can form a basis for rectifying the lack of systematic attention to M&A leadership.

Lack of Attention to Leadership in M&A Literature

A review of the academic and practitioner literatures on M&A reveals that discussions of the primary determinants of M&A process and outcome rarely even mention leadership and, when they do refer to leadership, they tend to focus exclusively on a highly rationalized notion of strategy development. Consider, for example, Bower's summary of key insights that can be derived from the research literature about M&A (Bower, 2001): (1) acquirers pay too much; (2) friendly deals done using stock perform well; (3) CEOs fall in love with deals and then don't walk away; (4) integration is hard, but a few do it well consistently. In another summary of the lessons about M&A's key influences, Arndt, Thornton, and Foust (2000) suggested a set of sources of M&A failure: (1) inadequate due diligence; (2) lack of strategic rationale; (3) unrealistic expectations of synergies; (4) paid too much; (5) conflicting corporate culture; (6) failed to move quickly enough to integrate. Where is leadership in these lists of key issues? The answer is that these fairly representative commentaries sometimes mention leadership, but largely neglect it.

Why has leadership been neglected in M&A writing? There are a number of sensible explanations for why leadership has been neglected despite its obviousness. M&A research has largely drawn from the disciplines of economics and sociology for its theoretical and empirical focus. These disciplines tend to mention leadership issues only in passing. Those whose focus is the organizational aspects of M&A have tended to study cultural fit or the compatibility of other organizational attributes, referring to leadership issues only incidentally. Because of these disciplinary roots, research on M&A has tended to stress the analysis of a number of important issues other than leadership, including firm valuation and financial performance, strategic fit, organizational fit, and the management of M&A postintegration processes. Although the practitioner literature suggests that top leadership focuses on fiscal and legal aspects of M&A and top management leadership talent is in short supply (Schein, 2001), the surprising net result is that there has been little systematic attention to the effect of leadership on M&A performance.

How Has Leadership Been Addressed in the M&A Literature?

Much of the literature on M&A has completely ignored leadership. For example, an article by Aiello and Watkins (2000) on "The fine art of friendly acquisition" includes not a single mention of the term. The M&A literature sometimes goes further than merely ignoring leadership issues, actively denying the potentially positive role leaders can play in M&A, for example, when Ashkenas, Demonaco, and Francis (1998, p. 169) assert that "the business leader's very position of authority often limits his or her ability to facilitate integration."

However, we would not wish to suggest that M&A research has entirely ignored the topic of leadership—an implication that would be inaccurate as there have in fact been a few cases in which leadership has been addressed substantively in the M&A literature. We discuss three ways that the M&A literature has discussed leadership, albeit sparsely.

First, leadership is often cited in the M&A literature. But when noted, it is treated in an almost off-hand way that seems to reflect the need to acknowledge what is an obviously important factor, while sidestepping the need to address the issue substantively. "Acquisitions are a revealing litmus test that highlight the quality of leadership" (Haspeslagh and Jemison, 1991), a "proper outlook [must be] modelled and managed at the top" (Marks and Mirvis, 2001, p. 90), and "successful integration needs strong leadership" (Setzer, 2000, p. 9) are all quotations illustrative of general references to leadership with few details or real analysis.

Second, a highly rationalized view of M&A leadership as the work of "great strategists" has been cited frequently enough that Gemini Consulting referred to this characterization as "Myth #5: Top management must first set the strategy and then align the organization behind it" (Davidson, 1996, p. 39). The general conception of leadership is of activities that can be planned in a highly rational manner and then implemented through a command and control management approach. Most of these writers focus on the importance of creating an integration team that focuses early on planning for building organizational capabilities, structures, management systems, and relationships (Galpin and Herndon, 2000; Marks and Mirvis, 2001; Tetenbaum, 1999). Sociocultural needs are spoken to by these authors in that they address the need to manage culture, and attend to the psychological states of organization members as they endure the organizational combination experience. A theme that runs throughout the prescriptions of these contributors is the need to plan early and comprehensively to bring about the required results in the combination, including paying specific attention to group processes and change management issues.

Third, the important role of leadership has been acknowledged by focusing on the negative effects of the lack of good leadership. Initiated by early work on the role of "hubris" (for example, Roll, 1986) and "over-confidence" (Jemison and Sitkin, 1986a) in M&A, some writers have emphasized the role of "CEO ego" in distorting appropriate M&A practice. For example, Marks and Mirvis (2001, p. 83) argue that "CEO ego was the primary force during M&A ... the bigger the ego of the CEO, the higher the premium."

The only example in the M&A literature we could find that even attempted to systematically assess M&A leadership issues was a Bain & Company effort (Gadiesh et al., 2002, pp. 14–15) to identify a range of leadership characteristics that might be associated with successful M&A outcomes. Their observations, derived from their own consulting practice, emphasize the importance of decisiveness ("closing the deal"), serving as a symbol and creating momentum ("crusading for the new entity"), fostering a sense of focus ("establishing and communicating the strategic vision"), motivating organizational members ("cheering on the troops"), and providing key cultural and operational guidance ("captaining change through integration"). These practice-focused observations and recommendations on leadership suggest a set of cause–effect relationships between acquisition requirements and the potentially facilitating role of leadership in providing positive direction and/or removing barriers to M&A success.

Thus, although the practitioner M&A literature frequently refers to corporate leaders and their actions, the specific mechanisms by which M&A leaders make a difference have not been systematically explored by either practitioners or scholars. In the next section, we begin to address this issue by turning our attention to a new model of leadership and its potential for understanding M&A leadership.

A Model of Leadership Applied to M&A

In developing a generic model of leadership, Sitkin, Lind, and Long (2001) have proposed that leadership is distinct from management, although the same individual can fulfill both kinds of responsibilities simultaneously. As shown in Figure 9.1, they proposed that there are six essential dimensions to effective leadership, each of which has a specific effect on followers: *personal leadership* fosters loyalty, *relational leadership* engenders a sense of trust and justice, *contextual leadership* helps to build community, *inspirational leadership* encourages higher aspirations, *supportive leadership* forges an internalized sense of self-discipline, and *stewardship* raises an internalized sense of responsibility. We will apply this model to the M&A context to discuss the applicability of each of these dimensions to M&A.

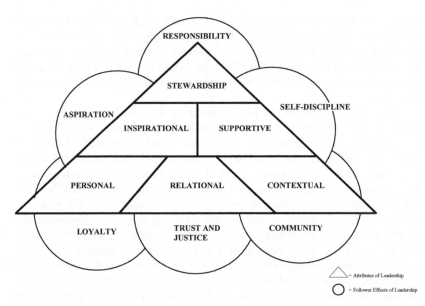

FIGURE **9.1** Six-Dimension Integrative Model of Leadership (Sitkin, Lind, and Long, 2001)

Personal Leadership in M&A

Personal leadership refers to the idea that it matters that a leader conveys to other organizational members who s/he is, including a sense of personal vision, values, emotions, and beliefs. For leaders to have "credibility" (Kouzes and Posner, 1993), they must be seen as having persona, character, identity—in other words, they must make palpable to others the kind of person they are. For example, can others predict how an individual will react when a particular value is violated? Do they have a sense of what that person really believes in and what the person disagrees with? Some people anger easily, or always see the humor in a situation. Some make a specific practice or value their "personal mission" such that others can anticipate how they will react to particular events. When effective and admired, we may hear "in our mind's ear" a leader's tone of voice, verbal expressions, or repeated messages voiced by others within or outside the organization. When this occurs, the leader has developed personal leadership. Others can see (even if they do not always understand or agree with) their vision, values, beliefs, and style—and feel they know the leader, even if they have never met face-to-face.

During M&A, a familiar and seemingly predictable leader can be a comforting anchor in a turbulent sea of change. The M&A experience can be so disconcerting and uncertain that the sense of predictability conveyed by a known entity can be received positively, even when we might disagree with the specific choices made.

Yet the personal side of leadership is largely absent from the M&A literature. A rare reference to some aspects of personal leadership in M&A situations can be found in Haspeslagh and Jemison's description of an "institutional leader" as communicator of "vision and purpose," including need to "recognize and address... and articulate new purpose for the combined firms" (Haspeslagh and Jemison, 1991, pp. 132–33) Gemini Consulting (1998) offers another rare instance of M&A writing reflecting this idea when they refer to shared vision, personal commitment, clear and well-articulated decisions, involvement and visibility, and role modeling as important attributes in M&A. When Haspeslagh and Jemison (1991) describe Johnson & Johnson's $3.7 billion acquisition of Depuy, by noting the "surprise" that the leader was a "lightning rod for many people's emotions," they capture both how important this issue is for many acquisitions, and also just how neglected the importance of this dimension has been in theory and practice.

Relational Leadership in M&A

Relational leadership emphasizes the important role of the leader in forging strong ties with individuals in the organization. The idea of building the organization through an endless series of dyadic interpersonal relationships is a daunting one when one considers how huge and geographically dispersed many of today's large organizations are. How can a leader foster interpersonal connections, build a shared sense of understanding, or establish an emotional connection and accessibility when they lead an organization of 100,000 employees spread across scores of countries, speaking different languages? How can a leader create emotional connection with individuals s/he has never met and may never meet? The key to relational leadership is to convey that the leader cares about and understands the individual organizational member, and that the individual member feels that they "know" the leader. This is simultaneously extremely difficult and extremely simple to accomplish. It is difficult for obvious reasons, but can be accomplished by fostering a sense of mutual understanding in which followers feel they know their leader and the leader knows them. Relational leadership rests on a sense of interpersonal ties that feel honest and accessible and human.

Sometimes the relational aspect of leadership has been reflected in writing on M&A. Ashkenas and Francis (2000, 112–13) capture this dimension in their description of the Texas Instruments/Unitrode merger, in which there was an explicit effort on the part of Texas Instruments' leaders to build "social connections" by emphasizing shared language and culture.

Haspeslagh and Jemison (1991, 134–35) identify "interpersonal leadership" as important for helping members of merging firms to "develop, understand, and embrace the acquisition's purpose" and "to see their role in it." Gemini, in presenting its approach to M&A processes (Davidson, 1996; Gemini Consulting, 1998), implicitly recognizes the importance of relational leadership when they encourage M&A managers to establish relationships in order to "build buy-in and coach people through difficulties." When people feel they have a real relationship with their leaders, the comfort and sense of connection it provides can help them remain focused and committed in getting through the inevitable difficulties that M&A processes present.

Contextual Leadership in M&A

Contextual leadership involves creating the situational conditions that enable organizational members to focus and be effective. By creating "enabling" structures and norms (Adler and Borys, 1996; Sitkin 1995), leaders provide the contextual infrastructure that allows individuals and subgroups in the organization to be successful. This is the leader as architect (Greenhalgh, 2001)—not only in the sense of physical structure, but also in the sense of task (or procedural) structure, and social (or normative) structure. By creating facilitating contextual conditions, leaders simplify, focus, and create a sense of coherence.

This simplification function can be especially critical when organization members encounter a complex and confusing environment, as is so typical of M&A. Within the M&A literature this notion has been captured in descriptions of leaders as the chief community builder and architect of the organization's structure, process, and culture. For example, when Pablo (1994) refers to the M&A leader as a "master designer," she captures the role of the leader as an architect of enabling conditions. As part of the Electrolux acquisition of Zanussi, leaders helped to create a positive organizational identity that encouraged members to want to be associated with the new venture. Thus, they built the "conditions" necessary to foster an effective "transfer of affiliation" (Haspeslagh and Jemison, 1991, p. 162).

Contextual leadership involves addressing typical M&A issues, such as redesigning rules, goals, measures, HR policies/procedures, symbols, and ceremonies (Galpin and Herndon, 2000). For example, Ashkenas and Francis (2000) pointed out that the Lucent acquisition of Ascend Communication involved leadership initiatives that included designing the "structure within which the team could function effectively," providing a "road map to help people see the work ahead," and creating common tools, measures, and project management discipline to build a sense of organizational or project coherence.

Contextual leadership in M&A focuses on the aspects of leader behavior that involve sociological influence rather than psychological or interpersonal influence. Leadership does not only involve interpersonal interaction or personal qualities, but also involves acting upon the organizational environment in a way that enhances the effectiveness of the organization and its members. When M&A activity occurs primarily in a small subsidiary of a large corporation, or occurs through a series of small acquisitions that cumulatively result in significant organizational changes, the most important actions that firm leaders may take are ones that create the conditions that allow others to succeed.

Inspirational Leadership in M&A

Inspirational leadership involves building the desire for greatness or excellence by raising expectations and the acceptance of challenges, enthusiasm, and confidence. Leadership is often described in terms of how charismatic leaders (Conger and Kanungo, 1998) can inspire others to admire or emulate them. But Sitkin, Lind, and Long (2001) focus clearly on how inspirational leadership is not based on the image of charisma or charm, but on the effect of a leader in engendering greater aspirations among those who follow. Inspirational leaders, in this sense, see things as they could be when others do not, articulate persuasively how the seemingly unrealistic and unattainable is, in fact, possible and worth pursuing. Inspirational leadership involves raising the bar and creating a sense of enthusiasm for reaching, for embracing the challenge, and for taking the risk, for winning.

Several M&A examples helpfully illustrate the crucial role that inspirational leadership played in organizations that pursued challenging acquisitions. Loral Corporation CEO, Bernard Schwartz, led his organization to stretch for previously unattainable targets and to acquire firms in segments of their defense electronics industry that were not previously part of their experience or expertise base (Jemison and Sitkin, 1986b). In demonstrating inspirational leadership, Schwartz created a step-by-step strategy for building his company's acquisitive strategy and concomitant capabilities. When he identified a particularly attractive acquisition target believed to be out of reach of Loral's current capability, he bolstered the perceived and actual capacity of his firm's staff by making two smaller and less challenging acquisitions. This initiative helped to position the firm to both purchase his original target, the "crown jewel" of the industry, and to manage it effectively. Throughout, Schwartz saw his leadership role as not only seeing as possible what others viewed as impossible, but also as articulating what and how the organization's members should aspire to greater—and attainable— goals. By creating the sense that challenging goals are attainable and that the firm had the capability and the plan for attaining them, Schwartz was able to generate the action and enthusiasm the firm's employees needed to overcome tough obstacles. That is the essence of inspirational leadership.

Although currently in disrepute for his general managerial actions, nobody has questioned the ability of former Tyco International/CIT's CEO Dennis Koslowski to motivate individuals to do that which they would not do without his influence (Symonds, 2001). Although he may have applied his considerable leadership abilities in getting people to exceed legal barriers, Koslowski appears to understand the importance of getting people to believe in their abilities to accomplish things they had previously thought were impossible. In terms of our focus here on inspirational leadership in M&A activities, Koslowski was quoted as describing the effect he wanted to impart to his staff and employees regarding Tyco acquisitions: "It is crucial we push growth coming out of the box... I want people to say 'Wow, this is a real step up'." In doing this, he inspired people to significantly raise their aspirations for themselves and their organization. And, thus, although he is far from a role model in other respects (see "Stewardship" described below), Koslowski nonetheless does provide an excellent example of how inspiring leadership can have significant effects on the aspirations that can so significantly affect firm performance.

Supportive Leadership in M&A

Supportive leadership involves making others aware of pressing organizational problems and secure enough in their own capacity to take appropriate corrective action. Supportive leaders provide the resources and feedback necessary to foster a sense of acceptance, security, and efficacy—both in one's own ability and in the organization as a collective. Supportive leadership does not imply "sugar-coating" tough feedback or failure, but necessitates the provision of the financial, procedural, developmental, and emotional support for the organization and its members to succeed. Whereas inspirational leaders "raise the ceiling," supportive leaders "raise the floor" (or provide a ladder or springboard). Specifically, supportive leadership involves ensuring that employees have the training, resources, and encouragement needed to make reaching that new and higher ceiling possible.

Discussions of supportive leadership in the M&A literature are quite limited. One illustration is provided by GE Capital's response to the challenge presented by its acquisitions of Gelco in the 1980s and U.K.'s Burton Group in 1991. During the initiatives, the organization created an Integrating Manager position with the specific intent to provide support to those living through the acquisition. The role of the Integrating Manager was to build "connective tissue" that helped each side "understand" the other—by bridging, explaining, and translating (Ashkenas, Demonaco, and Francis, 1998). Thus, while undertaking the challenging job of bringing together the operations, in both of these cases GE leadership consciously tried to provide elements that would be helpful in making these operations work.

Perhaps the clearest example is a negative one—illustrating the problematic circumstance created by the absence of supportive leadership. Specifically, Haspeslagh and Jemison (1991, p. 133) highlight the importance of this dimension when they capture its absence among financial services executives who were quoted as saying, "We were cast adrift . . . There was not support for us within the firm and nobody understood what we are . . . No instruction except to make money."

Stewardship in M&A

Firms are institutional ships and require symbolic leadership at the helm, with the leader acting as steward of the institution. As Selznick (1957) and Gardner (1968) noted, leadership involves a personal acceptance of the idea that an institution involves deeply held, even treasured, community values and that the highest calling of the leader is to honor and protect those values.

The stewardship role of leadership also involves two other functions: balance and personification. The multifaceted nature of organizational life and leadership makes it important for leaders to play the role of chief integrator and balancer, insuring that the multiple elements of leadership described here are drawn together and effectively balanced for a particular situation. Thus, for organizations to achieve work/life balance, or to appropriately balance the community's interests and the firm's, it is essential that the stewardship function is effectively performed. It is also important for the leader to imbue in others a sense of personal responsibility (ethics, values, and commitment to the broader community good) to the whole and a level of actionable understanding for what is needed, so that each member has the ability and desire to act in a way that advances a greater good.

In the context of M&A, leaders as stewards create what Galpin and Herndon (2000) refer to as "accountable others." These leaders make concrete "the mutual responsibility of all employees, but alert and bind them to everyone else's responsibility . . . this will create a social conscience" (Clemente and Greenspan, 1998, p. 199). Thus, when Verizon was created, CEO Ivan Seidenberg helped to crystallize the continued importance of customer service from one part of the Bell legacy, while also sustaining the important role that Verizon could play in promoting communication innovation. Both were foundational aspects of the firm's institutional identity, as each formed an important piece in the creation of a common foundation when Bell Atlantic and GTE merged.

Sometimes stewardship involves representing one of two firms' core values and history. Sometimes it involves forging an entirely new, shared sense of institutional values. Stewardship is especially significant given the challenges that today's firms and leaders face.

Implications for Leadership in M&A

We have identified a number of ways that leaders can affect M&A processes and outcomes. Admired, credible leaders can imbue those whom they lead with the necessary level of commitment, confidence, and comfort to work the leader to take the organization forward. Leaders can incite a sense of purpose, trust, and community that allows organization members to become focused in pursuing challenging goals, effectively balancing work life issues, and embracing a sense of responsibility and accountability.

The key message of this chapter is that leadership in M&A can make a significant, positive impact, but needs to be taken beyond broad generalities. Both researchers and practitioners need to distinguish myths from realities and focus on critical, leverageable M&A leadership issues. To enhance that objective, we have outlined the beginnings of a theoretically rich and practical framework in order to better understand and enact leadership that can make a positive difference in M&A performance.

References

Adler, P., and Borys, B. (1996). Two types of bureaucracy: Enabling and coercive. *Administrative Science Quarterly*, 41:61–89.

Aiello, R. J., and Watkins, M. D. (2000). The fine art of friendly acquisition. *Harvard Business Review*, Nov/Dec: 100–7.

Arndt, M., Thornton, E., and Foust, D. (2000). Let's talk turkeys: Some mergers were never meant to be. *Business Week*, December: 44.

Ashkenas, R. N., Demonaco, L. J., and Francis, S. C. (1998). Making the deal real: How GE Capital integrates acquisitions. *Harvard Business Review*, Jan/Feb: 165–77.

Ashkenas, R., and Francis, S. C. (2000). Integration managers: Special leaders for special times. *Harvard Business Review*, Nov/Dec: 108–17.

Bastien, D. T., and Van de Ven, A. H. (1986). Managerial and organizational dynamics of mergers and acquisitions. Discussion Paper #36, Strategic Management Research Center, University of Minnesota.

Bower, J. (2001). Not all M&A's are alike—and that matters. *Harvard Business Review*, 79(3): 92–101.

Buono, A. F., and Bowditch, J. L. (1989). *The Human Side of Mergers and Acquisitions*. San Francisco: Jossey-Bass.

Calder, B. J. (1982). Attribution theory of leadership. In Staw and Salancik (eds.), *New Directions in Organizational Behavior*. Malabar, FL: Robert E. Krieger, pp. 179–204.

Clemente, M. N., and Greenspan, D. S. (1998). *Winning at Mergers and Acquisitions: The Guide to Focused Planning and Integration*. New York: John Wiley & Sons.

Conger, J. A., and Kanungo, R. N. (1998). *Charismatic Leadership in Organizations*. Thousand Oaks, CA: Sage Publications.

Davidson, M. (1996). Mergers and acquisitions: Beware their siren call. *Across the Board*, October: 36–40.

Drucker, P. F. (1954). *The Practice of Management*. New York: Harper & Row Publishers.

Finkelstein, S. (1986). *The Acquisition Integration Process*. Working Paper, Columbia University.

Gadiesh, O., Buchanan, R., Daniell, M., and Ormiston, C. (2002). The leadership testing ground. *Journal of Business Strategy*, March/April: 12–7.

Galpin, T., and Herndon, M. (2000). *The Complete Guide to Mergers and Acquisitions: Process Tools to Support M&A Integration at Every Level*. San Francisco: Jossey-Bass.

Gardner, J. W. (1968). *No Easy Victories*. New York: Harper & Row Publishing.

Gemini Consulting (1998). *M&A Integration: The Key to Creating Value*. Cambridge, MA: Gemini Consulting.

Greenhalgh, L. (2001). *Managing Strategic Relationships: The Key to Business Success*. New York: The Free Press.

Haspeslagh, P. C., and Farquhar, A. B. (1987). The acquisition integration process: A contingent framework. Presented at the *Seventh Annual International Conference of the Strategic Management Society*, Boston.

Haspeslagh, P., and Jemison, D. B. (1991). *Managing Acquisitions*. New York: Free Press.

Hitt, M. A., Harrison, J. S., and Ireland, R. D. (2001). *Mergers and Acquisitions: A Guide to Creating Value for Shareholders*. New York: Oxford University Press. Howell, R. A. (1970). Plan to integrate your acquisitions. *Harvard Business Review*, 49: 66–76.

Isaacs, W. (1999). *Dialogue and the Art of Thinking Together*. New York: Currency/Doubleday.

Jemison, D. B., and Sitkin, S. B. (1986a). Acquisitions: The process can be a problem. *Harvard Business Review*, March/April: 107–16.

Jemison, D. B., and Sitkin, S. B. (1986b). Corporate acquisitions: A process perspective. *Academy of Management Review*, 11(1): 145–63.

Kitching, J. (1967). Why do mergers miscarry? *Harvard Business Review*, 45: 84–107.

Kotter, J. (1996). *Leading Change*. Boston, MA: Harvard Business School Press.

Kouzes, J. M., and Posner, B. Z. (1993). *Credibility: How Leaders Gain and Lose It, and Why People Demand It.* San Francisco: Jossey-Bass.

Larsson, R. (1989). Organizational integration of mergers and acquisitions. *Lund Studies in Economics and Management 7*, Lund, Sweden: Lund University Press.

Larsson, R., and Finkelstein, S. (1999). Integrating strategic, organizational, and human resource perspectives on mergers and acquisitions: A case survey of synergy realization. *Organization Science*, 10(1): 1–26.

March, J. G., and Simon, H. A. (1958). *Organizations.* New York: John Wiley & Sons.

Marks, M. L., and Mirvis, P. H. (2001). Making mergers and acquisitions work: Strategic and psychological preparation. *Academy of Management Executive*, 15(2): 80–92.

Meindl, J., Ehrlich, S., and Dukerich, J. (1985). The romance of leadership. *Administrative Science Quarterly*, 30(1): 78–102.

Meyer, J. W., and Rowan, B. (1977). Institutionalized organizations: Formal structure as myth and ceremony. *American Journal of Sociology*, 83: 340–63.

Nahavandi, A., and Malekzadeh, A. R. (1988). Acculturation in mergers and acquisitions. *Academy of Management Review*, 13(1): 79–90.

Pablo, A. L. (1994). Determinants of acquisition integration level: A decision-making perspective. *Academy of Management Journal*, 37(4): 803–36.

Pfeffer, J. (1981). Management as symbolic action. In Staw and Cummings (eds.), *Research in Organizational Behavior*, Vol. 1. Greenwich, CT: JAI Press.

Roll, R. (1986). The hubris hypothesis of corporate takeovers. *Journal of Business*, 59: 197–216.

Sales, A. L., and Mirvis, P. H. (1984). When cultures collide: Issues in acquisition. In Kimberly and Quinn (eds.), *Managing Organizational Transitions*. Homewood, IL: Richard D. Irwin, Inc.

Schein, L. (2001). *Managing Culture in Mergers and Acquisitions.* New York: The Conference Board (Research Report R-1302-01-RR).

Selznick, P. (1957). *Leadership in Administration.* New York: Harper & Row.

Setzer, M. (2000). *Deutsche Bank and Bankers Trust: How to Manage the Integration Effectively.*

Shanley, M. T. (1987). *Acquisition Management Approaches: An Exploratory Study.* Unpublished doctoral dissertation, University of Pennsylvania.

Sitkin, S. B. (1995). On the positive effect of legalization on trust. *Research on Negotiation in Organizations*, 5: 185–217.

Sitkin, S. B., Lind, E. A., and Long, C. P. (2001). *The Pyramid Model of Leadership.* Durham, NC: Duke University.

Symonds. W. C. (2001). The most aggressive CEO. *Business Week*, May 18, 69–77.

Tetenbaum, T. J. (1999). Beating the odds of merger and acquisition failure: Seven key practices that improve the chance for expected integration and synergies. *Organizational Dynamics*, August: 22–36.

Walsh, J. P. (1987). *Performance from Diversification by Acquisitions: Effects of Acquisition Integration.* Working Paper, Amos Tuck School of Business Administration, Dartmouth College.

Yunker, J. A. (1983). *Integrating Acquisitions.* New York: Praeger.

Executive Commentary on Chapter 9

WILFRIED MEYER

Mergers and acquisitions (M&A) are more than bigger balance sheets, new niches, and smarter synergies; they are complicated, emotional events that shake up and reshape the businesses they combine. M&A are at the core, human events. They topple long-standing relationships, and along with the new organization charts, they bring new ways of doing things. Change is always in the wind. Out with the old. In with the new.

Where are the business leaders as this new mix of cultures and customer and employee relationships are being defined? Some are pumping out due diligence reports; some are burning the midnight oil at negotiation tables. Others are pouring over the legalese in the counter proposals, and still others are crunching numbers. Always crunching the numbers.

Who is making the calls regarding how the new business will really *work* when the deal is done? Who will marshal all the competing interests, and referee the turf battles when the ink is dry? Who will sort through the clashing cultures and inspire a realigned and often fearful workforce to follow the new path? Who will *move* the new organization to the Promised Land and validate the M&A strategy?

Probably not the accountants or the lawyers or the marketing guys. Not alone anyway. They will all help, for sure. But the job of getting from point A to point B, and to *sustain* however success is defined for the new enterprise, belongs to the *business leader*.

My company is German-based and we are pushing five years into an acquisition of a large and respected American business. It has been quite a ride. We are a successful M&A: We were the flagship in EBIT performance for the entire Siemens portfolio last year, and our cash flow more resembled a tsunami. We are performing at benchmark levels in our global employee opinion surveys, and are continuing to improve each year. Not all our customers necessarily love us, but they are loyal and we are improving market positions even in these most difficult of times in the power generation industry. We have already paid back the investment for the acquisition.

That though is yesterday, for the most part. We are indeed facing some very stiff challenges in our business for tomorrow, and we will have to deal with them. And five years out, we are still in the postclosure acquisition phase, which means there are more than just loose ends to tie down: There are fundamental organizational, cost, and strategic issues that are yet in play. But the point is that I think we have been successful as an M&A, so far, for precisely the same reasons why we will hopefully be successful for the future in our business: the quality of our leadership, and its focus on the human side of the M&A.

Sim Sitkin and Amy Pablo have crafted a leadership model from their work, and say it may have some useful implications for enhancing the potential for successful M&A performance. Maybe so. Maybe some other leadership models are effective M&A success-boosters, as well. It is hard to argue that the characteristics that the authors articulate are not relevant to success. After all, who can throw stones at effective stewardship, or inspirational or motivational psychology, or any of the other blocks in the "Attributes of Leadership" pyramid that emerge in the authors' work? They are solid attributes. They are observable, tested, and verified. There are some other points, though, from my experience, that relate to this notion of "Leadership" and M&A success.

First, I am convinced that a base issue for the leadership, however it is described, is actual M&A experience. A consultant can help; but a consultant is not a substitute. You relearn some old things in some new ways when you *live* an M&A: such as the value of patience, the payoff of real team building, and the critical need for communications. In my own experience, I have listened and worked with the consultant "experts," and then seen firsthand how the advice doesn't always work as it is described in the PowerPoint presentations—especially when the leadership of components of the rollout and integration is in the hands of those who haven't managed change before, or those who do not have a real understanding of how profound the issue of culture is in integrating old entities into a new, and suddenly very organic enterprise. So I would add at least these two elements to the leadership model: firsthand experience and cultural perspective.

Here is a glimpse of this cultural "context" or perspective, from my recent (and ongoing) M&A experience. Our M&A was set in a truly global context: where there were once two international, former competitors— one based in the United States and one in Germany—now there is just one company operating in more than 100 different countries. When I think of leadership in "context" though, and with the notion of "personal leadership" as the authors describe, I think that "personal leadership" can look quite differently, and be valued differently, as seen through German, or American, or Chinese lenses. There are different views and ways of individual decision making, and there are different views and ways of more consensual, decision-making practices. The point is that there is a *difference*, and one size may not fit all in how the leader goes about "leading." The point is for me that whatever characteristic is examined must also be examined through overlays and prisms. And it is important that the leader has either the capability or the advisors to help him or her understand these leadership nuances through these prisms, and be able to operate in the way that is most effective to lead. Culture for me is one such prism.

I also think of leadership as a skill set or capability in the "basket" of human characteristics and interactions that together are the "souls" of the old organizations, and will be needed to mesh and compliment each other as well as inspire and drive the new organization forward, as the "heart" of the new enterprise. I would therefore consider leadership as a subset of a larger "human" component when looking at successful M&A activities. I think that what we really need to examine is a true "due diligence" of the human assets (leadership capability is one human asset) when assessing the potential of an M&A. Technical and commercial skill sets and the breadth and depth access of the "knowledge management" of an organization are other "human components." And there are others: Reward and recognition systems; pay for performance philosophies; succession planning issues; big issues effecting how people work, how they lead and how they are led, how they interact with each other, and with their customers.

Knowing how enterprises actually work also helps define how an M&A might work. If you are able to understand the human interactions and knowledge and skills, including its leadership badges and its leadership warts, plans and strategies can be made to help the new enterprise survive and prosper.

In my experience, our M&A did not come to these understandings in a real planned way, but I think we came to understand their importance when we started dealing with communication and trust issues, political infighting, and other large distractions for the work of making the M&A work. These "human" issues became critical and core as the integration started, and continue as issues to manage and to lead as the integration continues.

The test of leaders, then, in an M&A goes beyond the numbers and reshuffling the organization charts: it is anticipating, dealing with and learning from the human issues that are the way the business goes to work after the deal is cut. I think the leadership studies and the model the authors present are important in helping to understand the leadership dynamics of the M&A, but the root of success is really imbedded in understanding the range of human potential as well as human shortcomings as the deal comes together.

We did do some leadership "things" right, in my view, before as well as after the M&A event. The original American CEO is running a big piece of our new company as one of a four-member Board. From the very beginning, we struggled hard and finally were able to articulate a vision. We began a careful exchange of key management back and forth. We globalized our executive compensation programs. We developed a single employee feedback (opinion survey) mechanism. And we developed a common platform for defining what we needed in our future leadership. This platform is unique in some regard to our business, but not so unique in some regards to the leadership characteristics that the authors point to in their pyramid.

I believe that although leadership may be often "overlooked" in M&A literature, it surely cannot ever be underestimated nor should the entire "human asset" side of the M&A equation.

10 Psychological Communication Interventions in Mergers and Acquisitions

ANGELO S. DENISI AND SHUNG JAE SHIN

Mergers and acquisitions (M&A) continue to be an important part of the management landscape, and therefore scholars and practitioners continue to be interested in understanding what makes some M&A activities more successful than others. One factor that has been identified as being critical to management of human resources during the M&A process is communications. Once a merger, or acquisition, is announced, the stress levels of employees begin to climb (cf. Schweiger and DeNisi, 1991). In a merger situation, there will almost certainly be redundancies and so some employees will lose their jobs. If an acquisition is anticipated, there will also be redundancies, although the threat of job loss is presumably even greater for employees in the acquired company. In any event, the uncertainty about the future can lead to increased stress, decreased job satisfaction, and may lead to some employees seeking other employment opportunities (cf. Schweiger and DeNisi, 1991). The absence of communications from top management will lead to rumors and false stories, all of which can lead to even more stress and uncertainty.

But communications with employees during M&A activities can do more than just provide information. Communications about dates of announcements and plans can help reduce anxiety and uncertainty, but these forms of communications may be viewed as "instrumental communications," which have a somewhat limited function. Specifically, instrumental communications provide employees with important information that can reduce uncertainty, but there may be other types of communications that can serve other useful functions during the process.

Schweiger and DeNisi (1991) introduced and tested the effectiveness of a more strategic form of communications, which they termed a "realistic merger preview." This form of communications, based on a body of research (discussed briefly below) dealing with realistic *job* previews, attempts to do more than to simply convey information. Instead, the realistic merger preview allows employees to ask questions and make queries through a "merger hotline," and the intervention really involved creating an open communications system to function during the merger. Schweiger and DeNisi (1991) found that their intervention reduced stress and dissatisfaction, as well as intentions to quit, when compared with a control facility (also involved in the merger) where information was transmitted, but a more open system was not created.

What was the key to this realistic merger intervention? As noted above, the design of this intervention was based on the research literature on realistic job previews. These previews provided realistic information to either job applicants or new employees, in an effort to reduce subsequent turnover and increase job satisfaction and commitment. Although we cannot adequately review that literature here, there are excellent recent reviews available (for example, Phillips, 1998). *How do* realistic job previews actually work? Meglino and his associates (Meglino et al., 1988) compared several different hypothesized mechanisms underlying realistic job previews. Although they found some support for several proposed mechanisms (some of which are not relevant to the M&A context), two mechanisms that found support are worthy of note.

First, realistic job previews work, in part, because by communicating realistic information about the job, the organization communicates that it is honest and can be trusted. These perceptions result in the organization seeming more attractive, which reduces turnover and increases satisfaction and commitment (cf. Dugoni and Ilgen, 1981). If such a process could operate during M&A activity, realistic previews could serve an important role, because it is critical (as will be argued below) that employees find the new (either merged or acquired) organization to be attractive in order that they can become committed to the new organization and, eventually, identify with that organization.

Meglino et al. (1988) also found support for a mechanism based on volition. This proposed mechanism suggests that when employees decide to accept a job after being given complete information, they feel that they are making an informed decision that results in greater commitment to the decision (cf. Salancik, 1977). Again, such a mechanism could be important in the context of M&A, as employees who feel they have been given full information (which would be reinforced by the ability to ask questions) would then be more likely to feel that any decision to remain with the company would be one made with full information. As it would be a truly "volitional" decision, the employee would be more committed to the decision (and the organization) and remain more satisfied.

In this chapter, we propose a model that focuses on the importance of communications in M&A, one that limits itself to the broader type of communication needs, which Schweiger and DeNisi (1991) called "realistic merger previews." We do not intend to suggest that other types of communication interventions are not realistic or are not meant to reduce uncertainty. In fact, others have suggested that early communications are important for the success of M&As, and are effective in reducing uncertainty (for example, Bastien, 1987; DiFonzo and Bordia, 1998; Marks and Mirvis, 1985). We concur, but we further suggest that communication interventions designed to increase the attractiveness of the organization, as well as commitment to and attachment with the organization are more critical for managing human resources during a merger or acquisition.

Specifically, we will refer to these types of communication interventions as "psychological communications" interventions, as their intent is to influence some of the psychological aspects that are important during the M&A process. When we use that term, we mean interventions that provide clear and accurate information to employees about the progress of the merger or acquisition, including clear and accurate information about the consequences for the employees. These interventions should also include opportunities for two-way communications, and should also incorporate messages from top management indicating an understanding and compassion about what the employees are going through. In addition, psychological communication interventions help employees to experience better intergroup relations, which lead them to build more favorable identities with their newly merged organization. Through these processes, we will argue that these types of communications can also help to "prime" a new identity in employees—an identity that is related to the new, merged organization and is a positive association with the new entity. These types of interventions, then, are designed to reduce uncertainty and stress *and* to prime higher order identification with the new organization by building attachment and commitment to the new organization. Thus, we can think about "psychological communication interventions" as having two separate components—a realistic information component and a priming communications component.

But how exactly might these psychological communication interventions work to increase the chances of a merger or acquisition being successful? To explain that process, we propose a model that focuses upon the psychological processes experienced by employees during M&A activity. The model outlines ways in which psychological communication interventions can affect the ways in which employees think about themselves, their coworkers (both new and continuing), and the new organization of which they are a part. Figure 10.1 shows the model, which illustrates (1) how the psychological states such as perceived uncertainty and loss of control influence intergroup cognitions (which will be defined) in corporate mergers; (2) how

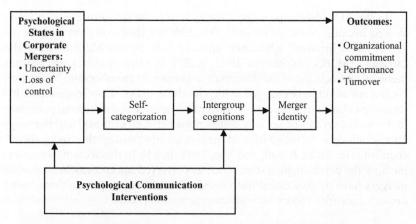

FIGURE **10.1** A Psychological Process During Postmerger Implementation: Roles of Psychological Communication Interventions

intergroup cognitions affect the perceived favorability of identities with the merged organization; and (3) how psychological communication interventions help to minimize the level of intergroup cognitions and develop a favorable social identity on the part of employees. We will further discuss how, if those cognitions and perceptions are properly managed, the M&A is much more likely to be successful.

Psychological States and Intergroup Cognitions in Corporate Mergers

A merger or an acquisition is essentially the process of two organizations coming together to form a new organization. Because part of a working person's identity is tied to the organization where he or she is employed, it is important for everyone involved in M&As to change the way they think of themselves and others following the creation of the new organization. In fact, the nature of intergroup relations between the two sets of employees has been suggested as one of the most important aspects of the process of integrating the two organizations into one (for example, Haunschild, Moreland, and Murrell, 1994; Hogg and Terry, 2000; Mottola et al., 1997; Rentsch and Schneider, 1991). Because of the very nature of a corporate merger (that is, merging two previously independent organizations), it is likely that employees' premerger organizational membership is salient in a corporate merger. Such a situation is likely to engender competitive and antagonistic intergroup relations and intergroup rivalry between the two merging companies (Haunschild et al., 1994), which easily result in employees' intergroup cognitions.

In the AOL–Netscape merger, for example, the integration process was slowed because Netscape's employees identified their company as "the inventor of the Internet" while they regarded AOL as "the McDonald's of the Internet" (Marks and Mirvis, 2001, p. 87). In other words, given the antagonistic perception of the difference in premerger membership, Netscape's employees might have engaged in high levels of "us vs. them" cognitions. Intergroup cognitions, then, are "thoughts, motives, or other mental processes that concern groups (especially distinctions between groups)" and that negatively influence the integration of the two groups through the "us vs. them" cognitions (Schaller, Rosell, and Asp, 1998, p. 11). In this section, we examine how the psychological states such as perceived uncertainty in corporate mergers have dysfunctional outcomes such as intergroup cognitions based on social identity theory and self-categorization theory.

Psychological States in Merger Processes

There are several characteristics of corporate mergers that bring about merger-related psychological states. First, a corporate merger represents an event where employees (especially those of the acquired company) do not have a sense of control. Specifically, changes in their work places may be imposed by an acquiring company (Fried et al., 1996), and the employees have no choice but to accept the changes or to leave. These situations lead the employees to feel loss of control, or even helplessness (Ashforth, 1989; Fried et al., 1996). Second, employees in acquired companies often feel uncertain about their futures. They may be faced with changes in jobs, in relationships with their coworkers, and even changes with their family (Fried et al., 1996; Ivancevich, Schweiger, and Power, 1987). To make matters even worse, executives of the acquired companies tend to adopt a crisis-management orientation because of the uncertainty of the situation (Marks and Mirvis, 1986, 1997a). They tend to increase centralization and cut off large amounts of communication in order to protect their own position and power. This aggravates the situation and so the subordinates feel even more uncertainty, insecurity, and loss of control, and search for rumors to lessen the uncertainty (Fried et al., 1996; Marks and Mirvis, 1997b). The above psychological states relate closely to self-categorization processes of the employees, which in turn result in intergroup cognitions.

Self-Categorization Process in Corporate Mergers

Social identity theory (SIT) and self-categorization theory can provide some insight into what employees are thinking and feeling through the M&A process. First, a person's self-concept is conceived of as a cognitive structure consisting of a set of concepts subjectively available to a person in attempting to define him/herself (Hogg and Abrams, 1988). SIT demonstrates that self-concept is composed of both personal and social identities (Ashforth and Mael, 1989; Tajfel and Turner, 1979; Turner, 1982). Personal identity refers to beliefs about one's characteristics such as skills, abilities, attractiveness, and so on, whereas social identity (one's collective self-conception) comes from one's knowledge of membership in a social group, as well as one's emotional attachment to that membership (Tajfel, 1981). Social identities are produced through social categorization: "Social categorizations define a person by systematically including them within some, and excluding them from other related categories" (Turner, 1982, p. 20).

One of the prime motivations for social identity processes, in particular self-categorization, is uncertainty reduction (Hogg, 2000): social categorization of self that cognitively absorbs self into ingroup prototypes (Turner, 1985). Self-categorization reduces uncertainty about oneself and others "by producing group-distinctive stereotypical and normative perceptions and actions" (Hogg and Terry, 2001, p. 4). Hogg and Terry (2001) argue that self-categorization reduces uncertainty by "assimilating self to a prototype that describes and prescribes perceptions, attitudes, feelings, and behaviors." These authors also argue that such prototypes are more likely to be activated during times of great uncertainty—such as during M&A.

Specifically, it is likely that perceived uncertainty and loss of control that occur during M&A make self-categorization more salient and more important to the employees. Because self-concept influences individuals' subsequent perceptions and behaviors (Tajfel and Turner, 1979), certainty in self-concept provides individuals with "confidence in how to behave and what to expect from the social environment within which one finds himself" (Hogg and Terry, 2000, p. 124). Given the uncertainty and sense of loss of control that accompanies M&A, employees may engage in social identity processes in order to maintain self-concepts that guide their behaviors in such turbulent social environments. Therefore, those psychological states produced in corporate merger processes lead employees to engage in higher levels of self-categorization process.

Furthermore, merger contexts provide a clear situational cue for the social categorization of ingroup and outgroup. Ashforth and Mael (1989) propose that distinctiveness of the group's values and practice, prestige of the group, and salience of the outgroup(s) are likely to be related to forming a social or group identity. A corporate merger may alter the psychological process of forming social identity by making the members' premerger company more distinctive and those of the other company in the merger more salient as an outgroup. Thus, because of the salience of the ingroup and outgroup boundary provided by merger contexts, the employees identify themselves based on their group membership (for example, acquiree and acquirer). In other words, merger contexts bring distinctive social category memberships and these "psychological groups" are constructed through self-categorization (Tsui, Egan, and O'Reilly III, 1992).

As social identity becomes salient, individual self-perception tends to become more membership-oriented. This depersonalization produces collective action, which represents a shift from action in terms of differing personal identities to one in terms of more shared social identity (Brewer and Weber, 1994; Hogg and Turner, 1987; Spears, Doosje, and Ellemers, 1997; Turner et al., 1994). When social identity becomes salient, individuals' attitude and behavior are likely determined by their membership in the social group. In other words, as a result of self-categorization and social comparison, individuals feel less individual and more representative of the social category as well, and they tend to engage in more intergroup cognitions such as ingroup favoritism and stereotyping.

Intergroup Cognitions in Corporate Mergers

According to SIT, individuals seek self-enhancement in social identity processes. The level of self-esteem can be augmented by enhancing either personal identity (for example, achieving individual accomplishments) or positive social identity (for example, belonging to an eminent group). Thus, the distinction between groups resulting from social categorization leads to intergroup cognitions (for example, ingroup favoritism), which is quite common even in the absence of any realistic conflict of interest between groups (Tajfel and Turner, 1979). Tajfel (1979) refers to motivation for positive social identity producing a drive for ingroup superiority as "the sequence of social categorization–social identity–social comparison–positive ingroup distinctiveness" (p. 184). After categorizing themselves into certain social categories, individuals engage in ingroup favoritism for self-enhancement and maintenance of a positive self-concept in comparison with relevant others (Abrams and Hogg, 1988). In corporate mergers, where the level of conflict between the two groups is relatively high, the level of social comparison and ingroup favoritism for a positive self-concept (in comparison with the other group) would be problematically high.

For example, when Citicorp merged with Travelers, employees of the new corporation, Citigroup, spent a lot of time trying to work out who were better, those from Travelers or those from Citicorp. Apparently employees on both sides of the issue wasted energy and time in doing social comparison and ingroup favoritism to maintain a higher status of social identity.

The previous arguments imply that intergroup cognitions are likely to occur in corporate merger contexts. Intergroup cognitions (which begin with the cognitive representations of "us vs. them") tend to cause subsequent negative outcomes (Gaertner et al., 1993). For instance, during the merger implementation, the "us vs. them" cognition may foster distrust of the other party. Inaccurate attribution or judgments about outgroup members' behavior may be based on inappropriate information such as the organization's status in the merger (acquirer or acquiree), on the actions of a few people (that is, the executives), or on ingroup rumor (Schweiger and DeNisi, 1991). Furthermore, misperceptions and negative expectations resulting from stereotypes tend to produce distrust, tension, and anxiety during the integration process.

In addition, intergroup cognitions such as ingroup favoritism and outgroup discrimination would spoil the atmosphere for the cooperation needed to achieve the goals of the merged organization. For example, ingroup favoritism may lead members of each organization to expect members of the other organization to favor their own and to engage in defensively motivated noncooperative behavior that can heighten intergroup distrust and suspicion (Kramer and Messick, 1998). In sum, these intergroup cognitions exacerbated by high degrees of realistic conflict in corporate merger contexts tend to result in feelings of hostility and anxiety. These feelings have been shown to inhibit organizational members' commitment and cooperation (Bachman, 1993; Buono, Bowditch, and Lewis, 1985). Thus, we argue that intergroup cognitions should be dealt with in corporate mergers because the nature of merger contexts invokes such cognitions easily and may ultimately have a great impact on the success of merger implementation.

Intergroup Cognitions and Favorability of the Merged Organization Identity

Intergroup cognitions negatively affect postmerger implementation not only by directly impacting employees' attitudes and behavior, but also by affecting their new organizational identity. The organization is a particularly influential source of social identity in its members' lives, that is, it is fundamentally linked to its members' social, economic, and psychological well-being. Therefore, companies usually provide a critical social category for individuals to form a collective identity (Ashforth and Johnson, 2001). As members of an organization, employees usually develop and internalize the organizational identity, which establishes harmony and commitment within the organization (Ashforth and Mael, 1989). Especially in merger situations, where the visibility of membership becomes high, the organizational identity becomes salient to the members (Ashforth and Mael, 1989; Hogg and Terry, 2000) and hence becomes an important source of social identity and self-concept. In this section, we will explain how intergroup cognitions impact employees' organizational identity in corporate merger contexts.

Organizational Identity in Merger Contexts

The concept of organizational identity was introduced by Albert and Whetten (1985). They defined organizational identity as a set of attributes that its members use to describe what is central, distinctive, and enduring about their organization (Albert and Whetten, 1985). Meanwhile, it is important to notice that perceived organizational identity matters in the relationship between organizational identity and members' attitudes and behaviors (Dutton, Dukerich, and Harquail, 1994). Perceived organizational identity is a set of a particular individual member's beliefs about his/her organization (Dutton et al., 1994). In other words, whereas the collective organizational identity is at the organizational level, perceived organizational identity is at the individual level. Because an organizational identity emerges through social interactions among organizational members and other stakeholders (Scott and Lane, 2000), what matters to employees' attitudes and behavior is the perceived organizational identity rather than collective beliefs regarding the central, distinctive, and enduring attributes of an organization (Dutton et al., 1994). Dutton and her colleagues propose that the more attractive one's perceived organizational identity, the more strongly he or she identifies with the organization. Organizational identification, defined as perceived oneness with an organization (Mael and Ashforth, 1992), is strongly influenced by perceived organizational identity (Dutton et al., 1994). Furthermore, positively perceived organizational identity enhances self-esteem, self-continuity, and feelings of distinctiveness.

Often, in corporate mergers, employees are forced to give up their premerger identity and to identify with a new postmerger organization. Schweiger et al. (1987) suggest that the employees can become disoriented when they experience loss of organizational identity. Furthermore, loss of organizational identity in corporate mergers may lead to lower levels of organizational commitment and identification (Ashforth and Mael 1989; Mark, 1994). Thus, loss of organizational identity in M&A situations can be inevitable and harmful to both the organization and the employees. Furthermore, given the context-dependent nature of social identity, it is imperative to examine how to manage employees' organizational identity during merger implementation. In other words, to make a merger successful, the organization needs to appropriately manage its employees' organizational identity. We will refer the perceived organizational identity during postmerger implementation as "merger identity."

There are cases, however, where it is difficult for employees to give up their premerger identity, and there are other cases where they simply do not wish to do so. When Phillip Morris acquired General Foods Corporation in 1985, this latter problem seemed to apply. Employees at General Foods thought of themselves as people who made "wholesome" products such as Jell-O and Maxwell House coffee. When they were acquired by Phillip Morris, these employees had to come to terms with now being employees of a firm that sold cigarettes and beer (Miller Brewing Company had already been acquired by Phillip Morris). Unfortunately, a move by Phillip Morris to try to build a new merger identity (see below) was to continue a long-standing policy of handing each employee a carton of cigarettes every Friday. This had the effect of strengthening the General Foods premerger identity, and Phillip Morris had problems "digesting" General Foods for a while.

Merger Identity

We define merger identity as transitional organizational identity perceived during merger implementation processes. A merger identity is developed based on how an employee perceives the merging process. In other words, merger identity is a set of perceived attributes that employees use to describe merger processes implemented by the new, merged organization. As perceived organizational identity is closely related to the level of employee organizational commitment, merger identity may have a significant impact on employees' attitudes and behaviors toward merger implementation. Because it usually takes a long time for an employee to develop a new identity with the new, merged organization, during the transition period of the merging process merger identity would be directly influential for employee attitudes toward the new, merged organization. If an employee has a favorable merger identity, he/she will commit him/herself more to merger implementation.

Merger identity reflects the context-dependent nature of an individual's organizational identity during the period of merger implementation. The characterization of identity as an enduring or stable notion is problematic especially when the organization is changing (Gioia, Schultz, and Corley, 2000). Organizational identity is revised when the organizational structure, culture, or boundaries change (Dutton et al., 1994), and corporate mergers usually cause changes in these areas (especially of the acquired organization). Thus, in a corporate merger, employees may develop a new organizational identity of the newly merged organization. The nature of that new organizational identity, however, depends on the nature of merger implementation.

In a corporate merger, the employees of both the acquired and the acquiring company may be forced to abandon one or more of their premerger values and norms in order to accept those of the merged company; furthermore, it will take time to build an identity with the new organization. Thus, it is natural that M&A threaten loss of organizational identity. Because organizational identity is one of the major parts of self-concept, as discussed before, loss of organizational identity is "like an anchor being taken away"

(Schweiger et al., 1987). It is also one of the most common merger stressors (Nahavandi and Malekzadeh, 1993). Mael (1988) suggests that loss of identity is associated with loss of a mentor, decreased job involvement and satisfaction, and increased turnover. In addition, giving up their premerger identity may be experienced as "surrendering" to the acquirer.

Thus, members often resist developing a new identity in order to preserve their premerger identity (Nahavandi and Malekzadeh, 1993). Mottola (1996) examined the effects of relative group status with their alumni in a scenario-based field experiment. He found that the equal-status condition, where equality of status is based on each group's superiority on different dimensions, resulted in the participants' highest identification with the merged organization. These studies suggest that a threat to and/or loss of organizational identity in a corporate merger may cause employees to develop unfavorable identities with the merged organization during the period of merger implementation. Therefore, to maintain a committed workforce, the merged organization should be able to manage appropriately employees' transitional identity during the integration period (that is, merger identity). In other words, if employees develop favorable merger identities, then they may highly commit themselves to the merger implementation. In addition, to help employees to have favorable merger identities, the merged organization needs to minimize the threat of loss of organizational identity, which we will discuss in the next section.

Intergroup Cognitions and Merger Identity

In corporate mergers, the intergroup cognitions may threaten the loss of organizational identities because of the following reasons. Firstly, in a corporate merger the salience of dual premerger identities exists (Hogg and Terry, 2000). As we discussed earlier, two previously independent organizations merge in a corporate merger, and employees are forced to build a new organizational identity. They are likely to hold their premerger organizational identity, not only because they tend to continue to define themselves in terms of membership of the premerger organization owing to the inertial cognitive process (Tsui et al., 1992), but also because they engage in social identity processes given the high level of uncertainty.

Secondly, in corporate mergers, employees become worried about intergroup relations due to the social identity process, in particular social comparison. They may pay more attention to the intergroup-related thoughts and information because the existence of intergroup relations becomes salient, and also because they think that their fates now depend more on the nature of the intergroup relations than before the merger. For example, the employees of the acquiring company may feel threatened if the intergroup relations are unstable (more mobility for the employees of the acquired company). On the other hand, the employees of the acquired company may fear job loss if they expect the other party (the acquirer) to have control over them. Intergroup cognitions may threaten existing identities because with intergroup cognitions employees tend to pay more attention to intergroup relations rather than a new, more inclusive organizational identity and to be afraid of losing their identity by the others in the merger. Finally, because it takes time to build an identity with the new organization, during the period of integration employees tend to be more vulnerable to experiencing loss of identity, which is more exaggerated by intergroup cognitions.

As discussed before, a threat of loss of organizational identity may cause merger identity to be unfavorable during the merger implementation. Therefore, we argue that intergroup cognitions are likely to lead the employees to have an unfavorable merger identity. In other words, intergroup cognitions caused by a self-categorization process may threaten existing identities and lead to an unfavorable merger identity and accordingly inhibit employees from committing themselves to their jobs by letting them focus on maintaining their existing organizational identities. Thus, it is beneficial (to both the organization and the employees) to minimize threat to loss of organizational identity aggravated by intergroup cognitions in corporate mergers. In turn, this helps employees to develop a favorable merger identity.

Summary

Corporate mergers (or acquisitions) produce a great deal of uncertainty for employees. These conditions make their social identities more salient (and more important) as a means of dealing with the uncertainty. But, an important part of an employee's social identity is their organizational identity. At the same time as the employee needs to have a clear social identity to rely upon, the changes that are taking place can threaten their organizational identity. Thus, it is important for us to know how to deal with the transitions of organizational identity caused by corporate mergers. If the (new) organization is not able to help the employee develop a positive "merger identity" (that is, an identity with the new organization during the period of merger implementation), then less commitment to the merger implementation will occur, which can seriously threaten the success of the merger. If, on the other hand, the organization can help employees to maintain their stable and constructive self-concepts, the new, merged company can keep them motivated and committed to their jobs. Thus, we argue that managing employees' merger identity is critical to the success of corporate mergers, and that merger identity is influenced by intergroup cognitions in the merger process.

Specifically, if employees engage in intergroup cognitions, they may have difficulty in developing a favorable identity of the new organization because of (a) the salience of dual premerger identities; (b) the increased level of anxiety about intergroup relations; and/or (c) the threat to their existing organizational identity. In turn, employees may lose the stability of their self-concept and begin to commit to dysfunctional attitudes and behaviors (such as lowered organizational commitment, reduced identification, and higher turnover). Therefore, the newly merged organization needs to manage its employees' merger identities in order to keep their self-concepts unwavering to ensure commitment to the merger implementation. Because self-concept is "an interpretive structure that mediates how people behave and feel in a social context" (Dutton et al., 1994, p. 242), the instability in employees' self-concepts may lead to confusion and frustration in their social lives and work.

Psychological Communication Interventions and Corporate Mergers Revisited

At the outset of this chapter, we suggested that communications were critical for helping employees to get through the M&A process. We also emphasized the importance of a specific type of communications, which we termed "psychological communication interventions." These interventions provide clear and accurate information *and* allow two-way communications with employees. But, in addition to transmitting information, these interventions also send the message that the new organization cares about the employees and is sympathetic with what they are going through. Furthermore, psychological communication interventions help employees to build a favorable identity with the merged organization by minimizing intergroup cognitions. Thus, we described these communications as having both an accurate information component and a priming component, and we noted that both of these components were important for understanding how these interventions functioned. We therefore return to these different types of communication interventions, and discuss how each can aid in the psychological process proposed earlier, arguing how psychological communication interventions may well hold the key to more successful M&A. Figure 10.2 helps to illustrate the role psychological communications can play.

Realistic Information and Uncertainty Reduction

"The biggest reason for failure of change efforts was due to employees' learning of the change from outsiders" (Richardson and Denton, 1996, p. 203). An important role for any communication intervention, then, is to provide realistic information that can reduce uncertainty. As a result, there have been a number of studies demonstrating how communications can

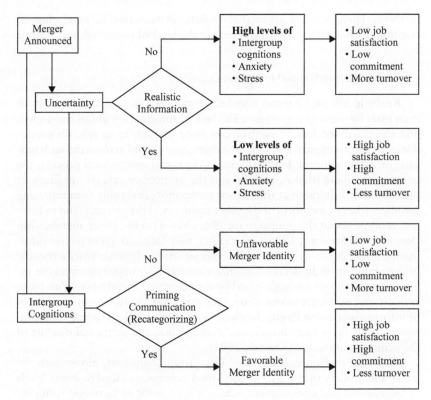

FIGURE **10.2** Flow Chart Explaining the Roles of Psychological Communications in Corporate Mergers

facilitate a merger or acquisition, by reducing uncertainty before, during, and after M&A (Difonzo and Bordia, 1998; Meyer, Allen, and Topolnytsky, 1997; Richardson and Denton, 1996; Schweiger and DeNisi, 1991). Moreover, successful communication may be contingent on the proper management of uncertainty resulting from changes induced by the intended M&A (Difonzo and Bordia, 1998).

As illustrated in Figure 10.2, when realistic information is not provided, employees may seek other sources of information such as rumors and informal communications (Napier, Simmons, and Stratton, 1988), which have been found to have detrimental effects on the change efforts (Richardson and Denton, 1996). Schweiger and DeNisi (1991) show that realistic communication through a merger preview program significantly reduces dysfunctional outcomes of the merger such as perceived uncertainty and stress, decreases in job satisfaction and commitment, and increases in intentions to leave. Therefore, we argue that realistic information of psychological communication interventions can reduce the level of perceived uncertainty.

Realistic Information and Intergroup Cognitions

Realistic information can also help employees to avoid (or at least, to minimize) intergroup cognitions. The lack of information about themselves and the perceived loss of control can force employees to rely on group-distinctive stereotypical and normative perceptions and actions through self-categorization process. Furthermore, in the social comparison process, the ingroup members (that is, members of the original company) are likely to use subjective criteria to evaluate their group more favorably than outgroup members (that is, members of the other company in the merger), and to form a stereotype about the outgroup members based on the group membership (Stephan and Stephan, 1996), especially if they lack enough objective information about the other group and merger situations. In other words, the role of communication in decreasing uncertainty is also important because intergroup cognitions are aggravated by the perceived uncertainty. With more realistic and authentic information, they don't have to rely on other sources of information; accordingly, they will be less vulnerable to intergroup cognitions such as ingroup favoritism, stereotyping, and irrational distrust of the acquiring company (Kramer, 1994).

As noted in Figure 10.2, these intergroup cognitions, along with the stress and anxiety that is part of the M&A process, can lead to lower levels of satisfaction and commitment, which in turn leads to increased turnover. Although some employees may lose their jobs as part of the M&A process, the organization does not want employees to choose to leave, because the better (more valued) employees are likely to have the most mobility and thus are most likely to quit. Realistic communication, then, can make the M&A process more effective by reducing intergroup cognitions, anxiety and stress, and their related outcomes.

Communication Interventions and Priming Effects

As noted in Figure 10.2, psychological communication interventions can also facilitate the priming of personal identity and higher order identity (re-categorizing), which can reduce intergroup cognitions. Because of the very nature of corporate mergers, collective identity (that is, social or organizational identity) is usually more salient than personal identity (Tsui et al., 1992), but as the collective identity most salient to an employee is probably the identity with his or her former organization (rather than with the new organization), reliance upon collective identity can lead to increased levels of intergroup cognitions. It is therefore helpful if the merged company could shift the employees' attention from collective identity to personal identity through psychological communication interventions, especially during the early stage of merger processes.

For example, employees with high individual ability may be more enthusiastic about the merger if they know there are opportunities for upward mobility (Ellemers, et al., 1988). Therefore, psychological communication interventions may help by providing them with valuable information, such as opportunities for upward mobility and other individual-based information regarding staffing, compensation, and career development. By helping employees to focus on personal identity during the early stage of merger processes, these interventions may succeed in reducing intergroup cognitions and increasing employees' commitment (Brewer and Gardner, 1996).

While priming personal identity focuses on individuality, recategorization (that is, priming a more inclusive identity) focuses on building up a common identity among the employees of the two merging organizations (Gaertner et al., 1993). Recategorization of "us vs. them" into "we are one" minimizes intergroup cognitions in a corporate merger. Gaertner and his colleagues (1993) proposed common identity theory, which argues that if members of different groups are induced to conceive of themselves as a common group rather than as two separate groups, the members will fall into less intergroup bias. Similarly, if employees of the merged organization are more inclined to perceive the new, merged company as one rather than two, they may engage in less intergroup cognitions. By *priming* the new merged organization's identity (one common identity) rather than premerger organizational identity ("us vs. them") merger managers can reduce employees' intergroup cognitions. In turn, the employees feel more favor toward their merger identity because there is no more threat to their organizational identities resulting from intergroup cognitions.

For example, communication interventions that emphasize the common fate of the employees without regard to their original membership will greatly reduce employees' intergroup cognitions in corporate mergers. In addition, if the merged company communicates the desirability of interactions with their counterparts of the other company, it may lead the employees to think they are working together for a common goal. In addition, emphasizing accomplishments that are achieved together may result in turning skepticism about the other company into more positive feelings about the acquisition and the potential that the two firms might achieve.

Even the use of words referring to different levels of self-concept (for example, personal and collective identity) and to different group status (for example, ingroup and outgroup status) can heavily affect individuals' attitudes and evaluative feelings. For instance, Brewer and Gardner (1996) imply that priming of different levels of self-concept (personal, relational, and collective) can lead to different perceptions of other people and groups. In a set of three experiments, they demonstrated that activation of collective identities (using "we and "us") lowered the threshold for perceived similarity of ambiguous information to their own views. In addition, Perdue et al. (1990) showed that common collective pronouns referring to ingroup (for example, "us" or "we") helped participants to build more inclusive common identity and to unconsciously have positive emotional significance. They demonstrated that words referring to ingroup categorization generated strongly positive evaluative and affective responses, and that ingroup and outgroup pronouns influenced social information processing by introducing evaluative (positive and negative) biases automatically into the perception of others. These results imply that collective nouns used in communications can mediate judgments and perceptions of members of the other organization in a merger by the processes of semantic priming and higher order semantic conditioning (Perdue et al., 1990). Therefore, in communications during the merger implementation, priming more inclusive social identity to employees is likely to be critical to dealing with intergroup cognitions.

Psychological Communications and Attraction

Finally, psychological communication interventions can serve to make the new organization more attractive to the employees. As noted earlier, the original intervention tested by Schweiger and DeNisi (1991) relied upon the literature on realistic job previews for its theoretical underpinnings. Research in the area of realistic job previews has indicated that these interventions operate through a number of mechanisms. Two of the most important for this discussion relate to making the organization more attractive to the (prospective) employee. In the case of M&As, psychological interventions should provide full information to the employee and allow the employee to ask questions and obtain any further information desired. By indicating its willingness to discuss any and all aspects of the merger or acquisition, the organization communicates that it can be trusted, and honestly deals with employees.

As illustrated in Figure 10.2, all of this can make the organization more attractive to the employees. The attractiveness of the new organization is further enhanced when intergroup cognitions are reduced, and this should also be an outcome of psychological communication interventions. Therefore, these interventions should help insure that employees will develop a new favorable organizational identity during the integration period. Such a positive merger identity, along with the increased attractiveness of the new organization that results, leads to increased commitment and reduced turnover.

This open and full information can also operate to make the employee feel that any decision to remain was purely volitional. Those employees who do elect to remain, then, are more likely to be committed to make the new enterprise work, and less likely to leave in the future. Thus, psychological communication interventions can also help make the new organization more attractive to employees by portraying itself as honest, as well as an organization that allows employees to make fully informed decisions.

Conclusion

Consistent with the theme of this volume, and its emphasis on the role that sociocoginitive factors play in the M&A process, we have proposed a model for managing human resources during M&A, which focuses on intergroup cognitions and merger identity. This model is presented and discussed in the context of communication interventions during the M&A process because we believe that (a) intergroup cognitions and merger identity are critical factors in determining the success of any M&A activity and (2) we believe that certain types of communication interventions might be useful in producing low intergroup cognitions and a strong, positive merger identity. We propose that if a newly merged organization is faced with integration-related problems such as employees' resistance to change, lower levels of commitment to the new organization, and higher rates of employee turnover, then the organization will be unlikely to achieve the goals of the merger.

If an organization can communicate effectively (relying upon what we termed "psychological communication interventions"), it can reduce employees' perceived uncertainty and intergroup cognitions, and ultimately help them to build more favorable social identity with the newly merged organization. Thus, effective communications can replace social identities based on premerger organizations with a new identity based on the postmerger organization. In this process, employee commitment and attachment should increase, as well as cooperation among employees so that everyone will be working toward a successful outcome for the merger or acquisition.

It is our hope that the proposed model and framework might provide some insights for organizations who are about to engage in some type of M&A activity. We also hope that this approach can lead to additional research in the area. Despite the best efforts of a number of scholars and practitioners, we still do not understand enough about the factors that contribute to the success or failure of a merger or acquisition. Our model can generate a number of testable hypotheses and research questions for subsequent research. If some of these issues can be addressed, a deeper understanding of how to better manage human resources during M&A may emerge.

References

Abrams, D., and Hogg, M. (1988). Comments on the motivational status of self-esteem in social identity and intergroup discrimination. *European Journal of Social Psychology*, 18: 317–34.

Albert, S., and Whetten, D. A. (1985). Organizational identity. *Research in Organizational Behavior*, 7: 263–95. Greenwich, CT: JAI Press.

Ashforth, B. E. (1989). The experience of powerlessness in organizations. *Organizational Behavior and Human Decision Processes*, 43: 207–42.

Ashforth, B. E., and Johnson, S. A. (2001). Which hat to wear? The relative salience of multiple identities in organizational contexts. In Hogg and Terry (eds.), *Social Identity Processes in Organizational Contexts*. Philadelphia, PA: Psychology Press, pp. 31–48.

Ashforth, B. E., and Mael, F. (1989). Social identity theory and the organization. *Academy of Management Review*, 14(1): 20–39.

Bachman, B. A. (1993). *An Intergroup Model of Organizational Mergers*. Unpublished doctoral dissertation, University of Delaware.

Bastien, D. T. (1987). Common patterns of behavior and communication in corporate mergers and acquisitions. *Human Resource Management*, 26(1): 17–34.

Brewer, M. B., and Gardner, W. (1996). Who is this "we"? Levels of collective identity and self representations. *Journal of Personality and Social Psychology*, 71: 83–93.

Brewer, M. B., and Weber, J. G. (1994). Self-evaluation effects of interpersonal versus intergroup social comparison. *Journal of Personality and Social Psychology*, 66: 268–75.

Buono, A. F., Bowditch, J. L., and Lewis, J. W. (1985). When cultures collide: The anatomy of a merger. *Human Relations*, 38: 477–500.

DiFonzo, N., and Bordia, P. (1998). A tale of two corporations: Managing uncertainty during organizational change. *Human Resource Management*, 37: 295–303.

Dugoni, B. L., and Ilgen, D. R. (1981). Realistic job previews and the adjustment of new employees. *Academy of Management Journal*, 24, 579–91.

Dutton, J. E., Dukerich, J. M., and Harquail, C. V. (1994). Organizational images and member identification. *Administrative Science Quarterly*, 39: 239–63.

Ellemers, N., van Knippenberg, A., de Vires, N., and Wilke, H. (1988). Social identification and permeability of group boundaries. *European Journal of Social Psychology*, 18: 497–513.

Fried, Y., Tiegs, R. B., Naughton, T. J., and Ashforth, B. E. (1996). Managers' reactions to a corporate acquisition: A test of an integrative model. *Journal of Organizational Behavior*, 17: 401–27.

Gaertner, S. L., Dovidio, J. F., Anastasio, P. A., Bachman, B. A., and Rust, M. C. (1993). The common group ingroup identity model: Recategorization and the reduction of intergroup bias. In Stroebe and Hewstone (eds.), *The European Review of Social Psychology*, Vol. 4. London: Wiley, pp. 1–126.

Gioia, D. A., Schultz, M., and Corley, K. G. (2000). Organizational identity, image and adaptive instability. *Academy of Management Review*, 25: 63–81.

Haunschild, P. R., Moreland, R. L., and Murrell, A. J. (1994). Sources of resistance to mergers between groups. *Journal of Applied Psychology*, 24: 1150–78.

Hogg, M. A. (2000). Social identity and social comparison. In Suls and Wheeler (eds.), *Handbook of Social Comparison: Theory and Research*. New York: Kluwer Academic/Plenum Publishers, pp. 401–21.

Hogg, M. A., and Abrams, D. (1988). *Social Identifications: A Social Psychology of Intergroup Relations and Group Process*. London: Routledge.

Hogg, M. A., and Terry, D. (2000). Social identity and self-categorization processes in organizational contexts. *Academy of Management Review*, 25: 121–40.

Hogg, M. A., and Terry, D. (2001). Social identity theory and organizational processes. In Hogg and Terry (eds.), *Social Identity Processes in Organizational Contexts*. Philadelphia, PA: Psychology Press, pp. 1–12.

Hogg, M. A., and Turner, J. C. (1987). Intergroup behaviour, self-stereotyping and the salience of social categories. *British Journal of Social Psychology*, 26: 325–40.

Ivancevich, J. M., Schweiger, D. M., and Power, F. R. (1987). Strategies for managing human resources during mergers and acquisitions. *Human Resource Planning*, 10(1): 19–35.

Kramer, R. M. (1994). The sinister attribution error: Paranoid cognition and collective distrust in organization. *Motivation and Emotion*, 18(2): 199–230.

Kramer, R. M., and Messick, D. M. (1998). Getting by with a little help from our enemies: Collective paranoia and its role intergroup relations. In Sedikides, Schopler, and Insko (eds.), *Intergroup Cognition and Intergroup Behaviors*. Mahwah, NJ: LEA, pp. 233–55.

Mael, F. (1988). *Organizational Identification: Construct Redefinition and a Field Application with Organizational Alumni*. Unpublished doctoral dissertation, Wayne State University, Detroit.

Mael, F., and Ashforth, B. E. (1992). Alumni and their alma mater: A partial test of the reformulated model of organizational identification. *Journal of Organizational Behavior*, 13: 103–23.

Marks, M. L. (1994). *From Turmoil to Triumph: New Life After Mergers, Acquisitions, and Downsizing*. New York: Lexington Books.

Marks, M. L., and Mirvis, P. (1985). Merger syndrome: Stress and uncertainty. *Mergers and Acquisitions*, 20(1): 70–6.

Marks, M. L., and Mirvis, P. (1986). Merger syndrome: Management by crisis. *Mergers and Acquisitions*, 21(1): 50–5.

Marks, M. L., and Mirvis, P. (1992). Rebuilding after merger: Dealing with "survival sickness." *Organizational Dynamics* 21(2): 18–32.

Marks, M. L., and Mirvis, P. (1997a). Revisiting the merger syndrome: Dealing with stress. *Mergers and Acquisitions*, 31(6): 21–7.

Marks, M. L., and Mirvis, P. (1997b). Revisiting the merger syndrome: Crisis management part 2. *Mergers and Acquisitions*, 32(1): 34–40.

Marks, M. L., and Mirvis, P. (2001). Making mergers and acquisitions work: Strategic and psychological preparation. *Academy of Management Executive*, 15(1): 80–92.

Meglino, B. M., DeNisi, A. S., Youngblood, S. A., and Williams, K. J. (1988). Effects of realistic job previews: A comparison using an "enhancement" and "reduction" preview. *Journal of Applied Psychology*, 73, 259–66.

Mottola, G. R. (1996). *The Effects of Relative Group Status on Expectations of Merger Success*. Unpublished doctoral dissertation, University of Delaware.

Mottola, G. R., Bachman, B. A., Gaertner, S. L., and Dovidio, J. F. (1997). How groups merge: Anticipated commitment to the merged organization. *Journal of Applied Social Psychology*, 27: 1335–58.

Myer, J. P., Allen, N. J., and Topolnytsky, L. (1997). Commitment in a changing world of work. *Canadian Psychology*, 39(1/2): 83–93.

Nahavandi, A., and Malekzadeh, A. R. (1993). *Organization Culture in the Management of Mergers*. Quorum Books.

Napier, N. K., Simmons, G., and Stratton, K. (1989). Communication during a merger: Experience of two banks. *Human Resource Planning*, 12: 105–22.

Perdue, C. W., Dovidio, J. F., Gurtman, M. B., and Tyler, R. B. (1990). Us and them: Social categorization and the process of intergroup bias. *Journal of Personality and Social Psychology*, 59: 475–86.

Phillips, J. M. (1998). Effects of realistic job previews on multiple organizational outcomes: A meta-analysis. *Academy of Management Journal*, 41: 673–90.

Rentsch, J. R., and Schneider, B. (1991). Expectations for postcombination organizational life: A study of responses to mergers and acquisition scenarios. *Journal of Applied Social Psychology*, 21: 233–52.

Richardson, P., and Denton, D. K. (1996). Communicating change. *Human Resource Management*, 35(2): 203–16.

Salancik, G. R. (1977). Commitment is too easy. *Organizational Dynamics*, 6: 62–80.

Salancik, G. R., and Pfeffer, J. (1978). A social information processing approach to job attitudes and task design. *Administrative Science Quarterly*, 23: 224–53.

Schaller, M., Rosell, M. C., and Asp, C. H. (1998). Parsimony and pluralism in the psychological study of intergroup processes. In Sedikides, Schopler, and

Insko (eds.), *Intergroup Cognition and Intergroup Behaviors.* Mahwah, NJ: Lawrence Erlbaum Associates, pp. 3–26.

Schweiger, D. M., and DeNisi, A. S. (1991). Communication with employees following a merger: A longitudinal field experiment. *Academy of Management Journal,* 34(1): 110–35.

Scott, S. G., and Lane, V. R. A. (2000). Stakeholder approach to organizational identity. *Academy of Management Review,* 25: 43–62.

Spears, R., Doosje, B., and Ellemers, N. (1997). Self-stereotyping in the face of threats to group status and distinctiveness: The role of group identification. *Personality and Social Psychological Bulletin,* 23: 538–53.

Stephan, W. G., and Stephan, C. W. (1996). *Intergroup Relations.* Westview Press.

Tajfel, H. (1981). Social stereotype and social groups. In Turner and Giles (eds.), *Intergroup Behavior.* Oxford, UK: Blackwell, 144–67.

Tajfel, H., and Turner, J. C. (1979). An integrative theory of intergroup conflict. In Austin and Worchel (eds.), *The Social Psychology of Intergroup Psychology.* Monterey, CA: Brooks-Cole, pp. 33–47.

Tsui, A. S., Egan, T. D., and O'Reilly III, C. A. (1992). Being different: Relational demography and organizational attachment. *Administrative Science Quarterly,* 37: 549–79.

Turner, J. C. (1982). Towards a cognitive redefinition of the social group. In Tajfel (ed.), *Social Identity and Intergroup Relations.* Cambridge, UK: Cambridge University Press, pp. 15–40.

Turner, J. C. (1985). A self-categorization theory. In Turner, Hogg, Oaks, Reicher, and Wetherell (eds.), *Rediscovering the Social Group: A Self-Categorization Theory.* Oxford, UK: Blackwell, pp. 42–67.

Turner, J. C., Oakes, P. J., Haslam, S. A., and McGarty, C. (1994). Self and collective: Cognition and social context. *Personality and Social Psychology Bulletin,* 20: 454–63.

Executive Commentary on Chapter 10

MARK JONES

The most consistent theme in studies of mergers and acquisitions (M&A) is that for the predicted shareholder value to be realized, the success of the postmerger integration process is critically important. It is often further argued that the creation of a single "new" organization "culture"—be it an integration of the two existing cultures or the acquiring organization culture subsuming that of the acquired business—is the most important single aspect of post-M&A integration. It is asserted that there is a direct causal link between this and the realization or prevention of increased shareholder value.

This is a central assumption of DeNisi and Shin's argument when they propose that psychological communication interventions are a key tool that can lead to "low intergroup cognitions and a strong, positive merger identity" and therefore increased likelihood of meeting merger goals.

Even the most positive merger experiences are not without their share of uncertainty and stress. Hindsight will almost always reveal how much more successful they could have been with a clearer common understanding of the communications strategy, if communication had started sooner and been addressed with greater transparency, consistency, and frequency.

As soon as employees become aware of an impending merger, they are typically thrown into a period of great uncertainty. Reactions and emotions vary from a sense of general trepidation to one of personal loss (especially within an acquired organization). Even those in an acquiring organization will often privately be dealing with feelings of insecurity as a new source of competition for their jobs is created. The overriding sense for most, however, is associated with loss of control. The vacuum of information typically available to employees once a merger or acquisition is announced simply compounds this sense.

Management's response is typically reactive rather than proactive and is often constrained by what they perceive they can tell employees because of legal, competitive, or commercial constraints on disclosure of information prior to closure of the deal. In most cases, management is overcautious about what they can reveal and in any event, as suggested by DeNisi and Shin, employees have an uncanny ability to find the information they need from other less reliable sources.

Management teams will often engage in lengthy debates about how much detail of postmerger restructuring can be disclosed to employees. Meanwhile even as these deliberations are in progress, employees of both organizations will be openly discussing the options and their impact through Internet "chat rooms."

Twenty-first-century communications channels mean that rumors and false information spread in minutes to vast numbers of employees. Stress and uncertainty are created at enormous speed. Furthermore, once created, the effort and time needed to mitigate against them is hugely disproportionate to that which created them. I would contend therefore that management time invested in utilizing models such as that proposed here and in applying a proactive communications strategy will have a rapid payback. It is however rarely an investment that is adequately addressed.

As speed of information provision is so important, intranet-based communication channels can be a key tool organizations can use to manage information-based communications (key messages, job opportunities, and so on). However, the intranet is a less effective management tool for dealing with psychological communication interventions, particularly those that benefit from a two-way exchange. The majority of employees want to receive key pieces of information from their immediate boss and to have the opportunity to question that information and receive an immediate response from someone they trust.

Management must, of course, be prepared to deal with the consequences of being more transparent in information provision. The examples of "realistic merger preview" through the provision of "job preview" deals with one aspect of employees' need to regain a sense of control. Once employees understand what their options are, they can make choices (that is, decide whether this is a job they want) and shape their future. This, of course, may mean a decision to leave, which, considered in isolation, may not appear to be in the new organization's interests. I would still argue however that giving employees a sense of control through the provision of reasonably detailed job information is more likely to create a productive and positive outcome for the merger and the business overall than when this is not the case. Generally speaking, once uncertainty is removed and employees have regained a degree of control, they will commit to the success of the business even if they do not see themselves as part of its long-term future. (The proviso is of course that they perceive they will be treated fairly and professionally in leaving the organization.) The majority of people will accept significant personal change if they perceive that the process that led to it has been "fair."

For those who stay, the role that psychological communication interventions play in creating a new organizational identity is critical. In conversations with employees who originated from an organization that was acquired over a decade ago, it was clear that large elements of the identity of the acquired organization remained. Even after many years an "us and them" undercurrent was preventing the combined organization from leveraging some of the potential synergies. The ability of employees to hold their premerger organizational identity as a result of the inertial cognitive process combined with strong social identity created by high levels of uncertainty can clearly be sustained over many years!

The proposition that "as perceived organizational identity is closely related to the level of employee organizational commitment, merger identity may have a significant impact on employees' attitudes and behavior towards merger implementation" resounds strongly with my own experience. During a major acquisition, it was planned that large parts of the acquired organization would be transferred intact into the acquiring company while other groups of employees would be absorbed but into unknown roles. Employees from those units that were to be transferred intact displayed a general sense of purpose and commitment to the change, and even at an early stage, they began to take on some elements of the acquiring organization's "identity." Those who lacked clarity about their future positions and had no sense of future organizational identity became solely focused on personal outcomes. As they could not answer the question "what's in it for me," they typically became dysfunctional and resistant to change.

Although there has been extensive research and writing on success and failure in M&A, DeNisi and Shin's assertion that "we still do not understand enough about the factors that contribute to success or failure [in M&A's]" remains true. We need further research and testing of these and other models on the subject. Those working in human resources and other related areas of the business inherently believe and understand that proactively managing the human element of postmerger integration has to start early with the rest of the premerger activity. It has to be treated equally with other aspects of pre-M&A due diligence and financial evaluation. All too often, however, it is addressed as one of the reactive outcomes of the M&A decision. To change this, we need stronger arguments and evidence to convince the business decision makers of this logic. This model and framework is a positive step in that direction.

11   Developing a Framework for Cultural Due Diligence in Mergers and Acquisitions

Issues and Ideas

SUSAN CARTWRIGHT AND SIMON McCARTHY

The underperformance of mergers and acquisitions (M&A) continues to be the focal point of much debate and attention. However, there is little argument that those who consistently gain from M&A activity are the divesting shareholders of the target firm and the lawyers and "marriage brokers" involved in the deals. While overall some sectors, for example, banking and insurance, tend to record higher success rates than others in terms of enhanced shareholder value, the success of a few top performers often masks the failure of the majority (Financial Times, August 2000). According to a recent report (KPMG, 2000) 83 percent of all deals fail to deliver shareholder value and an alarming 53 percent actually destroyed value. The report concludes that underperformance is the outcome of excessive focus on "closing the deal" at the expense of attending to factors that will ensure its success.

The factors that influence the decision to "close the deal" are invariably overtly of a financial and strategic nature. The attractiveness of an acquisition target or a potential merger partner has much to do with availability, price, projected economies of scale, and strategic fit. It is also not uncommon for M&A activity to be motivated by executive greed or fear of obsolescence (Cartwright and Cooper, 1996). As FitzRoy, Acs, and Gerlowski (1998) observe, executive remuneration and compensation are both closely related to organizational size.

There have been numerous studies that have examined the relationship between financial performance and the strategic fit of the combining organizations (Chatterjee et al., 1992; Lubatkin, 1987; Singh and Montgomery, 1987). Such studies have failed to find a consistent relationship and have inadequately explained the large variance in performance amongst mergers where the strategic fit was considered to be good. This is not surprising for the simple reason that strategic fit is not the only determinant of financial performance but one of a number of complex interrelated factors. In an attempt to better grasp an understanding of this complex phenomenon, an increasing range of management researchers have contributed to try and explain the unsatisfactory outcomes that result from many mergers. A number of studies have examined the impact of structural variables such as acquisition type and the relative size of the combining firms (Buono and Bowditch, 1989; Haspeslagh and Jemison, 1991). Others have focused on the role of process management and managerial competence (Hitt, Harrison, and Ireland, 2000).

Over the last decade, considerable effort has been expended in raising the profile of human factors in M&A and the issue of culture fit. In a recent study of chief executives of Fortune 500 companies (Schweiger and Goulet, 2000), the ability or competence to manage human integration was rated as a more important factor to an M&A success than financial or strategic factors. Yet the issue of cultural compatibility, at best considered a desirable "add on," is still a factor rarely assessed in any depth during the due diligence process. When Daimler and Chrysler merged in 1999, the event was described as the biggest ever automerger and the year's smartest deal (Fortune, January 1999). As the partners' markets scarcely overlapped, the strategic fit was considered to be perfect. Yet, despite the synergistic potential, within two years, the combined company was worth less than Daimler Benz was before the merger and the hostile relationship between the United States and German management groups was widely reported in the business press (The Economist, 13 December 2000). Clearly the challenges of integrating the entrepreneurial style of a U.S. business with the conservatism of a German company proved more difficult than expected (Schoenberg, 2000). Experiences such as this serve to emphasize the importance of target or partner selection based on additional and different criteria from traditional practice (Jemison and Sitkin, 1986).

This chapter considers current theories and research evidence that have attempted to understand and investigate the contribution of culture fit to the management and financial performance of M&A. It also discusses the way in which researchers and practitioners can potentially conduct some form of "gap analysis" to identify the areas of cultural difference that are likely to impact on the integration process.

What Is Meant by Cultural Compatibility or Culture Fit?

Researchers and practitioners differ considerably in the way in which they define and conceptualize culture and the methods they use to access, assess, and interpret the culture of a given group, organization, or nation. However, there is consensus that culture is underpinned by a set of, often unconscious, assumptions, values, and beliefs that are manifested in observable symbols, rituals, and normative patterns of behavior. Because cultures provide stability, order, and a sense of cohesion, they are often difficult to change or displace, particularly if they are well established and there is strong cultural attachment.

Theories of social attraction suggest that individuals are initially attracted to others whom they perceive to be similar to themselves. Physical proximity also plays a role in that regular contact with others is a determinant of friendship patterns. Collectively, groups tend to form stereotypical attitudes toward other groups which they perceive to be very different from themselves. In most cases, such attitudes are negative in their orientation. The problem of integrating two, often previously rival workforces and their cultures and getting them to cooperate and work toward a common goal is a major challenge for M&A management. There is always the inherent danger that in the process the acquirer or dominant partner will destroy the very attributes that initially attracted it to the selected target. Fear of change and self-protection amongst managers and employees of both combining organizations invariably leads to a closing of ranks. This increased cohesiveness occurs whether or not the takeover or merger is considered to be friendly or hostile, and regardless of whether or not individuals see it as a threat or an opportunity. Characteristically, employees focus on perceived cultural differences rather than similarities and see each other as competitors, reckoning that gains on one side will be matched by losses on the other side. A "we" and "them" mentality seems to inevitably develop and territorial battles ensue over a range of major and often minor issues. What may appear a minor issue to one party could mean a great deal to the other. Furthermore, it is posited that cultural differences are exacerbated by a lack of cultural sensitivity and cultural arrogance amongst those responsible for M&A management.

From the perspective of social identity theory, culture is socially constructed and confers identity and defines meaning by its content. M&A trigger a search for continuing social identity and distinctiveness whereby members of both organizations construct an understanding and description of themselves in order to emphasize differences between the two. As Kleppestø (1998) points out, the essence of identity is determined by social comparison with others; without "others" there can be no "self." In many cases, this is an emotional rather than an intellectual or rational process. Therefore, it is argued that even in cases where there is little measurable difference in the objective content of two cultures, integration may still be difficult because differences will be socially created to legitimize continued identities (Larsson, 1993).

Much of the behavioral research into M&A had its beginning in the United States and the United Kingdom. The focus of cultural analysis was predominantly concerned with the extent to which the combining companies had similar organizational cultures (Buono and Bowditch, 1989; Graves, 1981; Levinson, 1970; Sales and Mirvis, 1984). Success measured in terms of employee support, motivation, and attitudes was considered to be dependent on the extent to which the combining cultures integrated or conflicted and the speed with which the merged organization was able to establish internal coherence.

Few studies have directly examined the relationship between culture fit and financial performance. However, one such study (Chatterjee et al., 1992) based on a sample of thirty U.S. firms did demonstrate that the capital market's perceptions about the earnings impact of a related merger are associated with the acquired managers' perceptions of cultural differences between their senior management team and that of the acquiring organization. As M&A activity has become increasingly international, the focus has widened to consider the issue of foreign ownership and the differences between national business cultures as affecting the management practices in operating countries. To date, the complex interplay between national and organizational culture and its relative importance remains perplexing. Larsson and Risberg (1998) suggest that attractiveness in the selection of international M&A is strongly linked to perceived similarity and physical proximity in that organizations tend to invest in neighboring territories or those with which they have the closest economic, linguistic, and cultural ties. Studies of international managers (Cartwright and Price, 2002; Cartwright, Cooper, and Jordan, 1995) also confirm that given a choice, organizations would prefer to partner or be acquired by a foreign national culture which they perceive to be more similar to their own and are highly avoidant of cultural distance. This study found preference clusters closely conformed to Hofstede's dimensions (Hofstede, 1980). According to Cooper and Kirkcaldy (1995), in the absence of detailed knowledge or direct experience of a potential merger partner or acquisition target, cultural stereotypes play an influential role in selection decisions in the same way that customer purchase decisions are affected by country-of-origin (COO) or product country image (PCI) effects.

There have been a number of studies that have sought to investigate the cultural dynamics of international M&A and their impact on employee behaviors and financial performance. Often these have based their findings on a single example rather than multiple cases, making it difficult to generalize as to whether the reported outcome reflects a national, as opposed to a corporate practice, effect. Studies based on multiple cases tend to suggest that the influence of organizational culture overrides national cultural differences. Schoenberg and Norburn (1998) in a study of 129 European cross-border acquisitions found that other than attitudes toward risk-taking, national cultural differences had little impact on financial performance. Other studies (Cartwright and Cooper, 1996; Very, Lubatkin, and Veiga, 1997) have also found that irrespective of nationality if the buyer's culture is perceived as being relatively less controlling, then it is more likely to be perceived as being more attractive and hence more acceptable.

The question of subcultures within an organization, or regional differences within national cultures, which doubtless exist, adds a further layer of complexity to the issue. However, this issue has perhaps conveniently received cursory acknowledgment and little research attention.

While Chatterjee et al. (1992) found that financial performance was linked to culture fit and cultural tolerance in decision making, they acknowledge that account needs to be taken of situational factors. As Bower (2001) observes, not all M&A are alike and consequently, therefore, not amenable to a "one size fits all" approach. A good cultural fit can only be judged when a decision has been made as to the chosen M&A integration strategy or marriage terms. Haspeslagh and Jemison (1991) suggest that degree of integration depends upon the need for strategic interdependence and the need for organizational autonomy. In terms of integration strategies (Napier, 1989), M&A are generally conceptualized as falling into three types: extension, redesign, and collaborative. Generally, when organizations decide to extend their activities into other, that is, different business, areas, cultural differences matter less, as the acquired business usually continues to operate separately, at least in the short term. However, in redesign M&A, the strategy of the acquirer or dominant merger partner is to absorb and assimilate both the activities and culture of the acquired or weaker merger partner into its own. In these circumstances, cultural differences may present a major obstacle to the "cloning" process. Similarly, genuine or collaborative mergers intended to benefit from the creation of a new "best of both worlds" culture are dependent on some degree of cultural consensus and mutual respect if they are to be successful.

The typology of integration strategies proposed by Haspeslagh and Jemison (1991) has been extensively discussed in the M&A literature. They present four possible integration strategies:

1. *Preservation*—the maintenance of separate operations, identities, and culture.
2. *Absorption*—the assimilation of the operations, identity, and culture of the acquired company into that of the acquirer.
3. *Symbiotic*—the gradual blending and integration of the two operations, identities, and cultures.
4. *Transformation*—the reinvention of a new organization requiring radical and significant changes in the operations and cultures of both.

This typology has similarity with both the typologies of Napier (1989) and Nahavandi and Malekzadeh (1988). While Napier (1989) and Haspes-lagh and Jemison (1991) conceptualize culture change as driven by business needs, Nahavandi and Malekzadeh (1988) emphasize that when two cultures come together, it is the perceptions of the organizational members of their own and each other's cultures that determines the outcome and direction of any cultural change.

Cartwright and Cooper (1996) suggest that compatibility is contingent on this cultural encounter and does not have to mean similarity. They draw the analogy with interpersonal partnerships in that those who are most similar in terms of values and personal characteristics may feel initially more comfortable about the union but do not necessarily forge the strongest and most enduring relationships. Similarly, in M&A, if the intention of an absorption approach is to achieve "economies of sameness," this is likely to be easier to achieve if the cultures are more similar. However, symbiotic or radical transformational change may only come about through the negotiation and energistic potential created by cultural differences. Schoenberg (2000) echoes this point in stating that "cultural differences should not automatically be associated with negative consequences." Instead, he argues that more specific research is needed to establish the areas of difference that are most relevant and hence predictive of future integration problems. In this way, M&A managers could more accurately assess the risk, magnitude, and severity of the problems they might face and the key competencies needed to overcome such problems, thus highlighting the importance of preliminary planning activities and the establishment of appropriate transition management structures play in M&A integration.

Evidence from Child, Faulkner, and Pitkethly (2001) attributes the success of the acquisitive Cisco Systems as being the result of meticulous planning in respect of HRM issues and an anticipatory culturally sensitive integration strategy, which may in part explain the findings of Larsson and Risberg (1998) that cultural similarity alone is not predictive of financial success.

Assessing Cultural Fit

The concept of culture due diligence in the evaluation of the suitability of a potential acquisition target or merger partner is theoretically appealing, but difficult to apply in practice. The confidential nature of negotiations means that even if the issue of culture fit is considered at the decision-making stage, the basis on which such an assessment can be made is reliant on a very limited range of data, for example, information gleaned from interactions between the buying and selling teams, corporate literature, organizational folklore, and secondhand reports from individuals with previous or current contacts with the organization. Although there are examples (Cartwright and Cooper, 2000) where merger talks have been aborted because of radical cultural differences between the negotiating teams, such circumstances are still a rarity.

The possibility of conducting some form of culture audit either prior to or immediately following any agreement to purchase presents an attractive way forward. There are a variety of questionnaire measures designed to assess culture at an organizational (Denison, 2001) and at a national level (Hofstede, 1980, p. 1991). However, as Sparrow (2001) points out, although culture audits are useful, particularly in measuring change, many audit tools assess dimensions that have no relevance or proven link to performance outcomes.

In the context of M&A there is a need for an integrated measure that can be used both domestically and internationally, which captures areas of difference that are linked to M&A outcomes. To be useful, such an instrument should also have the capability to be applied at all organizational levels— be it top teams, regions, or departments. The existence of such a measure would enable decision makers and managers to assess whether any identified differences in culture are critical, desirable, or irrelevant to the proposed integration strategy. Such an approach mirrors the use of personality tests in personnel selection to assess the "goodness" of the person-job fit. Typically, personality tests provide information about a candidate measured against multiple dimensions of personality. Such information is interpreted in the light of job requirements. The presence of certain traits will be critical to the selection decision, others may be desirable but not absolutely necessary, and some will be irrelevant to the effective execution of the job role.

The development of such an instrument if completed by the buying and selling teams would make the concept of cultural due diligence a workable possibility in

- establishing the extent of differences or gaps between combining organizations in those aspects or dimensions of culture that have proven links to integration problems which impact on performance;
- deconstructing stereotypical cultural attitudes;
- establishing a means of placing value on the cultural assets of a potential target or partner;
- informing a culturally sensitive integration plan from the outset, which could be further refined by extended and more local use of the instrument postmerger to target culture differences at department or subculture level.

Elements of this approach and the origins of a developmental methodology can be found in a study by Forstmann (1998) who designed a questionnaire

to assess the relationship between cultural differences and integration problems in the context of an international acquisition. The study involved a
large North American acquisition made by a German chemical company.
On the basis of 135 questionnaire responses, Forstmann plotted the cultural differences between the German parent and the acquired company's
operational units in Canada, United States, Belgium, and France. The questionnaire comprised of eleven cultural dimensions described as challenge, ac-
complishment, reasons, own approach, cooperation, freedom, access, time,
contribution, identity, and security. It included six potential problem areas, namely, organization, planning, control, information systems, personnel
management, and general management. The choice of cultural dimensions
included in the questionnaire was influenced primarily by existing measures
of national culture (Hofstede, 1991; Trompenaars, 1993).

However, the rationale for the inclusion or exclusion of either the chosen cultural dimensions or the problem areas is not explained. Perhaps,
more importantly, the questionnaire design does not draw upon the more
specific context-bound findings reported in the M&A literature. Given earlier comments, although this work lays important foundations for future
research and development, the measure used may be insufficiently comprehensive. In the following section we discuss the factors that may need to be
incorporated into a culture due diligence measure which integrates both organizational and national cultural perspectives and which have been linked
to performance outcomes.

Potential Factors for Assessing Culture Fit
and Integration Problems

The factors briefly described below are not presented as being the definitive or only factors that may be pertinent to the issues of cultural fit and
integration problems. They are however chosen for inclusion here because
of considerable evidence (of both a quantitative and qualitative nature) that
indicates that they could be relevant to M&A issues and that therefore such
a possibility is worthy of investigation.

Degree of Internal Integration

Internal integration refers to the extent to which relationships within an
organization are cooperative, well coordinated, and positively promote the
sharing of information and ideas and achievement of common objectives
and goals. A high degree of internal integration is likely to be manifested
in a high level of cultural consensus and effective team working. Effective
team working has consistently been linked to high-performing organizations

(Huselid, Jackson, and Schuler, 1997). A lack or low level of internal integration is conducive to the proliferation of strong subcultures and competitive relationships between functional and departmental groups, which produces organizational tensions and conflict. The result of this may be that energy is directed so much toward problems of internal integration that the merged organization is distracted from its core business and the external environment in which it operates.

At an international level, Trompenaars and Hampden-Turner (1997) suggest that western cultures tend to emphasize the divisions of labor at the expense of cross-functional/departmental cooperation. Internal integration is thus likely to vary on a micro level from organization to organization within a single nation as well as more broadly speaking between nations.

High levels of internal integration are a potential cultural asset associated with learning organizations (Senge, 1990), which may be destroyed by an insensitive and less well internally integrated acquirer.

Autonomy and Involvement

Autonomy and involvement refers to the extent to which individuals have the authority and freedom to exercise control and make decisions about the way in which they perform their jobs and feel that they are informed and aligned with what is going on in the organization. Cartwright and Cooper (1996) found support for their model that autonomy is associated with cultural attractiveness and is highly valued by organizational members. In a review of recent M&A studies, Schoenberg (2000) identifies a strong link between decreased autonomy and poor M&A performance.

Autonomy is dimension measured by most organizational culture questionnaires (Denison, 2001) and in terms of national culture measures is associated with power distance (Hofstede, 1980).

Adaptability: Speed, Innovation, and Risk

Speed, innovation, and risk are suggested as being the three key components reflecting an organization's ability to adapt, develop, and survive.

Speed refers to the length of time for decisions to be made and the ability to react quickly to changes in the environment and even predict them before they occur. At the same time, account needs to be taken of the quality of those decisions.

Innovation and creativity also have strong links with performance (Flynn and Chatman, 2001) and are areas where differences between organizations in their encouragement and attitudes toward creative and novel ideas can lead to integration problems as in the case of Daimler-Benz. Adaptability and innovation inevitably involve risk. Like autonomy, attitudes toward risk-taking have been demonstrated to have a proven link with M&A performance (Schoenberg and Norburn, 1998) and are important sources of cultural difference.

Attitudes toward risk-taking has been identified as a factor that differentiates between organizations (Deal and Kennedy, 1982) and between national cultures (Hofstede, 1980). Both Smit (2001) and Denison (2001) highlight the importance of adaptability as a key component of organization culture.

Employee Welfare, Fairness, and Trust

Employee perceptions of justice or fairness concerning how they are treated with regard to pay, promotions, and individual consideration has important consequences for organizational performance generally (Colquitt et al., 2001). In a study of cross-national M&A, employee perceptions that the merger had reduced the objectiveness of the performance and reward procedures has been found to be significantly related to increased stress levels (Very, Lubatkin, and Veiga, 1997).

Employees who feel that they are treated fairly and with respect are more inclined to exhibit high levels of organizational citizenship behaviors (OCBs) and do things for the organization over and above that which they are contractually obliged to do (Guest, 1998). Perceptions of fairness are linked to both procedural justice (how fair the organizational processes and procedures are) and distributive justice (how fairly the rewards are distributed).

Concern for employee welfare, investment in training, and attitudes toward fairness and trust differ between organizations, and at a national level (Hofstede, 1980) feminine cultures like Sweden place a greater emphasis on employee welfare and quality of work life than do masculine cultures like the United Kingdom.

Diversity

Ethnocentricity has been consistently identified as a barrier to M&A integration (Cartwright and Cooper, 1996) and relates to the tendency to evaluate that which is different as being wrong or abnormal. Therefore, diversity is a factor worth considering in the context of M&A integration in that the more diverse and culturally inclusive an organization is in terms of the composition of its workforce (for example, ethnic origins, gender, age, education, social background), the more able it might be to cope with the integration of further diversity. Diverse heterogeneous organizations or cultures have the potential advantage over more homogeneous organizations or cultures of being able to generate a wider range of solutions to problems and dilemmas. They are also likely to be less inclined toward negative cultural stereotyping. Research by Smit (2001) identifies openness to ideas and positive attitudes toward diversity as being a key aspect of healthy work groups. At a national level, the cultural membership of European countries varies significantly in terms of the diversity of its membership, for example, contrast the Netherlands with Poland. This may be important in the context of M&A in that the more diverse a country is, the more likely that organizations in that country will be culturally sensitive and accepting of others different to themselves. However, as many a civil way demonstrates, diversity is not synonymous with harmony and where on paper a society or organization appears diverse, the reality of how they integrate or "get along" may be very different.

However, we believe that in many cases diversity in the context of an M&A partner is likely to be a positive cultural asset.

Potential Integration Problem Areas

The list of possible integration problem areas is extensive and would need to be established by analyzing the collective experiences of a range of managers at different levels in organizations and business sectors, perhaps by interview. Forstmann found that cultural differences had a high discriminatory power in relation to problems in the area of planning, information systems, and personnel management. Personnel management problems were defined as concerning incentives, qualifications, personnel development, and evaluation. Problems in the area of morale and stress have been strongly linked to the M&A outcomes (Panchel and Cartwright, 2001; Very, Lubatkin, and Veiga, 1997).

Intercultural Training and Competence

Assuming that a practical, reliable, and valid measure of culture fit could be developed and the conduct of cultural due diligence did become a reality, its use could be limited by the abilities and competencies of those required to act on the information and sensitively manage the integration.

Managers have different management styles that may be a reflection of their personality or be the outcome or adaptation to organization processes and influences. Kakabadse and Myers (1996) conducted a study of European executives and concluded that senior managers exercised four different styles of management in the boardroom. However, they concluded that only the management style of French and German managers was consistent in conforming with stereotypical national characteristics.

In the context of M&A, managers need to have a heightened awareness of the impact of their managerial style on others and the limitations of their own cultural paradigm as it affects the way in which members of that culture interpret what goes on around them. Therefore, some form of communication and intercultural awareness training may be necessary to prepare negotiators and managers for interacting with employees who may be feeling angry, upset, insecure, and/or who do not share the same culture. The literature on expatriation (Jordan and Cartwright, 1988; Tung, 1993) highlights the importance of selecting managers for overseas assignments who are open to experiences, culturally sensitive, and attune to the normative patterns and rules of social engagement in the host country. Such individuals are to be preferred to domestically successful "trouble shooters" whose approach lack adaptability and so may not effectively transcend cultural boundaries. Personal qualities such as patience, interpersonal tact, empathy, and a low need to control people and situations are also valuable. Such qualities may also be equally important in domestic M&A as well as international M&A. In the context of international M&A, linguistic skills are also an important consideration, largely ignored by English-speaking countries (Torrington, 1984). In the BASF acquisition of Boots Pharma, the German company invested heavily in intercultural and language training at all organizational levels, both in the United Kingdom and Germany (Cartwright and Cooper, 2000). Unfortunately, the take-up rate for language training amongst U.K. employees was rather low. Kakabadse and Myers (1996) suggest that international teams should rotate the country in which meetings are held—and ideally the language in which the meeting is conducted.

Conclusion

As a future research agenda, it is important to consolidate the three strands of literature and research relating to organizational culture, national culture, and M&A experiences if we are to advance understanding of the variance in M&A performance.

Without such consolidation, research studies will continue to explore the various possible cross-cultural permutations between countries with insufficient generalizability to be useful to practitioners.

To inform the management and practice of M&A, as a research community, we need to *merge* our own knowledge and perspectives and move to a more multidisciplinary approach that embraces diversity.

Finally, in this merging of knowledge and perspectives, we need to acknowledge that the existence of a good cultural fit between merger partners alone will still be an insufficient guarantee of wealth creation without skilled, detailed, and comprehensive human integration planning and communication.

References

Bower, J. L. (2001). Not all M&As are alike—and that matters. *Harvard Business Review*, 79(3): 92–101.

Buono, A., and Bowditch, A. (1989). *The Human Side of Mergers and Acquisitions*. San Franscisco: Jossey-Bass.

Cartwright, S., and Cooper, C. L. (1996). *Managing Mergers Acquisitions and Strategic Alliances Integrating People and Cultures*, 2nd edn. Oxford: Butterworth Heinmann.

Cartwright, S., and Cooper, C. L. (2000). *HR Know-How in Mergers and Acquisitions*. London: CIPD.

Cartwright, S., Cooper, C. L., and Jordan, J. (1995). Managerial preferences in international merger and acquisition partners. *Journal of Strategic Change*, 4, 263–69.

Cartwright, S., and Price, F. (2002). Managerial preferences in international merger and acquisition partners revisited: How are they influenced? In Cooper and Gregory (eds.), *Advances in Mergers and Acquisitions*, Vol. 2. London: JAI.

Chatterjee, S., Lubatkin, M., Schweiger, D., and Weber, Y. (1992). Cultural differences and shareholder value in related mergers: Linking equity and human capital. *Strategic Management Journal*, 13, 319–34.

Child, J., Faulkner, D., and Pitkethly, R. (2001). *The Management of International Acquisitions*. Oxford: Oxford University Press.

Colquitt, J. A., Conlon, D. E., Ng, K. Y., Porter, C. O. L. H., and Wesson, M. J. (2001). Justice at the millennium: A meta-analytic review of 25 years of organizational justice research. *Journal of Applied Psychology*, 86(3): 425–45.

Cooper, C. L., and Kirkcaldy, B. D. (1995). Executive stereotyping between cultures: The British v. German manager. *Journal of Managerial Psychology*, 10(1): 3–6.

Deal, T., and Kennedy, A. (1982). *Corporate Cultures: The Rites and Rituals of Corporate Life*. Reading, MA: Addison-Wesley.

Denison, D. (2001). Organizational culture: Can it be a key lever for driving organizational change? In Cooper, Cartwright, and Early (eds.), *The International Handbook of Organizational Culture and Climate*. Chichester: Wiley.

FitzRoy, J., Acs, Z. J., and Gerlowski, D. A. (1998). *Management and Economics of Organization*. Europe: Prentice Hall.

Flynn, F. J., and Chatman, J. A. (2001). Strong cultures and innovation: Oxymoron or opportunity. In Cooper, Cartwright, and Early (eds.), *The International Handbook of Organizational Culture and Climate*, Chichester: Wiley.

Forstmann, S. (1998). Managing cultural differences in cross-cultural mergers and acquisitions. In Gertsen, Soderberg, and Torp (eds.), *Cultural*

Dimensions of International Mergers and Acquisitions. Berlin: Walter de Gruyter.

Graves, D. (1981). Individual reactions to a merger of two small firms of brokers in the re-insurance industry—A total population survey. *Journal of Management Studies*, 18(1): 89–113.

Guest, D. E. (1998). Is the psychological contract worth taking seriously? *Journal of Organizational Behaviour*, 19(Special Issue): 649–64.

Haspeslagh, P. C., and Jemison, D. B. (1991). *Managing Acquisitions*. New York: Free Press.

Hitt, M. A., Harrison, J. S., and Ireland, R. D. (2000). *Mergers and Acquisitions: A Guide to Creating Value for Shareholders*. New York: Oxford University Press.

Hofstede, G. (1980). *Culture's Consequences*. London: Sage.

Hofstede, G. (1991). *Cultures and Organisations*. London: McGraw-Hill.

Huselid, M., Jackson, S., and Schuler, R. S. (1997). Technical and strategic HRM effectiveness as determinants of firm performance. *Academy of Management Journal*, 49(1): 171–88.

Jemison, D., and Sitkin, S. B. (1986). Corporate acquisitions: A process perspective. *Academy of Management Review*, 11(1): 145–63.

Jordan, J., and Cartwright, S. (1988). Selecting expatriate managers: A review. *Leadership and Organization Development Journal*, 19(2).

Kakabadse, A., and Myers, A. (1996). Boardroom skills for Europe. *European Management Journal*, 14(2): 189–200.

Kleppestø, S. (1998). A quest for social identity–The pragmatics of communication in mergers and acquisitions. In Gertsen, Soderberg, and Torp (eds.), *Cultural Dimensions of International Mergers and Acquisitions*. Berlin: Walter de Gruyter.

KPMG (2000). Dealwatch. Amsterdam: KPMG.

Larsson, R. (1993). Barriers to acculturation in mergers and acquisitions: Strategic human resource implications. *Journal of European Business Education*, 2(2): 1–18.

Larsson, R., and Risberg, A. (1998). Cultural awareness and national versus corporate barriers to acculturation. In Gertsen, Soderberg, and Torp (eds.), *Cultural Dimensions of International Mergers and Acquisitions*. Berlin: Walter de Gruyter.

Levinson, H. (1970). A psychologist diagnoses merger failures. *Harvard Business Review*, March/April, 84–101.

Lubatkin, M. (1987) Merger strategies and stockholder value. *Strategic Management Journal*, 8: 39–53.

Nahavandi, A., and Malekzadeh, A. (1988). Acculturation in mergers and acquisitions. *Academy of Management Review*, 13: 79–90.

Napier, N. (1989). Mergers and acquisitions, human resource issues and outcomes: A review and suggested typology. *Journal of Management Studies*, 21: 271–89.

Panchel, S., and Cartwright, S. (2001). Group differences in post-merger stress. *Journal of Managerial Psychology*, 16(6): 424–34.

Sales, A., and Mirvis, P. (1984). When cultures collide: Issues in acquisition. In Kimberly and Quinn (eds.), *New Futures: The Challenge of Managing Corporate Transition*. Homewood, IL: Irwin.

Schoenberg, R. (2000). The influence of cultural compatibility within cross-border acquisitions: A review. In Cooper and Gregory (eds.), *Advances in Mergers and Acquisitions*, Vol. 1. New York: Elsevier Science Inc.

Schoenberg, R., and Norburn, R. (1998). Leadership compatibility and cross-border acquisition outcome. Paper presented to *18th Annual Strategic Management Society International Conference*, Orlando.

Schweiger, D. M., and Goulet, P. K. (2000). Integrating mergers and acquisitions: An international research review. In Cooper and Gregory (eds.), *Advances in Mergers and Acquisitions*, Vol. 1. New York: Elsevier Science Inc.

Senge, P. (1990). *The Fifth Discipline: The Art and Practice of the Learning Organization*. New York: Double Pay Currency.

Singh, H., and Montgomery, C. (1987). Corporate acquisition strategies and economic performance. *Strategic Management Journal*, 8: 377–86.

Smit, I. (2001). Assessment of cultures: A way to problem solving or a way to problematic solutions? In Cooper, Cartwright, and Early (eds.), *The International Handbook of Organizational Culture and Climate*. Chichester: Wiley.

Sparrow, P. R. (2001). Developing diagnostics for high performance organization cultures. In Cooper, Cartwright, and Early (eds.), *The International Handbook of Organizational Culture and Climate*. Chichester: Wiley.

Torrington, D. (1984). *International Human Resource Management*. London: Prentice Hall.

Trompenaars, F. (1993). *Riding the Waves of Culture*. London: Economist Books.

Trompenaars, F., and Hampden-Turner, C. (1997). *Riding the Waves of Culture: Understanding Cultural Diversity in Business*, 2nd edn. London: Nicholas Brealey Publishing.

Tung, R. L. (1993). Managing cross-national and intra-national diversity. *Human Resource Management*, 23(4): 461–77.

Very, P., Lubatkin, M., and Veiga, J. (1997). Relative standing and the performance of recently acquired European mergers. *Strategic Management Journal*, 18, 593–614.

Executive Commentary on Chapter 11

MAX OTTE

By now, it is an established fact that culture plays a crucial, if not THE crucial role in mergers and acquisitions (M&A) performance. After providing us with an overview of the literature on the disencouragingly complex relationship between corporate and national cultural fit and M&A performance, Cartwright and McCarthy present a framework to address the issue of cultural due diligence in M&A.

Indeed, the relationship of culture to M&A performance is almost impossible to disentangle: national and corporate cultures (that in addition may vary across corporate units and hierarchy levels), implicit and explicit parts of culture, the objective of the merger (extension, redesign/assimilation, autonomy), and strategic fit, all may have a bearing on the outcome. To add to this orrery, a common definition of "culture" is still not found. We do have a number of widely accepted dimensions to measure "culture," but we disagree when we are to put them together in a comprehensive model.

Cooper and McCarthy point out the major factors that may influence M&A performance: internal integration, autonomy, speed, risk-taking, welfare, fairness and trust, as well as diversity. All may play a significant role—but then, they may not. To sum up, as the chapter of two of the foremost academic experts on the topic reflects, the current state of research does not yet allow the operationalization of an applicable, comprehensive, proven, and tested set of tools for cultural due diligence that would be of help to practitioners.

In the absence of such scientifically proven and operationally tested methods (and in the hope and confidence of fast progress), let me state some practitioners' axioms (derived solely from intuition, experience, and gut feelings) that may provide guidelines for those currently faced with actual M&A challenges.

Constitutional Management

I base my proposals on the notion of *constitutional management* as developed by Peter Drucker[1]: management is, first and foremost, the job of getting the right things done in the right sequence. It can be learned and practised and is a priori not dependent on corporate or national culture. The tasks and responsibilities of good management are the same in the United States, Germany, or China, ExxonMobil or Microsoft.

Functional and Dysfunctional Cultures

Nonetheless, culture does have, of course, a *pervasive influence* in management. (It seems obvious—and Cartwright and McCarthy see it similarly—that corporate culture dominates national culture). There are *functional* and *dysfunctional* corporate cultures—just as there are sick and healthy organisms (Scott-Morgan).[2] Functional cultures are the result of good management, dysfunctional cultures are the result of bad management. In functional cultures, the operating mode and systems support the corporate mission and goals. Inevitable contradictions present in every company are minimized and tensions channelled to productive purposes. Trust results from consistence and coherence of words and actions on all levels. If consistency dominates, commonly shared expectations and interpersonal—organizational—knowledge emerge. This may even be the case in a cutthroat culture, if it is consistent.

The first task of a due diligence would therefore be to uncover if a culture is functional or dysfunctional. Here, an a priori framework is not extremely helpful—a company's culture and systems must be measured against its own mission and goals and be tested for consistence. This implies the necessity of treating every company as an individual case. The good news: a person with some experience in management and the industry will normally be able to tell after just a few interviews if things are largely in order or if something is going badly wrong.

The examination should extend right to the top management level of the acquiring firm. There is a German saying that goes "the fish begins to stink at the head." If the top level is largely out of sync with the rest of the organization, the culture will sooner or later become dysfunctional. Some companies may be extremely robust against top-level incompetence or even compensate for those shortcomings, but those are rare cases. And in the case of executive greed, fear, or megalomania, due diligence is useless.[3] Then, only a psychotherapist can help.[4]

Appropriate and Inappropriate Cultures

For many industries, products, or services, there exist *appropriate cultures* and there exist inappropriate cultures. The second task of a cultural due diligence would be to find out whether companies have appropriate or inappropriate cultures for the mission they set out to achieve (or would want to achieve jointly).

I posit that "appropriateness" is largely independent of national culture as for example measured by Hofstede. Large differences in the ratings on Hofstede's four dimensions of national culture can also be found with the employees of any larger organization. And while an organization as a whole may be more "masculine" or "feminine," respectively more "individualist" or "collectivist" according to Hofstede, these dimensions do not relate to specific business models. In my opinion, even "authority distance" does not necessarily relate to specific business models: a networked consulting culture may have a very low authority distance, but the opposite could also be true. Hofstede's "uncertainty avoidance" does, however, have a direct bearing whether a culture is appropriate for a certain industry or business.

A rather small number of variables will suffice to clarify if a culture and a specific business model or situation does fit. The simple two-dimensional model with which Deal and Kennedy reignited the culture debate in the early eighties is still very pertinent in my opinion. On the basis of speed and degree of risk-taking, the authors lay out four prototype cultures[5]:

1. "bet your company" (expert culture; high risk, slow),
2. "tough guy macho" (fast deals; high risk, fast),
3. "work-hard-play hard" (sales-oriented, basic services; low risk, fast), and
4. "process" (bureacracy; low risk, slow).

It seems relatively obvious, for example, that in the fast-paced world of investment banking, in the late 1990s you needed a b-type culture. This is why American and not German or Japanese banks dominated the field. In many German companies, the "expert culture" dominates. As the pace of business is picking up, "expert cultures" may become an endangered species despite their merits.

Treacy and Wiersema[6] presented three "disciplines of excellence" of which a company may pick a primary and a secondary discipline, but not all three if it wanted to become an excellent company:

5. customer intimacy
6. operational efficiency
7. innovation

Microsoft, for example, is operationally efficient and occasionally innovative, but no one has accused it of customer intimacy.

Taking a slightly different approach, Goffee and Jones[7] are more concerned with measures of coherence. On the basis of the degree of networking and solidarity, they distinguish between

8. networked (high sociability, low solidarity),
9. communal (high sociability, high solidarity),
10. mercenary (low sociability, high solidarity), and
11. fragmented (low sociability, low solidarity) cultures.

This leaves us with eleven cultural prototypes. Points (4) and (11) are clearly dysfunctional cultures: a slow culture with little risk-taking will always lead to failure in business. A nonnetworked culture with low solidarity is also a recipe for failure. A communal culture, (8), asks too much from a business organization and rarely works. The remaining eight applicable prototypes may be reduced further in number. For example, a networked culture is often an expert culture, a sales- or service-oriented culture is often a mercenary culture. An operationally efficient culture is normally a work-hard–play-hard culture.

So let's try to regroup and reduce the number of workable combinations:

1. An expert culture ("bet your company") is normally also a networked culture and a culture of innovation. It could also be an operationally efficient culture.
2. A sales or service culture ("work-hard–play-hard") is normally operationally efficient and mercenary. It could also be customer intimate.
3. A deal-oriented culture ("tough guy macho") is mercenary or networked. It may be innovative or customer intimate, but it will rarely be operationally efficient.

After due diligence has established whether a culture is functional, the second step would be to ascertain the "operating mode" of each of the combining companies according to the relatively simple prototypes described above. If the acquirer is aware of its own operating mode and the requirements of the industry, the result of such an exercise could be the makeover of either the acquiring or acquired company's culture, no change, or the creation of a "new" company. If operational efficiency is called for, but a company prides itself on its expertise in product development, it will need a culture makeover.

The relationship to the goals of the merger—extension, autonomy, or makeover—is NOT one-directional. A culturally sensitive acquirer may change its goals in the process of due diligence. The acquirer may even use the acquisition for its own makeover, as Deutsche Bank used its acquisition of Bankers Trust to accelerate its change into an Anglo-Saxon-style investment bank.

Due Diligence, Cultural Sensitivity, and the Integration Process

A major merger that includes operational integration is always a time of great uncertainty. Even if strategies and cultures seem to fit, and especially if they seem to be rather similar or mutually supportive, much can go wrong. The complexity of challenges cannot be planned. What can be established beforehand is a clear code of conduct and communication as well as a roadmap. Even between similar companies, a major merger should almost always be used as a possibility to reinvent the combined company and to think innovatively and boldly about the future. Only such "one-company measures" based on a common view of the future will make the merger work. If the integration work is reduced to a best-of-two-practices benchmarking exercise, it will soon become an "us vs. them"—and then the acquirer will dominate.

Goals must be ambitious, but attainable. Compare the brilliantly executed Novartis merger to the seemingly well-executed DaimerChrysler merger that soon ran into trouble. Vasella was bent on remaking the company and creating one of the absolute top players in the pharmaceutical industry. On the other hand, even if the combined DaimlerChrysler is undoubtedly one of the largest automotive companies, 1.3 billion dollars in cost savings is not exactly an ambitious target for a 140 billion dollar company. In fact, it is less than 1 percent of sales.

To find inspiring goals that have just the right balance between vision and the attainable and to execute the integration, beginning with the top and stretching into the organization, is the true test of a top management team. It depends largely on management practices, openness, and soft skills. Schrempp's much touted integration tool (his information system with which he was supposedly able to track progress on all projects and that allegedly impressed Eaton very much) was, in the end, not much more than the attempt to substitute technology for leadership. Schrempp's style is very American. Yet, the DaimlerChrysler top management team did not come together and open conflict was the result. If the team at the top does not know how to deal with culture issues (and chances are that it doesn't), then due diligence and training further down the levels of the company are exercises in futility.

Notes

1. Peter Drucker (1992). *Management—Tasks, Responsibilities and Practices*. New York: Harper Business.

2. Peter Scott-Morgan (1994). *The Unwritten Rules of the Game*. New York: McGraw-Hill.

3. S. Cartwright and C. L. Cooper (1996). *Managing Mergers, Acquisitions and Strategic Alliances—Integrating People and Cultures*. Oxford: Butterworth Heinemann.

4. Michael Maccoby (2001). Narcicisstic leaders. *Harvard Business Review*, 78(1): 68–77.

5. Terrence E. Deal and Allan A. Kenney (2000). *Corporate Cultures—The Rites and Rituals of Corporate Life*. New York: Perseus Publishing.

6. Michael Treacy and Frank Wiersema (1997). *The Discipline of Market Leaders—Choose Your Customers, Narrow Your Focus, Dominate Your Markets*. New York: Perseus Publishing.

7. Rob Goffee and Gareth Jones (1996). What holds the modern company together? *Harvard Business Review*, 74(6): 133–48.

PART IV *Learning from Experience: Case Analyses of*
Sociocultural Processes in Mergers and Acquisitions

12 Managing Human Resources to Capture Capabilities
Case Studies in High-Technology Acquisitions

SAIKAT CHAUDHURI

Corporate acquisitions involve the integration of physical assets, organizational processes, and people (Capron, Mitchell, and Swaminathan, 2001; Karim and Mitchell, 2000; Shrivastava, 1986). In these transactions, the combination of the assets and processes, or task integration, by which the resources and activities of the firms are assimilated, is clearly essential to being able to conduct business operations and thereby to create financial gains from a deal (Birkinshaw, 1999; Birkinshaw, Bresman, and Hakanson, 2000; Haspesplagh and Jemison, 1991; Shrivastava, 1986). Many times, the blending of the employees from both sides to generate interaction and productive cooperation amongst them, namely the human integration to achieve organizational cultural convergence and shared identity, motivation, and goals (Bastien, 1994; Buono and Bowditch, 1989), is a necessary enabler to allow the commencement of business operations, but is not a direct driver of value, as the target brings competitive advantage from capabilities rooted in distinctive assets and processes rather than people's unique abilities. Deals to enhance market share by obtaining customers, capital equipment, and infrastructure, such as airline takeovers, telecommunication service provider mergers, regional bank buyouts, or steel plant acquisitions, as well as purchases geared toward consolidation by streamlining operations, such as oil company mergers, are examples of acquisitions where this is often the case.

In some takeovers, however, the integration of people takes on a direct role in realizing deal-specific and longer term financial and associated gains, because specialized employees are a critical component of the competencies purchased. Without the people's successful integration in terms of shared identity, motivation, goals, and work culture, products from the acquisition cannot be developed, manufactured, or sold. A prevalent example of such buys are acquisitions in the high-technology industries, characterized by short product life cycles and high degrees of uncertainty (Eisenhardt, 1989; Fine, 1998; Mendelson and Pillai, 1999), where companies have bought other firms fervently over the past decade to supplement internal innovation efforts amidst continuously and rapidly shifting markets and competitive landscapes (Birkinshaw, 1999; Chaudhuri and Tabrizi, 1999; Puranam, 2000). Such innovation-oriented deals, most visible in the communications equipment and information technology sectors, reached record levels in the 1990s, though they have been active for some time (Bower, 2001; Chakrabarti, Hauschildt, and Süverkrüp, 1994; Chakrabarti and Souder, 1987; Hitt et al., 1996; Hoskisson, Hitt, and Ireland, 1994).

In these high-technology acquisitions, the objective of the buyers has been to either gain new technologies and associated engineering skills that can be applied in new products being developed, or to obtain innovative products that fill gaps in the current product line or fulfill presently unserved needs in the market, and are often to be sold in conjunction with other products. Fundamentally, the value from these deals derives from the financial returns of newly created or bought products, both in the short term and in the long run, though other benefits such as receiving employees which end up having high impact on a technical or managerial front, or accrued learning, may also be gained.

The integration process drives the value creation in these acquisitions by preserving, transferring, and commencing the application of the engineering, manufacturing, and sales capabilities from the target organization to develop, produce, and sell the products resulting from the acquisition. These specific competencies are important in these cases because the technological sophistication and uncertainty of products means that they are complex to not only build, but also to manufacture, sell, and support. The capabilities reside in not only physical assets and organizational processes, but to a large extent also in the people of the target.

The Critical Role of Human Integration

Capabilities comprise the collective knowledge of an organizational unit, comprising explicit and tacit components (Leonard-Barton, 1992, 1995). Explicit knowledge comprises the technical and organizational understanding and techniques, which is codified and can be accessed through verbal communication and written documentation (Winter, 1987), and is embodied in the complementary physical assets and formal processes of the firm. Tacit knowledge, on the other hand, is the expertise and skills that are based on accumulated experience and resides in the memories of individuals, and is embedded in the people's nonformalized but routinized actions and interactions with each other (Leonard-Barton, 1992, 1995; Nelson and Winter,

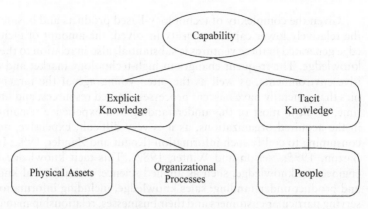

FIGURE **12.1 Sources of Capabilities**

1982; Winter, 1987). Figure 12.1 summarizes this conceptualization of capabilities.

Inherent in both the explicit and tacit knowledge is the culture, the norms, and the values that guide the organization (Schein, 1986). For example, physical assets such as products are created with modular architectures by companies that value decentralized work to drive innovation and fast responsiveness to markets. Similarly, processes with overlapping stages reflect norms of cross-functional information exchange in firms that believe such interaction will improve the product quality in changing markets (MacCormack, 2001). Finally, people embody culture in the manner they work and routinely interact with others, using norms and values to guide their decision making, communication, and other actions in the development, production, and sales of products (Schein, 1986).

Effective integration in high-technology deals thus entails the combinatorial fusion of the knowledge bases of the acquirer and the target such that they develop, produce, and sell the products intended from an acquisition (Ahuja and Katila, 2001). From this perspective, integration creates value from an acquisition through a three-stage process: the preservation, transfer, and application of knowledge from the acquired organization. Knowledge is first preserved to ensure that the specialized understanding and techniques in the target are maintained and available to be utilized by the acquirer. Subsequently, this knowledge is transferred from the target to the appropriate place in the acquiring organization so that it can be exploited. Finally, the knowledge is applied to create, manufacture, and sell innovative products from the acquisition. Task integration, the combination of physical assets and formal processes, is the mechanism by which the explicit knowledge is captured. However, human integration, the blending of the people, is the process by which the tacit knowledge is extracted.

Given the complexity of technology-based products and businesses and the relatively lower capital intensity involved, the amount of tacit knowledge generated in these ventures is substantial, also in relation to the explicit knowledge. The frequent changes in high-technology market and competitive environments, as well as the often young age of the target companies that generally have nascent processes, limited resources, and little slack time, result in most of this understanding and experience remaining tacit in the acquired organizations, as it is very difficult, expensive, and time-consuming to codify such information (Kogut and Zander, 1992; Leonard-Barton, 1995; Nelson and Winter, 1982). This tacit knowledge includes engineering knowledge, such as applied science, technological know-how, and product understanding; sales knowledge, including information about serving particular customers and their businesses, relationship management, brand management, and channel management skills, experience with geographic market characteristics, domain expertise, and consulting abilities; manufacturing knowledge like design for manufacturability know-how, production feasibility expertise, scaling methods, and experience with various quality standards; and the management skills to apply each of these functional knowledge sets to commercial ends.

Therefore, the integration of employees of the target company into the acquiring organization, especially in the product development, sales, and manufacturing functions, actually represents the assimilation of the substantial specialized tacit knowledge that is at the core of the competencies in high-technology firms. Viewed in this light, human integration creates value from an acquisition through the preservation, transfer, and application of tacit knowledge from the target, which, in conjunction with explicit knowledge, is used to build, make, and sell innovative products and solutions. Effective integration of human resources hence translates into a substantial contribution to the preservation, transfer, and application of capabilities.

Integration Strategy for Human Resources

Without this tacit knowledge, it is consequently not possible to access and utilize the capabilities from a high-technology acquisition. As tacit knowledge resides in people, the target employees in these types of buyouts are strategic resources that directly influence value creation from the acquisitions, as without them, critical know-how is lost and products cannot be created, produced, or sold. As such, the human integration is necessarily a strategic exercise, to be viewed along analogous dimensions as suggested by scholars for task and overall integration (Chaudhuri and Tabrizi, 1999; Haspesplagh and Jemison, 1991; Jemison and Sitkin, 1986; Kitching, 1967; Larsson and Finkelstein, 1999; Napier, 1989; Pritchett, 1985; Puranam, 2000; Ranft and Lord, 2002).

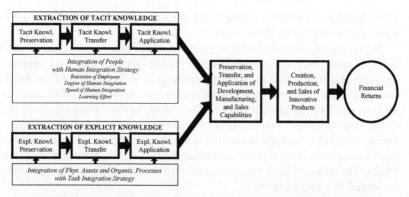

FIGURE **12.2** Role of Integration Processes in the Value Creation from Acquisitions

In this vein, four critical dimensions of a human integration strategy are the retention of employees, the degree of human integration, the speed of human integration, and the learning effort engaged in. Employee retention regards the decision of which and thereby how many target people to keep following the acquisition. Degree of human integration refers to the desired end state in the level of interaction, cooperation, cultural convergence, shared motivation and goals, and common identity amongst the employees of both sides. Speed of human integration refers to the rate at which the level of contact and interaction of the employees is to be propagated. Learning effort comprises the amount of energy and resources to be spent for transmitting tacit knowledge between the target and the acquiring people.

All of these strategic decisions affect the manner in which the tacit knowledge from the bought organization is preserved, transferred, and applied, because the integration process affects the capabilities embedded in the purchased organization (Chaudhuri and Tabrizi, 1999; Haspesplagh and Jemison, 1991; Puranam, 2000; Ranft and Lord, 2002). In their effect on knowledge extraction, there are tradeoffs inherent in these components. Figure 12.2 indicates the role of human integration strategies and processes in the value creation from high-technology acquisitions.

The approach to target employee retention involves tradeoffs of the benefits and costs of preserving tacit knowledge. As this type of understanding and experience is by definition embedded in people, retaining target workers represents preserving that knowledge, and serves as a prerequisite to being able to transfer and apply it. Therefore, if people are not kept or leave because of dissatisfaction at the changes taking place, which often occurs (Cannella and Hambrick, 1993; Lubatkin, Schweiger, and Weber, 1999; Marks and Mirvis, 2001), the value of the merger may be lost (Birkinshaw,

1999; Brockner, 1992; Chaudhuri and Tabrizi, 1999; Ernst and Vitt, 2000; Ranft and Lord, 2000; Slowinski et al., 2000).

Retention of a handful of select individuals is often insufficient in these deals, because tacit knowledge is often rooted in groups such as engineering, manufacturing, and sales teams, not just in individuals (Huber, 1991). Groups enable teams to draw upon the collective knowledge, skills, and experiences of its individual members. Over time, as they work together, they divide tasks in unique ways so that individual members develop expertise in various areas that is useful in conjunction with the abilities of team members and not necessarily on its own (Leonard-Barton, 1995; Nelson and Winter, 1982). Therefore, a high retention rate ensures that the tacit knowledge is preserved in a complete form.

However, retaining large numbers of target employees also comes at a substantial cost, because of at least two reasons. First, retaining people with such specialized knowledge often requires significant financial and nonmonetary incentives (for example, Chaudhuri and Tabrizi, 1999; Ranft and Lord, 2000). Second, relatively large numbers of target employees to integrate means more effort needs to be devoted toward the assimilation process because of greater and more complex coordination needs, at the expense of resources and time that could otherwise be directed toward the creation, production, and delivery of goods and services (Ahuja and Katila, 2001; Asquith, Bruner, and Mullins, 1983; Clark and Ofek, 1994; Jarrel and Poulsen, 1989; Kusewitt, 1985; Loderer and Martin, 1990; Lubatkin, 1983; Sherer and Ross, 1990).

The degree of human integration involves tradeoffs around, on the one hand, enhancing the transfer and application of the target's tacit knowledge, and on the other hand, preserving the target's tacit knowledge. A high degree of interaction and cooperation as well as a strongly converged work culture, identity, and set of goals allow for benefits of economies of scale and scope, tighter control, efficient coordination, and thereby focused effort, which translate into effectively transferred and applied tacit knowledge from the target.

On the other hand, a low degree of human integration, that is, a high degree of autonomy, enables the preservation of tacit knowledge, which could otherwise be diluted if people's work habits as well as nonformalized but routinized interactions were disrupted (Boyd, 1990; Chaudhuri and Tabrizi, 1999; Haspesplagh and Jemison, 1991; Puranam, 2000; Ranft and Lord, 2000, 2002; Zollo and Singh, 2000). This is because the tacit knowledge rests as much in specialized relationships as in the body of abilities itself (Badaracco, 1991; Grant, 1996; Leonard-Barton, 1992), which could be interrupted by a high level of assimilation with acquirer employees.

These groups are often tightly coupled systems in which disturbing individual linkages can dissipate the tacit knowledge that resides in them

(Leonard-Barton, 1995; Nelson and Winter, 1982) even if all employees belonging to the original group are retained. Moreover, while cultural convergence can lead to efficiency in transferring and applying tacit knowledge, it can also dilute the preservation of such understanding and experience because the differences in work habits norms, and values that guide actions and interactions of people may also be a source of specialized skills amongst the purchased employees, in contrast to the general view that cultural dissimilarity leads to value destruction in acquisitions (for example, Buono and Bowditch, 1989; Chatterjee et al., 1992; Datta, 1991; Harrison, 1972; Marks and Mirvis, 1986, 2001; Slowinski, 1992; Weber, 1996).

Likewise, the speed of human integration also involves promoting tacit knowledge transfer and application against ensuring its preservation. On the one hand, fostering contact and interaction quickly is desirable to be able to enjoy the benefits of merging sooner by transferring and applying the target's tacit knowledge early, instead of dissipating value through indecision and thereby lack of concentrated effort (Covin et al., 1996; Schweiger and Ivancevich, 1985; Smith and Hershman, 1997), which is especially pressing if high premiums have been paid. In this vein, fast human integration is also better to minimize the uncertainty of target employees and reduce "postmerger drift" in terms of effort and pain (Ashford, 1988; Marks and Mirvis, 1986, 2001; Shirley, 1973; Tetenbaum, 1999), and to demonstrate the value of the combination to both sides (Chaudhuri and Tabrizi, 1999; Dessler, 1999; Robinson, 1998), which leads to smooth and focused transfer and utilization of the target's tacit knowledge. In contrast, slow integration has the benefit of avoiding sudden disruption to the purchased employees' work life, which can result in a demotivated workforce and thereby dilution of the tacit knowledge preservation, as well as potential efforts to transfer and apply it (Birkinshaw, 1999; Birkinshaw, Bresman, and Hakanson, 2000; Empson, 2000; Ranft and Lord, 2002).

Finally, the choice of learning effort to be expended involves a tradeoff around the benefits and costs of transferring and applying tacit knowledge from the target. Such learning leads to expansion of an organization's tacit knowledge base, but it also requires resources, time, and effort, which could otherwise be directed toward the development, manufacture, and sales of goods and services. Therefore, this decision is important for both effectiveness and efficiency purposes (Begley and Yount, 1994; Zollo and Singh, 2000).

A Contingent Approach to Human Integration

Therefore, when collated, current scholarship collectively identifies these tradeoffs in terms of impact on tacit knowledge preservation, transfer, and application, within each of these strategic variables. However, present theories do not resolve them, making the development of appropriate integration strategies for human integration difficult. The question then becomes, which circumstances favor each tradeoff one way or the other? Furthermore, although these four aspects of integration have been treated independently by scholars thus far, how do the relationships between them influence the resolution of the tradeoffs and thereby the creation of an optimal strategy in each case?

We can approach this problem by considering the core of the human integration process, namely, the type of tacit knowledge exchange required, in order to achieve a given acquisition objective in terms of developing, manufacturing, and selling products. In doing so, it is useful to think of the human integration taking place at a functional level, as competencies are often located there, and devising assimilation strategies for each function (Chaudhuri and Tabrizi, 1999), though scholars in the past have generally done so at the organizational level (for example, Haspesplagh and Jemison, 1991).

In each function, the tacit knowledge flow can be of four types: from the acquirer to the target people; from the target to the acquirer employees; both simultaneously; or none at all. Retention of employees is valuable if the tacit knowledge of the target needs to be preserved, either to be transferred to and applied by acquirer employees, or to be directly applied. Thus, if tacit knowledge exchange is required either from the target to the acquirer or bidirectionally, a high retention rate of the target employees is needed to be able to preserve the tacit knowledge before it can be transferred to the acquirer and applied there. Similarly, in the case where the target is working on disconnected (but useful) matters from the acquirer and there is no tacit knowledge exchange required between them, the target employees need to be retained so that the experience is preserved and can be applied without interruption. However, in the situation where tacit knowledge flow is needed from the acquirer to the target only, the retention rate of purchased employees can be low, as their implicit understanding is not necessary to be preserved; keeping the employees is useful in that case only if they provide needed manpower.

Once the retention decision is made, the strategy for degree of human integration of the kept people is analogous. Autonomy of the target people is valuable if, and as long as, tacit knowledge needs to be preserved, as their integration leads to more efficient transfer and application of this experience. Therefore, if implicit knowledge exchange needed is from the acquirer to the target only, there is no need to preserve the tacit knowledge, and a high degree of human integration is most efficient. If, on the other hand, the tacit knowledge flow required is from the target to the acquirer, then the target employees' understanding needs to be preserved to enable it to be transferred, but at the same time, it needs to be transmitted. In that case, it is necessary to have a medium level of human integration, such that there is sufficient autonomy to preserve the tacit knowledge, and simultaneously, the target people can interact with the acquiring employees to transfer the understanding and apply it.

Similarly, when the tacit knowledge exchange required is bidirectional, although the need for knowledge flow from the acquirer to the target favors high employee integration, this is countered by the need to preserve the knowledge of the target people before it can be transmitted to the acquirer; a medium level of human assimilation achieves the preservation as well as the transfer and application concurrently. Finally, in the situation where the target is working on disconnected matters from the acquirer and there is no tacit knowledge flow required between them, the target people can be left with low integration with the purchasing workers, to enable preservation and application of the implicit experience without its transfer.

The approach for integration speed is related to the degree of human assimilation. In the situation where it is efficient to have a high degree of employee integration, namely, where there is tacit knowledge exchange required from the acquirer to the target only, the integration can proceed quickly, as there is no need to preserve the target implicit knowledge. In contrast, in the case where there is a low degree of human integration needed, that is, when there is no tacit knowledge exchange required, the rate of assimilation of the target people with the acquiring people is optimally very gradual, to maximize preservation and application of the target experience directly without any transfer. Finally, in circumstances where there is a need to have a medium level of employee integration, that is, when there is knowledge flow needed from the target to the acquirer or bidirectionally, the integration should likewise be medium-paced to balance the preservation of the tacit knowledge in the purchased organization's people with its transfer and application.

The learning effort to be invested in to transfer and apply the tacit knowledge also depends on the knowledge flow required, and is related to the retention, degree of integration, and speed of integration. In the case where there is no or virtually no exchange required, there is no or little learning needed. In the situation where the only exchange necessary is from the acquirer to the target, it can also be low, if not many target people are retained; if many employees of the purchased organization are retained, more effort can be expended. In those instances where the tacit knowledge flow necessary is from the target to the acquirer or bidirectional, high learning effort is required to effectively and expeditiously transmit the implicit understanding and experience.

In summary, the tacit knowledge exchange required to fulfill the acquisition objective in terms of creating, producing, and selling innovative products determines the employee retention needed, learning effort to be

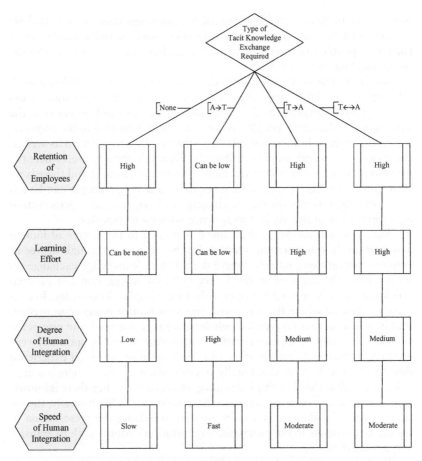

FIGURE **12.3** Contingent Human Integration Strategies at the Functional Level

engaged in, appropriate degree of human integration, and optimal speed of human integration. Figure 12.3 graphically illustrates the resulting contingent human integration strategies at the functional level to preserve, transfer, and apply the target's tacit knowledge as needed to create value.

Using this framework, two case studies illustrate how the integration of the purchased human resources can be managed strategically to appropriately preserve, transfer, and apply the tacit knowledge in them. These examples show how the implicitly residing know-how in the employees, which constitutes a critical element of the product development, manufacturing, and sales capabilities inherent in the target organization, can be harnessed toward innovation activities. The first case is Cisco Systems' acquisition of

Grand Junction Networks, while the second is IBM's takeover of Lotus Development Corporation.[1] Both acquisitions have contributed significantly to their acquirers' long-term profitability with the introduction of new product lines.

Cisco's Acquisition of Grand Junction

In September 1995, San Jose, CA, based Cisco, the maker of communications network equipment and known to be an active acquirer, announced the acquisition of Grand Junction for $348 million in order to fill an important product gap. Grand Junction, based in Fremont, CA, was founded in 1992, employed 85 people, and was the first to create and market Ethernet desktop switching products. Cisco's LAN switching products from its workgroup business unit (WBU) addressed the backbone and workgroup market segments, while Grand Junction would bring complementary fast Ethernet hubs, adapters, and switches for the desktop, as customers were rapidly migrating to desktop switches. Together, they would be able to develop and provide complete Internet-working solutions to their small and medium business customers faster than their competitors.

By the day of the announcement, the top executives at Grand Junction were informed of details of their new employment arrangements. Furthermore, at the announcement, senior managers of Cisco, including WBU General Manager Mario Mazzola, as well as Grand Junction, including CEO Howard Charney, addressed Cisco employees in the acquiring business unit as well as the target employees, explaining to them the strategic vision of the acquisition and the process for determining the purchased people's new positions, in an interactive session that included Cisco employees who had come into the organization from acquisitions themselves.

During the period between the deal's announcement and its close, Cisco formed an integration team including Cisco's business development staff, some of its human resources and IT personnel, and Mazzola and Charney. Impressed by the individual talent and recognizing the strong team dynamics amongst employees, Cisco decided to absorb all of Grand Junction's employees, offered them salaries similar to their prior contracts plus attractive stock options in Cisco, and gave them titles and responsibilities commensurate to what they enjoyed previously. No one refused the offer. Moreover, during this time, the integration team developed and communicated to all the acquiring and purchased employees the product road maps, as well as revenue projections and other goals, in addition to the new organizational structure postclose.

After the acquisition closed, Cisco placed Grand Junction into the WBU as its desktop division. The firm made Charney vice-president of this division, reporting to Mazzola, who reported to Cisco CEO John Chambers.

Charney kept his engineering and product marketing teams under his authority, while all other functions, including manufacturing, sales, finance, and customer service, were combined with the corresponding Cisco functions, whose heads oversaw both their original as well as the new employees. All Grand Junction employees were relocated from Fremont to Cisco's San Jose campus, and all Grand Junction labeling was transitioned to Cisco's name.

In the product development function, comprising the engineering and product marketing areas, the integration team discouraged mass direct interaction of the Grand Junction desktop division with the other WBU employees and channeled communications through the business development staff to prevent the latter from overwhelming the former. At the same time, they paired the Grand Junction engineers with "buddies" from Cisco, who would sit in offices near them, and enlighten them on how things were done at Cisco, while observing how the Grand Junction employees would go about their tasks.

Furthermore, to promote product innovation as envisioned from the merger, the integration team quickly commenced the joint development of the next generation Grand Junction desktop Ethernet switch to be interoperable with the other WBU products. In doing so, the integration team introduced the leaders of the product development teams on either side to initiate the engineering process, and subsequently other relevant individuals on both sides as work on the Catalyst-2000 progressed, in a phased manner. During the joint development project, one momentous occasion occurred when the desktop switches developed by the Grand Junction team failed in the first test because of a software glitch, which Cisco employees through their experience were able to quickly identify and fix.

In manufacturing, which was outsourced both at Cisco and at Grand Junction, the former's team, which had substantial experience in producing other LAN-switching products, proceeded immediately to help the latter to implement a significant ramp-up in output, by keeping those target suppliers that were on Cisco's approved vendor list, dropping those that were not, and adding ones with larger capacities and the requisite qualifications. Cisco's manufacturing people taught their counterparts their Oracle-based manufacturing system software through training, after transitioning Grand Junction to it.

In sales, the ten Grand Junction sales people, who had been utilizing small-scale indirect and direct channels to market their products, were immediately introduced to Cisco's massive direct sales staff, which had tremendous experience in selling such switching gear to a large set of customers globally. The Cisco team taught their large-scale forecasting methods as well as direct sales model to the Grand Junction employees through individual interaction and group sessions, while gaining insights on the unique features of desktop switching products through formal training events and associated materials, to which the Grand Junction employees contributed.

After the integration was completed and in the following years, it became clear that the Grand Junction acquisition was an overwhelming success. The first joint product from the acquisition was developed on schedule, manufactured efficiently and to a large scale, and sold to a large set of customers, establishing Cisco as the market leader in LAN switching in general, and desktop switching in particular, with approximately double the revenue and even higher margins for the products than Grand Junction had enjoyed before the merger. Since then, several generations of the Catalyst-2000 series have been created, and today, the WBU products constitute approximately 60 percent of all of Cisco's revenues.

Lessons from Cisco

When Cisco bought Grand Junction, its objective was to jointly develop new products based on the target device such that they could be part of a system that included other related Cisco equipment, and bring the array of offerings to Cisco's broad set of customers. Thus, the knowledge flow required in product development was bidirectional, as integrated product creation demanded Grand Junction employees to understand the functionality it needed to incorporate into its desktop switches to be an effective member of a suite of backbone, workgroup, and desktop devices, while Cisco engineers needed to be familiar enough with the Grand Junction product to be able to convert it to the same platforms and standards as the rest of the equipment. In sales and manufacturing, in contrast, the only knowledge exchange needed was overwhelmingly from Cisco to Grand Junction, as these were exercises in areas where Cisco had vast experience and economies of scale and scope, and it would be most efficient for Grand Junction to adopt Cisco's practices and systems.

Consequently, in product development, Cisco ensured a high retention of employees, strong learning effort, medium degree of human integration, and moderate speed of human integration to preserve the tacit knowledge of Grand Junction but also to transfer and apply it effectively and efficiently. Giving generous salaries with attractive stock options to be vested in future, that is, strong financial incentives, led to satisfaction, long-term commitment, and focus in the Grand Junction employees, as did the offer of equivalent or promoted positions within Cisco, as well as the crucial role accorded to Grand Junction in realizing the vision of the merger's product output. Such responsibility and high relative standing encouraged them to stay, as it represented recognition of their abilities and an expressed need for them as well as respect and clear direction without uncertainty, leading to psychological ownership and hence a desire to work on the task at hand

(Hambrick and Canella, 1993; Lubatkin, Schweiger, and Weber, 1999; Ranft and Lord, 2000; Sales and Mirvis, 1984). High retention hence translated into the preservation of the tacit knowledge.

To transfer and apply this tacit knowledge, Cisco implemented a strong learning effort, by having a one-on-one partner system to allow employees to casually communicate understanding of their ways of doing things and allow for the informal observation of work actions and productive interactions with others, and by embarking on a joint project, as working toward a common goal allows for conscious and subconscious communication and observation of tacit ways of doing things, and necessitates mutual adaptation by members of the two sides, besides for motivating both sides by showing them the value of merging quickly (Chaudhuri and Tabrizi, 1999). High learning effort thus led to efficient transfer and application of the tacit knowledge.

To support the preservation and simultaneous transfer and application of the implicit understanding, the degree of human integration was enacted at a medium level. Placing the Grand Junction group in the WBU and in the same geographical location as the Cisco people, together with committed, powerful, and experienced leadership comprising senior executives from both sides, allowed for enough interaction and joint work for tacit knowledge transfer and application to occur, but as Grand Junction's engineering team was kept separate but within the WBU, there was no full immersion, and this prevented disruption of the tacit knowledge in Charney's team.

Likewise, the moderate speed of human integration also supported transfer and application of the tacit knowledge balanced by its preservation. Frequent communication and active matching of employees enhanced the rate of interaction and thereby propelled transmission and utilization of the implicit understanding, while buffering by the business development staff and matchmaking being done in phases slowed down the interaction and ensured the tacit knowledge's preservation.

On the contrary, in the sales and manufacturing functions, where knowledge flow was needed only from Cisco to Grand Junction, the acquirer adopted a strategy of high retention, simple learning, high degree of human integration, and fast human integration to preserve and transfer only the minimal amount of tacit knowledge necessary from the target and otherwise push forward utilization of acquirer knowledge. As there was some tacit knowledge unique to making and selling Grand Junction's desktop switching products despite their similarity to the backbone and workgroup devices, Cisco used attractive financial incentives, equivalent positions, and promise of a role in the merged entity to successfully retain employees in the sales and manufacturing functions to preserve the implicit techniques.

At the same time, though, the learning effort in these areas consisted of only some basic training sessions and events to transfer the little unique expertise needed by the acquirer from the target and the teaching of standard methods by codifying some of the tacit knowledge. As preservation of target tacit knowledge was not a major concern, the degree of human integration was high, enacted through full integration of the employees into the respective acquiring functional departments at the same location, with no target leadership in place, which led to maximum interaction and productive cooperation using the acquirer's tools and methods. Similarly, the speed of human integration was kept high, by communicating often and matching everyone at once.

Thus, applying these various mechanisms in desired ways allowed Cisco to enact human integration strategies in each function to preserve, transfer, and apply tacit knowledge of the target most effectively to realize the acquisition objectives. This contributed to the effective use of Grand Junction's capabilities, leading to the strong value creation from the deal. Other situations require different strategies to be effective, as the next case will demonstrate.

IBM's Takeover of Lotus

In June 1995, Armonk, NY, based mainframe and computer services giant IBM successfully executed a hostile bid for Cambridge, MA, based Lotus for $3.5 billion, to jump into a fast-growing market and initiate a transformation of IBM's strategy and culture. Lotus, with its 4,500 employees, had developed corporate network enabling software (so-called "groupware") known as Lotus Notes. While IBM was strong in hardware, especially mainframe computers and associated consulting and services, the firm was looking to strengthen its software competence through Lotus. Lotus needed resources to promote its products in its attempt to set an industry standard.

Together they could provide back-end and front-end, hardware and software, and hence comprehensive solutions for network computing, to challenge software-makers like Microsoft and Oracle. At the same time, this could provide an opportunity for IBM to shift its then bureaucratic and stodgy image by aggressively pursuing a new and fast-growing market. Given Lotus CEO Jim Manzi's open opposition to the deal and weeklong search for a white knight, as well as past records of IBM's acquisitions, industry analysts surmised at the time of announcement that IBM would smother the innovative culture of Lotus and not recoup the amount it paid.

Immediately after the deal's announcement and Manzi's reluctant acceptance of the offer a week later, IBM CEO Lou Gerstner and Senior Vice President for software John Thompson, along with Manzi, visited Lotus in Cambridge and its Notes subsidiary Iris Associates in Westford to explain to all employees their strategic vision and their intention to not change anything for Lotus but provide support for the success of Notes, in the hopes of convincing the target people to stay. Nonetheless, not believing IBM's intentions and fearing IBM dominance and layoffs, many Lotus employees left shortly thereafter, including ten senior executives and CEO Jim Manzi, whose acrimonious takeover battle with Gerstner brought with it too much baggage and varied opinion.

However, Gerstner and Thompson were able to convince a core contingent of Lotus workers to stay, most notably the Iris Associates group, not through financial incentives or titles as they had already received those when Lotus had bought them earlier, but with the promise of making Notes successful by providing resources, marketing expertise, and access to many global corporate customers to sell such a complex product on a large scale in pursuit of their dream of seeing Notes as a widely adopted platform. Those retained included the two single-most indispensable Lotus employees: Notes creator Ray Ozzie (who stayed until late 1997), and CTO John Landry, technology guru and sound business visionary.

After the deal closed, IBM kept its promise. It kept Lotus as a separate subsidiary in its existing facilities with its original name and corporate regulations, including compensation plans and benefits. Former Lotus Vice Presidents Michael Zisman and Jeff Papows became the CEO and COO respectively, and reported to Thompson, who reported to Gerstner. Zisman had worked closely with IBM for fifteen years, and Papows knew Lotus and Notes inside out. Other than the new Lotus CFO, not a single IBM person filled Lotus ranks in the first six months. Those who had left were replaced by Lotus employees, not IBM people. Meanwhile, Landry became a close adviser to Gerstner. To control interaction, Thompson assigned a person in his office to be a full-time gatekeeper of all communications between the companies for the first year, to avoid an overwhelming flurry of well-intentioned suggestions from IBMers.

In product development, IBM terminated all internal development projects that might compete with Lotus. Lotus was allowed open access to IBM's vast research and development technologies, and utilized several features such as voice recognition in its development of new versions of Notes. Also, although the IBM and Lotus sides were to develop separate products, in pursuit of promoting the understanding to facilitate complementary software to be built, IBM commenced a small joint development project between the two sides, by having engineers migrate back and forth, which even resulted in the creation of Java-based suite of productivity applications called eSuite, for network-based computing.

In the sales function, after six months of limiting interaction to allow Lotus to become accustomed to the new arrangements, IBM sent 600 of its people to help Lotus' sales force, to provide Lotus sufficient resources to ramp-up its sales, especially to IBM's large set of customers, and cross-sell IBM and Lotus products. IBM and Lotus salespeople doubled up on accounts to jointly conduct sales calls. Subsequently, after IBM sales-people had understood Lotus' product and Lotus' salespersons had gotten to know IBM's customers, account management slots could be individu-ally allocated with executives from either side. In manufacturing, IBM even consolidated its own software production into Lotus' facilities, noting their superior operating efficiencies.

Over time, through its relationship and joint marketing with Lotus, IBM's software strategy not only developed around network-based com-puting, but extended into the Internet, much under the influence of Landry, who convinced Gerstner of its importance. The firm also purchased the companies Domino and Tivoli to be able to combine distributed middle-ware from Lotus with Domino Web servers and Tivoli systems manage-ment to provide complete software solutions for Internet commerce, which when coupled with IBM's hardware and consulting led to comprehensive e-business offerings. Simultaneously, as IBM's software division developed itself around Notes, it was infused with the more open, less formal, and very entrepreneurial Lotus culture, which further cross-pollinated into the hard-ware division as it was pooled into solutions, especially as IBM's powerful sales force navigated all three areas.

Despite the hostile start to the acquisition and unfavorable predictions by industry analysts, three years after the merger, the deal met nearly all strategic and financial projections, and IBM built a leadership position in the networked desktop computing market, receiving mention in the same breath with Microsoft and Oracle. Before the merger, fewer than 3 million copies of Notes were sold, and within three years, 20 million copies were sold, while Lotus' workforce grew to twice its size. Annual attrition rate at Lotus was at this point 6 percent, less than the 11 percent prior to the merger. Moreover, for every dollar of revenue from Notes, IBM made another two dollars in hardware, service, support, and consulting. Thus, the Lotus acquisition catalyzed IBM's transformation from the mainframe-manufacturer Big Blue to the Internet-oriented e-business provider New Blue, which could offer complete hardware and software solutions.

Insights from IBM

IBM's integration approach differed from Cisco's strategy both in form and in execution, given the different objectives behind the deal. Lotus had a product that IBM was seeking to sell as a technically stand-alone applica-tion alongside IBM's software, rather than as part of an integrated system. Thus, there was virtually no knowledge exchange required in product de-velopment, while the desire to cross-sell the independent products and other services demanded bidirectional knowledge flow in the sales function so that the respective sales forces could understand the sales consulting and service required for these different complex products. In manufacturing, as Lotus was a focused software company, IBM could benefit from knowledge flow from Lotus to IBM.

Therefore, in product development, IBM implemented high retention, minor learning effort, low human integration, and slow human integration to maximize preservation and direct utilization of tacit knowledge at Lotus without its transfer. As tacit knowledge preservation was critical, it was necessary that the relevant people—in this case the Notes developers—stayed. The loss of the other engineers and executives hence did not matter as much. As financial incentives would not work, by allowing the Iris Associates individuals to continue working in positions and tasks as previously, and by aligning the acquisition strategic vision with theirs, namely to make Notes a widely used product, IBM was able to retain Ozzie and his team. Furthermore, IBM did not spend much time with learning effort so that Lotus engineers could concentrate on Notes, and only employed a small joint project to create eSuites to have basic understanding between developers on both sides to allow them to build complementary products, but not conduct any major tacit knowledge transfer.

The degree of human integration was limited by having the Lotus engineers be in a separate organizational unit in a separate location, so as to foster no potential disturbance to their interaction and hence maximize tacit knowledge preservation an direct utilization in developing Notes. Likewise, the pace of human integration was kept very slow by buffering communication through Thompson's office. Only the active leadership of Landry led to some interaction at the top levels where there was a little more human integration, paving the way for IBM to steer toward network computing and subsequently Internet products.

In contrast, in the sales function, where bidirectional knowledge flow was required to be able to scale Lotus Notes' marketing and cross-sell other IBM products with it, the integration strategy adopted was one of high retention, high learning effort, medium human integration, and moderate speed of integration to balance tacit knowledge transfer and application with preservation. IBM offered the same financial incentives, positions, and important role in realizing the strategic vision to the Lotus sales staff, and was able to retain a large enough critical mass as a result. Simultaneously, to fulfill the objective of scaling and cross-selling, IBM engaged in a high learning effort by engaging in large-scale joint sales projects and account management between salespersons of both sides, in order to accelerate tacit knowledge transfer and application.

The degree of human integration supported these imperatives. To keep the tacit knowledge of selling such complex products as Notes intact, the degree of human integration was limited by keeping Lotus as a separate organizational unit in a different location, while at the same time having acquired executives Zisman, Papows, and Landry working with IBM top manager Thompson to promote interaction amongst the two sides. Similarly, the speed of human integration supported these efforts. By actively matching employees one-to-one by doubling account management, the rate of inter-action was increased and knowledge transfer and application could ensue, while buffering the sales organizations from each other for a long time en-sured that the tacit knowledge was first preserved. Once preserved, these heavily activated mechanisms to transmit and apply tacit knowledge by the large and powerful IBM sales and consulting force paved the way for IBM to shift its entire strategy around network computing and eventually the Internet, with a corresponding aligned entrepreneurial culture part of the tacit knowledge gained from Lotus.

In manufacturing, given Lotus' sole focus on producing software, IBM saw benefits in receiving knowledge from Lotus. As such, through financial incentives, maintenance of similar positions, and an important role in the merged organization, IBM was able to keep the Lotus workers in this area, leading to the preservation of tacit knowledge associated with manufactur-ing. The learning effort expended was high, as IBM needed to learn, and was enacted by the largest possible joint project: the consolidation of IBM's production into Lotus' facilities, leading to transfer and application of the target's tacit knowledge.

The degree of human integration was aligned with these needs, as the combination of the facilities into the same location promoted tacit knowl-edge transfer and application, while lower-powered leaders from both sides prevented full interaction and hence dissipation of the implicit understand-ing. The speed of human integration had a similar effect. While matching everyone at once with each other accelerated interaction and thereby tacit knowledge transfer and application, the initial buffering first preserved it.

Thus, by enacting these various mechanisms to implement a human inte-gration strategy, IBM was able to preserve, transfer, and apply as necessary the tacit knowledge in each of the functions to create value from its acquisi-tion as envisioned in the takeover. The demands of this situation contrasted with Cisco's challenge, and moreover, in IBM's case, an important compo-nent of the tacit knowledge in Lotus was in the latter's culture of doing things, which had to be delicately managed.

Implementing Human Integration Strategies

In high-technology acquisitions, the integration process creates value by preserving, transferring, and applying the capabilities from the purchased or-ganization in the buying company, in order to develop, manufacture, and sell innovative products that yield financial returns to the acquirer. Capabilities comprise explicit and tacit knowledge, and while explicit knowledge is captured by combining physical assets and organizational processes, tacit knowledge is extracted by assimilating people. Therefore, the integration of employees actually represents the preservation, transfer, and application

TABLE **12.1** Executing Human Integration Strategies

Dimensions of Human Integration Strategy	Tactical Mechanisms for Implementation
Retention of employees	▪ Financial incentives
	▪ Nature of work and position
	▪ Vision for merged entity
Degree of human integration	▪ Organizational design and identity recognition
	▪ Geographical location
	▪ Leadership
Speed of human integration	▪ Communication
	▪ Buffering
	▪ Matching
Learning effort	▪ Training
	▪ Partner system
	▪ Joint projects

of the tacit knowledge in the target, which is generally a substantial component of the capabilities in such takeovers, given the rapidly changing environments and the difficulties in codifying such understanding and experience.

In these types of mergers, the target people thus represent strategic resources that directly influence value creation from the acquisitions, because without them, products cannot be created, produced, or sold. As such, their integration is a strategic exercise, analogous to the integration of physical assets and organizational processes. Human integration strategies comprise the dimensions of employee retention, degree of human integration, speed of human integration, and learning effort, all of which affect the manner in which the tacit knowledge from the bought organization is preserved, transferred, and applied. In terms of their effect on knowledge extraction, there are tradeoffs inherent in each of these components, and the desirable design of the comprehensive strategy depends upon the tacit knowledge exchange required. The direction of the tacit knowledge flow required determines the necessary retention, learning effort, degree of integration, and speed of integration of the people.

The Cisco and IBM case studies illustrate the impact of different human integration strategies aligned with varying acquisition-objective-based tacit knowledge exchange contexts, and identify various tactics and mechanisms to implement each of the strategic dimensions, which are compiled in Table 12.1. These levers can be used to control the amount of retention of target employees, their degree of integration, speed of integration, and the magnitude of learning to create the most effective and efficient human integration process in the acquisition at hand.

Strong financial incentives, work and positions tailored to target people's desires, and a vision of the merged entity that includes an important role for the target all enhance retention. Likewise, a postmerger organizational design that integrates target functions more tightly with the acquirer counterparts and emphasizes identity recognition of the target in terms of new organizational membership in lieu of closer linkage to their heritage, closer geographical location of buying and acquired employees, and assimilation and postintegration operational leadership with high-level purchased and acquiring executives all facilitate greater human integration. Similarly, frequent communications by the acquiring people with the target employees, little buffering, and more employee-matching increases the pace of human integration. Finally, more training, one-to-one partnering systems, and joint integration and business projects improves learning between the employees. Use of these mechanisms in a correspondingly reverse manner, of course, creates the opposite effect on each of the strategic dimensions.

Beyond High-Technology Acquisitions

The lessons derived here apply not only to acquisitions in high-technology industries, but to any merger that involves the purchase of capabilities with large tacit knowledge components. This is often the case with acquisitions in professional services such as investment banking, consulting, and advertising, with mergers in pharmaceuticals and biotechnology, with combinations in media and entertainment, besides for buyouts in automotive and other engineering sectors. In these acquisitions, human integration strategies can simply be applied to each of the relevant functions. Strategic human integration, coupled with similarly intended task integration of physical assets and organizational processes, is the means by which value is created from these types of deals.

Note

1. The cases have been compiled using information gathered from public sources as well as personal interviews with employees at the firms, and are part of the extensive data I have been collecting in my research on high-technology acquisitions since 1998.

References

Ahuja, G., and Katila, R. (2001). Technological acquisitions and the innovation performance of acquiring firms: A longitudinal study. *Strategic Management Journal*, 22(3): 197–220.

Ashford, S. J. (1988). Individual strategies for coping with stress during organizational transitions. *Journal of Applied Behavioral Science*, 24(1): 19–36.

Asquith, P., Bruner, R., and Mullins, D. (1983). The gains to bidding firms from merger. *Journal of Financial Economics*, 11(1–4): 121–39.

Badaracco, J. L., Jr. (1991). *The Knowledge Link: How Firms Compete Through Strategic Alliances*. Boston, MA: Harvard Business School Press.

Bastien, D. T. (1994). A feedback loop model of postmerger performance. *Management Communication Quarterly*, 8(1): 46–70.

Begley, T. M., and Yount, B. A. (1994). Enlisting personnel of the target to combat resentment. *Mergers and Acquisitions*, 29(2): 27–32.

Birkinshaw, J. (1999). Acquiring intellect: Managing the integration of knowledge-intensive acquisitions. *Business Horizons*, 42(3): 33–42.

Birkinshaw, J., Bresman, H., and Hakanson, L. (2000). Managing the post-acquisition integration process: How the human integration and task integration processes interact to foster value creation. *Journal of Management Studies*, 37(3): 395–425.

Bower, J. (2001). Not all M&As are alike—and that matters. *Harvard Business Review*, March: 93–101.

Boyd, R. G., Sr. (1990). How employee thievery can plague an acquisition. *Mergers and Acquisitions*, 24(4): 58–61.

Brockner, J. (1992). Managing the effects of layoffs on survivors. *California Management Review*, 34(2): 9–28.

Buono, A. F., and Bowditch, J. L. (1989). *The Human Side of Mergers and Acquisitions: Managing Collisions Between People, Cultures and Organizations*. San Francisco: Jossey-Bass.

Canella, A. A., and Hambrick, D. C. (1993). Effects of executive departures on the performance of acquired firms. *Strategic Management Journal*, 14: 137–52.

Capron, L., Mitchell, W., and Swaminathan, A. (2001). Asset divestiture following horizontal acquisitions: A dynamic view. *Strategic Management Journal*, 22: 817–44.

Chakrabarti, A., Hauschildt, A. J., and Süverkrüp, C. (1994). Does it pay to acquire technological firms? *R&D Management*, 24(1): 47–56.

Chakrabarti, A. K., and Souder, W. E. (1987). Technology, innovation and performance in corporate mergers: A managerial evaluation. *Technovation*, 6(2): 103–114.

Chatterjee, S., Lubatkin, M. H., Schweiger, D. M., and Weber, Y. (1992). Cultural differences and shareholder value in related mergers: Linking equity and human capital. *Strategic Management Journal*, 13(5): 319–34.

Chaudhuri, S., and Tabrizi, B. (1999). Capturing the real value in high-tech acquisitions. *Harvard Business Review*, 77(5): 123–30.

Clark, K., and Ofek, E. (1994). Mergers and a means of restructuring distressed firms: An empirical investigation. *Journal of Financial and Quantitative Analysis*, 29(4): 541–65.

Covin, T. J., Sightler, K. W., Kolenko, T. A., and Tudor, R. K. (1996). An investigation of post-acquisition satisfaction with the merger. *Journal of Applied Behavioral Science*, 32(2): 125–42.

Datta, D. K. (1991). Organizational fit and acquisition performance: Effects of post-acquisition integration. *Strategic Management Journal*, 12: 281–97.

Dessler, G. (1999). How to earn your employees' commitment. *Academy of Management Executive*, 13(2): 58–67.

Eisenhardt, K. M. (1989). Making fast strategic decisions in high-velocity environments. *Academy of Management Journal*, 32: 543–76.

Empson, L. (2000). Merging professional service firms. *Business Strategy Review*, 11(2): 39–46.

Ernst, H., and Vitt, J. (2000). The influence of corporate acquisitions on the behaviour of key inventors. *R&D Management*, 30(2): 105–19.

Fine, C. (1998). *Clockspeed*. Boston, MA: Perseus Books.

Grant, R. M. (1996). Prospering in dynamically competitive environments: Organizational capability as knowledge integration. *Organization Science*, 7: 375–87.

Hambrick, D., and Canella, A. (1993). Relative standing: A framework for understanding departures of acquired executives. *Academy of Management Journal*, 36(4): 733–62.

Harrison, R. (1972). Understanding your organization's character. *Harvard Business Review*, 50(3): 119–28.

Haspeslagh, P. C., and Jemison, D. B. (1991). *Managing Acquisitions*. New York: The Free Press.

Hitt, M. A., Hoskisson, R. E., Johnson, R. A., and Moesel, D. D. (1996). The market for corporate control and firm innovation. *Academy of Management Journal*, 39(5): 1084–119.

Hoskisson, R. A., Hitt, M. A., and Ireland, D. (1994). The effects of acquisitions and restructuring (strategic refocusing) strategies on innovation. In von Krogh, . Sinatra, and Singh (eds.), *The Management of Corporate Acquisitions: International Perspectives*. Houndmills: Macmillan, pp. 144–69.

Huber, G. (1991). Organizational learning: The contributing processes and the literatures. *Organization Science*, 2: 88–115.

Jarrel, G., and Poulsen, A. (1989). The returns to acquiring firms in tender offers: Evidence from three decades. *Financial Management*, 18(3): 12–9.

Jemison, D. B., and Sitkin, S. B. (1986). Corporate acquisitions: A process perspective. *Academy of Management Review*, 11(1): 145–63.

Karim, S., and Mitchell, W. (2000). Path-dependent and path-breaking change: Reconfiguring business resources following acquisitions in the U.S. medical sector, 1978–1995. *Strategic Management Journal*, 21: 1061–81.

Kitching, J. (1967). Why do mergers miscarry? *Harvard Business Review*, 45(6): 84–101.

Kogut, B., and Zander, U. (1992). Knowledge of the firm, combinative capabilities and the replication of technology. *Organization Science*, 3: 383–97.

Kusewitt, J. B. (1985). An exploratory study of strategic acquisition factors relating to performance. *Strategic Management Journal*, 6: 151–69.

Larsson, R., and Finkelstein, S. (1999). Integrating strategic, organizational, and human resource perspectives on mergers and acquisitions: A case survey of synergy realization. *Organization Science*, 10(1): 1–26.

Leonard-Barton, D. (1992). Core capabilities and core rigidities. *Strategic Management Journal*, 13: 111–125.

Leonard-Barton, D. (1995). *Wellsprings of Knowledge*. Boston, MA: Harvard Business School Press.

Loderer, C., and Martin, K. (1990). Corporate acquisitions by listed firms: The experience of a comprehensive sample. *Financial Management*, 21(3): 69–79.

Lubatkin, M. (1983). Mergers and the performance of the acquiring firm. *Academy of Management Review*, 8(2): 218–25.

Lubatkin, M. H., Schweiger, D. M., and Weber, Y. (1999). Top management turnover in related M&As: An additional test of the theory of relative standing. *Journal of Management*, 25(1): 55–73.

MacCormack, A. (2001). Product-development practices that work: How Internet companies build software. *Sloan Management Review*, 42(2): 75–84.

Marks, M. L., and Mirvis, P. H. (1986). The merger syndrome; when companies combine, a clash of cultures can turn potentially good business alliances into financial disasters. *Psychology Today*, 20(10): 36–42.

Marks, M. L., and Mirvis, P. H. (2001). Making mergers and acquisitions work: Strategic and psychological preparation. *Academy of Management Executive*, 15(2): 80–94.

Mendelson, H., and Pillai, R. R. (1999). Industry clockspeed: Measurement and operational implications. *Manufacturing and Service Operations Management*, 1(1): 1–20.

Napier, N. K. (1989). Mergers and acquisitions, human resource issues and outcomes: A review and suggested typology. *Journal of Management Studies*, 26(3): 271–89.

Nelson, R., and Winter, S. (1982). *An Evolutionary Theory of Economic Change*. Cambridge, MA: Harvard University Press.

Pritchett, P. (1985). *After the Merger: Managing the Shockwaves*. New York: Dow Jones-Irwin.

Puranam, P. (2000). *The Management and Performance of Technology Grafting Acquisitions*. Working Paper, The Wharton School.

Ranft, A. L., and Lord, M. D. (2000). Acquiring new knowledge: The role of retaining human capital in acquisitions of high-tech firms. *Journal of High Technology Management Research*, 11(2): 295–321.

Ranft, A. L., and Lord, M. D. (2002). Acquiring new technologies and capabilities: A grounded model of acquisition implementation. *Organization Science*, 13(4): 420–41.

Robinson, W. (1998). Finding easy money on the target's shop floor. *Mergers and Acquisitions*, 33(3): 35–8.

Sales, A. L., and Mirvis, P. H. (1984). When cultures collide: Issues in acquisition. In Kimberly and Quinn (ed.), *Managing Organizational Transitions*. Homewood, IL: Dow Jones-Irwin, pp. 107–33.

Schein, E. (1986). *Organizational Culture and Leadership*. San Francisco: Jossey-Bass.

Scherer, F., and Ross, D. (1990). *Industrial Market Structure and Economic Performance*, 3rd edn. Boston, MA: Houghton Mifflin Company.

Schweiger, D. M., and Ivancevich, J. M. (1985). Human resources: The forgotten factor in mergers and acquisitions. *Personnel Administrator*, 30(11): 47–61.

Shirley, R. C. (1973). Analysis of employee and physician attitudes toward a hospital merger. *Academy of Management Journal*, 16: 465–80.

Shrivastava, P. (1986). Postmerger integration. *Journal of Business Strategy*, 7(1): 65–76.

Slowinski, G. (1992). The human touch in successful strategic alliances. *Mergers and Acquisitions*, 27(1): 44–7.

Slowinski, G., Rafii, Z., Tao, J., Gollob, L., and Krishnamurthy, K. R. (2000). Integrating R&D organizations in a merger and acquisition. *Research Technology Management*, 43(5): 11–12.

Smith, K. W., and Hershman, S. E. (1997). How M&A fits into a real growth strategy. *Mergers and Acquisitions*, 32(2): 38–42.

Tetenbaum, T. J. (1999). Beating the odds of merger and acquisition failure: Seven key practices that improve the chance for expected integration and synergies. *Organizational Dynamics*, 28(2): 22–36.

Weber, Y. (1996). Corporate cultural fit and performance in mergers and acquisitions. *Human Relations*, 49(9): 1181–201.

Winter, S. (1987). Knowledge and competence as strategic assets. In Teece (ed.), *The Competitive Challenge: Strategies for Industrial Innovation and Renewal*. New York: Harper and Row, pp. 159–84.

Zollo, M., and Singh, H. (2000). *The Impact of Knowledge Codification, Experience Trajectories and Integration Strategies on the Performance of Corporate Acquisitions*. Working Paper, The Wharton School.

13 The CNH Global Case

Building Social Capabilities to Win in Global
Acquisitions, Joint Ventures, and Alliances[1]

PIERO MOROSINI

Overview

The exceedingly high failure rate of acquisitions worldwide over the last three decades of the twentieth century suggests that our conventional theories explaining why acquisition activity occurs might have failed as well. Quite disturbingly, very similar empirical evidence and arguments seem to also apply to international joint ventures (JVs) and alliances.[2] Indeed, this dismal performance track record has legitimately raised the question: Are international acquisitions, JVs, and alliances about creating value at all?

In this chapter we will examine in detail the case of CNH Global's construction equipment, which raises these issues from a remarkably different perspective to what most conventional value-creating theories maintain. By building strong social "connecting tissue" fast between the joining target companies, JV counterparts, and alliance partners, CNH Global aims at creating real value after the deal while at the same time implementing a highly unusual global growth strategy.

Some readers will agree with CNH Global's executives that it is possible to create value through acquisitions, JVs, and alliances, but only at the expense of building strong social commonalities between the companies involved in these transactions. In order to do this successfully after the deal is done, these readers will find CNH's unusual execution approaches quite compelling. However, other readers will disagree, perhaps arguing in favor of either the more gradual and "hands-off" approaches or the harsher, more assertive alternatives that have been traditionally elicited when integrating cross-border acquisitions, JVs, and alliances after the deal.

In the following sections the reader will not find a conventional case study portraying either an immaculate "success" story or yet another example of a devastating "failure." Rather, executives, practitioners, and academics alike will be able to judge for themselves whether or not an innovative and challenging strategy of global growth through acquisitions, JVs, and alliances can be successfully underpinned by the building of strong social capabilities between the joining companies.[3]

At any rate, the issues raised by this highly relevant case example underlie the need for executives and academics alike, to reach out beyond conventional theories in this area in order to find creative alternatives that might improve the performance of acquisitions, JVs, and alliances in the future. Given the overwhelming importance gained by international acquisitions, JVs, and alliances in the eve of the new millennium, this undoubtedly constitutes one of today's central challenges in global management theory and practice.

CNH Global: Building a Global Player Through M&A, JVs, and Alliances Across Borders

The construction equipment (CE) business of Fiat New Holland (CNH Global's predecessor) was extremely weak during the early 1990s. As a CNH Global executive summarized it:

> We [Fiat New Holland] had 40% of the Italian CE market but very little elsewhere, especially in the US, which represented over 40% of the world market in both volume and value. Secondly, we simply did not have heavy excavators in our product portfolio, although they accounted for 50% of the total CE market. Third, we neither possessed nor had access to hydraulics technology, which is most crucial for excavators, especially the heavy type.

Ten years later, however, CNH Global had become one of the world's leading CE manufacturers, with nearly US$4 billion in annual revenues, profitable economic results, 10,000 employees, and 1,700 dealers worldwide. CNH Global boasted a complete product portfolio in CE, ranking number one in the world in light and medium CE, and third in heavy excavators, with an overall market share surpassed by only Caterpillar and Komatsu (refer to Figure 13.1). Construction equipment revenues amounted to $3,785 million in 1999, up 7 percent from 1998. Growth had mostly been achieved through a series of global acquisitions, JVs, and alliances of a hitherto unprecedented scale in the CE industry, involving major players in the European, North American, and Japanese markets. Although the integration of these entities had not been completed by 2000, the turnaround achieved thus far had been remarkable.

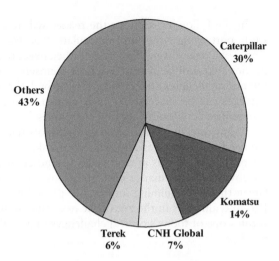

FIGURE **13.1** Global Construction Equipment Market Shares (Q2 2002) (*Note*: 100 percent = $40 billion; Salomon Smith Barney, 2002)

The Unlikely Beginnings of a Truly Global Player

Historically, Fiat had been a pioneer in the agricultural equipment (AG) and CE businesses in Italy, France, and Spain through its Fiatagri and FiatGeotech divisions. In 1972, Fiat established a JV with U.S.-based Allis to manufacture and distribute AG in North America and Brazil. A CNH Global executive said:

> [The Fiat–Allis JV] ... was not a very successful story. We had built a manufacturing plant in the US as part of this JV, dealing with both AG and CE businesses, but we got out of North America as a result of the lack of success of the Fiat–Allis JV.

In 1989, Fiat acquired Ford New Holland—itself the result of a 1986 merger between Ford Tractors and New Holland—and in 1991 it consolidated its AG activities globally under the name Fiat New Holland. The acquisition gave it access to around 900 dealers carrying industrial products, and a product portfolio of tractor loader backhoes (TLB), skid steer loaders (SSL), tractor loaders, and telehandlers. The same CNH Global executive remarked:

> Ford New Holland was a very strong player in AG, especially in the UK and North and South America, but had a very weak presence in continental Europe or Asia. And you could say exactly the opposite of Fiatagri. The [postacquisition] integration [between Fiat and Ford New Holland] was very

successful even if we really had to merge five companies [FiatGeotech, FiatAgri, Fiat–Allis, Ford Tractors, and New Holland] and at least as many national cultures!

However, until the early 1990s Fiat New Holland had remained a marginal player in the CE industry. At the time, most of the large AG manufacturers, such as Caterpillar and John Deere, were also strong in the CE business, although the two industries had different customers and were driven by substantially different industry forces. Nevertheless, Fiat New Holland executives saw strategic opportunities in the CE industry during the early 1990s:

> We found that strong synergies were possible between AG and CE. Important pieces, not just components, could be shared between both businesses. For example, Fiat Iveco's diesel engine, an excellent piece developed for tractors, could be utilized in both AG and CE vehicles, and a few products such as the skid steer loaders were used by both construction and agricultural workers. On the other hand, both CE customers and [distribution] channels were rather fragmented.

The Fiat–Hitachi JV

To expand its CE business beyond Italy, in 1986 Fiat had entered a JV with Japanese Hitachi to import heavy excavators from Japan into the European Union (EU). Large Japanese CE manufacturers had been in search of European partners for some time in order to avoid the EU's antidumping tariffs on Japanese products and to secure a manufacturing foothold in Europe, which represented 28 percent of world demand in CE.

Fiat's JV with Hitachi was joined by Sumitomo. It was named Fiat–Hitachi Excavators SpA and began operations in 1987, with Fiat having a 51 percent stake, Hitachi 44 percent, and Sumitomo 5 percent. In the period from 1987 to 1990, sales rose from L 150 billion (lire) to L 400 billion and its share of the European excavators market went up from 7 to 13 percent.

The JV's operations were entirely controlled by Italian management. Fiat's executives had responsibility for finance, purchasing, human resources, logistics, and sales and marketing, as well as managing a sales and distribution network covering Europe, Africa, and the Middle East. Hitachi's management coordinated the "industrial" functions of engineering, manufacturing, and quality. "Coordinated" was the operative word, as Fiat–Hitachi Excavators SpA relied solely on Italian personnel, backed up by a dozen Japanese engineers acting as technical consultants plus a controller, a marketing expert, and an executive vice president who represented Hitachi on the board of directors.

Following the creation of Fiat New Holland in 1991, the JV with Hitachi gave the company access to the key hydraulics technology for heavy excavators and an improved market position in Europe. However, the United States remained a major CE market where Fiat New Holland did not have a strong presence. The Fiat–Hitachi JV explicitly excluded the North American markets, and John Deere, a rival company in the AG business, already had a similar arrangement with Hitachi in the U.S. market. During the mid-1990s Fiat New Holland concluded that in order to stay in the CE business, a competitive presence in the United States was indispensable. Through the more extensive New Holland AG dealerships in the United States, the company was able to offer a strong portfolio of products in the light CE segment. However, this was not enough to survive in the U.S. CE market, as the local dealers definitely preferred to work with "full-line" competitors such as Caterpillar. A company executive noted:

> In 1995 we realized that we had to have a heavy excavator in the US or get out of the CE business.

The Acquisition of Orenstein & Koppel

Fiat New Holland acquired German Orenstein & Koppel's (O&K) CE business in November 1998. This allowed it to launch a full range of excavators in the United States under its existing New Holland brand. A Fiat New Holland executive observed:

> It was very simple. Only the Germans and the Japanese had excavator technology. So, in order for us to offer a full range of excavators in the US, we had to secure access to either a Japanese excavator technology source different from Hitachi or a German one.

O&K's excavator business had an interesting profile: Once O&K's elevator activities had been divested to Kones in Denmark and its mining equipment to Terex of the US, the remaining business activities showed a strong product range within heavy CE. O&K had nineteen basic models of heavy CE, of which it sold 1,802 units in 1997. In addition, 79 percent of O&K's sales were in Western Europe, with Germany being the largest market (47 percent of sales in 1998). Total sales amounted to €412 million in 1998. The complementarity between New Holland and O&K in terms of product range and geographical match made a strong case for the acquisition.

Then, in early 1999, Fiat New Holland's management decided to give O&K a change of direction: All of O&K's lines of excavators would continue to be produced at O&K's Berlin-based manufacturing plant, but products were to be sold in different ways across different geographic regions worldwide. In Germany and Europe, O&K's brand would still be sold through the same channels as before. But for the U.S. market, the O&K excavator was to be customized and sold under the New Holland brand.

Developing New Holland's Product Offering in the United States

The New Holland brand was to lead the development of Fiat New Holland's presence in the North American CE market. Following the 1998 O&K acquisition, New Holland's product range was very rapidly completed with multiple models targeting high potential segments in both light and heavy CE. Thus, a comprehensive range of New Holland CE was on offer in the United States: excavators made in Berlin, loaders and bulldozers from Lecce (southern Italy), telehandlers from Imola (San Marino, central Italy), and graders from Brazil. A truly multinational supply chain was set in motion, with seventeen models of light segment product offerings launched in 1998–1999, and thirteen models of heavy segment product offerings launched in 1999.

In the medium term this wave of new product launches and the broadening of existing model lines was set to continue. For the light CE product range, the number of models was planned to increase from 24 in 1997 to 47 in 2002, of which 23 were additional models and 11 were renewed. These included midi wheel excavators, midi crawler excavators, mini crawler excavators, mini wheel loaders, backhoe loaders, skid steer loaders, and telehandlers. For the heavy CE products, 38 different models covering six key product lines would increase to 53 models in 2002, of which 15 were additional models and 30 were new. These products included crawler excavators, wheel excavators, wheel loaders, dozers, crawler loaders, and graders.

Restructuring the Dealer Network in the United States

During 1999, New Holland's product range in the united States was becoming more complete than ever before in the company's history. The next step was to optimize its existing distribution channels. This had become a priority as New Holland's distribution dealerships for light CE had traditionally been very fragmented: Just 50 out of its 900 U.S. dealers sold more than 50 units of New Holland light CE every year. For a manufacturer interested in competing on a global scale this presented a clear handicap. In addition, New Holland had historically sold its heavy CE through five "master distributors" that had a negligible share of the U.S. market, as the following figures show: 1.6 percent crawler loaders, 1.5 percent wheel loaders, 0.6 percent dozers, and 4.1 percent graders.

The company decided that only the New Holland brand would remain in the United States. The contracts with the master distributors would be phased out over a few years. New Holland dealers were to sell New Holland brands exclusively, and *either* CE *or* AG. Fiat New Holland's commitment to provide a full product range allowed it to select the best performers from its existing dealer base as well as lure new dealers away from its more specialized competitors. The number of exclusive New Holland dealers was to be significantly reduced to 125 for CE and about 150 for AG. New Holland Construction would continue selling tractors, while New Holland Agriculture would continue selling skid steer loaders and tractor loader backhoes.

The Merger with Case: CNH Global is Born

On May 16, 1999, Fiat New Holland announced the acquisition of U.S.-based Case Corporation. The merged company, renamed CNH Global, would have revenues worth $12 billion in both the AG and CE businesses, and would surpass global market leader Caterpillar in numbers of AG units manufactured. However, the analysts remained skeptical. One of them remarked:

> Long-term, it is an excellent deal. In the CE industry, a complete range of products is driven largely by scale. The industry leader, Caterpillar, offers both wide product range and volume. But both Fiat New Holland and Case already are considered "full liners" in CE. They will face a real challenge in integrating the company under one umbrella.

An investment banker familiar with the deal commented:

> The acquisition is expected to dilute earnings until 2001. As for the cost savings from the deal, estimated by Case and Fiat New Holland at $400 million to $500 million a year, these will probably take a few years to realize.

The Kobelco Alliance

In March 2001 CNH Global made public its plans to enter a global alliance with Japanese Kobelco Construction Machinery (wholly owned by Kobe Steel) to develop, produce, and market crawler excavators. Founded in 1999, Kobelco was the world's fourth largest producer of hydraulic excavators.

Under the agreement, which was finalized in January 2002, CNH Global purchased a 20 percent stake in Kobelco Construction Machinery, with an option to buy a further 15 percent. Additionally, CNH Global obtained a 65 percent interest in Kobelco America. Kobelco in turn acquired all of CNH Global's CE operations in Australia, Asia, and China, as well as exclusive rights to distribute CNH Global's CE product offering in Japan and the Asia-Pacific region.

CNH Global president and CEO Paolo Monferino described the alliance:

> This alliance is of strategic importance for our current and future position within the global construction equipment business. The introduction of the new [crawler] excavator technology will allow CNH [Global] the global reach we require to be competitive in today's [CE] market. A best-in-class product offering, economies of scale, purchasing and manufacturing efficiencies, and a stronger and wider distribution network are the key success factors of the newly announced alliance.[4]

At the same time, CNH Global and Hitachi Construction Machinery agreed to end their European JV in July 2002, with a transition period extending through 2003 (for the purposes of customer service). CNH Global acquired Hitachi's stake in the Fiat–Hitachi venture. Kobelco Construction Machinery then formed a JV with CNH Global named Fiat–Kobelco Construction Machinery SpA. The JV would produce crawler excavators using Kobelco technology—to be sold under both the Fiat–Kobelco and Kobelco brands from January 2003—as well as heavy CE previously sold under the Fiat–Hitachi brand. CNH Global held a 75 percent stake in the JV, Kobelco a 20 percent stake, with Sumitomo Corp. holding the remaining 5 percent. Through the JV, Kobelco was able to establish manufacturing operations in Europe, while CNH Global was able to further extend its product offering.

Another advantage of the global alliance for CNH Global was greater market access for its full range of CE products via Kobelco's strong distribution network. Kobelco's interest in the alliance lay in becoming a full-line supplier, and in strengthening its presence in Europe. Through this global alliance, in the words of Tsuguto Moriwaki, Kobelco's president and CEO:

> Kobelco will become a full line supplier of construction equipment in Japan and the Asia Pacific region, with the addition of CNH's broad product offering which serves all industry segments in specific customer needs... Kobelco will also have access to state of the art manufacturing plants in Europe.[5]

CNH Global CE's "Multibrand and Multichannel" Strategy

Following Fiat New Holland's 1999 acquisition of Case, Fausto Lanfranco, who had led the Fiat–Hitachi JV since 1996, became president of CNH Global's CE business. The new company's top management immediately set about designing a strategic direction for the business that would make sense of its unlikely mix of multiple brands, national and corporate cultures, customer groups, and organizational functions and geographies.

On the one hand, the new strategy was to reflect the fact that at the dawn of the twenty-first century there were very few truly global customers in the CE market. Large CE customers certainly had international reach, but they were typically concentrated in one particular geographic region and clearly favored one CE brand above all others. Moreover, the use of specific kinds of CE varied strongly along national cultural and climatic lines. For example, Japanese building companies preferred to use "angled" excavators, whereas German ones generally bought "rubber-wheeled" excavators.

On the other hand, the new CNH Global strategy had to take into account the major role that CE dealers played in reaching and selling to the customers. Jim McCullough, Senior Vice President of CNH Global's CE business, commented:

> [. . . CE] customers are looking for more than equipment. They're looking for the relationship with their equipment dealer—the professional partnership that encompasses total solutions, including service, parts, warranty and financing that go months and years beyond the sale. They're looking for a partner they won't outgrow as they expand their business to include larger construction and utility projects, highway and road-building and more.[6]

All the exclusive CE dealership contracts were brand-based, and if CNH Global were to combine two brands in one, it would risk losing half of its dealers and the associated sales volumes. As the New Holland and Case brands had a strong presence in different geographic areas, CNH Global decided to pursue a "multibrand and multichannel" strategy for its CE business. Lanfranco remarked:

> From the outset we realized that CNH Global's strategy in the construction business could be encapsulated in two words: multi-brand and multi-channel. This approach was radically different from our major competitors like Caterpillar, Komatsu, Volvo or JCB who sold all over the world under a single brand name through a single type of distribution channel.

CNH Global's multibrand approach meant that it would sell its CE under the Case and New Holland brands in the United States, under Fiat–Hitachi, O&K, New Holland Light, and Case in the EU, and under both the Case and the New Holland–Allis brands in South America. Maintaining these different brands allowed the company to use all of its existing dealership networks. Thus, multichannel distribution meant that CNH Global could reach different CE customers through different dealership networks offering their distinct brands.

At the same time, CNH Global decided to create global CE "product development platforms" in order to manufacture different product lines while sharing fundamental parts. Lanfranco observed:

> A CNH Global line of CE products is highly differentiated per brand, distribution channel, customer segment or region. But a CNH Global [CE manufacturing] plant is not differentiated. We even share some components and the same suppliers in many cases. In fact, our "multi-brand, multi-channel" strategy forced us to drastically rationalize and transform our [manufacturing] plants, so that we could manufacture differentiated product lines on the same [global] platforms.

CNH Global intended to apply the multibrand, multichannel strategy to its CE business on a global scale, as described by McCullough:

> [This] is also the strategy we will follow in our new alliance with Kobelco Construction Machinery. Construction equipment users tend to be brand loyal. They take tremendous pride in the equipment they own and operate, and they want to be recognized for making smart choices. Case and New Holland have loyal followers. Both have unique attributes. Both have well-established dealer networks. And both are in a position to benefit from the shared strength of CNH Global through manufacturing synergies, research and development.[7]

The Need for Product Differentiation

Product differentiation became a centerpiece of CNH Global's multi-brand, multichannel strategy for its CE business. The company approached this concept from two different and complementary perspectives. Lanfranco explained:

> "Upstream" product differentiation means that we manage multiple [CE] brands and multiple [CE] distribution dealerships that serve different customer groups. "Downstream" product differentiation means that we have to share manufacturing components without erasing the essential differences between product lines or product brands "as perceived by the customers." So, differentiation does not mean that we essentially produce the same products—only painting them differently for some time and later on selling everything under a single brand. However, differentiation does not mean entirely different products either.

Some types of product differentiation did not necessarily need to be expensive in order to be effective in generating a differentiated customer perception of a specific product family belonging to the same brand. For example, a great deal of "soft" product differentiation could be achieved through the external shape and the design of an excavator, or by the way it felt to the user when sitting inside the cabin of a backhoe loader. McCullough explained the rationale for product differentiation:

> This strategy makes sense because by maintaining distinct brands, we retain the market share represented by the brands. Globally, we [CNH Global] are No. 1 in light to medium construction equipment and No. 3 in Excavators. Driven by brand strength, our growth shows we are offering more options for customers. And we're serving differing customer bases with differing values and needs. Our strategy allows buyers to choose the brand and dealer best able to meet their business needs.[8]

Building a New Global Organization Across Boundaries

In the space of a few years, CNH Global's revenues, profits, and economic value added in the CE business increased significantly, despite particularly challenging market conditions. Between 1995 and 2000, CNH Global's CE business went from $0.7 billion to $4 billion in annual revenues. As a result of its global strategic repositioning (refer to Figure 13.2), by 2002 the company had become one of the few truly global "full-line" CE players, joining the ranks of Caterpillar, Komatsu, and Volvo.

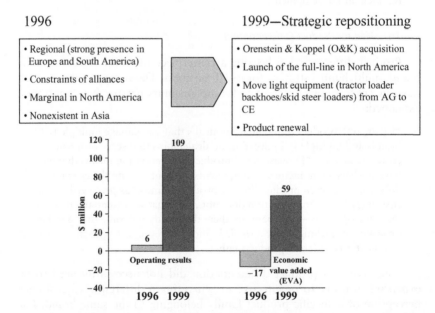

FIGURE **13.2** CNH Global's Strategic Repositioning and Economic Results 1996–1999 (CNH Global, 1999)

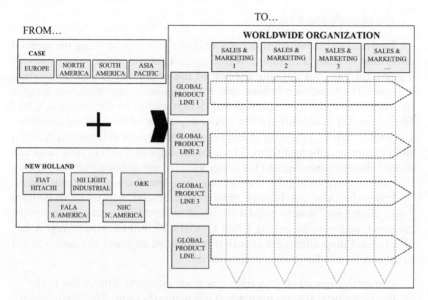

FIGURE **13.3** Organizational Changes in CNH Global's Construction Equipment Business (CNH Global, 1999)

These results reflected a series of unprecedented execution efforts at CNH Global. In the 18 months between October 1999 and March 2001, CNH Global's management had to simultaneously integrate the CE businesses of the German Orenstein & Koppel (O&K) and U.S.-based Case. During the same period, CNH Global had also formed a JV with the Japanese firm Kobelco in the CE business.

CNH Global was the first large-scale competitor in the CE business to attempt a multibrand and multichannel strategy worldwide. Although brands, marketing, and distribution would continue to be managed separately under this strategy, manufacturing product lines would become increasingly global. The organizational blueprint CNH Global designed to support the implementation of this strategy was in essence a matrix organization (refer to Figure 13.3).

The new matrix organization needed to be operational in a very short time. In order to accomplish this, CNH Global carried out a sweeping worldwide reorganization of its CE business during 1999 and 2000. The challenges were particularly daunting because of the existing cultural, geographic, and organizational differences. The approach CNH Global's CE managers put together to rapidly convey the new strategic, managerial, and marketing spirit throughout the organization was called *map alignment.*

The Map Alignment Approach

Lanfranco realized from the outset that the company's key managerial talent had to share a common mental map. This would eventually provide a powerful basis for aligning the rest of the organization with a common purpose. The basic idea behind this map alignment approach was simple: In order to execute a complex global design within its CE business, CNH Global needed to identify the key leadership cadre of the new organization, and build a strong degree of cohesiveness, cooperative relationships, and a shared purpose amongst them. These leadership cadre will in turn "cascade down" the main messages to the lower levels of the organization and ensure that a strong degree of cohesiveness was also created amongst all employees.

From the outset, it became clear that a crucial step to implementing "map alignment" was to build a common understanding of certain words, concepts, and notions among CNH Global's 10,000 CE employees. A key idea behind map alignment was that it intended to foster the involvement of *all* employees. Lanfranco commented:

> Putting this mental map together was made extremely difficult due to the diverse cultural systems from which our managers came. The Anglo-Saxon cultural systems tended to favor linear thinkers, for example, whereas the Mediterranean way of communicating was more multi-active. So, when American executives from Case had to build a common map together with their Italian colleagues from New Holland, their different ways of thinking easily became a big issue. For instance, Italian managers often would consider linear thinkers, with their distinct pattern of speaking and listening, as offensive. But American executives tended to regard the Mediterranean's multi-active way of communicating as chaotic.

Implementing Map Alignment

During the first half of 1999 Lanfranco selected seven executives from the top management of the CE businesses of former Fiat New Holland, Fiat–Hitachi, Fiat–Allis, Case, and O&K to join him in forming an executive team. This team defined the new organizational blueprint for CNH Global's CE business: A matrix organization with two fundamental structural dimensions—on the one hand, the GPL (Global Product Leaders) dimension and, on the other, the local brands and distribution channels.

In addition, a few concrete, pragmatic, and relevant business issues were identified that were critical to the implementation of the new organization. For example, one issue was the global logistics system for the CE business; another was closures of CE manufacturing plants. The executive committee members expected that the urgent need to address these issues would force CNH Global managers in the CE business to develop a common understanding—a common mental map—of the business while simultaneously implementing the company's strategy.

Next, the executive team chose twenty "global managers" from among the top performers of former Fiat New Holland, O&K, and Case. These managers were asked to lead cross-functional projects addressing the business issues the executive team had previously identified. The global managers were given complete freedom to choose their own project teams as long as a balance of culture and geography existed, that is, a certain number of team members had to come from Latin America, a few from Europe, others from North America, and so on. Similarly, a certain number of project team members had to come from Case, others from O&K, some from Fiat–Hitachi, and so forth. Filippo Polifroni, head of human resources (HR) construction equipment, CNH Global, recalled:

> To pick the first 20 global managers was simple because we already knew most of these people. We chose individuals who were experts in their fields and excellent coaches at the same time. People who were open minded and patient to make sure that key messages were understood by others. Then we had to trust these 20 and rely on other people who were new to their positions. This was important because these teams were incredibly crucial to build the new organization of CNH Global's CE business as one company. And in the end you would be surprised to see how little Italians, and how little former Fiat New Holland people, were represented amongst the key cadre of 250 global managers we ended up with in early 2000.

The twenty cross-functional project teams addressed key issues such as global manufacturing platforms, product development processes, procurement and supply chain processes, knowledge sharing on a global scale, and multibranding, to name but a few. The 250–300 global managers involved in these project teams came from different functions and not only addressed the key global processes that were crucial for managing the CE business as a truly integrated operation but also introduced and managed the company's new GPL-based structure. Polifroni commented:

> In the end we achieved map alignment through a cascading effect: First the top 8, then the next 20, then the next 200 to 300. Like three sequential, concentric circles, three waves implemented between September and October 1999 and the spring of 2000.

Working Inside CNH Global's CE Cross-Functional Project Teams

Each of the twenty cross-functional project teams organized itself as it wished. At the beginning some teams had problems understanding CNH Global's strategy for the CE business. Former Case and New Holland employees, for example, were used to the concept of a single global brand and found it difficult to understand how the company would execute a multibrand strategy. Therefore, the project team looking after multibrand strategy implementation went into great detail, looking at every single product line and model, discussing and deciding what components could be shared with which product line and what components had to remain different. Moreover, it analyzed and decided which distribution channels would be allocated to each product line, targeting different customer segments with different dealership networks, marketing mixes, and marketing tools. One project team member said:

> The strength of the map alignment concept was that the way in which product differentiation, multibrand and multichannel strategies were implemented was born within and across our 20 project teams. It was not a top-down process.

The cross-functional project teams also developed a common vocabulary for key terms. The word "logistics" for example had different meanings for different people. For some former New Holland managers this meant the operational flow of materials along a specific supply chain, that is, for manufacturing trucks. However, for a number of former Case executives "logistics" meant "transportation services." There were similar differences across many other terms such as "product marketing," "brand management," and so on.

From defining a common vocabulary, the cross-functional project teams moved on to gaining a common understanding of CNH Global strategy for the CE business. This was also approached as a process of mental alignment around pragmatic, relevant business issues. Polifroni explained:

> We deliberately avoided organizing meetings—big or small—where you talk about strategic visions, common values, behaviors and processes in abstract terms. Instead, we sought to gather groups of high performing professionals and gave them concrete, limited and specific business issues to address.

As a next step, the cross-functional project teams defined the key global processes and procedures that were required to implement the company's strategy. The company's executive team deliberately chose to let these processes evolve from the previous map alignment exercises. Thus, only after a cross-functional project team had developed a sufficiently strong degree of map alignment and a common understanding of their strategic orientation, would they move to address the key global processes and organizational structures that were needed.

There were very few large meetings where all the global managers came together. Instead, the eight-strong CE business executive team was constantly "on the road" visiting the twenty project teams wherever they happened to be. Most project team members did not work full-time on these initiatives; typically, they continued to work on their "normal" assignments as well, "so that the factories were running at the same time," as one project team member put it. Many of the project teams utilized the premises and resources of Isvor Fiat—CNH Global's corporate university—to carry out their project work. Polifroni summarized the company's approach to map alignment:

> Most companies start with setting out their strategy, vision and mission, then define the global processes & organization and only then focus on execution of key projects/tasks. We did it exactly the opposite. We started with map alignment within specific business problems and a very general idea of an organizational blueprint. In the beginning the two key words for us were "common understanding" and "sharing" the meaning of key terms. Once we had achieved that common, shared understanding, we agreed on a common direction to follow, and the global organization and processes just followed naturally from this initial common understanding.

Establishing CNH Global's Organizational Building Blocks

The company implemented English as the official language. When it came to business issues, all the global managers had to speak and write to each other in English, even if the interaction took place between people of the same nationality. In the CE business, CNH Global also set a common and explicit expatriate and repatriate policy for its global manager group. This facilitated continuous transfers and rotations of key managers across countries and functions. To accelerate the flow of management control information, the company implemented a "common hub" IT network, where different IT systems—ranging from varying e-mail platforms to the different financial performance measurement systems of the various acquired companies—could converge and "talk to each other."

Lanfranco and his executive team put together the company's "book of values" and presented it to hundreds of managers at the first of the two annual conventions that were organized in 2000. These annual conventions were a key part of the company's corporate communication program to foster common values, together with monthly newsletters, a dedicated intranet, and videocassettes that were made available to both CE and AG employees.

Because CNH Global's multibrand and multichannel strategy for CE relied heavily on managing multiple brands, product differentiation, and brand-based distribution channels all over the world, the company also created a "book of brands." The substance of each brand—its DNA, as managers at CNH Global called it—was to be identified, understood, and codified in this "book of brands," which was accessible to all company employees.

The "book of brands" provided clear guidelines that reflected a proper understanding of the value inherent in each of the company's brands. Once the "DNA of a brand" had been explicitly defined and managers understood it, modifications to the brand could be undertaken. In turn, this helped managers determine the right degree of product differentiation across the company's full range of product lines. If product differentiation was too low, the brands risked converging and separate dealer networks could find themselves competing for the same customer segments. However, if product differentiation was too high, the potential for cost efficiencies and scale economies in purchasing, manufacturing, and the like might be lost.

CNH Global encouraged the use of video conferences and conference calls to coordinate the various activities across its global CE organizational structure. One global manager commented on this practice:

> [Within CNH Global's CE business] we choose to travel relatively little, except for the top executive team. Instead, we are incredibly big users of video conferences. I believe that each of our 300 global managers in the CE business has got at least one videoconference scheduled every day. To the point that in 2001 we had to install four new video-conferencing positions at [former] Fiat–Hitachi's Torino offices, which can simultaneously engage 60 people.

Lanfranco also instituted monthly business reviews and product development committees to monitor the key activities and initiatives of the CE business. The committees included Lanfranco himself as well as members of the executive team and global managers for whom the topic under review was relevant. Typically, both the reviews and the committees would be conducted on the same day each month at a different manufacturing plant location. During the morning, the business review would involve monitoring management and business goals with key executives responsible for all the company's brands and geographic markets. During the afternoon, they would carry out a similar process with those responsible for global product lines. Polifroni observed:

> We have 15 manufacturing plants today [in 2001], spread across Latin America, North America and Europe. The fact that we do these reviews in a different plant every month is also an opportunity for top management to keep track of what's going on in each of these plants, roughly once per year.

Creating Common Product Platforms

Although CNH Global's CE product offering was typically differentiated by brand, customer segment, or region, manufacturing would be highly standardized worldwide. To achieve this goal, the company's strategy was based on global product development platforms, where differentiated product lines that shared a series of key pieces, components, and suppliers were manufactured.

The implementation of global product development platforms would entail significant rationalization of CNH Global's CE manufacturing plants. In 2000, the company operated with fifteen plants across North America, the EU, and Latin America. Within the next three to five years, this number was to be reduced to only nine plants covering all three geographic regions. Within each manufacturing plant, entirely different brands and differentiated product lines would be manufactured on the same global product development platform. This was to be one of the first truly global standardized manufacturing platform overlays in the automotive industry. In addition, CNH Global's worldwide platform strategy represented an innovative, flexible response to the cyclical manufacturing overcapacity that had historically characterized the CE industry.

Moving Forward

An internal survey carried out early in 2001 at CNH Global recorded the highest degrees of overall employee satisfaction within the CE business. In particular, employees within the CE areas manifested an extremely high degree of commitment to the company's vision and strategy, as well as a tremendous degree of managerial cohesion. Lanfranco observed:

> Map alignment accelerated the process of building a cadre of global leaders which worked very effectively across cultural, geographic and organizational differences. They all had developed a common understanding of where CNH [Global's CE business] wanted to go and with which organization.

However, as 2001 ended, new challenges appeared on CNH Global's competitive horizon. A looming economic slowdown of global proportions suggested that the company would have to deliver results in difficult market conditions and against competitors with considerably less complex organizations. One analyst summarized the company's imminent challenges:

> The real test of CNH Global's "multi-brand, multi-channel" strategy in the construction equipment business is whether it can work in practice, both in good years and in bad ones. Can they smoothly coordinate their different brands, channels and manufacturing plants across their multiple cultures, geographies and companies? Or is it going to take them multi, multi years to get there?

Best Practice

Can superior competitive performance be achieved by building social capabilities across a global constellation of acquisitions, JVs, and alliances?

CNH Global's remarkable journey of global growth through cross-border acquisitions, JVs, and alliances represents an original approach based on building strong social capabilities fast across the joining companies' organizational and cultural boundaries. These social capabilities are deemed to be highly strategic as they are expected to create real value through the blending of the joining companies' key capabilities into superior, highly competitive products and services.

1. *A "social capabilities" perspective can result in broader, more holistic approaches to strategic growth through acquisitions, JVs, and alliances.* Within its core business of agricultural equipment manufacturing, CNH Global developed the social capabilities to quickly combine the knowledge, brands, and expertise stemming from cross-border acquisitions, JVs, and alliances. This gave the company the confidence to set upon a challenging "multibrand and multichannel" growth strategy within the construction equipment industry—although the latter had little potential for technological and manufacturing synergies vis-à-vis CNH Global's core business. Likewise, by focusing on developing a strategic set of social capabilities, your company executives might be able to find more imaginative and profitable ways to grow beyond their core businesses by stretching the boundaries of the industries they traditionally compete in.

2. *Building social capabilities is about creating a strong "common glue" first, between a company's global array of acquisitions, JVs, and alliances.* What sets CNH Global's approach to integrating acquisitions, JVs, and alliances apart from most other companies is its emphasis on developing strong commonalities and a shared sense of identity from the outset amongst the joining companies' key leadership cadre. As a result, a "common glue" is created amongst the members of a multicultural leadership group through a process called map alignment. The latter starts off by harmonizing the mindset, vocabulary, and ways of working and addressing problems within the context of pragmatic business projects. As a second step, a business strategy and functional processes are developed by the joining companies' key managers. Only then a new organizational structure is devised that suits both the "common glue" and the formal processes that have emerged in the process of map alignment. This approach is radically different from conventional acquisition integration undertakings across borders. The latter usually start from designing and communicating a business strategy, followed by the design of a new organizational structure and functional

processes, and only then a process of "roll-out" execution will typically unfold.

3. *A company's ability to create value through acquisitions, JVs, and alliances might rely on "simple" organizational capabilities that are extremely difficult to develop across boundaries.* The experiences of CNH Global suggest that creating a suitable social context where groups of managers from widely diverse cultural backgrounds can comfortably share their insights and build new knowledge might be central to the success of cross-border acquisitions, JVs, and alliances. In the absence of such a social context, a company's attempts to gain competitive advantages by combining strengths globally through acquisitions, JVs, and alliances will be lost along cultural, functional, and organizational divides. Building a social context across boundaries relies upon seemingly "simple" things that can nevertheless become extremely difficult to implement. Examples of these include instilling a common language and a common understanding of business terminology, or creating a common problem-solving approach amongst a group of culturally diverse managers. However, quite paradoxically, many companies typically overlook these "simple" social aspects following the conclusion of an acquisition deal and instead move directly to implement "one-off" financial, marketing, and technical synergies between the joining players.

4. *Building strong social capabilities within your company might constitute the best platform for future success in acquisitions, JVs, and alliances.* The experiences of CNH Global highlight that the same social capabilities that are critical to coordinate a company's assets and resources across international boundaries might also be crucial for undertaking a successful journey of cross-cultural acquisitions, JVs, and alliances. Therefore, the best place for a company's executives to start such a journey is to ask to themselves and find a response to the question: How strong is our company's "common glue"?

Notes

1. The author expresses special thanks to the contributions and support of Giovanni Testa and Salvatore Garbellano, executives at ISVOR FIAT in Turin, Italy. This chapter is based on a case research carried out by Professor Piero Morosini at IMD, Lausanne, together with IMD Research Associates Hans Huber, Deepak Khandpur, and Sophie Linguri.

2. As it is well known amongst executives and academics alike, although global acquisitions, joint ventures, and alliances grew at an unprecedented rate during the last two decades of the twentieth century, well over half of them failed. (For a comprehensive review of the empirical evidence on M&A performance

322   Learning from Experience: Case Analyses

track record see P. Morosini (1998). *Managing Cultural Differences*. Oxford, U.K.: Pergamon.

3. Here, "success" is measured as to whether or not the acquisition, JV, or alliance creates value for the bidding (or JV and alliance partner) companies following the conclusion of the deal. For publicly quoted companies, this is usually measured in market value capitalization. For privately held companies, value can be measured in company growth and/or in economic value added (or similar approaches to company valuation based on either its cash flow or its earnings before taxes and depreciation figures—EBITDA).

4. CNH, Kobe Steel and Kobelco Finalize Global Alliance, Press Release, January 10, 2002, Available at: http:www.cnh.com.

5. CNH, Kobe Steel and Kobelco Finalize Global Alliance, Press Release, January 10, 2002, Available at: http://www.kobelco.co.jp/column/topics-e/messages/137.html.

6. Interview with Jim McCullough, senior vice president, construction equipment, CNH Global. *Construction Equipment*, July 26, 2002, Available at: http://www.coneq.com/cnh.asp.

7. Op. cit.

8. Op. cit.

14 Integration Processes in Cross-Border Mergers
Lessons Learned from Dutch–German Mergers

RENÉ OLIE

Introduction

The purpose of this chapter is to explore the managerial challenges in international mergers, when two companies of approximately equal size and strength yet different national origin join forces to be united into a single economic entity. In most literature the terms *merger* and *acquisition* are used interchangeably and employed in a rather loose way to indicate a situation in which the two organizations are brought together in varying degrees to form one organization. Here, I propose to make a clear distinction between the two types of organizational combination because they represent different strategic activities and pose different managerial challenges and problems, particularly after the deal has been concluded.

The basic feature of a merger is the sense of equality, interdependence, and mutual accommodation. Typically, the two organizations unite into a single organization with a common and coequal identity (Bastien and Van de Ven, 1986). In most mergers neither of the two parties has the power to unilaterally impose its own structure and culture on the other company. They have to develop a "third culture" composed of the amalgamation of the two originals or, at least, a strongly modified version of one of the originals. The absence of a dominant frame of reference puts great demands on the compatibility of the two managerial visions and the styles or "cultures" of the two organizations involved, as potential discord cannot be solved through the bargaining power of one of the two companies, as in acquisitions.

Because the organizational parties regard themselves as coequals, symbols of corporate identity such as board leadership, corporate names, and location of head offices gain special significance. Especially in so called "mergers of equals" the initial configuration is often characterized by parity. This parity can be applied to the overall distribution of management positions, the composition of the new management board, the issue of presidency, new investments, and the location of the new head office.

In comparison with domestic mergers and acquisitions, international mergers face several obstacles that are unique to the cross-national situation. Legal difficulties are one set of stumbling blocks of merging across borders. For example, there is no legal institution providing for international de jure mergers by which two legal entities from two different countries are integrated into a single legal entity with a supranational identity and regulations. In the absence of such an institution, a legal merger between two national firms implies that one national company is dissolved and its assets and liabilities are transferred to the other company, or that both national companies are absorbed by a new company established in one country and structured according to the national laws of that country. A problem is that the dissolution of one national company suggests a company with one dominant national group, which obviously runs counter to the idea of partnership.

A further complicating factor in consolidating cross-border mergers are existing disparities in national traditions in corporate governance and worker participation. Two-tier board systems, in which the executive and controlling function are completely separated (for example, in Germany, Sweden, and the Netherlands), exist alongside systems in which these two functions are integrated in one enlarged Board of Directors (for example, in the United Kingdom and the United States). While in French, British, and American firms it is customary to have a single president or CEO with far-reaching authority, in other countries such as Germany and the Netherlands, management boards bear a collective responsibility. The chairman in this system is often a primus inter pares. Another significant difference between national governance systems is how they balance the interests of the firm's stakeholders. In the United States and the United Kingdom, the shareholder is preeminent (Prowse, 1994). In contrast, German companies are defined in law as social institutions with public responsibilities for other stakeholders, including the local community. Likewise, some countries have institutional systems of worker participation and representation— even at the highest level such as in Germany—and others have looser systems.

In addition, international mergers are more likely to bring together people with different values, expectations, and beliefs about the workplace (Hofstede, 2001). Large national culture differences between the countries of origin will diminish the likelihood that managers from both countries will have similar orientations to organizational life and risk-taking. This may increase miscommunications and frictions, and hamper the development of a united policy.

Another stumbling block to a smooth integration of companies from different countries is national identity. Particularly where major national companies are involved that have a major national reputation and a central place in the economic history and current development of a country, the maintenance of existing national identities may be important, notably in sectors where the public sector is a dominant buyer and gives some advantage to "local" companies, or where state ownership prevails. But also for those inside the organization, nationality is a crucial issue. Perhaps even more so than organizational membership, nationality is a meaningful source for social identity. For this reason, company boards, head office location, corporate identity, and company language tend to be especially politically sensitive in a merged organization, as they often determine the perceived nationality of the organization.

To sum up, given their specific properties, mergers not only involve an entirely different integration process, but are much more difficult to establish than most acquisitions. Furthermore, an international merger involves the combination of two organizations that are embedded in two different national cultural and institutional contexts that affect the ways these organizations are managed, structured, and functioned. The more divergent these contexts are, the more difficult it will be to consolidate them. On the positive side, international mergers combine two organizations that have developed specific routines and capabilities in their national context, which may provide additional sources of synergy. In the remainder of this chapter we will discuss how these issues played a role in three cross-border mergers.

Three Examples of Cross-Border Mergers

The cases that we will explore in greater detail concern three Dutch–German "mergers of equals": Enka Glanzstoff[1] in the chemical fiber industry, VFW–Fokker in the aerospace industry, and Estel, the merger of Hoesch and Hoogovens in the steel industry. The first merger took place between the Dutch AKU and the German Glanzstoff. A Dutch holding company was formed holding the shares of the Dutch and German company. A few months later, as the newly formed holding company merged with a Dutch chemical company to form AKZO (now AkzoNobel), the Dutch–German fiber company effectively became a Dutch–German division of a Dutch holding company. The second merger concerned Europe's first transnational aircraft company, formed in 1969 and dissolved ten years later. The Dutch company Fokker, the only indigenous aviation company in the Netherlands, was a relatively small aircraft company, but with an excellent reputation and well established in the market for medium-sized civil aircraft. Under pressure of the Dutch government to reduce its dependency on public funds for the development of new aircraft and to build a strong international position, it had started to look for a foreign partner. The German company VFW was mainly involved in military projects and was largely dependent upon public funds. This relatively secure position made it an attractive partner for the Dutch company wanting to broaden its financial basis. In addition, VFW had a new jet aircraft under development, the VFW 614. This aircraft would be the first German civil airplane in a very long time. As the company lacked experience in this field, the German company hoped to market the aircraft through the Dutch sales organization and benefit from this company's marketing and after-sales experience. The third merger took place between Holland's major national steel enterprise Hoogovens and the German company Hoesch. The Dutch steel company, with its coastal position, was ideally situated for the supply of raw materials and the shipment of its finished products to overseas markets. The German steel company Hoesch, located in the heart of an industrial region, was well situated to meet the demands of the large German market for finished products. The merger created the second largest steel enterprise on the European continent and the first binational enterprise of its kind in Europe.

As in many other cases, the three mergers proved not really successful. This was partly due to the economic situation. Shortly after their inception, each of the companies resulting from these mergers went through a major crisis in its industry. But more importantly, the postmerger implementation proved a much more difficult task than expected. VFW–Fokker's internal cohesion was a problem from the very beginning, while in the merger between Hoogovens and Hoesch the initial optimism about the merger gradually turned into disappointment, disillusion, and resentment. But even in the more successful Enka Glanzstoff merger, the integration of the two companies was a long and difficult process. The emerging economic crisis divided the company into a Dutch and a German camp, and in the mid-1970s, six years after its beginning, the merger seemed not far from falling apart entirely. Eventually, the mergers in the aerospace industry and in the steel industry both fell apart after a marriage of ten years. The third merger, Enka Glanzstoff, survived despite internal turmoil during the first few years. A detailed account of these cases can be found in Olie (1996). Before we start analyzing the factors that contributed to the success or failure of these mergers, we first discuss how the companies involved structured their merger, and solved the issues of national balance.

Consolidation of the Merger

A central issue in discussions concerning all of the mergers was the degree of management influence each partner would have in the future company. In each combination, the partners differed in terms of size, turnover, profitability, manpower, reputation, management potential, and experience, but there was only a small power or resource differential, which ruled out a clear acquisition of one partner by the other. In fact, a 50-50 partnership appeared the only way a merger could be realized in these three cases.

As explained earlier, one set of obstacles companies encountered in realizing a cross-border merger are the legal intricacies stemming from national differences in governance structures, worker participation traditions, fiscal regimes, and political influences, as well as other reasons of a national-psychological nature. Complex legal structures are therefore often necessary to formalize the union. This was particularly true for the steel and the aircraft merger. In view of the equality of the two partners and their status as major national companies, a direct legal merger by which one of the two national identities would disappear was obviously unacceptable to either partner, even if such a merger form had been available.

Eventually, Hoogovens–Hoesch and VFW–Fokker used similar legal frameworks to structure their merger (see Figure 14.1). This framework comprises a network of five different companies. The most important company in the network is the central management company that has complete ownership of the two national companies, which are transformed into operating companies. The founding companies in turn were transformed into pure holding companies, each holding 50 percent of the shares of the central management company.

The Dutch and German holding and operating companies in both mergers were structured according to the national laws and customs of the country in which they were domiciled. This allowed each constituent firm to conform to the respective national laws, customs, and developments regarding board structure, worker participation, salary structure, tax laws, and social security schemes.

Whereas the establishment of a central management company was one way, another way in which the management of VFW–Fokker and Hoogovens–Hoesch tried to achieve unity of command was by creating a large number of personal unions between key positions in the legal framework. For example, in Hoogovens–Hoesch steel merger this overlap was created between the Estel management board and the management boards of the operating companies. In both mergers these overlaps were mainly national. Top managers of the corresponding nationality filled membership positions on the boards of the national holding and operating companies. This emphasis on national overlaps proved to have a strong negative effect

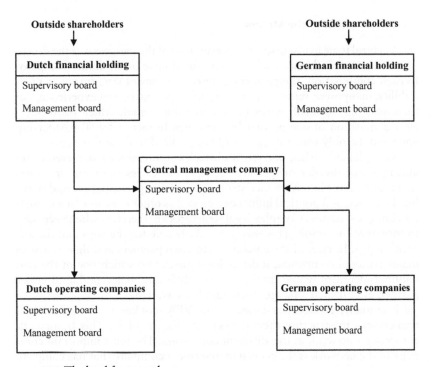

FIGURE **14.1** The legal framework

on the psychological integration of the two organizational groups, as we shall see below.

The organizational framework, the way in which the two partner organizations would be joined together to form an economic unit, differed substantially among the three mergers. The strongest interdependence between the partner organizations was in Enka Glanzstoff. Two central product divisions were created: one with its central point in Holland (industrial fibers) and one managed from the former Glanzstoff headquarters in Wuppertal, Germany (textile fibers). Departments with similar activities were put together. As a result, some departments moved from the German to the Dutch head office, and vice versa. This entailed a considerable exchange of personnel.

The weakest interdependence was in VFW–Fokker, mainly because the two partners did not have to merge every aspect to realize their strategic objectives. Following the legal structure, the two organizations were combined under the general direction of the central management company. This central unit was responsible for the policy-making of the new group, while the two national operating companies were responsible for the engineering, production, and financing of national aircraft projects. The only subsidiary with cross-border responsibilities was a newly based subsidiary to market the commercial aircraft (two Dutch, one German) of the company. As a result of Fokker's experience in this field, the Dutch-based marketing subsidiary was mainly staffed by Dutch employees.

Hoogovens and Hoesch took an intermediate position between these two extremes. As economies of scale and an efficient division of labor were potential advantages, especially in steelmaking, far-reaching coordination and operational integration of units in each business was expected to pay off. But another reason for strong integration was to establish a cohesive organization. Therefore in contrast with the legal framework, the organizational structure of Estel cut across national lines. A temporary coordination structure was created, which, as in Enka Glanzstoff, grouped activities along product lines. The core of this structure were four coordinating groups that would manage related areas on either side of the border. Because the organizational structure did not correspond to the legal format, the coordination groups possessed no formal administrative authority over the firms they were supposed to manage. After a period of two to three years this structure was supposed to be replaced by a more permanent organization that would better combine the legal and organizational structures. Two coordination groups were officially located in the Netherlands, while the other two had their official domicile in Germany. But unlike Enka Glanzstoff, this did not lead to the large-scale transfer of staff across the border, as managers of the coordination group retained their operational management responsibilities in the constituent companies. International staffing was principally restricted to the central head office, as in VFW–Fokker.

In both Enka Glanzstoff and Hoogovens–Hoesch, the divisional management teams were each dominated by one nationality. This largely reflected the strengths of the original companies. Thus, in Hoogovens–Hoesch, the divisions of Steel Processing and Trade were "German," while the coordination group "Diversification" was a predominantly Dutch affair. A notable exception was the coordination group "Steel," the most important division of Estel. In this sector both companies possessed similar operations and, therefore, management had an equal representation of Dutch and German staff. Particularly in this division, major conflicts between the Dutch and German management ensued as we shall see.

The Binational Identity

As the two partners in each merger regarded themselves as coequals, each party was concerned that the new organization should reflect a true mixture of the two organizations, symbolized in the leadership of the new

TABLE **14.1** The binational identity in the three mergers

	The Fiber Merger Enka Glanzstoff	The Aviation Merger VFW–Fokker	The Steel Merger Estel
Management board	National parity for seven years	National parity	National parity
Board leadership	Binational leadership for three years Single board leadership after seven years	German chairman; Dutch vice chairman	Dutch chairman; German vice chairman
Head office	Dual head office	New head office in Germany	New head office in the Netherlands
Corporate identity	Enka + Glanzstoff (three years); Enka Glanzstoff (three to eight years); Enka (after eight years).	VFW–Fokker for the whole company; Fokker–VFW for the Dutch units; Verenigte Flugtechnische Werke-Fokker for German subunits.	Estel for the whole company; Hoesch + Hoogovens for the national subunits (eight years); Estel Hoesch + Estel Hoogovens for the national subunits (after eight years).

organization, its new name, the location of its headquarters, as well as other identity-defining organizational aspects. Table 14.1 summarizes how these issues were solved in each merger.

In each merger the first management board was largely a consolidation of the original premerger boards. In the short or long run, this often resulted in a top-heavy management board, eventually leading to board changes. Consistent with the dominant practice in both Germany and the Netherlands, the joint boards of the three merged companies aimed at unanimity in decision making and operated under a system of collegiate management in which the chairman functioned as a primus inter pares. The most far-reaching form of parity was in Enka Glanzstoff. Each national company had its own chairman with a vice chairman who was the chairman of the partner company. Together these two persons fulfilled the chairmanship role for Enka Glanzstoff as a whole. Board meetings were held alternately in Germany and the Netherlands under the leadership of the chairman of the corresponding nationality.

Fairness and balance between the Dutch and the German interests also permeated the rest of the organization. Enka Glanzstoff and Estel both tried to find a national balance in the location of their divisions. Similarly, VFW–Fokker based two of its central units in Germany (the company's head office and the German operating company) and two in the Netherlands (the marketing subsidiary and the Dutch operating company). When operations were of equal size, such as in Estel's steelmaking activities, there was a balanced distribution of management positions across the two nationalities so far as possible. To further minimize resistance, Hoogovens–Hoesch and Enka Glanzstoff initially worked with a binational leadership combination of supervisor and deputy. In VFW–Fokker, where integration was minimal, this construction did not exist.

Another aspect having significant implications for the identity of the new firm is the location of the new head office. For Enka Glanzstoff, which had decided to retain both head offices for the time being, this issue remained an occasional point of discussion for almost ten years. The steel merger and the aviation merger, by contrast, worked with a single head office from the very beginning. The head office location was based on a mixture of political, psychological, legal, and practical considerations. For example, the stronger economic position of Hoogovens and the fact that the Netherlands would lose control over its only steel industry were important considerations pointing in the direction of the Netherlands as domicile for the new steel company. In VFW–Fokker, a German-based headquarters was a Dutch concession in return for the 50-50 balance. The importance of German public procurement for the new company was another argument for this decision. However, to underline the neutral position of the binational head office, the top management of both merged organizations considered it important to choose a site close to the national border and roughly halfway between the two major production sites.

Two other issues that tend to have national overtones in international combinations are company language and corporate identity. While language appeared to be a minor issue in all three combinations, corporate identity tended to be far more sensitive. Original company names were retained, partly for marketing reasons, but mostly because any change in cherished corporate identities was very difficult. Although all three merged companies eventually considered changing their corporate identities to create a stronger sense of unity between the different parts and to achieve a clearer corporate identity, only Enka Glanzstoff was really successful, although even in this case it took several years to realize.

In VFW–Fokker the name for the merged company was a combination of the original company names. The name order, however, depended on the country of the subunit's location. Aircraft, however, were marketed under the original company names. In the steel merger, the two national operating companies kept their original names, but the group as a whole adopted the name Estel. Steel products, however, were marketed under the names of Hoesch or Hoogovens, depending on the producing company. In 1981, the family name Estel was added to the names of the operating companies and their subsidiaries. But even then, nearly nine years after the merger, the renaming process evoked strong emotions.

As seems generally to happen in mergers, despite the many attempts to symbolize the binational character and the coequal status of the two partner firms, the national balance was often perceived differently by the two management groups. The merged steel company Estel, for example, was viewed as a venture with a strong Dutch influence, because its leading man was Dutch and its head office was located in the Netherlands. The relatively better performance of the Dutch operating company further reinforced the idea that there was a dominant Dutch influence in Estel. A similar awareness developed among the German management in the aviation merger. Many at VFW felt that they were subordinate to Fokker in terms of experience and reputation. This feeling increased when the German aircraft project VFW 614 failed to satisfy the German need for success, and the central management, under the leadership of a new Dutch chairman, started to interfere more with the management of the German subunit. In the chemical fiber merger, both national groups were very much concerned about their position, but it was the Dutch, in particular, who felt that they were losing influence. In particular, the ending of national parity after a period of seven years, the German board chairmanship, and the concentration of the board in one location confirmed ideas among the Dutch staff that a clear shift in power was taking place between the two nationalities.

Only in Enka Glanzstoff did the initial configuration develop significantly in the direction of greater unity while maintaining its binational character. The change of the corporate name to Enka is indicative of this development, as is the concept of binationality in management. The emphasis on strict parity evolved into a policy of keeping a national balance to the extent that each nationality would be able to retain an active role and to participate directly in policy decisions. The dual chairmanship of Enka Glanzstoff was replaced by a single chairman. Board meetings stopped alternating between two locations and the agreement to invest according to a fixed ratio was abandoned. The other two mergers demonstrated fewer such changes: national parity was maintained even when inefficient.

Restraining and Supporting Factors

After have described how the three mergers tried to solve the problems that are inherent in most mergers, and international mergers in particular, we will now analyze the factors that contributed to or hindered a smooth consolidation process. Some of these factors are external, such as economic and political developments, while others are internal, such as the role of top management. Starting with the external conditions, we will discuss, respectively, economic and political developments including the role of various external stakeholders, the merger logic, the role of internal stakeholders, organizational and cultural compatibility, the merger framework, and the role of top management.

Business Conditions and the Role of External Stakeholders

A common factor in all these mergers is that they took place against the background of significant economic decline and instability in the 1970s. The economic recession in combination with the changing political climate had a significant impact on the fortunes of the three Dutch–German mergers. Each of these mergers had been established in a period of relative prosperity, but soon faced a recession not previously experienced in their industry. As in many European countries, the social and political context of the firm made it difficult to pursue a dramatic and speedy restructuring. For example in Enka Glanzstoff, an early rationalization program to concentrate production in fewer locations and to close inefficient plants failed due to strong opposition in the Netherlands. From the mid-1970s new reorganization plans were more successful. Between 1974 and 1985 employment in the Enka Glanzstoff Group decreased from 44,500 to 27,500. In the steel merger such drastic measures followed much later. Initially the crisis in the steel industry was not interpreted as having structural causes. But the continuing depressed state of the European steel market and the heavy losses of the obsolete German steelworks in Dortmund made more drastic reductions in production capacity unavoidable. Management inertia and strong opposition from the worker representatives in Germany were among the major reasons why the restructuring process of the Dortmund steelworks only made slow progress.

After the deep recession of the mid-1970s the situation improved slightly in both the chemical fiber and the steel industry. But 1980 saw another sharp downturn. The merged companies in the two industries saw themselves forced to accelerate a far-reaching reorganization of their core business to restore the profitability of the whole group, if they wanted to survive. The year 1981 marked a turning point for both companies. With the help of its holding company AKZO, Enka Glanzstoff managed to live through this financially dramatic period and further improved its product structure. For Estel, on the other hand, further heavy losses in 1981 severely threatened its financial capacity and it was obliged to call for public aid. When the appeal for joint action by the German and Dutch governments failed, the German half of Estel opened talks with its German competitor Krupp about closer collaboration. These developments marked the industrial disintegration of the binational concern.

Although VFW–Fokker's losses were only a fraction of the losses incurred by the other two merged companies, they were as threatening to the merged company's existence. A particular problem was the German aircraft project VFW 614 which suffered from a number of setbacks. When the aircraft was finally launched in 1975, it did not sell. The predicament of the German operating company was compounded by similar poor sales results in the military sector. As a result, VFW–Fokker was also forced to seek government support to avert bankruptcy. But in this case, as for Estel, the attitude of the German federal government proved a considerable stumbling block for further cooperation within the binational framework.

Besides the unquestionably stronger political influence on their development, what further distinguishes the two failed mergers from the more successful Enka Glanzstoff is the diverging economic performance of the Dutch and German operating units. In both of the failed mergers the Dutch partner did relatively well, whereas the German partner faced increasing financial difficulties. In the aircraft merger the Dutch-designed commercial aircraft were moderately successful, whereas the German aircraft proved a commercial failure. In the military segment, a similar pattern emerged. This development resulted in the politically awkward situation of the Dutch unit having to expand its workforce, whereas the German part was forced to reduce its workforce. The steel merger showed the same pattern. The major losses were incurred by the German steelmaking unit. Owing to their energy-intensive and labor-intensive nature the old open hearth plants at Dortmund, Germany, became increasingly economically obsolete and caused significantly higher operating costs on the German side.

The differing performance of the two partner organizations was a major source of tension in both mergers. In the aviation merger the German side was under the impression that the Amsterdam-based sales force pushed only Dutch-designed planes. In the steel merger the mounting losses in Dortmund were perceived by many on the Dutch side as being due to management failures, while the Germans believed that the Dutch were systematically trying to weaken the German unit for the benefit of their own company. In contrast, in the successful Enka Glanzstoff merger the deteriorating economic conditions affected operations in Germany and the Netherlands to more or less the same degree. This enabled management to keep a national balance in both staff and production capacity reductions. A second reason why the crisis did not have the same negative effect in this case was that the national companies in the fiber merger did not operate as profit centers, as in the other two cases, but principally as legal entities. The strong integration of the Dutch and German organization in Enka Glanzstoff meant that the German-based product divisions also controlled Dutch production plants, while Dutch-based divisions coordinated German plants. This construction made it difficult to attribute negative performance, for example, in textile fibers, to one side in particular.

In sum, the three mergers were in part victims of economic and structural changes in the world economy. These changes had a dramatic effect on their financial performance and constrained management efforts to create a cohesive unit. In all three mergers the sense of crisis increased dissatisfaction with the merger and led to scapegoating between the partners. But, remarkably, for the chemical fiber company the crisis soon turned into a positive factor. Whereas in this merger the crisis was considered a major reason for the successful economic integration of the two partner organizations, in the other two mergers it had the opposite effect, particularly when the performance of the national subunits started to diverge.

If diverging economic performance was one aspect that hindered co-operation in these two mergers, national industrial policies were another. Political influence in the fiber merger was minimal, but it was quite significant in the other two mergers. Government subsidies and diverging national industrial policies proved a major obstacle to the smooth functioning of these binational companies. Indeed, in a sense it was the immediate cause of their dissolution.

The Merger Logic

Research on mergers and acquisitions underlines the importance of strategic fit, that is, the degree to which the acquired or merged companies augment or complement the acquiring firm's or partner firm's strategy and the degree to which additional value is created (Jemison and Sitkin, 1986; Larsson and Finkelstein, 1999). On the face of it all three combinations seemed highly compatible in this respect. AKU and Glanzstoff had similar product lines, but operated in different geographical markets. In VFW–Fokker it was the complementarity of product strengths that determined the added value of the merger. Fokker was well established in the market for medium-sized civil aircraft with its successful turbo-prop aircraft and recently launched jet aircraft, while its German counterpart was mainly involved in military projects. The industrial logic of the merger between Hoesch and Hoogovens was also primarily based in the complementary strengths of the two partners. The merger would permit an economic division of labor: concentrating primary steelmaking in the coastal centers, and the manufacturing of sheet and other semifinished products in the German inland centers.

Unfortunately, reality proved very different from each management's expectations. Many of the expected benefits were not realized because of the changing economic and political situation. The assumption that the two partners together would have greater opportunities for development than either partner alone was seriously questioned in all three mergers. For example, the merger between Hoesch and Hoogovens was based on the assumption of sustained growth, but an efficient allocation of production capacity through the economic division of work could hardly be realized under the prevailing conditions of overcapacity. As a result of the decline in demand, the rationale of the internal transfers from Hoogovens to Hoesch increasingly came under pressure. Many came to feel that the merger was working against them. While in Hoesch they believed that their sacrifices of production capacity were only for the benefit of their Dutch partner, on the Dutch side many felt that the merger only constrained their own development. A similar discrepancy between expected and realized strategic benefits troubled the relations between the partners in VFW–Fokker. Fokker's hopes for a stronger financial basis did not materialize. Its partner's strengths in the military sector quickly evaporated when the German government decided to cut several of VFW's defense programs for budgetary reasons, and no major new programs could be acquired. VFW also failed to obtain the results it had counted on. Its civil aircraft was a dismal failure, which many attributed to insufficient marketing support on the part of the Dutch partner.

Changing economic and political conditions were one reason that merger partners failed to realize their objectives. Overestimation of strategic benefits was another. This appeared to be a particular problem in the aircraft merger where a quasicompetitive situation existed between the Dutch and German civil aircraft. This was at the root of VFW–Fokker's demise ten years after the merger. On this point, VFW and Fokker proved to be only superficially congruent. The competition between the three civil planes put VFW–Fokker in an extremely awkward position and became a strong source of German frustration. In hindsight one could say that an early cancelation of the German aircraft project could have prevented many of the problems at a later stage. However, the project had been a major reason for VFW's interest in a merger with Fokker, and the vested interests in the project made its cancelation hardly feasible. As a result the merger was burdened by an effectively insoluble problem.

Internal Stakeholders

Mergers and acquisitions are usually the products of the visions of one or a few influential actors at the top of the organization. These ideas may not always gain strong support from other internal stakeholders, including management and workforce, for various reasons.

There was resistance in all three Dutch–German mergers, but the level of noncooperation was most dramatic in VFW–Fokker. Many, particularly on the Dutch side, resented the merger. From their own perspectives Dutch local managers disagreed with the need for a merger, felt that it could not bring them any gains, and showed little enthusiasm for the prospective cooperation partner. Having been successful in developing their own aircraft, the Dutch management was somewhat dismissive of their German partner. In their efforts to maintain the integrity of the local company, the Dutch operational management was quite successful in obstructing any attempt that would curb its autonomy. VFW seemed more in favor of a merger, but its management became increasingly dissatisfied with its role in the combination.

The Estel steel merger also lacked widespread support but resistance was felt more equally on both sides. Resistance was particularly manifest in steelmaking, the activity most directly affected by the merger. On the German side this reluctance appeared to originate from the fear that a merger with a firm with a more advantageous location and more efficient production structure could only work against them. They shared these concerns with the local workforce. Their fears about losing codetermination rights and the viability of Dortmund as a steel-producing location, already a major obstacle during the merger negotiations, remained a consistent theme throughout the merger. These concerns motivated them to oppose several integration attempts and to defer drastic reorganizations of the Dortmund steelworks. Opposition on the Dutch side was intimately linked with a wish to preserve the company's identity and the belief that the Dutch side did not really need the partner company.

In all three mergers resistance and antimerger feelings increased over the years, especially when economic performance declined. In Enka Glanzstoff many started to feel that the merger only led to greater inflexibility and sluggishness. Similar feelings emerged in VFW–Fokker, but with far more serious consequences. In Estel, too, the rapidly deteriorating economic situation in the mid-1970s created several conflicts of interest between the Dutch and German local managements and permitted strong antimerger feelings to develop. This caused partisan interests to dominate over company interests, and a situation of mistrust and competition developed. The actual nonintegration of the two sales organizations, largely a result of an unwillingness of managers to give up their favored sales approach and to relocate their sales organization, contributed considerably to the "in-house" competition in the steel sector.

Because Estel and VFW–Fokker used similar setups for their mergers, they had one central problem in common. This concerned the relationship between company headquarters and the national operating units. In the aircraft merger the managers of the national subunits tended to regard their units as separate. What they shared was their aversion to the central management company. Recruiting staff for company headquarters in Düsseldorf proved a major problem, and it was not always possible to attract the best people. Also in Estel, the operational units tended to picture the central head office as a top-heavy construction with little added value. The reluctance to work at central headquarters was particularly strong among the Hoesch staff. Fearing that they would lose their jobs if the merger did not work out, most Hoesch staff members were reluctant to be relocated in the Dutch-based head office. Many of them retained their offices in Dortmund and went only for meetings to the Netherlands.

Because it had retained both national headquarters, Enka Glanzstoff did not have these staffing problems. In addition, there were no powerful national subsidiaries which could develop as a countervailing power to the central unit. The operational units in Enka Glanzstoff consisted of relatively small production sites spread across Germany, the Netherlands, and several other countries in Europe. Potential resistance under these conditions could not have the same impact as in the other two mergers, where major operations were geographically concentrated in two large self-contained national subunits.

Organizational Identity and Cultural Compatibility

A topic that has received much attention in the merger and acquisition literature is that of organizational fit. Organizational fit refers to the compatibility of administrative practices, leadership styles, organizational structures, and organizational cultures (Jemison and Sitkin, 1986). Firm-specific characteristics created various problems in the three mergers.

Organizational differences had the biggest impact in the case of sales organizations, particularly in Estel. The German company sold a wide range of products to a large number of firms, mostly small and medium-sized. Most of this was sold through a separate trade organization with an extensive network of sales agencies. Hoogovens sold a more limited range of products directly to a few large, and mostly foreign, customers without the intervention of a trade organization. In combination with the generally negative attitudes of each sales staff toward the merger, these different sales approaches presented an insurmountable barrier to integration.

Another important obstacle to integration was organizational identity, which provides the members of an organization with a sense of pride, satisfaction, and belongingness. The companies in these mergers had strong distinct identities, except for VFW, the German aircraft manufacturer. VFW was in fact an amalgam of different company identities. Its Dutch counterpart, on the other hand, had a strong and clear image based on the company's rich history and its successes in civil aircraft manufacturing. In particular, the company's products acted as an integrating force and encouraged strong identification with, and loyalty to, the firm. Products were perhaps less important sources of identification for the other companies, but they were all companies full of tradition. The fact that these were large, important firms, a fact of which the Dutch were particularly conscious, made these organizations even more distinctive in the eyes of their members. As a result, organizational members in all three mergers had difficulty in shedding their old and cherished loyalties in favor of the new identity. Changes in corporate names, corporate head office locations, or board compositions were a strong source of tension, even in the successful merger.

Many of the problems of integrating the Dutch and German organizations also appeared to stem from disparities between the two home nations. The different legal systems, national traditions regarding worker participation and corporate governance structures, and their implications for structuring and managing the new organization have been highlighted in previous sections. But disparities also emerged in other areas, such as management qualifications, international scope, and commercial and production orientation. These aspects reflected many of the characteristics that are considered typical for German and Dutch firms and management. For example, all three Dutch companies generally had a greater international scope and a relatively stronger market orientation, which mirrored the traditional dependence of the Dutch economy on foreign markets and its commercial outlook. The German companies for their part had a much stronger manufacturing orientation. They were largely organizations dominated by engineers. These differences were generally not strong sources of incompatibilities. Indeed, they could be considered as potential sources of synergy. More fundamental were the diverging ideas and expectations in other areas. For example, the two national groups appeared to differ sharply in the degree in which they preferred to stick to the organizational blueprint, and their preference for clearly structured tasks and well-defined responsibilities. In the Dutch companies there was generally much less insistence on the importance of defining and specifying the functions and roles of organizational members. The Dutch chemical fiber and steel organizations in particular were characterized by improvization and individual initiative. This informal style was also reflected in a readiness to bypass the formal hierarchy and to make use of informal contacts to get things done. Their German partners, by contrast, appeared to have a penchant for tradition and a high level of concern for form and order.

Another area in which conflicting management styles existed concerned decision making. For the Germans, meetings had a strong task-oriented character. They were primarily means to state clear goals and to assign tasks. Germans appeared strongly committed to a decision or strategy once it had been stated. The Dutch decision-making style, by contrast, reflected more the societal tendency of creating balances. Meetings were perceived as a platform for exchanging ideas and information rather than as a simple preparation for further action. Consensus-building was an important value that made decision making and implementation much slower and more time-consuming than the German management in Glanzstoff and Hoesch was used to.

While for the German managers the contrasting decision-making styles were a source of frustration, frustration for the Dutch managers arose from the different conceptions of authority. The Dutch leadership style was distinctly more participation-oriented. It was based on consensus and accommodation rather than assertiveness. While Dutch managers expected their decision making or authority to be challenged by subordinates, German managers considered authority to be "a right of office" as their job was to make decisions. German subordinates were generally more afraid to voice their disagreement with their superiors.

Another consistently found difference between the two national groups concerned interpersonal styles. Although this difference may seem trivial to an outsider, for many inside the merged organizations it had a strong significance. For the Dutch managers, informality of style and atmosphere and intimate forms of address between superiors and subordinates were the rule, whereas the German organizations were characterized by a high degree of formality. In accordance with the German business culture, it was not uncommon for German managers to interact for years on a formal basis, whereas in the Netherlands the norm is to be on a first-name basis immediately. This formal attitude appeared cool to the Dutch, and was often interpreted as a sign of social distance.

Postcombination efforts were much stronger in the fiber and steel merger. This may explain why these cultural differences appeared to be a potent source of conflict in these mergers, but not in the aviation merger despite the different traditions and backgrounds of the partner firms. Particularly in the Estel merger, national and organizational culture differences were regarded by the Dutch as the principal reason why the merger had failed or could not be forged into a cohesive entity. But even in the successful merger Enka Glanzstoff, it was a long time before the presence of the two cultures was seen as enriching the binational organization.

The Merger Framework

Cultural and organizational differences in themselves would be sufficient to make the integration process difficult, but there were several other, more structural sources for conflict in these mergers. Particularly in both the aviation and the steel merger, the merger framework had institutionalized many of these sources of conflict.

The VFW–Fokker organization was basically federal in character, as we have seen. It pooled Fokker and VFW's interests under a joint top authority, leaving most of the existing organizations intact. The two operating companies retained their separate identities, management and responsibilities, as well as their aircraft projects. Like the management boards, the supervisory boards remained uninational in order to maintain the national identities of the firms. It is no wonder, under these conditions, that the two operating companies developed a strong subunit orientation, in which each unit pursued its own goals and saw itself and the other subunits as separate, rather than as complementary units in search for a common goal. Especially because each national subunit still considered the aircraft programs they performed as their own, Fokker–VFW International, which was responsible for sales of Dutch and German civil aircraft, became the focus of strong interunit tensions. The German local management felt that competition with the Dutch aircraft was the basic reason for the poor sales performance of its own aircraft. It believed that the predominantly Dutch sales force was pushing only Dutch-designed planes. For its part, the Dutch local management considered its own aircraft, the only viable aircraft project of the group. Marketing attention for the VFW 614 was a waste of time and could only be at the expense of their own aircraft. To maintain control over what it perceived as its own aircraft, the Dutch local management strenuously frustrated any attempts of the marketing management to pursue an independent course.

In the steel merger, Estel, the coordination structure that had been developed in anticipation of a more permanent organization, appeared to be equally ineffective in promoting interfirm cooperation. This was most evident in the steelmaking sector, where close coordination between the two national steelmaking units was required to realize the envisaged economic division of work. As mentioned, steelmaking activities were managed by a team consisting of managers from the constituent companies under the supervision of Estel board members. Its task was to pursue a joint policy with respect to sales, purchasing, and marketing and to allocate resources and coordinate investments. However, rather than a single management body whose members felt collectively responsible for steelmaking, the managers from the constituent companies acted as representatives of their individual steel plants. This was to some extent because of their lack of identification with the merger, but was largely attributable to the structure itself. First of all, the management team of the coordination group "Steel" was not a unified body. For example, the supervision of both sales and production was split between a Dutch and a German manager. More important, the coordination structure was informal. The teams did not possess any formal authority, so it was difficult to guarantee implementation even if the members were able to reach consensus on a joint policy. The Hoesch steel management, in particular, demonstrated a strong preoccupation with their legally defined responsibilities for the German steelworks. The unwillingness of the German management to shift its loyalties to the coordination group may have had both cultural and structural origins. Apart from the general strong preference of German managers for clear, hierarchical structures, the Hoesch steel works was managed by a company in its own right. Its management was formally accountable to its own supervisory board, and the five-year term of their appointments reinforced their loyalty to this company. After three years the management structure for the coordination group Steel was changed to create a more efficient organization. Because the

Estel board appeared divided (along national lines) over the consolidation strategy for steelmaking, a difficult compromise was reached which did not in fact reduce the potential for conflict. It continued a situation in which each group had identifiable interests and separate identities and governance structures. The steel crisis showed the weak spots of this construction. The recession in the industry reinforced the perceptions of both groups that they were competing for the same market share. Heated discussions ensued and the interaction between the two groups became extremely awkward as each national subunit lobbied for its own interests and for cutbacks to fall on the other unit. The effective nonintegration of the two sales organizations owing to their sharply different sales and marketing strategies and their resistance to change contributed considerably to the interunit tensions.

The third merger, Enka Glanzstoff, was the only merger that was not characterized by pervasive interunit struggles. Like Estel, Enka Glanzstoff had created divisions to manage its operations on an international basis. But unlike Estel, the old company structures were not retained but replaced by an integrated structure. The divisions were integrated management bodies consisting of a management group that sat and worked together to coordinate product activities across Europe. Each division management team contained a mix of both nationalities, although one nationality dominated. Dutch managers were relocated to Germany and German managers moved to Holland. Most departments were placed under single command within a relatively short period, although many of these departments continued functioning as separate units for a much longer time. In spite of differences in sales and marketing approaches, it was considered important to establish an integrated sales function to avoid organizational conflicts. By using common names for its products, Sales had an important function in stressing the new company identity to the outside world. In time a single integrated organization developed with two head offices housing central staff departments and product groups working for the entire organization. The product groups operated through production sites irrespective of their location. Personnel management is the only area in which this integration has not been pursued. Employment contracts are geared to the local conditions, allowing different salary structures, pension funds, and so on for Dutch and German employees. The exchange of personnel has been strongly reduced over the years. As a result, each head office is now characterized by uninational staffing.

Top Management

Top management has a pivotal role in a merger, as it has to give direction to the new company and to symbolize and promote its unity. Cooperation at lower levels cannot be expected to thrive if top management is divided in itself, or fails to provide any direction. In all three mergers top management was not entirely successful in these tasks for various reasons.

Lack of continuity in management was one reason. Some key actors in the decision-making and negotiation process retired immediately after the merger, while others left within one or two years. The potential danger of these management discontinuities is that the commitment, the personal rapport, and the confidence that is shared between key decision makers may be lacking among their successors. Such a situation arose in the steel merger Estel. After the early death of the powerful merger champion, the chairman of the German company, the binational board of Estel became unbalanced and a leadership vacuum developed on the German side. An important reason was the mixed support on the Hoesch board for the merger. The economic recession did not stimulate new loyalties, as in Enka Glanzstoff, but increased the doubts among these people, especially when Hoogovens initially made greater losses than Hoesch.

A second reason for lack of cohesion among top management in these mergers was the split loyalties of board members. This applied, for example, to Estel where nationality-based appointments kept a natural relationship with the national home base alive. Another reason was the "linking pin" system between the central board, the boards of the subsidiary companies, and the management of the coordination groups. Although initially developed to promote the integration of the partner organizations, this system also created a potential political arena, where one option was traded against another. The top management level was no longer a neutral body making decisions independently, and considering the benefits of the whole firm instead of its parts. Mainly as a result of the lack of full support and the divided loyalties of its members, the Estel board never managed to develop into a powerful center that symbolized the unity of the two partners. The different views between Dutch and German board members on the consolidation of Estel manifested the growing disunity between the two partners. This national divide was not only psychological but also physical, as most German managers concentrated on responsibilities in their home organizations and only drove to Holland for weekly meetings in the central head office.

Divided company loyalties also hindered the integrated functioning of Enka Glanzstoff's top management. Although the two company boards were identical in membership to ensure a uniform integrated company policy, this setup could not prevent each nationality feeling greater responsibility toward the national subunits than to Enka Glanzstoff as a whole. An important weakness concerned the chairman's position. Initially, the chairmen of the two national companies were jointly responsible for the group as a whole. This was quickly found ineffective because it slowed down decision making where fast decision making was required. After two years the double chairmanship was therefore replaced by a single chairman for the whole group and two chairmen for each separate national unit. This setup helped Enka Glanzstoff to develop a stronger organizational identity, but cohesiveness of its top decision-making unit remained weak. The precarious economic situation in the mid-1970s eventually provided the basis for a more effective and cohesive top management. The three chairman's positions were combined in one person and the board was reduced from seven to five members. Managerial skill and team spirit instead of nationality became primary selection criteria for board membership. Another measure that appeared to increase the cohesiveness of this board was the concentration of top management in the German head office. Under skillful leadership of its German chairman, this board managed to overcome the existing national divide in the company. The board functioned for more than seven years with the same composition.

A third reason for ineffective top management in the three mergers was management itself. This was most evident in VFW–Fokker. The most important problem in this case was the failure of top management to give any direction to the merger. The merger enjoyed the support of most top managers, but these failed to inspire lower echelons and translate the whole merger idea into concrete plans. The outspoken opposition to the merger from the Dutch local management went largely unrecognized, or was ignored. Its passivity as regards internal affairs caused a loss of morale among those who felt committed to the merger and encouraged local managers who questioned the merger to pursue their own goals. The crisis of leadership at the top of the organization encouraged the strongest operating unit to compete for control and challenge the authority of top management. The Dutch operating management successfully lobbied for a position on the central management board. In 1975, following a long discussion about reorganizing the whole company, a new board structure was created, consisting of four full-time members supplemented by three part-time members, namely the leading managers of the three subunits. The hope that the new linking pin structure would encourage the development of a company-wide perspective among operational management proved illusionary. The central board lost its neutral position and became even more powerless vis-à-vis its Dutch operating unit than before.

A similar lack of management power could be observed in Estel. The Estel board was seriously handicapped by a German management that was partly uncommitted and partly unable to enforce a more Estel-oriented strategy upon its constituency. The Dutch worries about the leadership vacuum on the German side eventually resulted in the appointment of a new German top manager to the board after eight years, whom they hoped would overcome opposition to change and develop a strategy that would promote Estel's interests, and not just the interests of Hoesch. Indeed, this person initially presented himself as a champion of Estel and managed to enforce a restructuring program on the ailing Dortmund steelworks. But in time he started to place Hoesch interests over those of Estel.

One remaining question about top management relates to the effects of binational parity, that is, the fact that the two partners had an equal say in the management of the merged company. Many considered this parity as fundamentally wrong for a merger as it slowed down decision making, eventually resulting in deadlock situations or false compromises, giving priority to political arguments rather than economic considerations. This may be partly true. In a merger, compromises have to be reached to satisfy the interests of both partners. This seems especially important in the early period, to build trust between the partners. As noted, the equal division of management influence in these three mergers has to be considered as more or less a conditio sine qua non. In these three mergers, real deadlock situations between Dutch and German board members were quite rare. However, the conflicting opinions in Estel between Dutch and German members over the need for merger consolidation does show that the equal say of both parties in the combinations may lead to uneasy compromises. More importantly, this example demonstrates that national parity is a strong disadvantage if board members view themselves primarily as representatives of their original company and their opinions on the merger start to diverge. The development of Enka Glanzstoff as a binational company from the mid-1970s shows that selection of board members on the basis of competence and team criteria instead of nationality increased the effectiveness of the board and fostered the perception of common identity.

Evaluation of the Three Cases

Our analysis has shown that the success or failure of the three mergers cannot be attributed to any single factor, but is the result of many factors, external as well as internal. External factors included changes in market conditions and political developments. Internal factors included resistance to change, cultural and organizational diversity, structural factors, and managerial factors. A summary of the impact of these factors is provided in Table 14.2.

A comparison of the three cases shows why Enka Glanzstoff was more successful than Estel and VFW–Fokker. Although each merger faced a serious crisis, Enka Glanzstoff, unlike the other two mergers, did not have to face the diverging economic performance of its national units, or diverging national industrial policies. In Estel, the deteriorating economic conditions changed the basic rationale underlying the merger. In VFW–Fokker the economic deterioration showed that the merger was based on unrealistic expectations. In Enka Glanzstoff, on the other hand, the crisis fostered the perception that the two organizations could not survive separately. It

TABLE **14.2** Summary of the factors

	Fiber Merger Enka Glanzstoff	Aviation Merger VFW–Fokker	Steel Merger Estel
Business conditions	Unfavorable	Unfavorable: Leading to diverging national performances	Unfavorable: Leading to diverging national performances
External stakeholders	Strong union opposition	Strong political interference	Strong political and union interference
Merger logic	Strategic fit	Poor and changing strategic fit	Changing strategic fit
Internal stakeholders	Mounting resistance	Strong resistance among powerful actors	Increasing resistance among powerful actors
National and organizational characteristics	Strong diversity in organizational practices, identities, and cultures as a source of conflict	Strong identities as a source of conflict; not for organizational practices and cultures	Strong diversity in organizational practices, identities, and cultures as a source of conflict
Merger framework	Cross-border roles and tasks	No real integration: national distinctive roles and tasks	No real integration: national distinctive roles and tasks
Top management	Initially divided along national lines, but unified and determined after six years	Unified, but powerless	Initially unified, but increasingly divided along national lines after two years

provided the impetus for a radical reorganization of top management and the creation of a strong administrative unity. Another important reason for Enka Glanzstoff's survival is AKZO. The financial support of its holding company meant first of all that Enka Glanzstoff did not have to turn to external parties for assistance with the risk that it would become subjected to forces over which management has no control. In addition, the presence of the holding company put pressure on the two partners to find agreement among themselves. In the other two cases, cooperation and effectiveness hinged to a large extent upon the good will and management power of the two partners in the merger. It is significant in this respect that Enka Glanzstoff did not encounter the same level of resistance as the other two mergers. Although there was growing dissatisfaction with the merger after some years, it could not become a significant counter force in the absence of major power blocs.

Another difference is that both VFW–Fokker and Estel had developed organizational structures that were characterized by a high potential for interfirm conflict. Corporate identities, employment systems and staffing, aircraft projects, and governance structures all reinforced the impression that the two organizations were still to a large degree independent entities. The split obligations, and loyalties that rested primarily with the home base, were an additional reason why it was almost impossible to co-opt the services of leading managers, who already had strong doubts about the advantages of the merger.

Splitting up was not a realistic alternative for Enka Glanzstoff. Given the degree of organizational integration achieved, separation could only be accomplished at high cost, whereas the survival of the national units as independent producers was very unlikely. In the other two cases, in contrast, the comparatively low level of integration achieved of the two partner organizations made this a much more viable option. Splitting up appeared fairly easy and offered an attractive option for at least some of the company's stakeholders.

An important factor in this respect was leadership. While changes in management and the appointment of a skillful leader who gained the respect of both nationalities helped Enka Glanzstoff to find greater cohesion and unity, the other two mergers were characterized by insufficient leadership and a lack of commitment among key actors to make the merger work. Their management changes did not improve this situation much.

Conclusions

In this chapter we have focused on mergers, and on international mergers in particular. As opposed to acquisitions, mergers face particular challenges because of the sense of partnership that underlies mergers and which makes them more difficult to manage. Cross-border mergers face additional challenges. These find their origins in national disparities in cultures, institutional contexts, and national identities. Although these differences may have beneficial outcomes, in most cases they will add to the problems of building a cohesive new entity, as the three cases demonstrate.

The case studies have led to several conclusions about the factors that constrain or support the successful developments of mergers. A first general conclusion is that a merger is principally a dynamic process, with a high degree of uncertainty and predictability about the outcomes. In none of these cases, the final outcome could be traced back to a single factor. Although some factors were more important than others, their impact varied per case, and they typically gained their significance in relation with other factors. For example, interunit struggles were as much a result of the poor merger structure, the onset of the economic crisis, the failure of top management to act as a cohesive entity, as the existence of cultural differences. Essentially, the outcomes of these mergers were the product of a series of interactive factors. When looking at each of the factors specifically, starting with the business conditions, an important conclusion from the three case studies is that mergers need favorable conditions, especially in the early stages of their development, to build trust and confidence between the two groups. Stagnation or decline in an industry forces management to take difficult decisions concerning the divestment of activities and workforce reductions. This tends to put considerable pressure on a new firm that has not yet developed into a robust entity. In some cases, however, economic crisis may have a positive effect, provided that it does not affect the strategic rationale too much. Differences between group members become usually less important as they pull together to resist the threat. The case studies show that this requires two important conditions. First, it needs awareness among stakeholders that either company cannot survive independently, and second, that the merger is seen as irreversible. In other words, dissolution is impossible.

A second important determinant of success is strategic fit. Strategic fit provides the strategic rationale of the merger, but it also functions as integrating force as the recognition of mutual interest is an important binding element. Poor or changing strategic fit will reduce the effectiveness of the merger and hinder the integration of the two companies. In most merger analyses, strategic fit is approached as a static concept. The case studies make clear that strategic fit at one point in time can change into a strategic mismatch at a later stage.

Besides an accurate assessment of the synergetic benefits at the outset of the merger, potential synergies will result in superior performance only if these can eventually be realized through effective postmerger integration (Larsson and Finkelstein, 1999). But this often appears to be a major problem. One reason is that during the decision-making process organizational issues tend to be postponed to the implementation phase in the belief that these can be solved after the merger, or because ambiguity about the timing and purpose of the integration is considered functional in helping both parties to find agreement. However, such agreements in general terms can be a source of strong conflicts and disappointments as parties in the postmerger period find incongruities between their interpretations and expectations of the agreement and the other party (Jemison and Sitkin, 1986). The conflicts about the consolidation of the merger in Estel and the problems with the German aircraft project illustrate the significance of this point. Another reason for problems in the integration process is that integrating two separate companies with different traditions and backgrounds often proves to be a difficult and time-consuming process. Conflicts between the two organizational groups can frequently be observed during the postmerger situation. Again, the three case studies provide a perfect illustration. Both researchers and practitioners have tended to attribute this to the presence or absence of cultural fit. Although important, our cases suggest that cultural differences are neither a necessary nor a sufficient factor in this process. In the most unsuccessful case, the merger between Fokker and VFW, cultural differences had little to do with failure. The lack of internal cohesion and outspoken failure of this particular case was the result of a combination of external factors (unfavorable economic conditions, strong national political interests, poor strategic fit) and internal factors (incompetent top management, strong employee resistance, and an inappropriate merger framework). Also the other merger cases showed that implementation difficulties did not emanate from cultural factors alone. The perception of conflicting goals, scarce resources, and separate identities played an equally important role.

Finally, from the case experiences, it is clear that leadership is also a central factor in the success of a merger. Particularly in mergers, the effectiveness of top management is strongly dependent on cooperation and good will between the two partners. This means that the two partners must have a shared vision of the future of the new company, and a high commitment to this vision. High commitment is also needed to constrain resistance at lower levels. An essential factor in top management effectiveness is its capacity to unify its constituency to accept and implement the merger. One of the central tasks for top management in the merger process is to ensure that the loyalty of the management under them is committed to the whole business, and not just to whatever part they come from. This requires not only vision, but also the ability to communicate this vision.

A final conclusion is that mergers take time. Depending on the capital-intensiveness of the industry, it may take years to reorganize production and to realize economies of scale in production and other fields. For international mergers these costs will be even higher, as complete rationalization of production sometimes has to be sacrificed to the "twin" structure of the arrangement, or deliberately foregone because of the social consequences. In addition, people have to get used to working with foreign associates, learn to understand another company's ways of doing business, and develop new loyalties. All this is a matter of years, and a new generation of managers with a different perspective is often needed to promote the sense of unity in the new firm. The merger has to gain a self-sustaining momentum. Mutual trust and good will are essential elements of this process. A period of relative prosperity is a great help for the long-term success of a merger.

Note

1. In order to avoid confusion between the names Enka and Estel, we will use the name Enka Glanzstoff for the fiber merger; this was the official name of the merged company during the first eight years of its existence before its name was changed into Enka.

References

Bastien, D. T., and Van de Ven, A. H. (1986). Managerial and Organizational Dynamics of Mergers and Acquisitions. Unpublished Paper, University of Minnesota.

Buono, A. F., and Bowditch, J. L. (1989). *The Human Side of Mergers and Acquisitions*. San Francisco: Jossey-Bass.

Hofstede, G. H. (2001). *Culture's Consequences: International Differences in Work-Related Values*. Beverly Hills, CA: Sage.

Jemison, D. B., and Sitkin, S. B. (1986). Corporate acquisitions: A process perspective. *Academy of Management Review*, 11: 145–63.

Larsson, R., and Finkelstein, S. (1999). Integrating strategic, organizational, and human resource perspectives on mergers and acquisitions: A case survey of synergy realization. *Organization Science*, 10: 1–26.

Olie, R. L. (1996). *European Transnational Mergers*. Unpublished doctoral dissertation, Maastricht University, The Netherlands.

Prowse, S. (1994). Corporate governance in an international perspective: A study of corporate control mechanisms among large firms in the United States, the United Kingdom and Germany, *BIS Economic Papers*, 41.

15   DaimlerChrysler

A Case Study of a Cross-Border Merger

TORSTEN KÜHLMANN AND PETER J. DOWLING

Introduction

The announcement on May 7, 1998, that Daimler-Benz AG and Chrysler
Corporation intended to merge was major news in the global business
community. This high degree of publicity is not surprising. Both Daimler-
Benz and Chrysler were considered to be a part of the national heritage
in their respective countries—Germany and the United States. Daimler-
Benz's solid engineering skills symbolized Germany's industrial resurrec-
tion after World War II while Chrysler was renowned as a car manufacturer that offered innovative yet affordable products to the American consumer. However, in addition to the reputations of the companies as icons of the world automobile industry, as Table 15.1 shows,
the DaimlerChrysler merger also contains many elements of a "business
thriller."

This merger has spawned a large number of articles in the business
press and books with titles such as *Taken for a Ride: How Daimler-Benz
Drove Off with Chrysler* (Vlasic and Stertz, 2000); *Wheels on Fire: The
Amazing Inside Story of the DaimlerChrysler Merger* (Waller, 2001); and
Der DaimlerChrysler Deal (Appel and Hein, 2000). To date, however, management scholars have paid little attention to this event. It is the goal of this
chapter to correct this dearth of research on this topic. A particular emphasis is directed to the HR issues during the merger (Kay and Shelton, 2000;
Schuler and Jackson, 2001). Our chapter aims to give some preliminary
answers to three questions:

1. Which HR issues emerged in different stages of the merger process?

TABLE **15.1** The DaimlerChrysler Merger as a Business Thriller

- Secret meetings of top executives (Eaton and Schrempp)
- Code names ("Denver" and "Cleveland")
- Diversionary negotiations (Daimler-Benz and Ford)
- Influential characters in the background (Deutsche Bank manager Kopper)
- False promises (merger of equals)
- Fall of the crown prince (Stallkamp)
- A great deal of money

2. How have these issues been handled?
3. What part did the HR function play in the merger process?

We used several sources to tackle these questions as shown in Table 15.2.

To describe the merger process in a structured way, we propose a model comprising four phases: (1) targeting, (2) negotiating, (3) closing the deal, and (4) postmerger integration. We used this model because it reflects the way the process was reconstructed by one of the merging companies (Gaitanides and Sjurts, 1999). The model is also consistent with more scientific approaches to describe merger processes (for example, Hunt, 1990; Very and Schweiger, 2001). Applying the proposed model, the merger process starts with the screening of alternatives in support of a company's overall strategy. If a merger appears to be a promising option, suitable candidates have to be identified based on an analysis of their strengths and weaknesses using public domain information.

The second phase starts with a more thorough assessment of the potential benefits of the merger. A variety of issues have to be analyzed, for example, product–market combinations, tax regulations, antitrust legislation, compatibility of technical systems, human capital, and cultural gaps. Based upon these analyses, central aspects of the new company such as legal form and governance are negotiated. The second phase ends by officially announcing a merger.

The third phase emphasizes the elaboration of the legal framework for the merger as well as the planning of the required financial transactions for the merger to occur. In the last phase, the perspective turns to unifying strategies, operations, workforces, and cultures to enable plans to be put into action.

TABLE **15.2** Sources Used for our Case Study

- Books about the merger and its initiators
- Articles in journals and newspapers (Economist, Newsweek, Spiegel, Die Zeit, Zeitschrift Führung und Organisation)
- Information offered by DaimlerChrysler in its Internet-based archives
- Electronic publications about the DaimlerChrysler merger

The Process of the DaimlerChrysler Merger

Phase 1 of the DaimlerChrysler Merger: Targeting the Partner

As shown in Table 15.3, the first phase of the DaimlerChrysler merger started in 1997 when three separate studies, which had been carried out by internal experts as well as by the investment bank Goldman Sachs, all independently showed that Daimler-Benz would run out of profitable growth in the near future. The background for this prediction was

- intense price competition
- massive overcapacity
- new competitors
- rapidly changing customer preferences

In order to take the initiative in the inevitable consolidation process, several companies were considered as potential partners (General Motors, Ford, Toyota, Honda, Nissan, and Renault). All analyses showed that Chrysler was the obvious partner for Daimler-Benz. During this time Chrysler also examined several foreign companies to find a proper partner for an alliance. One goal of the alliance would be to move into the markets of Asia and Latin America. BMW and Daimler-Benz were also identified as promising candidates for a partnership.

The HR Dimension in Phase 1 of the DaimlerChrysler Merger

The assessments conducted during the screening of potential partners were limited to hard facts like market share, product programs, finance, and

TABLE **15.3** Chronicle of the DaimlerChrysler Merger (Phases 1 and 2)

1997	Both companies, Chrysler and Daimler-Benz, screen the automotive industry for potential partners.
January 12, 1998	Jürgen E. Schrempp, CEO of Daimler-Benz AG, contacts Robert J. Eaton, CEO of Chrysler Corporation, during the North American International Auto Show in Detroit and proposes a merger.
February 12–18, 1998	Initial talks regarding a possible merger involving only a small number of representatives and consultants from both companies.
March 2, 1998	Robert J. Eaton and Jürgen E. Schrempp meet in Lausanne, Switzerland, to discuss the organizational and executive structure of a possible merger.
March to April, 1998	Elaboration of the details of the merger.
April 23 to May 6, 1998	Teams negotiate the "Business Combination Agreement" and related contracts.
May 6, 1998	The merger contract is signed in London.
May 7, 1998	Worldwide announcement of the merger: Daimler-Benz and Chrysler merge to create one of the world's leading companies in Automobile, Transport, and Services (431,000 employees, 260 billion DM turnover).

technology. "Softer" people issues had not been discussed thoroughly. But it was these people issues that became very critical in the further course of the merger: widespread fears of job losses after the merger; the commitment of DaimlerChrysler to suspend layoffs for a certain time; loss of key talent; salary differences; and corporate and national culture gaps were all issues that contributed to misunderstanding and conflict. We do not argue that the partner choice would have been different if the "soft HR" facts had been given a larger weight in the targeting phase. But it can be assumed that giving more attention to HR issues would have sensitized the initiators of the merger to possible difficulties at an earlier point in time.

Phase 2 of the DaimlerChrysler Merger: Negotiating

Jürgen Schrempp was the first to suggest a merger to Chrysler. On January 12, 1998, he met Chrysler CEO Bob Eaton during the Detroit Motor Show at the head office of Chrysler in Auburn Hills, Michigan. The first conversation and also all further negotiations before the official announcement of the merger were kept highly secret. On the German side, only Jürgen Schrempp, his secretary Lydia Deininger, Rüdiger Grube, a corporate strategy advisor, Eckard Cordes, director of corporate development, and Alexander Dibelius, an investment banker from Goldman Sachs, were involved. The Chrysler team consisted of the CEO, Bob Eaton, Gary Valade, Chrysler's chief financial officer, the treasurer, Thomas Capo, and Steve Koch, an investment banker from Credit Suisse First Boston. Later, lawyers and merger experts of both companies were appointed. Everyone involved had to sign a confidentiality declaration that committed them to secrecy.

On March 2, 1998, Schrempp again met with Eaton at the General Motors Show in Lausanne, Switzerland. They reached an agreement on the first potential deal-breaker: the Chairmanship. They agreed to a cochairmanship for three years. After this period, Eaton would retire. Having agreed on the cochairmanship, they identified five issues that would have to be resolved as soon as possible:

- The location of the headquarters of the new company
- The overall financial structure of the company
- The composition of the executive board
- A joint business plan for the new company
- The name of the new company

After tough negotiations during March about the valuation of both companies, Schrempp and Eaton met on April 9 to determine the exchange ratio of assets. They agreed on a price of US$57.50 per Chrysler share, which meant a 28 percent premium added to the actual price at the N.Y. stock exchange. At this time, the shape of the merger also became clearer. The shareholders of both groups would exchange their shares for shares in the newly founded company.

On April 19, Schrempp informed the board of Daimler-Benz for the first time about the negotiations with Chrysler. Two days later Eaton and Schrempp met in New York and discussed the composition of the future board of the new company. The outcome was a board with a total of eighteen members. In essence, everyone from both the Daimler and Chrysler boards kept their positions. Up to this point, both negotiation teams had only included the CEOs, their finance and strategy executives, and several accountants, lawyers, and bankers. On May 4, Schrempp and Eaton met once again in New York. One important issue was still unresolved—the name of the new entity. Eaton wanted the name "Chrysler–Daimler-Benz" and Schrempp suggested "Daimler-Benz–Chrysler." As neither were willing to compromise, they parted without an agreed name. Only just before the announcement, the American side accepted the name *DaimlerChrysler* in exchange for another seat on the board for a Chrysler director (Dennis Pawley). On May 6, both parties signed the formal merger agreement and the following day Eaton and Schrempp informed the public about their plan to merge. The key messages emphasized shareholder value, job creation, and a *merger of equals*.

The HR Dimension of Phase 2 of the DaimlerChrysler Merger

HR issues continued to play a minor part during phase 2 of the DaimlerChrysler merger. Legal and financial aspects dominated the negotiations. The only exception was the discussion about the composition of the new board. Figure 15.1 shows the DaimlerChrysler board on "Day One" of the merger (November 17, 1998). The guiding principle for filling the board positions was "continuity." It was agreed that the chairmen from both Daimler and Chrysler would share their responsibilities in the form of a cochairmanship. It was also agreed that most members of the executive boards would hold their respective positions. Due to the strict secrecy established in phase 2, the corporate HR directors from both companies were not informed nor involved.

Phase 3 of the DaimlerChrysler Merger: Closing the Deal

Once the official announcement was made, a big advertising campaign began to explain the virtues of the merger to the shareholders of both companies. Several teams consisting of representatives from both companies spent

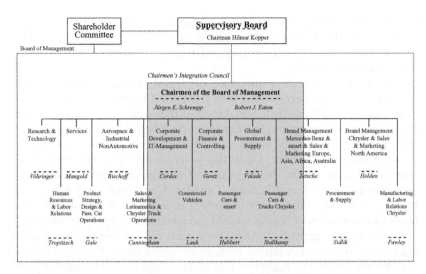

FIGURE **15.1** The First DiamlerChrysler Management Board

the northern summer of 1998 elaborating the details of the merger such as the locations for listing of the new shares, bonus payments for managers, and the location of production facilities. Table 15.4 outlines the key events of Phases 3 and 4 of the merger.

TABLE **15.4** Chronicle of the DaimlerChrysler Merger (Phases 3 and 4)

August 27–29, 1998	Management teams from Daimler-Benz and Chrysler meet in West Virginia and develop strategies for the merged company.
September 18, 1998	97.5 percent of Chrysler shareholders and 99.9 percent of Daimler-Benz shareholders approve the merger.
November 17, 1998	"Day one": DaimlerChrysler shares are traded at stock markets worldwide with the Ticker-Symbol DCX (Price per share US$68). The Management Board has eighteen members. Robert J. Eaton and Jürgen E. Schrempp are both Cochairman. Eight board members are from Chrysler, eight from Daimler-Benz, and two from the Daimler subsidiaries Dasa and Debis.
September 24, 1999	DaimlerChrysler reduces the number of its board members from eighteen to fourteen. Two Germans (Lauk and Tropitzsch) and two Americans (Stallkamp and Cunningham) leave the board. James Holden takes over the Chrysler business unit.
March 31, 2000	Robert J. Eaton, Cochairman of DaimlerChrysler, retires early.
October 26, 2000	DaimlerChrysler announces the results for the third quarter of 2000. Chrysler accounts for a loss of Euro 540 million.
October 30, 2000	Schrempp tells the London "Financial Times" that he does not consider the merger of the two automobile companies to be a "merger of equals."
November 17, 2000	James Holden, head of Chrysler, is replaced by Dieter Zetsche. In addition, the position of Chief Operating Officer (COO) is created at Chrysler and Wolfgang Bernhard is assigned to this position.

The joint management teams had identified a total of eighty-nine issues that had to be dealt with during the postmerger integration. These issues were bundled into clusters like product creation, global sales, manufacturing, global strategy, human resources and IT. One of the projects already in progress at the time of the meeting was the plan to use production capacity at Chrysler's plant at Graz, Austria, to manufacture Mercedes M-Class vehicles. The Daimler managers demonstrated how the project could save US$150 million by developing unified processes for assembling and painting. Another issue that had to be tackled was remuneration. The Chrysler top executives earned far more than their German colleagues. However, lower level German executives got paid more than their American counterparts. While Bob Eaton's annual salary amounted to US$9.7 million, Schrempp had to content himself with US$1.3 million. It was decided that the salaries for a small number of Daimler's top managers with international responsibilities would be increased to U.S. levels. For a broader group of German managers, a component of their salary would be linked to the company's profit and its share price.

On September 18, the shareholders of Daimler-Benz and Chrysler met in parallel national meetings in Stuttgart, Germany, and Auburn Hills, USA to decide on the merger. Overall, 99 percent of the Daimler shareholders and 97.5 percent of the Chrysler shareholders voted in favor of the deal. On November 17, 1998, only ten months after Schrempp had discussed the idea of a merger with Eaton, the new stock (DCX) was traded on seventeen stock exchanges around the world. When the 431,000 employees of DaimlerChrysler arrived at work that day, each one received a letter of congratulations from the two chairmen, a poster showing the new company's products and a Swatch watch. New DaimlerChrysler business cards were distributed that day. Employees were able to watch the opening ceremony at the New York stock exchange on the new DaimlerChrysler business TV-channel. The factory canteens in the United States offered wiener schnitzel and spätzle, while the German factory canteens had doughnuts and muffins on the menu.

The HR Dimension in Phase 3 of the DaimlerChrysler Merger

In the closing phase of the merger, HR issues became gradually integrated into the negotiation process. The first step was an internal marketing campaign emphasizing job security (and even job creation) to the employees of both companies. A letter signed by Eaton and Schrempp explaining the logic of the deal was sent to all employees. Information about the merger was also published on the intranet of each company and various Internet sites. The employees also watched prerecorded interviews with Schrempp and Eaton. The messages were kept simple with the aim to convince the workforce and unions in each company—hence the emphasis on jobs and job creation.

Another impetus to consider HR issues came from the American consultant Michael Hammer (author of "Reengineering the Corporation") who was invited to give a lecture to the two boards during a joint meeting in West Virginia. He outlined the critical factors for the eventual success of a merger. Among other factors, he noted the importance of cultural issues. Although there was an awareness among the board members that there would be cultural barriers, little systematic attempt had been made to help people overcome them. The most broadly discussed HR topic during this phase was remuneration and incentives. As noted earlier, German board members and top executives were paid less than their American counterparts. Commenting on this issue, Schrempp said in mid-1998 that "the German salaries will be brought in line, but there will be no Americanization."

Phase 4 of the DaimlerChrysler Merger: Postmerger Integration

During phase 4, executives at all levels and locations of the merged companies began working in mixed teams on 1,242 individual projects identified by the postmerger integration coordination team. Month-by-month reports summarizing progress of postmerger integration (measured in terms of hard facts) circulated within the company and were broadcast on the internal business TV-channel. By the end of 1999, 80 percent of the projects had been completed.

In September 1999, the DaimlerChrysler executive board was reduced to fourteen members. Two German board members were removed (Kurt Lauk, head of the commercial vehicles division, and Heiner Tropitzsch, head of human resources), whereas on the American side, Thomas Stallkamp, President of Chrysler and the leading candidate to succeed Jürgen Schrempp as Chairman, left the company. Ted Cunningham was downgraded to become the Executive Vice President, responsible for global sales of the American brands. Jim Holden was named the new President of the Chrysler division. After the restructuring of the board the German side held nine positions and the American side had five board members. Bob Eaton resigned as chairman on March 31, 2000. The original agreement indicated that he would serve as cochairman until 2001.

On November 17, 2000, DaimlerChrysler announced that Dieter Zetsche, head of the commercial vehicles division, would take over as President and CEO of the Chrysler group. Wolfgang Bernhard, another German, was appointed Chief Operating Officer of Chrysler. The context for Holden's replacement as President of Chrysler group was a sharp drop in profitability at Chrysler during the course of 2000 and a 20 percent decline in the DaimlerChrysler share price. At that time, the market capitalization of DaimlerChrysler was little more than that of Daimler-Benz *before* the merger. Intense competition in the U.S. auto market, big discounts offered by companies to stimulate sales, and the costs of launching new models had resulted in a loss of Euro 540 million in the third quarter of 2000.

The HR Dimension in Phase 4 of the DaimlerChrysler Merger

Within the postmerger integration there were only forty-three projects in the area of human resources. These projects covered topics such as corporate culture, employee profit-sharing, leadership styles, labor relations, global job evaluation, exchange programs, and management development. The board member responsible for human resources (Tropitzsch) was not included in the "Chairmen's Integration Council," the core of DaimlerChrysler's management structure during the postmerger integration phase. Within the first two years of the merger, DaimlerChrysler lost about twenty top executives, especially from the Chrysler side. Thomas Stallkamp and Jim Holden were the most prominent executives to leave Chrysler. There is little evidence of systematic attempts to prevent or reduce executive turnover during the integration process. However, communication with lower level employees was practiced quite effectively. Using the business TV-channel, intranet, and Internet, employees were regularly updated about upcoming changes. These communication activities consistently addressed the issue of job security. The prospects of job security and even job creation were key factors that convinced the worker representatives on Daimler's supervisory board to vote in favor of the merger.

The mixed teams working on integration projects constituted an ideal arena for learning and knowledge sharing. When the integration teams started, the members quickly noticed the difficulties and misunderstandings that arose from different cultural and national backgrounds. Examples of issues and problems that emerged include inappropriate humor, political correctness, perceived excessive formality, sexual harassment, private relationships, and documentation of meetings.

Both Daimler and Chrysler focused on the integration of businesses and technologies. Cultural issues were only addressed by top executives when making general statements to the media regarding the challenges of an international merger. The intercultural training offered by the company was short-term in nature and limited to the "Do and Don't" in encounters between Germans and Americans. It was not until the end of 2000 that DaimlerChrysler executives openly admitted that cultural differences had caused problems. As Chrysler's operating performance deteriorated in the third quarter of 2000, Manfred Gentz, the Chief Financial Officer, explained that the late intervention by the DaimlerChrysler management board, especially by the German board members, was due in part to the fear of being labeled as "always knowing better" and being seen as "evil Germans" by the American public. If this causal attribution is correct, a cultural problem may have cost the shareholders of DaimlerChrysler a great deal of money.

Human Resource Issues Identified from the DaimlerChrysler Merger

A summary of the HR activities which occurred during the Daimler-Chrysler merger are shown in Table 15.5.

From this case study we conclude the following:

1. The HR function played a minor part in the planning and implementation of the DaimlerChrysler merger. It was apparently assumed that people issues would create no special problems. The planning and closing of the merger was based on factors such as market share, technology, product strategy, legal frameworks and finance. These evaluations took place "behind closed doors". HR management was not involved in the process until the deal had been closed. This case study confirms a report of the Conference Board which reported that less than one third of HR executives had a major

TABLE **15.5** A Summary of HR Activities During the DaimlerChrysler Merger Process

Targeting the Seller	Negotiating	Closing the Deal	Postmerger Integration
Communications		Letter from Cochairmen Information campaign using intranet, Internet, and the DaimlerChrysler business TV-channel	Information campaign using intranet, Internet, and the DaimlerChrysler business TV-channel
Selection	Appointment of Management Board		Restructuring of Management Board
Compensation		Decision about remuneration of top executives	
Development		Sensitizing Management Board to cultural gaps Binational project teams	Intercultural training for executives Management exchange program

influence on how mergers were planned and implemented (Noe et al., 2000, p. 59). On the other hand there is accumulating evidence that reaching a merger's goals depends on the "people factor" or the "human capital" of the merging companies. The employees' expertise and skills, their willingness to accept the merger and to cooperate with their new colleagues, and the fit between the respective corporate cultures all significantly contribute to the success of a merger (Hubbard, 1999). In particular, little weight was given to the cross-border aspect of the merger. In fact, differences between the American and German national cultures became important obstacles to the integration of the two companies, although the cultural misfits took some time to appear.

Lesson 1—Involvement of HR management starting from the preacquisition analysis of candidates facilitates all phases of the merger process.

2. As the merger process developed pace, the scope of HR activities became broader. The involvement of HR management had been hampered by the fact that neither a HR due diligence nor a cultural due diligence could be performed prior to the merger. HR management was faced with the challenge of integrating two workforces, two HR strategies, and two corporate cultures without having timely access to detailed data about the human resources of the merger candidates.

Lesson 2—The evaluation of merger candidates as well as the integration of the merging companies requires a detailed database covering employee characteristics, working conditions, and HR systems.

3. At first, HR decisions focused on the top hierarchical levels. The high fluctuation of former Chrysler managers during the merger process indicates that the management potential of the target company (for example, leadership skills, cross-cultural competencies, commitment to a merged company) had not been thoroughly screened in the selection of managers for key positions. Over time, more and more lower level employees were addressed by HR activities. The communication policy towards the middle and lower hierarchical levels focused on the fears and concerns of the average employee: Will my job be secure? Will I be assigned to new tasks? Will I have to cooperate with new colleagues? Do I have to move abroad? Will my salary be cut? This focus was correct as the average employee during the transition period is not particularly interested in statements about the strategic advantages of a merger. But one can assume that the lack of specific communication in the first three phases of the DaimlerChrysler merger substantially undermined the credibility of the messages sent afterwards.

Lesson 3—Communication about the merger has to be rapid, specific, and truthful.

4. HR issues appear to have become a prominent argument for the explanation of merger problems within the echelons of DaimlerChrysler. It is plausible to argue that HR issues may be one of the major reasons that the DaimlerChrysler merger did not initially live up to expectations. However, it is possible that people issues are really only a partial explanatory factor. All too frequently, senior managers hasten to attribute a failure of merger processes to soft factors such as culture differences, power struggles, and excessive loss of key employees without providing sufficient analysis of other internal and external factors that also influence the merger process.

Lesson 4—HR problems are a common but usually incomplete explanation for merger difficulties.

5. The DaimlerChrysler merger supports the case to have the HR function integrally involved in strategy formulation and implementation of mergers. Contrary to the hopes of many HR academics, the integration of HR into strategic planning processes appears to be a long way from being achieved in many organizations. Top executives appear to keep on neglecting the importance of HR issues as a source of competitive advantage.

Lesson 5—Top managers do not appear to be convinced of the important contribution of human resource issues to a merger's success and the need for early involvement of senior HR managers in the merger process.

References

Appel, H., and Hein, C. (2000). *Der DaimlerChrysler Deal*. München: Heyne.

Gaitanides, M., and Sjurts, I. (1999). Der Merger of Equals muss letztlich ein Merger der Rationalen sein. *Zeitschrift Führung und Organisation*, 68: 349–57.

Hubbard, N. (1999). *Acquisition—Strategy and Implementation*. London: Macmillan.

Hunt, J. W. (1990). Changing patterns of acquisition behaviour in takeovers and the consequences for acquisition processes. *Strategic Management Journal*, 11: 69–77.

Kay, I. T., and Shelton, M. (2000). The people problems in mergers. *The McKinsey Quarterly*, 4: 29–37.

Noe, R. A., Hollenbeck, J. R., Gerhart, B., and Wright, P. M. (2000). *Human Resource Management: Gaining a Competitive Advantage*, 3rd edn. Boston: Irwin.

Schuler, R., and Jackson, S. (2001). HR issues and activities in mergers and acquisitions. *European Management Journal*, 19: 239–53.

Very, P., and Schweiger, D. M. (2001). The acquisition process as a learning
process: Evidence from a study of critical problems and solutions in
domestic and cross-border deals. *Journal of World Business*, 36: 11–31.

Vlasic, B., and Stertz, B. A. (2000). *Taken for a Ride: How Daimler-Benz Drove
Off with Chrysler*. New York: HarperCollins.

Waller, D. (2001). *Wheels on Fire: The Amazing Inside Story of the
DaimlerChrysler Merger*. London: Hodder and Stoughton.

16 The Importance of the Agreement Formation Process in Partnering with the Unfamiliar

The Case of Renault and Nissan[1]

HARRY KORINE, KAZUHIRO ASAKAWA,
AND PIERRE-YVES GOMEZ

Companies are increasingly forming alliances and joining forces in mergers with unfamiliar, often even unlikely, partners in the search for greater geographic coverage and complementary skills. How can such odd couples effectively cooperate in practice? They can—if they make the presignature, agreement formation process an integral part of their strategies.

In the wake of globalization, industry convergence, and technological upheaval, companies are increasingly concluding long-term cooperation and even merger agreements outside their traditional spheres of familiarity. The search for expanded geographic coverage, broader service to clients, and complementary skills has yielded some extraordinary new alliances and mergers: the Renault/Nissan strategic alliance in the automotive sector; the AT&T/NTT DoCoMo partnership in telecommunications; and the Fresenius/National Medical Care merger in health care are just a few prominent examples.

Odd couples abound. These are companies with little or no previous experience of working together. Often everything from management style to historic trajectory suggests they should be kept apart. Yet, they are joining their fortunes and establishing deep strategic interdependence. Although the theoretical gains to be had from such combinations are evident, the practice of creating successful partnerships between the unfamiliar is fraught with difficulty.

In this chapter, we focus our attention on strategic alliances. Strategic alliances imply long-term cooperation and often involve significant equity participation. Although they differ from outright mergers in that the participating firms maintain their individual legal identities, many strategic alliances bear a resemblance to mergers in terms of level of functional integration and administrative cooperation. This is particularly true of strategic alliances such as Renault/Nissan that aim for very close sharing of development, production, and cost management efforts.

Research has shown that the ultimate outcome of strategic alliances depends upon (a) the terms of the alliance agreement and (b) the evolution of intercompany coordination over time. Both the terms set by the partners and the evolution of coordination, in turn, are a function of the level of mutual trust. In partnerships between the unfamiliar, where there is little or no prior store of trust to draw upon, the alliance formation process is particularly important. The *experience* of presignature interaction conditions postsignature collaboration.

How do you approach a stranger with a view to building a long-lasting, effective partnership? Typically, there are cultural differences to be overcome and diverging world views to be reconciled. The initiator of the process worries about being seen as too aggressive; the recipient of an alliance proposal wonders how to play his or her cards. The process may yield knowledge that leads to a more refined evaluation of the alliance or it may hide knowledge and result in wildly overoptimistic (or overpessimistic) projections. Most importantly, perhaps, the alliance formation process in which executives from both sides form the first associations with each other sets the tone for the partnership. Negative routines established and bad precedents set in the alliance formation process are very hard to correct later on, once the partnership is under pressure to deliver results.

Renault and Nissan

Of the many odd couples being created today, the partnership between car-makers Renault from France and Nissan from Japan was perhaps one of the least likely to form. Although the case for an alliance between Renault and Nissan might have looked attractive on paper—geographic complementarity in market coverage, economies of scale in shared production activities, and potential for cross-learning in areas of different competencies—the obstacles to actually achieving these benefits were formidable.

Renault and Nissan had no history of doing business together, came from very different cultures, and had both seen their reputations tarnished in recent years—Renault by a failed attempt at merger with Volvo; Nissan by its declining market share and great financial difficulty.

Against all expectations, however, these two giants found each other and signed a far-reaching strategic tie-up, with equity participation and exchange of executives. Even more surprising, the partnership has borne fruit. Thanks to the recovery plan launched shortly after the alliance agreement was formalized, Nissan has become profitable again for the first time in six years and is developing an innovative new product line-up; over the same period, the two companies have enjoyed mutual benefits from platform sharing, technology transfer, and supply chain rationalization. Renault has increased its initial ownership stake in Nissan from 36 to 44 percent and Nissan has recently taken a 15 percent equity participation in Renault.

How did Renault and Nissan come together and what can be learned from their success? We have studied the nine-month Renault/Nissan alliance formation process in great depth, from first contacts to the signature of the alliance agreement, interviewing all the principal participants and consulting archival material of the two companies.[2] Based on unique data from both parties to the agreement, our study suggests how executives can use the alliance formation process to overcome the liability of unfamiliarity and sow the seeds for long-lasting cooperation.

In the case of Renault and Nissan, successful management of the alliance formation process hinged on the ability of the executives of the two companies to put the alliance process at the center of their respective strategies. First, they took a long-term, encompassing view at critical junctures in the process, rather than a short-term, bargaining perspective. And second, they used the process itself to initiate strategic changes within their organizations rather than waiting to initiate change until the signing of an agreement. In effect, the executives of both Renault and Nissan appeared to have postsignature collaboration in view throughout the alliance formation process.

The Alliance Formation Process: From Conceiving to Closure

The formation of the alliance between Renault and Nissan was divided into four temporal stages. Key events and interim agreements separated the stages and provided clear signposts for the executives involved. Each stage represented a new level of cooperation and served a particular purpose in the alliance formation process. On the basis of an interpretative analysis, we label the four stages conceiving, courting, commitment, and closure.

Conceiving: June 1998 to September 10, 1998

After failing to link up with Volvo in 1995, Renault remained in search of a partner with which to achieve broader geographic coverage and increased size. In 1998, the urgency of the search was heightened by the Daimler/Chrysler merger and Ford's purchase of Volvo Automobiles. As the musical chair game in the automobile industry speeded up, Asia appeared the most promising hunting ground.

In spite of advice against a direct approach, in June 1998, Renault president Louis Schweitzer wrote to Nissan president Yoshikazu Hanawa proposing broad strategic cooperation. He sent a similar proposal to the president of Mitsubishi Motor Cars.

While Mitsubishi was relatively slow to respond, Nissan's Hanawa answered quickly and positively. "[Bankers told us]...if you write to them, that's the best way to make sure of failure. Well, I wrote to Hanawa in June saying 'I believe we should be thinking strategically. Can we do that together,' and he answered in July," Schweitzer recalls. "I was impressed with Mr. Schweitzer's courageous decision to embrace a new business opportunity," says Hanawa.

After a framework for cooperation was defined by an advance team, Schweitzer and Hanawa held the first of twelve one-to-one meetings they were to have over the course of forming the alliance between Renault and Nissan.

"Mr. Schweitzer and Mr. Hanawa learned to trust each other very quickly. I think that this trust between the chairmen has lasted all the way through, with no stumbling blocks, deviations or betrayals," Renault's head negotiator Guy Douin observes.

Hanawa himself stresses this point: "With many people around, it is difficult to tell each other the truth, that is why I decided to negotiate alone. I think Mr. Schweitzer, on the other hand, was more careful about opening up to me because of the previous experience with Volvo. I believe the process leading up to an alliance is all about telling the truth; dishonesty only makes the process longer."

During July and August, negotiators from the two companies got to know each other and identified some twenty areas of potential synergy. On September 10, 1998, Schweitzer and Hanawa signed a memorandum concerning the evaluation of technical and financial synergies. The memorandum gave Renault negotiating exclusivity for Nissan Motor and established twenty-one joint study teams to examine the feasibility of the alliance.

Both Renault and Nissan took a very open-minded approach to partnership in the conceiving stage. Rather than beginning with the most familiar candidate in the pool of potential partners (for Renault, Mitsubishi, because of a history of cooperation in conjunction with Volvo; for Nissan, Ford, because of shared van development experience), both companies were prepared to start from scratch and think outside existing frames of reference. With its superior technology and size, Nissan was a huge challenge for Renault. Renault, on the other hand, could bring a true outsider's view to Nissan's organisation and operations.

Courting: September 10, 1998, to October 1998

"In a car company, when there's a problem, the problem normally rises from the engineering department. So engineers were selected from both sides to work on research topics for three months. Similar projects were performed for other departments as well," says Hanawa.

During the courting stage, nearly one hundred engineers and business specialists from each side worked together very closely, without any assurance of an outcome. These joint study teams quickly became deeply involved in sharing critical information about both companies. The coverage of their work was comprehensive—from platform integration to joint geographic presence—and provided hard evidence for alliance benefits.

"It was extraordinary in terms of synergies. We really believed in it, or at least those taking part in the negotiations did. Quite frankly, we were so complementary in terms of geography, products, personality . . . so we had great confidence," says Alain Dassas, a member of Renault's lead negotiating team. The spirit of discovery was shared among the top negotiators on both sides. T. Shiga of Nissan notes: "The kind of information that we were sharing with each other prior to the alliance agreement was a very rare case . . . since both sides had strong individual needs to make themselves stronger, the joint study took place sincerely. It was not just a handshake between the top managers."

In order to maintain confidentiality and control in the process, the teams did not communicate with each other or to the outside but reported directly to the head negotiators on both sides, who in turn kept Schweitzer and Hanawa regularly informed.

Progressing from the conceiving to the courting stage of the alliance formation process, the two companies threw out stereotypes about France and Japan and put big-company arrogance aside to concentrate on hard business facts. The heavy resource allocation to preagreement evaluation allowed the business managers to begin to overcome unfamiliarity and to find common ground, not in theoretical terms but in concrete synergies such as access to the Latin American market and sharing transmission technology. This patient investment in process, when the ultimate outcome of the alliance was still in doubt, yielded discoveries about the prospective partner but also provided a mirror for self-reflection. Both companies learned more about their own strengths and weaknesses.

Commitment: October 1998 to December 23, 1998

In October, Schweitzer prepared a two-page mock press release with the title "Nissan and Renault join forces," outlining the full scope of the agreement he envisioned. He discussed it with Hanawa at a face-to-face meeting. "We had to move closer strategically, but it could not be a simple acquisition or a merger, because a Franco-Japanese merger is no easy matter. . . . I suggested to him [Hanawa] that three people from Renault should become members of the Nissan board of directors: the COO, the VP product planning and the deputy chief financial officer. I only asked for those three.

I didn't ask for any other jobs except those three, and he [Hanawa] didn't try to argue about any of them," says Schweitzer.

"I did not agree with it [the mock press release] from the start of course. But I was not surprised. Through our discussions, I felt that Mr. Schweitzer always had a more comprehensive view of the partnership than I did," Hanawa notes.

Their meeting culminated in Hanawa's invitation for Schweitzer to speak at Nissan's Tokyo headquarters.

On November 10, Schweitzer, Douin, and Carlos Ghosn (who went on to become first COO, and then, in 2000, CEO of Nissan) made what Renault called the "big picture" presentation to the Nissan board. Drawing on the findings of the joint study teams and Renault's own experience in turnaround management, Schweitzer described in detail the full benefit of a large-scale collaboration for Nissan. No immediate response was forthcoming from Nissan but work in the joint study teams continued until mid-December.

In the commitment stage, both sides took make or break risks—in the words of Schweitzer, "ça passe, ou ça casse." "We knew we were playing with fire. We had the growing impression of being on slippery ground, not to say enemy territory... We weren't at all sure we could pull it off," says Douin.

When Schweitzer had fully articulated Renault's view in the mock press release, Hanawa invited him to show the Nissan board what Renault could do. Why did both executives act so boldly? With the personal relationship between Schweitzer and Hanawa established and with the work of the teams showing the hard benefits of an alliance, the time appeared ripe to both executives to go beyond talk and put stakes in the ground—for Schweitzer toward Nissan management and for Hanawa toward his own board.

"At the presentation, the participants were informed for the first time of the overall direction which the joint studies might be leading towards," recalls Hanawa. "But, to be frank, I myself was amazed at ... the level of research as well as the level of involvement with which Renault had progressed with the alliance plans. Because at Nissan, the negotiation was strictly kept between Mr. Schweitzer and I. This was the difference between Renault and Nissan. Renault knew exactly what they wanted from the beginning. I think our board only understood it as one possibility."

Bold, public action took the alliance process to another level of intimacy, making the cooperation much harder to reverse.

Closure: December 1998 to March 11, 1999

On December 23, 1998, Hanawa asked Renault to make an offer for *both* Nissan Motor (cars) and Nissan Diesel (trucks), formally terminated the negotiating exclusivity clause, and set a deadline of March 30, 1999, for concluding a deal. Nissan was effectively put in play, and DaimlerChrysler was mooted as Renault's main rival.

Throughout the due diligence process that followed, the lead negotiators continued to meet regularly. On March 10, 1999, DaimlerChrysler announced that it was no longer in the running for Nissan. Meeting their counterparts in Tokyo on the day after DaimlerChrysler's announcement, Renault negotiators upheld the terms of their original offer.

Says Schweitzer, "The decision we made during the final negotiations was not to change our position. It was an important choice on our part to say 'It's not because Daimler is no longer around that we are changing our proposal.' I decided not to [change the proposal] because I felt it would destroy the relationship of trust which was indispensable for us to work together... It seemed more important to show that we were loyal, stable and reliable partners."

The next day, Renault and Nissan went public with a signed alliance agreement that very closely matched Schweitzer's October mock press release. "The fact that we had agreed on the terms of equal position was important for me, as dominance destroys motivation," notes Hanawa.

Despite changed circumstances post-December 23, negotiators at both Renault and Nissan persevered. Renault continued its fact finding and did not waver from the mode or the spirit of interaction established earlier in the process. "Above all we tried—even if we didn't manage it 100 percent—to avoid putting ourselves forward as the company making an acquisition, the side that comes out on top. We always wanted to have due regard for form, to have due consideration for the Japanese... We kept in mind the lessons that could be learned from our previous experience [with Volvo]," says Jean-François De Andria of Renault's negotiating team.

Nissan continued to meet with Renault regularly and responded quickly to requests and proposals. "For Nissan, the negotiations and the execution of the alliance contract were a process and not an objective," observes T. Sugino of Nissan's negotiating team. "The objective was not to finalize the contract wording but to examine how to share best practices."

In effect, the long period of building familiarity between the two companies could not be matched by any new suitor. "Determining an alliance partner actually involves a lot of work, joint study teams, bottom-up reporting, etc... In view of all the work that was put into the study process with Renault, I imagine that evaluating another alliance deal at the same time would really be a major undertaking," says Nissan's Shiga.

Schweitzer held on to the original proposal in the strong belief that consistency was crucial for the long-term health of the alliance. He did not want doubt to enter into the relationship and sour the future.

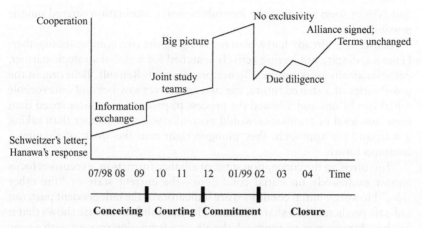

FIGURE **16.1** The Renault/Nissan Alliance Formation Process: A Timeline

Going Against Received Wisdom

Figure 16.1 above schematically summarizes the evolution of cooperation between Renault and Nissan in the alliance formation process. We observe that the development of cooperation from stage to stage was not linear, nor unidirectional. A great deal of effort and perseverance was required on both sides.

The sheer length of time devoted to the alliance formation process—nine months, in total—and the deep, personal involvement of the two companies' chief executives underlines the significance of the period of rapprochement. Both Schweitzer and Hanawa put the alliance process at the center of their respective strategic agendas. In this way, they could take a long-term perspective and go against received wisdom in managing the different stages of the alliance process.

Conceiving as Believing in a Shared Future

In the conceiving stage, instead of narrowly pursuing a deeper relationship with already familiar partners (to recall: for Renault, Mitsubishi; for Nissan, Ford), both Renault and Nissan actively encouraged novel relationships. The universe of potential partners was their opportunity space and they quickly got down to business with an unfamiliar partner. It would appear that both Schweitzer and Hanawa were less interested in the initial conditions that guide most partner searches than in the shape of a shared future. Mitsubishi might have looked better to Renault (and Ford to Nissan) from the point of view of prior experience but the executives of Renault and Nissan soon saw that the Renault/Nissan combination offered unique possibilities.

Schweitzer already had a plan for bringing the two companies together; Hanawa, despite not having actively searched for a global strategic partner, enthusiastically took up the alliance process with Renault. Believing in the possibilities of a shared future, the two executives saw beyond unfavorable initial conditions and allowed the process to proceed at a faster speed than their low level of familiarity would normally warrant. Rather than taking a wait-and-see approach, they plunged right into the work of shaping a common future.

Too often, in the conception stage of alliance formation, executives focus almost exclusively on initial conditions—the current state of "the other side." However, initial conditions are indicators of the independent past, not fail-safe predictors of a shared future. The Renault/Nissan case shows that it can be advantageous to approach the alliance formation process with a view to the future. Belief in a shared future allows even unfamiliar companies to move more quickly into a stage of courting, where courting aims at defining common advantage, rather than exposing individual weaknesses.

It should be stressed that taking a "believing is seeing" approach—rather than the more conventional "seeing is believing"—requires that both partners develop clear frames of reference for continuously testing their beliefs against reality. Both Renault and Nissan, both Schweitzer and Hanawa, had clear ideas of what they needed out of a strategic alliance and used the alliance formation process to rigorously test the other side's abilities to deliver on the promise of a shared future.

Courting as Intensive Fact Finding

In the courting stage, where prudence advises a top-level approach and careful guarding of company secrets, Renault and Nissan got down to facts and, through the joint study teams, deeply involved middle managers in the alliance formation process. Although they opened up the process to information sharing and learning across company boundaries, Schweitzer and Hanawa kept a very tight rein on their companies' negotiators and the joint study teams. The two executives took an approach that can best be described as both open and closely controlled.

It is worth noting that Daimler-Benz and Chrysler followed a much more traditional path in coming to their 1998 merger agreement: only a few top executives were involved in the process, and no joint study teams were formed until many months *after* signing.

The traditional path to partnership agreement can at best confirm the two sides' starting views of initial conditions. There is just not enough information sharing to go beyond a static evaluation. In the case of Renault and

Nissan, by contrast, the courting stage allowed for discovery. In this kind of a process, more facts come out, more people are involved, and more tacit knowledge is shared. The courting process becomes a living experiment of working together before signature and establishes the practical bases for future cooperation.

In theory, any strategic partnership between unfamiliar organizations can benefit from such an open exchange of facts and experiences prior to signature. The questions are how to ensure quality of information sharing and how to protect the process from leakage and unwanted publicity. For Renault and Nissan, clearly defining the tasks of the joint study teams was critical to information sharing. High priority, regular involvement of top executives, and the establishment of specific internal reporting lines reinforced the process and prevented it from getting out of control.

Commitment as Risk-Taking

In the commitment stage, both sides opened up and took big risks: Schweitzer's mock press release; Hanawa's invitation to talk to the Nissan board in Tokyo; and the "big picture" presentation. Rather than inching toward a commitment bargain by bargain, executives at Renault and Nissan explicitly acknowledged the need for dramatic action to cement the tie between the two companies.

Commitment is generally built incrementally, step by verifying step. It is a time-consuming process, one that takes place for the most part at the individual level of analysis. That being said, there are junctures in the life of a partnership where it appears necessary to take more radical action, articulating the extent of progress made and making a public statement. The transition sought especially by Schweitzer and, to a lesser extent perhaps, also by Hanawa was to higher levels of commitment and trust: from individual to organizational commitment; and from trust based on knowledge *of* the other side to trust based on identification *with* the other side. The symbolic and public nature of the events at this stage was clearly designed to bring the broader organizations into the process. The content of the mock press release and the "big picture" presentation aimed at demonstrating that Renault and Nissan had truly common interests in the alliance—not only did the two companies know each other, they could identify with each other.

The majority of strategic alliances need at some point to establish organizational commitment and identification-based trust. Of course, previously unfamiliar organizations cannot just jump from zero to this level of partnership. Only when the initial belief in a shared future has received sufficient corroboration in facts and the level of interaction between the partners is roughly symmetrical, does it make sense to initiate dramatic commitment steps. In a sense, the commitment stage is the time to put the relationship to the test and, through the test of public articulation, to establish a different, common base for going forward.

Closure as Investment, Not Negotiation

In closure, finally, when negotiating practice would suggest squeezing for better terms, Renault stayed the course and gave up the unique opportunity provided by DaimlerChrysler's dropping out to take advantage of Nissan. Rather than opening up negotiations again, Renault closed them down. Nissan was to be a fully motivated, equal partner, not a humiliated outpost of a new automotive industry empire.

Schweitzer and his team never lost sight of their fundamental objective, that is, to form a lasting, significant strategic alliance with Nissan. The failure to squeeze Nissan on terms is not a case of undue generosity or insufficient aggressiveness in the final hour. Rather, Renault's actions during closure demonstrated consistency of purpose. Any negotiation will have its twists and turns but negotiation tactics should not take precedence over the gains to be achieved through long-term cooperation.

Alliance Formation: An Opportunity to Launch Change

The guiding principle in managing critical junctures in the alliance formation process would appear to be the quest for long-term gain on both sides. Their ultimate strategic purpose(s) guides Schweitzer and Hanawa through the ups and downs.

The long-term perspective is also apparent in the way both companies used the alliance formation process to change themselves—the process of working with the unfamiliar adds value, independent of the ultimate outcome. Thus, Schweitzer used the alliance formation process to build the organization's confidence and enhance the company's standing in the automotive world. The ambition to take on one of the biggest names in the business and the mastery of challenges in the process (that is, joint study teams, "big picture" presentation) made the company a more serious player in the automotive industry partnership stakes. The process was not only concerned with learning more about Nissan, it also served to build up Renault.

Hanawa, too, used the alliance formation process to effect change inside his company. The work with Renault served as a mirror for demonstrating the full extent of Nissan's problems, helped promote new, younger managers (the lead negotiators), and isolated a board that had blocked major change in the past (the "big picture" presentation put the board in front of a fait accompli). Independent of the final outcome of negotiations, the alliance process with Renault brought fundamental changes to Nissan.

The Process Behind the Miracle

From the Wall Street Journal to the Harvard Business Review, newspapers and business magazines around the world have reported extensively in recent months on the successful turnaround of Nissan. Carlos Ghosn and his team have been described as miracle workers for the speed and scope of the changes they have achieved at Nissan. According to these reports, the secret of success appears to lie solely in adept management of postalliance integration. Based on our analysis of the alliance formation process, we can shed further light on the subject of Nissan's turnaround. In our view, the alliance formation efforts presaged and jumpstarted Nissan's turnaround.

Deep knowledge was built up in the joint study teams. Thanks to the very detailed engineering and marketing work done over the last three months of 1998, the true nature of the issues at Nissan was out in the open. Strengths, weaknesses, and complementarities had been precisely evaluated. Moreover, the process of working in joint study teams had helped establish a common language and protocol—it is no accident that the joint team structure was replicated after the signing of the alliance. In the process of becoming familiar, the two companies developed a way of learning from each other.

Resistance at Nissan was broken down during the alliance formation process. Hanawa adroitly bypassed the existing power structure by keeping the negotiations to himself and his personal lieutenants. When sufficient knowledge and confidence in the alliance was built, he effectively used Renault to present the truth about Nissan to his own executive board. Working with Renault in this fashion publicly exposed bureaucratic inefficiency and uncompetitive management. Continued resistance to change would have implied severe loss of face, and the majority of the executive board therefore stepped down after the alliance agreement was signed.

Entrepreneurial spirit was infused into Nissan in the course of building the alliance agreement. At a company where lack of critical review and mechanical agreement had been the norms of interaction for many years, the key managers involved in the alliance formation process saw themselves in the unflattering mirror of reality and got used to challenging the status quo. Moreover, through the work with Renault, these technology-focused managers began to develop a strategic view of the business. Most significantly, perhaps, younger people were put in charge of running the alliance formation process and gained the experience necessary to begin to drive change from the inside.

In short, when Ghosn came on the scene in the late spring of 1999, he *knew* what would be required and found a group of managers inside Nissan that was *ready* to follow his dramatic remake of the company.

The process of partnering with the unfamiliar represents a unique opportunity to do things differently—to break with received wisdom about collaboration and to change perspective on the organization itself. Partnering with the unfamiliar is both challenge and opportunity. The case of Renault and Nissan—the ultimate odd couple—demonstrates how challenge can be turned into opportunity, if the alliance formation process is put at the center of strategy.

For the better part of the 1970s and 1980s, both the practice and the study of bringing together companies were focused on *pre*signature contract negotiation and evaluation, with little attention to the social psychology of the process. By the early 1990s, the tide had begun to shift, and influential authors such as Haspeslagh and Jemison (1991), and later Doz (1996), stressed the importance of *post*signature coordination process in successful merger/acquisition and alliance management. Based on the research evidence provided by the case of Renault and Nissan—a highly successful strategic alliance with some characteristics of a merger—we would urge practitioners and researchers to keep the *whole* process in view, weighing *pre* and *post* appropriately. The process of integrating two companies does not stop or start at signature. As the case study indicates, the experience of presignature interaction conditions postsignature collaboration, particularly between companies without a prior history of working together. Pre and post are closely tied, by logic, of course, but also through the development of trust and cooperation. Bringing two companies together is a holistic process that requires a long-term, strategic perspective—all along the way.

Notes

1. This chapter was prepared for G. K. Stahl and M. E. Mendenhall (eds.). *Managing Culture and Human Resources in Mergers and Acquisitions.* Palo Alto: Stanford Business Books/Stanford University Press. It draws extensively on our earlier work (Korine, Asakawa, and Gomez, 2002). The financial support of the Strategic Leadership Research Programme at LBS, the *Rodolphe Mérieux* Foundation for Entrepreneurial Management at EM Lyon, and the overseas case development fund at Keio Business School are gratefully acknowledged. For teaching purposes, the case study series Renault/Nissan is available in English, French, and Japanese.

2. Data collection involved three trips to Renault headquarters in Paris and one trip to Nissan headquarters in Tokyo. Interviews lasted an average of two hours each and were held in the interviewees' native language, French or Japanese. All interviews at Renault were tape-recorded and subsequently transcribed; all interviews at Nissan were taken down in note form by three researchers, cross-checked, and transcribed. We followed a narrative approach, asking actors to recall the chronology of events. To guard against selective retrospective bias, we made use of previous interviews' results and firm-internal data to challenge the

interviewees' recollections. The resulting complete case history, including interview quotes and document citations, has been read and meticulously verified by both firms, with additional details provided as necessary.

References

Burgers, W. P., Hill, C. W. L., and Kim, W. C. (1993). A theory of global strategic alliances: The case of the global auto industry. *Strategic Management Journal*, 14(6): 419–31.

Das, T. K., and Teng, B.-S. (1998). Between trust and control: Developing confidence in partner co-operation in alliances. *Academy of Management Journal*, 23(3): 491–512.

Doz, Y. L. (1996). The evolution of co-operation in strategic alliances: Initial conditions or learning processes? *Strategic Management Journal*, 17: 55–83.

Doz, Y. L., and Hamel, G. (1998). *Alliance Advantage—The Art of Creating Value Through Partnering*. Cambridge, MA: Harvard Business School Press.

Gersick, C. J. G. (1989). Marking time: Predictable transitions in task groups. *Academy of Management Journal*, 31(1): 9–41.

Gersick, C. J. G. (1991). Revolutionary change theories: A multilevel exploration of the punctuated equilibrium. *Academy of Management Journal*, 33(1): 10–36.

Gulati, R. (1995). Does familiarity breed trust? The implications of repeated ties for contractual choices in alliances. *Academy of Management Journal*, 38: 85–112.

Hagedoorn, J., and Schakenraad, J. (1994). The effect of strategic technology alliances on company performance. *Strategic Management Journal*, 15(4): 291–310.

Haspeslagh, P., and Jemison, D. (1991). *Managing Acquisitions*. Cambridge, MA: Harvard Business School Press.

Korine, H., Asakawa, K., and Gomez, P.-Y. (2002). Partnering with the unfamiliar: Lessons from the case of Renault and Nissan. *Business Strategy Review*, 13(2): 41–50.

Langley, A. (1999). Strategies for theorizing from process data. *Academy of Management Review*, 24(4): 691–710.

Larson, A. (1992). Network dyads in entrepreneurial settings: A study of the governance of exchange relationships. *Administrative Science Quarterly*, 37: 76–104.

Lewicki, R. J., and Bunker, B. B. (1996). Developing and maintaining trust in work relationships. In Kramer and Tyler (eds.), *Trust in Organizations: Frontiers of Theory and Research*. Thousand Oaks, CA: Sage, pp. 114–39.

McKnight, D. H., Cummings, L. L., and Chervany, N. L. (1998). Initial trust formation in new organizational relationships. *Academy of Management Review*, 23(3): 473–90.

Parkhe, A. (1998). Understanding trust in international alliances. *Journal of World Business*, 33(3): 219–40.

Ring, P. S., and Van de Ven, A. H. (1992). Structuring cooperative relationship between organizations. *Strategic Management Journal*, 13: 483–98.

Ring, P. S., and Van de Ven, A. H. (1994). Developmental processes of cooperative interorganizational relationships. *Academy of Management Review*, 19(1): 90–118.

Schwenk, C. R. (1986). Information, cognitive biases, and commitment to a course of action. *Academy of Management Review*, 11(2): 298–310.

Yin, R. K. (1984). *Case Study Research: Designs and Methods*. Beverly Hills, CA: Sage.

17 Creating a New Identity and High-Performance Culture at Novartis

The Role of Leadership and Human Resource Management

CHEI HWEE CHUA, HANS-PETER ENGELI,
AND GÜNTER K. STAHL

> In these times of economic uncertainty and volatility, it
> gives me pleasure to present another year of record results
> and consistent growth—the sixth year since Novartis was
> formed from the merger of Ciba and Sandoz in
> 1996 . . . These good results are the fruits of a shared focus
> on clear, unchanged strategic goals and of the positive
> attitude and high level of commitment of our associates . . . [1]
>
> *Daniel Vasella, Chairman and CEO Novartis (2002)*

From the onset, the merger between Ciba-Geigy and Sandoz to form Novartis was poised for success because of the excellent strategic fit between the two companies. However, a good strategic fit only sets the stage for potential synergies to be reaped. Realizing the envisaged synergies and sustaining outstanding performance requires effective management of the sociocultural factors in the integration process because it is the people of the merged company who will deliver the results.

This case discusses the role of leadership and human resource management in managing the merger integration process, in creating a new identity and high-performance culture at Novartis, as well as in handling the challenges of postmerger integration. It shows that even in a well-planned and executed merger like Novartis, there are still challenges to be tackled.

The New Novartis

The mega-merger between Ciba-Geigy and Sandoz to form Novartis was officially completed on January 1, 1997, after regulatory approvals to merge were obtained from both the European Commission and the U.S. Federal Trade Commission. Before the merger, Ciba-Geigy and Sandoz were two leading Swiss corporations in the pharmaceuticals, chemical, and nutrition industries. It was executed as a "merger of equals" through an exchange of equity, and the positions for the executive boards of management and the board of directors were split equally between ex-Ciba-Geigy and ex-Sandoz representatives. Up to that time, the Novartis merger was the largest corporate merger in history. Novartis became not only the second largest corporation in Europe, but also the second largest pharmaceutical company in the world with 360 affiliates in more than 140 countries.

The chosen name, "Norvatis," was derived from the Latin words "novae artes," meaning "new skills." This reflected the commitment to realize the merger vision "to create the worldwide leader in life sciences focused on innovation in health care, agribusiness and nutrition; create a fast, focused, flexible company with a passion for competitiveness and implementation."[2] The operations of Ciba-Geigy and Sandoz in health care, nutrition, and agribusiness were integrated, whereas those that did not fit into Novartis' focus were divested. Several acquisitions were also made to strengthen the initially selected three core businesses and Novartis became the worldwide number one in life sciences and agribusiness, and number two in pharmaceuticals.

Preparing for the "Big Bang"

In the mid 1990s, the pharmaceutical industry was experiencing a very rapid technological change with the emergence of technologies such as biotechnology and genetechnology, making knowledge of life sciences crucial to industry players. The enormous cost for R&D was increasing and industry players were beginning to compete on a global level. The global pharmaceutical market was very fragmented, with top league players having only a market share of between 2 and 7 percent. Industry players' market shares depended heavily on one or two blockbuster products that may stumble in sales once the patent(s) elapsed. All these precipitated a trend of mergers and alliances, together with deep cost cutting and restructuring among industry players.

The starting point of the merger between Ciba-Geigy and Sandoz could be traced back to late 1995 when Marc Moret, President of the Board of Directors of Sandoz, proposed the idea of a possible merger between the two companies to the Honorary President of Ciba-Geigy, Louis von Planta. The latter then approached the acting President of Ciba-Geigy, Alex Krauer, and convinced him to start negotiations with his counterpart at Sandoz. Attracted by the vision of developing a new entity with strong pharmaceutical potential, Alex Krauer wasted no time and started the merger negotiations immediately. Faced with the dramatic industry changes, both Presidents of Ciba-Geigy and Sandoz were convinced that it would be impossible for Ciba-Geigy or Sandoz to survive alone in the mid-term and agreed that it was only a matter of time that the merger would have to occur. They remembered the visionary statement made by Carl Koechlin, "patron" of Geigy during the merger of Ciba and Geigy in 1971—"... and at a later stage it may well prove necessary for Sandoz to join forces with Ciba-Geigy." A merger between Ciba-Geigy and Sandoz clearly made both strategic and economic sense. With resources from both companies, the merged entity would be able to increase its innovative potential and have the critical mass to become an industry leader in R&D investments. Being in the same industry also meant that economies of scale and scope could be reaped.

The two Presidents with their entourage—made up of a few insiders and external consultants—did not dare to meet in their companies' hometown, Basel, to avoid any rumors. The two companies were still fierce competitors. Meetings between the two Presidents could only mean that they were preparing for a "big bang." Thus, these many clandestine meetings took place in a nearby rural area across the frontier in France.

Truly involved in the merger negotiations were only a handful of top managers from each company. Each company also engaged its own set of investment bankers, management consultants, and lawyers to conduct thorough due diligence. Right from the start, both sides shared a common vision to create a new stronger entity. Negotiations were fact-based and guided by the honest intention on both sides to create a "merger of equals" in all areas, and not only as a legal construct to save taxes. Such an intention helped to relax the atmosphere of the meetings and created a tone similar to those of discussions amongst colleagues. They spoke the same language and shared the same cultural background. Although both companies were industry rivals, they generally had been good neighbors separated only by the river Rhein over the last century. The overriding goal of completing the deal successfully quickly got them into a collaborative mode and laid the foundation for working together in the future.

The "Big Bang"

The official announcement of the merger was broadcast over the local radio in Basel, Switzerland, in the early hours of March 6, 1996, before the Swiss stock market opened and before both companies' employees arrived at their respective workplaces. The announcement took industry and financial analysts, and the employees of both companies by surprise. Other than the few top managers who were involved in the merger negotiations and those handpicked to lead the new organization and the merger integration planning, there were absolutely no leaks before the official announcement.

In fact, many of the country heads who had to announce the merger in their respective countries only knew about it the night before the merger was to be announced. The value of Ciba-Geigy's and Sandoz's stocks rose immediately after the announcement by 27 and 20 percent, respectively. On the other hand, employees who heard about the impending merger and the expected workforce reduction on their car radios arrived at their workplace anxious and bewildered.[3] Each of them was greeted with an eight-page information leaflet that revealed the name of the new company, Novartis; the designated CEO, Daniel Vasella; the reasons for the merger and expectations of the merged company; and a forty-page long document describing the economic and financial background of the merger in detail. Employee reactions to the pending merger were mixed. There was much excitement about the merger as the company would gain in size, presence, and resources. However, employees were also plagued with many uncertainties. Among their most pressing thoughts were, "Am I going to have a job in the merged organization? If I get a job, what will it be? How will my career be affected? Who will be my new boss and colleagues? What is the corporate culture and management style going to be like?" A statement in the merger agreement had heralded equal treatment and parity between the two companies, but as experience tells, true "mergers of equals" are rare.[4] Although it was true that Ciba-Geigy and Sandoz had a common Swiss cultural heritage, the two companies were fierce competitors whose corporate strategies and cultures were markedly different. Many wondered whether there was going to be a new corporate culture as signaled by the choice of a new company name or the initial balance of power would disappear, resulting in a loss of identity and autonomy for the members of the dominated firm. If the latter happened, would Ciba-Geigy's or Sandoz's culture and systems prevail?

Integration Planning and Implementation

Work on integration planning started immediately after the merger announcement. A "shadow" organization structure was built very quickly using a top-down approach. First, a steering committee consisting of potential Novartis executive committee members was formed. Then, within a couple of months, the top four layers of management positions were named. These decisions were made very quickly so that integration planning could proceed at the corporate, business, and country levels. By September 1996, the first round of personnel selection for both management and nonmanagement positions throughout the organization was completed.

A merger integration office (MIO) consisting of representatives from both companies was set up at the headquarters. It had about forty task forces. The guiding principles of the MIO were to plan the integration process comprehensively and to cascade the process down each layer of the

TABLE **17.1** Novartis Charter on Integration Process

- Focus on common objectives—respect each other's performance and do not drag on past weak performance of any of the two partners
- Trust each other—until proven differently—and build alliances with new people
- Fight the "we vs. them" syndrome decisively
- Be candid, simple, and clear when listening and explaining so that we understand each other better
- Be competent and fact based
- Agree of object (stick out your neck), but always commit to decisions taken and do not question them after having left the meeting room
- Stick to decisions unless there are important new facts
- Take the best solution of both companies and go beyond it—the successes for yesterday may prove to become obsolete dogma for today and tomorrow
- Be generous on borderline issues
- Resolve conflicts quickly by putting the issue on the table and focus on common objectives—avoid any conflict expansion and exacerbation, solve issues at the lowest level possible
- Inform and explain repeatedly especially during stressful times when concentration and memory often fail; you cannot overcommunicate
- Realize reductions are never "fair," work processes and company profitability are the main criteria in choosing site locations and defining work force reductions
- Take action—a decision that remains just an intention and is not rapidly followed by action is not only worthless but it also undermines credibility

SOURCE: *Novartis internal document*

organization in a systematic way; to act fast and communicate clearly; to follow up on all integration issues and decisions with the steering committee on a weekly basis; and to implement the integration process without interrupting normal business activities. A Novartis charter on the integration process was also drawn up to guide the decision-making process (see Table 17.1).

The main task of the MIO was to design the templates on how to plan and implement the integration process so that everything would be carried out in a consistent manner across the world. Each division also had an integration office with its own set of task forces and project teams to look into business issues. Altogether, there were 200 task forces and 600 project teams across the whole organization looking into functional and business issues. Whenever a major integration planning process was to be launched, those in charge were briefed thoroughly about the process at the headquarters. To ensure speedy integration planning, they only had two weeks to work on it back at their divisions or countries before they returned to the headquarters to present their recommendations to the steering committee. There were about 80–100 external management consultants supporting and coaching the task forces and project teams across the world. Because of the fast and comprehensive integration planning, Novartis managed to integrate 65 percent of its operations worldwide within three months of obtaining the regulatory approval to merge. To ensure that employees felt informed of what was going on, the MIO sent out regular updates on the integration process, sometimes even repeating the same information. It found repeating information useful as it helped to reinforce what was said and to reassure employees during such times of uncertainty.

The integration planning and implementation period proved to be very hectic and stressful for all managers and staff. Work was plentiful but time was short. To keep up with the tight deadlines, many had to work phenomenal hours, as many as 14 hours per day. The task forces kept everybody busy and pushed them to move forward with the merger. In general, employees had a positive attitude toward participating in the task forces because they felt that they had a share in shaping the future of the merged company. Nevertheless, the initial atmosphere at the task forces varied. For those task forces where representatives from both companies were already acquainted with one another, for example, through the merger negotiations or through interactions at business associations, they got down to working together immediately. But for some task forces where representatives from both sides did not have any prior interactions, the initial atmosphere was often cold and filled with mutual suspicion. One task force leader recalled that at the first meeting, there was a clear physical divide. All Ciba-Geigy representatives sat on one side of the table and all Sandoz representatives sat on the other. The task force leader made a conscious effort to ensure that seating arrangements were mixed at every meeting so that there would not be a "we vs. them" symbolic feeling. Despite the initial uneasiness, task force members realized that they had to start working together quickly because they only had a couple of weeks to come up with their recommendations. Hence, the task forces created opportunities for employees of both companies to get to know one another and to work together on common tasks as early as the integration planning phase. To ensure that integration plans were made seriously, those responsible for making them were also the ones responsible for implementing them. As one of the divisions' integration office head explained, "People were very careful in their planning because they knew that they were 'making their own beds' since they will be the ones implementing the plans."

Managing the Personnel Selection and Redundancy Process

Given the new strategic direction and the massive restructuring of all operations from top to bottom, the content of most, if not all, established functions underwent significant changes. The personnel selection process started with establishing new job profiles and then selecting personnel with the right skill sets to cater to the needs of Novartis.

The initial nominations of country heads and their direct reports around the world were made bilaterally by Ciba-Geigy's and Sandoz's division heads, and approved by the steering committee. The selection was based on the relative strengths and weaknesses of both companies' cadre of top managers, as well as the principle of a "merger of equals." Although performance and skill sets were the most important decision criteria, the selection process also sought to ensure that there was a somewhat balance of power between managers from both companies in Novartis. For example, the nominated country heads for the two most important markets were from Sandoz and the nominated country heads for the next three most important markets were from Ciba-Geigy. At the same time, nominations were made in such a way that the positions of power in each country were not dominated by managers from one company.

In selecting personnel for the rest of the managerial and rank-and-file positions in each country, corporate HR sets the guidelines for the local HR functions to follow. This was to ensure that each country had a standard selection process that was considered fair and transparent by employees. The process was also facilitated by external management consultants. Managers and staff had to submit their latest curriculum vitae and to interview for jobs. To ensure fairness, employees were evaluated by senior managers and HR managers from both companies based on a standard performance evaluation sheet designed by corporate HR. Although there was an implicit understanding that there should be a somewhat overall balance in composition between Ciba-Geigy and Sandoz personnel in the initial list of selected personnel, everybody was given equal chances regardless of the company they came from. No outstanding performer was made redundant just to adhere to numbers.

Line managers who had the responsibility of informing their staff about selection decisions were given a check-list designed by corporate HR to ensure that the communication process was handled appropriately. This was especially important in those sensitive cases where employees would have to be told that they would lose their current jobs and/or that they were not successful in their new job applications. To ensure continued performance during the integration phase, job holders whose contributions during the merger integration phase were crucial for either the existing operational business or integration success, but who were going to lose their positions, were kept motivated by the offer of a retention bonus of about 15–30 percent of their annual salaries upon achieving their targets.

Redundancies were managed in several ways. First, employees who were made redundant received a severance package that came with very generous financial compensation and an outplacement program. Managers were offered an individual outplacement program with a reputable outplacement company, whereas nonmanagement staff were offered an in-house group-outplacement program. Second, many employees nearing retirement age were asked to leave on an early retirement program. A few employees were also asked to leave on a pre-early retirement scheme. Third, a Novartis Venture Fund was set up in March 1996 as a social measure for redundant staff in the R&D units. Novartis decided to close certain R&D units because they did not fit into its new focus. The Fund gave entrepreneurial employees of these units a chance to turn their unit into their own companies by offering them part of the required capital in exchange for equity. Those working at the Fund also coached them on making business plans, getting more financing, and running the operations.

Creating a High-Performance Culture

Not only those employees who had to leave Novartis during the first few months of its existence had a difficult time, the same was true for the "survivors." They suffered from some of the symptoms of the "survivors' sickness." The symptoms included an almost complete loss of orientation, rupture of communication, lack of identification with the new company's values and cultural norms, insecurity regarding the new social intercourse, and a reduced feeling of togetherness. A new organization, a new boss, and a new location had destroyed employees' existing networks and interpersonal relations. Novartis leaders knew that their most urgent task at the beginning of the implementation phase was to build a new Novartis identity and to create a new corporate culture quickly. But what kind of culture should Novartis adopt?

One of the merger objectives was to build a company that is a "first league global player" in the industry. However, both Ciba-Geigy and Sandoz were "second league players." Combining two teams of "second league players" together would increase the size of the team but would not make the combined team a "first league player." Daniel Vasella, the designated CEO of Novartis, believed that Novartis needed a high-performance corporate culture to do so. Novartis managers had to be challenged to achieve the "slightly impossible" through setting tough goals and rewarding outstanding performance. To support this, corporate HR developed a rigorous performance appraisal system and a pay-for-performance compensation system.

Although it was clear that the initial list of selected managers and staff had a job at Novartis, it did not mean that they would be able to keep their jobs. Only those who proved themselves capable of "playing in the first league" would be kept. When it was found that a wrong selection decision was taken, the incumbent was replaced very quickly. New managers showing the potential of "playing in the first league" were also recruited and tested. Hence, Novartis leaders spent the first few years of the merger putting a "first league team" together. The hire-and-fire phenomenon created much uncertainty throughout the organization. Job security was low and employees were faced with changes in bosses. This meant that working relationships had to be reestablished as new bosses or colleagues came in. However, Novartis leaders believed that the short-term instability was worth the long-term benefit of having a top performer for the job.

Daniel Vasella was personally involved in the change process by communicating the high-performance organization concept, as well as Novartis' shared values and behaviors using various communication tools and platforms. He introduced it at the first Novartis top management conference in January 1997 and subsequently through numerous workshops with key managers and visits to Novartis' operations around the world. He made it clear that the organization had become bigger and more complex and a high-performance organizational culture was necessary for Novartis to become a successful global player in the competitive pharmaceutical industry.

Written Objectives, "Stretched Targets," and Shared Values

The new worldwide performance appraisal system was based on written objectives and targets. Each division was given the responsibility for the bottom line of its business and the Novartis Group Management focused on challenging each division's objectives to ensure high performance. Novartis managers around the world were asked to come up with four to eight objectives tailored to the specifics of their division, including shared objectives selected by their respective division's executive committee. All draft objectives had to be reviewed and approved by each manager's division head and the CEO. The objectives had to include basic ones on financial performance, competitive performance (mostly nonfinancial quantitative objectives), and integration performance. Additional objectives on people and organization performance, major functional process achievements, R&D performance, and special issues/initiatives such as a major product launch or an important country turnaround were also encouraged. Novartis managers also had to bear in mind the following questions when proposing their objectives: (1) Would somebody three layers down in your organization understand the objectives and implications for his or her job? (2) Do they cover what really matters in your industry and our success? (3) Are your objectives consistent with one another? Are your objectives consistent with the objectives of your division's executive committee members?

In setting their targets, Daniel Vasella demanded from his managers "stretched targets" that were "slightly impossible" to reach. "For each of your objectives, I would like you to set a measurable stretched target, one which is achievable with real effort, a bit high enough for you not to be certain you can achieve it or necessarily know today how you can get there," explained Daniel Vasella in his internal memorandum to managers on the written objectives exercise and the stretched target concept. As such, targets that were deemed to be easily achieved were strictly refused and the incumbent was asked for a revision of the targets. He also added that "as we will be increasing the variable portion of the incentive, people will still receive an incentive even if they do not reach each target, so people should not shy away from committing to 'stretched targets.' Our targets should be developed in a spirit of mutual trust and clarity. This is not a system to be 'gamed,' but one that allows us to help each other."

To inculcate Novartis' new corporate values and guide managerial behavior to support the high-performance culture, Novartis managers were also assessed on eight shared values and related behaviors in their annual performance appraisal: leadership, empowerment, customer/quality focus, competence, speed/action/simplicity/initiative, candor/trust/integrity, communication, and commitment/self-discipline.

The overall annual performance evaluation consisted of a simple matrix with two dimensions showing the combined ratings for achieving targets and displaying shared values and behaviors. The review also comprised of two sections—an appraisal by the superior and a self-assessment. The concept of a forced distribution for the overall rating was introduced. Out of the total appraised population, up to 10 percent could be performing stars, 15 percent good performers, 50 percent average performers, 15 percent below average performers, and 10 percent poor performers. It was felt that a forced distribution would give a clear signal that top management was serious in implementing a strong pay-for-performance culture because the overall rating was linked to individual manager's variable pay. The annual performance appraisal was also used as a platform for discussions with superiors (direct and next up) on career development plans and training needs.

Pay-for-Performance

The overriding goals of the strong pay-for-performance culture were to retain existing Novartis talent and to attract external talent by rewarding outstanding performance. Hence, Novartis' executive compensation system had to be performance- and shareholder-value-oriented, and competitive internationally with leading companies in the relevant markets.

An analysis of the existing executive compensation system revealed a number of weaknesses: (1) it lacked accountability for results; (2) had very limited possibilities to reward outstanding individual performance; (3) the small variable pay portion led to marginal impact of performance on compensation; (4) and it lacked long-term incentives that led to short-term focus. To remedy the shortcomings of the existing system and to live the new credo, "compensation is a tool used to focus on business performance and to reward individual performance," incentive payments were structured in such a way that managers would be motivated to deliver outstanding performance and to focus on both short-term and long-term business performance. When managers reached their "stretched targets" and were assessed to have had pursued the company's shared values and displayed the related behaviors, the amount of incentives paid would make them top-tier earners at Novartis in terms of total compensation. Depending on the management level and the market situation in each country, the target-payout would be 10–100 percent of annual base salary with a range from zero to double of the target. To ensure that managers considered both short-term and long-term effects in making decisions, incentive payments were made up of cash and a long-term element. The long-term element in top and upper management's incentive was in the form of shares and options, whereas middle and lower management received the annual incentive payments in a partially deferred way. Middle and lower management and professionals could also be granted stock options on an ad hoc basis. Full vesting of shares and options could only take effect after three years, and options could be exercised within a total of ten years.

Grappling with "Stretched Targets" and a Pay-for-Performance Culture

When the new compensation policy was applied in the first salary round in 1997, 100 percent of top and upper management and 57 percent of the middle and lower management had targets set for 1997. Initially, many Novartis managers found the new compensation policy very exciting. However, the exercise revealed the uncertainties they faced and the teething problems of the new system. For example, many managers voiced that the "ownership" of the compensation process was unclear. They did not understand what was to be considered under "corporate" and what was to be considered under "division."

Some managers found it difficult to grapple with the new "stretched target" concept as they felt that some stretches seemed really "impossible" to reach. Recalling the first stretched target setting process in 1997, Daniel Vasella admitted that, in some cases, the bottom line was probably pushed too hard. Some managers felt that they had already set their targets at growth rates well beyond expected market growth rates as requested, but they were still asked for more and there was no room for discussion. It was also felt that some managers were pushed harder than others. This resulted in a lot of resentment and some managers lost confidence.[5]

Despite the initial outcries, Novartis leaders felt that this was a good way to differentiate between managers who would try their best and those who give up easily. For the managers who thought that the "stretched targets" were impossible to reach but still possessed a positive attitude, the "stretched targets" made them think in unconventional ways. At the end of the year, they achieved better results than they had expected and realized that the experience of pursuing stretched targets was not as difficult as they had imagined. However, for those managers who thought that it was impossible and sat back and did nothing to try to achieve the "stretched targets," they obviously were unable to produce the results and were replaced.

Grappling with the New Management Style and Shared Values

Novartis leaders believed that a management style based on "command and control" combined with "strong and clear accountability" is the best migration route to becoming a high-performance organization. They also felt that this is especially crucial during the postmerger integration period where strong leadership is needed to provide a new direction and to guide behavior amidst all the uncertainties. However, implementing this brought out the underlying cultural differences between the two premerger companies as ex-Ciba and ex-Sandoz people experienced different levels of difficulties in adjusting to the new style. The new management style meant a radical change to the ex-Ciba-Geigy people who were used to a culture of pronounced empowerment. In 1990, Ciba-Geigy published VISION 2000—a declaration of economic, societal, and ecological values. It emphasized a human-oriented corporate culture, with empowerment as a key principle. This contrasted markedly with Sandoz's "command and control" culture. Given the difficulties of adjusting to such a 180° change in management style, it soon became obvious that within the top and middle management in corporate and pharmaceuticals, only a handful of ex-Ciba-Giegy managers could or would hold on to their jobs. On the other hand, ex-Sandoz people adapted much better as the new Novartis culture resembled the culture they were used to in many ways. They were tuned to meeting the numbers as they were accustomed to being governed by strict financial controls.

The need for fast decision making especially during the immediate postmerger integration phase also meant that ex-Sandoz people adapted better than ex-Ciba-Geigy people. At Sandoz, decisions were made relatively quickly with fewer people involved but implementation took more time. In contrast, decisions at Ciba-Geigy were made on a consensus basis with more people involved but implementation was quick. Novartis leaders knew that the best way was to have a balance between the two and sought to instill that as the integration progressed and when things become more stabilized.

Novartis managers were perplexed by the call for simplicity and empowerment—part of the new set of shared values and related behaviors that they felt contrasted markedly with actual practices. For example, as all external hires in Switzerland had to be approved by the executive committee, going through the whole approval chain did not seem simple to managers and they did not feel empowered to do things. Many managers also found it difficult to understand the meaning of empowerment in a command and control style of management and were unsure of how to behave. In such times of uncertainty, many managers looked at the top management's behavior for clues about the appropriate behavior. However, some managers felt that it was rather obvious that even some executive committee members were struggling with the issue of empowerment and control. As one senior manager who went through the merger described, "The first few years after the merger was a theoretical time. Most people were confused because they were not sure where the lines are drawn for empowerment and a top-down style of management. It was only through time and experience in the new culture that people slowly understood." In the case of some country managers, the top-down approach and tough pushing of "stretched targets" made them feel that headquarters did not trust them. This inevitably created some tensions in headquarters field relations.[6]

Building a Culture Based on Trust

Novartis leaders knew that it was inevitable that trust levels at the newly merged organization would be low. Trust is something that takes time to build up through working together and mutual evaluation of what is said and done. Being a merger of equals, regardless of which premerged company the nominated boss came from, half of the employees would know him or her and the other half would not. With a new organization, a new management team and a new immediate boss, there was little trust initially. The merger also brought about a lot of changes and uncertainties and employees often wondered what would the next wave of changes be and whether they would be negatively affected. Daniel Vasella addressed this matter upfront and highlighted the importance of building trust.

> Among all the corporate values, trust was the one that suffered most from the merger. . . . We must fill this vacuum as fast as we can, we must restore confidence. To create a culture based on trust takes time; it requires dedication and the right mindset. We must earn it by "walking the talk"

with candor, integrity, openness, and fairness, as well as with credible, consistent and convincing behavior. . . . Only in a climate of trust are people willing to strive for the slightly impossible, to make decisions on their own, to take initiative, to feel accountable.[7]

Novartis leaders sought to build trust through various ways. First, they went to great lengths to constantly update employees and managers on new developments, provide direction, and engage in open forums and credible behavior. An excellent example illustrating their credibility was the way they dealt with the closing down of a factory in Japan. The local management in Japan had requested for more time so that they could find a buyer who would accept the condition of hiring the existing factory employees. Daniel Vasella agreed to this and kept his word. This not only had a positive impact on the employees of the factory but also showed Novartis employees that the top management can be trusted.

Second, they tried to rebuild social networks and interpersonal relations so that trust can be established as people get to know one another better. For example, Novartis conducted corporate assimilation workshops for the top 500 managers around the world. The program had three modules and gave the top managers the opportunity to get to know one another through learning together and to build trust through team-building activities. A company intranet was also established to open up communication channels and to enable quick access of information and exchange of ideas.

Third, they took corrective actions quickly whenever it was deemed necessary. For example, the new HR systems that were implemented to support the new culture were fine-tuned as integration progressed.

Employee Receptiveness to the New Novartis Culture

In 1999, two years after the merger, Novartis engaged a survey company, International Survey Research (ISR), to conduct a global leadership survey to ascertain employee motivational levels and job satisfaction ratings. Target respondents were Novartis corporate executive group members. Two hundred forty executives around the world responded to the survey. The answers were compared to the global senior management norms that ISR had established from a screened management population of more than 20,000. There were ten topic areas, including performance management, compensation and benefits, leadership development and motivation, leadership and cooperation and trust.

The results of the survey showed that most Novartis managers' motivational levels and organizational commitment had improved since the merger. The pay-for-performance culture and executive compensation system had not only gained credibility and acceptance, but also seemed to have increased actual performance as respondents felt that superior performance was recognized and rewarded. By then, the managers who remained in the company were those selected for their current jobs based on the new requirements of Novartis and who could thrive in a high-performance culture based on written objectives and "stretched targets," and getting paid according to their performance. Moreover, a number of managers enjoyed an explosion of their individual remuneration when Novartis adjusted salaries up to global levels in its bid to become a competitive employer of talents in the global market. Teamwork was also mostly perceived to be excellent, and the majority of respondents felt that they were being treated with respect and fairness in their current jobs. Compared with external norms, Novartis management style was deemed to be "less bureaucratic, more decisive, less risk-avoiding, more task-oriented, more directive, more open with information as well as more persuasive."

However, the survey results revealed that some negative effects of the merger lingered on. Most respondents were still dissatisfied with their job security. A substantial number of respondents also believed that job stress had reduced their effectiveness. The company values seemed unclear to some respondents, possibly reflecting the ongoing struggle Novartis managers had in reconciling a top-down approach management style with the call for empowerment as a company value. Trust in higher levels of management remained weak. Based on the survey results, Novartis leaders started to address the various shortfalls that were identified. For example, at the Novartis Global Conference in January 2000, to help reconcile the perceived dichotomy between a top-down management approach with the call for empowerment, Daniel Vasella fine-tuned his views on leadership and urged Novartis senior managers to decide on a case-by-case basis when top-down and when bottom-up was the appropriate approach.

In 2001, a similar survey was conducted and improvements in ratings were found, most notably in the areas of leadership, cooperation, and trust. In other areas such as "achieving a sustainable balance between work and private life," and "identifying and alleviating stress related reduced effectiveness," there was room for improvement. To address these problems, Novartis started to include workshops on time management, work-life balance, and positive stress management in its training programs.

Novartis Performance and Merger Synergies

Novartis' success in implementing a high-performance culture can be seen by comparing its pre- and postmerger financial results (see Tables 17.2 and 17.3). Before the merger announcement in March 1996, the combined global head count of both Ciba and Sandoz was 134,000 and their combined sales was CHF 35.9 billion. Novartis' business and personnel restructuring

TABLE **17.2** Profile of Ciba-Geigy and Sandoz

	Ciba (in CHF Bn)	Sandoz (in CHF Bn)
Total turnover	20.7	15.2
Health care	8.0	7.1
Agribusiness	4.8	2.2
Nutrition	0	3.7
Industry chemicals	7.9 (spin off)	0
Construction chemicals	0	1.2 (spin off)
Net profit	2.2	2.1
Company capital	17.0	8.5
Number of employees	84,000	50,000

SOURCE: *Merger Announcement; Explanations to the Shareholders, March 1996*

TABLE **17.3** Novartis Financial Results and Head Count Between 1997 and 2001

	2001	2000	1999	1998	1997
Total turnover	32.0	35.8	32.5	31.7	31.2
Percentage change relative to preceding year	−10.5%	10.3%	2.4%	1.7%	−13.9%
Pharmaceuticals	20.2	18.2	15.3	14.5	14.1
Percentage change relative to preceding year	11.2%	18.8%	5.3%	2.8%	21.5%
Generics	2.4	2.0	1.8	1.5	1.5
Percentage change relative to preceding year	23.3%	8.2%	19.2%	5.3%	18.0%
Consumer health	6.7	6.5	5.8	5.8	5.9
Percentage change relative to preceding year	2.5%	13.2%	−0.6%	−1.3%	−1.0%
CIBA vision	1.8	1.4	1.6	1.5	1.4
Percentage change relative to preceding year	28.4%	−14.8%	8.4%	5.8%	18.0%
Animal health	1.0	1.1	0.9	0.9	0.9
Percentage change relative to preceding year	−11.2%	16.8%	2.9%	0.9%	6.2%
Discontinued agribusiness and industry	–	6.7	7.1	7.5	7.4
Net profit	7.0	7.2	6.7	6.0	5.2
Percentage change relative to preceding year	−2.6%	8.3%	10.8%	15.4%	126.0%
As a percentage of sales	21.9%	20.1%	20.5%	19.0%	16.7%
As a percentage of average equity	17.8%	19.5%	19.4%	20.7%	20.7%
Equity	42.2	36.9	37.2	31.4	26.8
R&D expenditure	4.2	4.7	4.2	3.9	3.7
As a percentage of sales	13.1%	13.0%	13.1%	12.3%	12.0%
Pharmaceuticals R&D expenditure	3.4	3.3	2.8	2.6	2.6
As a percentage of pharmaceuticals sales	17.1%	18.2%	18.6%	18.0%	18.6%
Number of employees at year end	71,116	67,653	81,854	82,449	87,239
Sales per employee (in CHF)	455,603	431,219	393,711	369,337	350,905

SOURCE: *Novartis Annual Report 2001. Values are in CHF billions unless indicated otherwise*

were made very quickly after the merger. In fact, Novartis reduced the global head count to 87,239 by the end of 1997 through cutting 12,000 jobs within its continued activities, and spinning off various noncore businesses. By 2001, Novartis sales were CHF 32.0 billion with a heavily reduced global head count at 71,116. Besides making redundancies, Novartis also hired new employees who possessed the skills Novartis needed. There were 1,200 new hires between 1996 and 1998, and another 3,500 in 2001.

The restructuring costs for creating Novartis were estimated at CHF 4.284 billion—total expenses for restructuring and outsourcing measures. In 1996 alone, the restructuring costs amounted to CHF 4,126 million, of which CHF 1,945 million was for severance pay. Right at the beginning, Daniel Vasella had set an ambitious goal to reap merger synergies of CHF 1.8 billion over the first three years—CHF 630 million in year 1, CHF 720 million in year 2, and CHF 450 million in year 3. Despite the ambitious target, by the end of its first year, Novartis had already reaped 65 percent of the envisaged merger synergies for its first three years.

Novartis' outstanding financial performance was also mirrored in its stock price. Novartis' market capitalization shot up to CHF 175 billion at the end of December 1997 from CHF 75 billion on March 5, 1996 (the day before the merger announcement). Compared to the Swiss stock market performance index (SMI), which showed an increase of 19.5 percent between January 1996 and December 1997, Novartis' market capitalization recorded a phenomenal growth rate of 52 percent during the same period. In 1998, Novartis' market capitalization kept pace with the SMI at an annual growth rate of 12 percent. But Novartis' market capitalization was adversely affected in 1999 with a decrease of 18 percent while the SMI showed a minimal increase of 0.32 percent within the same period. Since 2000, Novartis' stock consistently outperformed the SMI. In 2000, Novartis' stock was favored against the other blue chip stocks and its market capitalization recorded an annual growth rate of 27 percent compared to the SMI's growth rate of about 12 percent. In 2001, the Swiss stock market was bearish with the SMI indicating a drop of 21 percent while Novartis' market capitalization decreased only by 19 percent during the same period.

Implications for the Management of Mergers and Acquisitions

A "process perspective" on mergers and acquisitions suggests that while the initial strategic and financial conditioning factors in a merger or an acquisition form the upper bound on the degree of success that the combination can achieve, the management of the postcombination integration process will determine the extent to which that potential is realized.[8,9] The case of the Novartis merger clearly supports this view. The high degree of strategic fit gave Novartis a good starting point. However, this strategic fit was only "half the battle won"; execution was critical.

A number of lessons can be learnt from this case: First, as employees are likely to suffer a loss of orientation in the postmerger integration phase, strong leadership is crucial in formulating and communicating a vision for employees to work toward to. Daniel Vasella provided direction through his strong leadership in the difficult months following the merger by constantly communicating the new high-performance organization concept and a set of shared values and related behaviors to employees at all levels of the organization.

Second, the case illustrates that the integration process, where a new corporate culture and company systems have to be implemented, must be speedy as people expect changes during this period and are more likely to accept them. Novartis leadership's decisiveness and a top-down management style ensured that quick decisions were made, and integration planning and implementation was carried out very quickly within a matter of months. If decision making during integration is slow or if top management changes its tune halfway, its credibility will be hurt and people are likely to think that they have a chance of succeeding in resisting the changes and revert back to their old ways. Nevertheless, management has to be able to recognize problems during integration implementation and take timely corrective actions.

Third, an important lesson to be learnt from the Novartis case is that a merger is a major disruption and an inevitable consequence is that trust levels at the newly merged organization would be low. Trust is something that takes time to build up through working together and mutual evaluation of what is said and done. Moreover, trust can be destroyed in an instant when a merger is announced unexpectedly. As can be seen in Novartis' case, it is highly important for the top management to build trust through open communication and credible behavior, and to facilitate the rebuilding of social networks and interpersonal relations. It not only takes a lot of effort, but also takes years to rebuild trust.

Fourth, effective HR policies and practices are a key factor for success in mergers. As employee morale and commitment usually suffer following a merger, an employee-friendly HR and reward system is crucial in retaining and motivating key employees. If key employees anticipate greater job satisfaction and increased prospects for compensation and promotion in the merged company, they will be much more likely to stay.[10] Moreover, the HR and reward system is a useful tool to support the creation of the desired corporate culture.

Fifth, the people selection and redundancy process has to be perceived as fair and transparent. Equal chances have to be given to everybody regardless of which premerged company they come from and what their current functions are to ensure that the process is fair and that people with the right skill sets and personalities are selected. Generous severance plans are expensive, but they have a strongly positive influence on the remaining employee's morale.[11] Being sensitive to the needs of those who suffer as the result of the merger is an effective means of building trust in management. To ensure continued performance during the integration period, retention bonus tied to achieving targets can also be used to motivate employees who are needed for the integration phase, but will lose their positions after that.

Finally, the Novartis case illustrates the importance of visionary leadership to the success of a merger. But creating a vision of the future is not enough. The vision must be credibly communicated and closely aligned with all aspects of the organization. As leadership gurus Collins and Porras put it, "building a visionary company requires 1% vision and 99% alignment."[12] Novartis is a prime example of a company that achieved continuous, sustainable performance following a merger through close alignment of its vision, strategy, culture, and management practices.

Notes

1. Novartis Annual Report 2002, Letter from Daniel Vasella.

2. Novartis internal document.

3. Employee reactions to the Novartis merger are described in S. Caudron (1996). Rebuilding employee trust. *Training & Development*, August: 18–21.

4. For example, S. Cartwright, and C. L. Cooper (1996). *Managing Mergers, Acquisitions, and Strategic Alliances: Integrating People and Cultures*, 2nd edn. Oxford: Butterworth & Heinemann, and D. B. Jemison, and S. B. Sitkin (1986). Corporate acquisitions: A process perspective. *Academy of Management Review*, 11: 145–63.

5. Novartis managers' reactions to the first stretched target setting process in 1997 are described in C. Knoop and S. Datar (1998). *Novartis (A): Being a Global Leader*. Boston, MA: Harvard Business School.

6. Novartis managers' difficulties in reconciling the shared values of empowerment, candor, and simplicity with the command and style of management are described in Knoop and Datar (1998). *Novartis (A)*, see n. 5.

7. H.-P. Engeli (1999). Klippen einer Fusion—Novartis International AG. Paper presented at the Conference, *Den Erfolg der Internationalisierung gestalten, Deutsche Gesellschaft für Personalführung (DGFP)*, Offenbach/Main.

8. P. Haspeslagh and D. B. Jemison (1991). *Managing Acquisitions: Creating Value Through Corporate Renewal*. New York: The Free Press.

9. A. L. Pablo, S. B. Sitkin, and D. B. Jemison (1996). Acquisition decision-making processes: The central role of risk. *Journal of Management*, 22: 723–46.

10. G. K. Stahl, P. Evans, V. Pucik, and M. Mendenhall (2004). Human resource management in cross-border mergers and acquisitions. In Harzing and van Ruysseveldt (eds.), *International Human Resource Management: An Integrated Approach*, 2nd edn. London: Sage, pp. 89–113.

11. I. Kay and M. Shelton (2000). The people problem in mergers. *The McKinsey Quarterly* (4).

12. J. C. Collins and J. I. Porras (1996). Building your company's vision. *Harvard Business Review*, 74(5): 77.

PART V *Lessons for Research and Practice*

18 Research on Sociocultural Integration in Mergers and Acquisitions

Points of Agreement, Paradoxes, and Avenues for Future Research

GÜNTER K. STAHL, MARK E. MENDENHALL, AND YAAKOV WEBER

Over the past thirty years, a growing body of research has investigated the antecedents that predict the performance of mergers and acquisitions (M&A). However, despite this extensive body of research, the key factors for M&A success and the reasons why so many M&A fail remain poorly understood. The results of a recent review of the M&A literature by King et al. (2004) are instructive in this regard. They employed meta-analytic techniques to empirically assess the impact of the four most commonly researched antecedent variables on postacquisition performance: acquisition by a conglomerate firm, degree of relatedness between the acquiring and the acquired firm, method of payment (cash vs. equity), and prior acquisition experience of the acquiring firm. King and his colleagues (2004) found none of these variables to be significant in explaining the variance in postacquisition performance, indicating that "existing empirical research has not clearly and repeatedly identified those variables that impact an acquiring firm's performance" (p. 196). They concluded that "[r]esearchers simply may not be looking at the 'right' set of variables as predictors of postacquisition performance" (p. 197), and recommend that future research pay more attention to nonfinancial variables that are currently underrepresented in theory and research that seeks to explain M&A activity and performance.

Although we agree with King et al. (2004) that "nonfinancial" variables significantly influence postacquisition performance, we do not believe these issues have been neglected in M&A theory and research. Quite the contrary, as the literature cited in the preceding chapters have illustrated, the "softer," less tangible social, cultural, and psychological aspects of M&A have received considerable research attention in recent years. Factors such as the social climate surrounding the merger or acquisition (Chapters 4, 15, and 16), the integration approach taken by the acquiring firm (Chapters 2, 8, and 14), the cultural dynamics between the combining firms (Chapters 5, 6, and 11), the amount and quality of communication (Chapters 3, 4, and 10), leadership and the creation of shared values (Chapters 9 and 17), learning processes (Chapters 3, 7, and 13), and human resource management practices and career development systems (Chapters 2, 8, 12, and 17) have been proposed—and demonstrated—to be of critical importance to postacquisition performance.

In contemplating possible future directions for scholars to consider in conducting research in the M&A field, we felt that it would be useful to isolate the major, broad trends in the research literature that seem to be emerging, and to briefly delineate patterns of emergent consensus and patterns of paradox. Based upon the analyses of the scholars who contributed to this book, and from our review of the extant literature, a clear consensus emerged on a number of key issues related to the management of M&A. These points of agreement are as follows:

CONSENSUS 1
Management Efficacy Trumps Precombination Factors

Whether an M&A fails or succeeds depends primarily on the management of the postcombination integration process. Although the initial strategic, financial and organizational conditioning factors form the upper bound on the degree of success that a merger or acquisition can achieve, the management of the postcombination integration process will likely determine the extent to which that potential is realized. One of the implications of this "process perspective" on M&A (Haspeslagh and Jemison, 1991; Hunt, 1990; Jemison and Sitkin, 1986; Pablo, Sitkin, and Jemison, 1996) is that precombination factors such as those examined in the meta-analysis (relatedness, method of payment, prior acquisition experience, etc.) of King et al. (2004) can only predict the success of an M&A if integration process variables are taken into account. The best laid plans for merging or acquiring do not ensure postcombination success; postcombination managerial competence is a critical variable to the success of M&A.

CONSENSUS 2
Level of Integration Influences Criticality of Sociocultural Process

There seems to be agreement that what constitutes "good" management in a particular M&A depends on the strategic logic behind the deal and the integration approach taken. Each of the various integration approaches discussed in the M&A literature (see Chapters 2, 3, and 8) have different managerial implications. In general, attention to cultural and people issues is most critical to M&A that require high levels of integration, because the higher the level of integration, the greater the extent of contact and degree of change in the acquired firm. The level of integration affects the emotions and attitudes of the acquired employees and may lower their commitment to and cooperation with the acquiring management (Haspeslagh and Jemison, 1991; Stahl and Sitkin, 2001; Weber, 1996; Weber, Shenkar, and Raveh, 1996), and eventually lead to higher turnover (Lubatkin, Schweiger, and Weber, 1999) and other negative outcomes.

CONSENSUS 3
Basic Personnel Practices Make a Difference

A large body of research indicates that the way employees react to an M&A depends primarily on the personal benefits and losses attributed to this major life event. This is why many authors in this book have stressed the importance of the quality of postacquisition reward and job security changes in determining employee reactions to M&A (see Chapters 2, 7, 8, 12, and 17). This research suggests that human resource management and career development practices can go a long way toward overcoming employee resistance and retaining key employees.

CONSENSUS 4
Extension of Sociocultural Factors into the Due Diligence Process

Although most M&A failures are linked to problems in postcombination integration, there seems to be agreement that cultural and people issues have to be considered at an early stage in the M&A process—as early as during the evaluation and selection of a suitable target and the planning of the postcombination integration phases (see Chapters 11 and 15–17). In the due diligence process, the assessment of the organization structure, corporate culture, and HR system in the company to be acquired is just as important as financial analysis and strategic fit considerations. Undertaking a human capital audit to ensure that the target company has the talent necessary to execute the acquisition strategy, identifying which individuals are key to sustaining the value of the deal, and assessing any potential weaknesses in the management cadre are key to the long-term success of the acquisition.

Research on Sociocultural Integration in M&A:
Unresolved Paradoxes

Despite the consensus that emerged from the research presented in this book and from our review of the literature, many questions about M&A productivity remain unanswered and underexplored. The authors of the chapters in this book have identified a number of gaps in M&A theory and research; however, we will not reiterate these gaps in this conclusion to the book. Rather, we will focus on those issues that have received ample research attention in the field, but have yielded inconclusive—and sometimes contradictory—results. The following list of paradoxes in M&A research is not exhaustive but illustrates that our current understanding of the process of sociocultural integration in M&A is limited.

Paradox 1: Culture Matters/Culture Does Not Matter

On the basis of the "cultural distance" hypothesis (Hofstede, 1980; Kogut and Singh, 1988), which, in its most general form, suggests that the difficulties, costs, and risks associated with cross-cultural contact increase with growing cultural differences between two individuals, groups, or organizations, it can be predicted that cultural differences are negatively related to postcombination integration outcomes. However, empirical support for the cultural distance hypothesis in the context of M&A is weak. While some studies found that cultural differences had the expected negative effect on financial performance, stock market performance, or other performance criteria, an equally large number of studies found cultural differences to be unrelated or even positively related to M&A performance (see Chapters 4 and 11; for recent reviews of this literature, please see Schoenberg, 2000; Schweiger and Goulet, 2000; Stahl and Voigt, 2004, in press).

Most executives and scholars intuitively sense that "culture matters," but *when* it matters, under *what* conditions it matters, and *how* it matters are not currently clear. Future research that isolates when culture moves, as a relevant factor, to figure and when it moves to ground, would be beneficial not just from a scholarly understanding, but for executives in their due diligence efforts and when seeking firms to acquire and with which to merge.

Paradox 2: Imperialism Is Bad/Imperialism Is Good

Some authors have suggested that asymmetrical power and imposition of control by an acquiring firm need not lead to conflict in M&A, that the integration approach taken depends on the strategic logic behind the deal, and that each integration approach has different managerial implications (see Chapters 2, 3, and 8). As noted by Evans, Pucik, and Barsoux (2002), the terms *absorption* and *assimilation* often carry a pejorative meaning; however, if managed well, an absorption approach to integration can be of benefit to the employees of the acquired firm. This is especially true when these employees are afraid of losing their jobs and see the dominant company as being a savior or having a more enlightened culture, or when they see a variety of positive outcomes in being associated with the acquiring company (better pay, more prestige, etc.).

Similarly, cultural arrogance and imposition of control by an acquiring firm need not be a "bad" thing from an ethical point of view either. As

Schreyögg has pointed out in Chapter 5, the general suspicion against a universal corporate culture (which, in most cases, implies imposition of control by one firm on another) tends to obscure the actual ethical question at stake: whether or not the values represented in the cultures are legitimate. Schreyögg uses the Bhopal tragedy to support his argument. Union Carbide was accused of applying different safety standards in its plants, and of not carrying out in India the safety regulations and training they used in the United States. From an ethical point of view, the universal, and not the pluralist, corporate culture would have been preferable, and thus cultural arrogance and imposition of control on the part of Union Carbide would have been the correct ethical approach to take.

Further investigation regarding the utility of the different integration approaches that firms can strategically utilize in M&A, and under which conditional configurations they should be applied, is an area of M&A research that cries out for more intensive and careful research.

Paradox 3: Experience Matters/Experience Doesn't Matter

On the basis of empirical research, it is unclear whether there is a significant learning effect, that is, whether more experienced companies have a higher probability of success when acquiring other companies. The chapters by Greenberg, Lane, and Bahde and by Björkman, Tienari, and Vaara in this book suggest there is a learning effect, and there is some evidence that previous experience tends to influence subsequent M&A and their performance (Finkelstein and Haleblian, 2002; Haleblian and Finkelstein, 1999; Hayward, 2002). However, the meta-analysis by King et al. (2004) as well as recent research conducted by Zollo and Singh (2004) found that prior acquisition experience by the acquiring firm was *not* significant in explaining variance in postacquisition performance.

Further research that probes with more specificity the systemic relationships involved in learning effects in M&A seems warranted in order to delineate the conditions upon which learning effect makes a difference or does not make a difference in postcombination success.

Paradox 4: Speed Saves/Speed Kills

Another key question that has not yet been answered adequately in the research literature is whether a high speed of integration leads to better outcomes than a low speed of integration. There is considerable disagreement regarding the relationship between speed of integration and integration outcomes in the extant literature. Buono and Bowditch (1989) argue that there is a "window of opportunity" during the first 100 days after an acquisition. During this time, they state that employees are open to change because they expect change, and are thus more willing to allow themselves to be malleable to new policies. Thus, the argument continues, management should move as quickly as possible to initiate new policies, procedures, strategies, and so on (Angwin, 2004; Bastien, 1987; Mitchell, 1989).

Conversely, others (Jemison and Sitkin, 1986; Shrivastava, 1986) argue that such speedy change initiatives in M&A are contributing factors to the high failure rates that are widely manifested in studies of M&A. Alternatively, Robino and DeMeuse (1985), on the basis of the findings of their research, argue that a moderate speed of integration is more effective in terms of generating positive postcombination outcomes. Others (Evans, Pucik, and Barsoux, 2002; Haspeslagh and Jemison, 1991) argue that speed is a variable that is moderated by various other intervening variables (for example, strategic intent behind the acquisition, and the nature of the integration approach that is deployed).

To date, the ideal speed of change, as well as factors that may influence it, are not well understood, and the popular notion that speed is necessary for M&A is based on anecdotes from the popular press. This is a critical area that needs intensive investigation from scholars in the field in order to gain a better understanding of the variables that influence the speed of integration decision and its ultimate effects on M&A efficacy.

Research on Sociocultural Integration in M&A: Avenues for Future Research

M&A have drawn the attention of many groups of scholars, each of which studies the subject from a unique perspective. Although the strategic management, organizational behavior, and to a lesser extent, the international management research perspectives pursue questions related to M&A, they approach the phenomenon from differing perspectives, with different sets of assumptions and with a variety of methodologies.

While sharing some definitions and terms, scholars writing about M&A generally refrain from entering each other's areas of expertise, thereby missing obvious opportunities for combined research that would lead to a better understanding of M&A. Although, on balance, strategic management research has not considered implementation problems, much research from other research streams, such as organizational behavior, have focused on the "people aspects" of implementation, while often neglecting strategic considerations. Organizational behavior research focuses on the impact of M&A on individuals, and attempts to provide a complementary explanation of M&A success/failure, namely, that the acquired management's and employees' commitment to, and cooperation with, the acquiring firm are contingent upon cultural fit. The major assumption is that without management and employee support, the expected performance from a merger is rarely realized. Combining multiple measures from diverse perspectives (that is, strategic management and organizational behavior) may lead to more robust explanations of surface paradoxes.

To illustrate this argument, consider the inconsistent findings extant in the strategic management research area regarding the relationship between firm-level measures of financial performance and the "strategic fit" of the combining firms. "Strategically fit" firms are those that share similar industries, products, markets, and technologies. Some scholars have hypothesized, but failed to find, a consistent relationship between performance gains and the merging firms' relatedness. There are as many published studies that find a "strategic fit" effect (Chatterjee, 1986; Lubatkin, 1987) as those that do not (King et al., 2004; Shelton, 1988; Singh and Montgomery, 1988).

It is likely, then, that strategic fit interacts with other systemic variables in the M&A in order to produce robust performance results. These variables that influence the efficacy of the strategic fit dimension may exist at differing levels of analysis that are not normally considered by scholars operating from the strategic management perspective; for example, measures of leadership dimensions (Chapter 9), level of trust (Chapter 4), communication intervention processes (Chapter 10), transfer of knowledge (Chapter 3), and HR practices (Chapter 2) may help explain some of the inconsistent findings discussed above.

In addition to the organizational behavior perspective, adding cross-cultural and human resource management perspectives to the strategic management perspective in research efforts will also likely be necessary in order to resolve the paradoxes that currently exist in the field. For example, frameworks that focus exclusively on the cultural issues involved in integrating merging or acquired firms, such as the "cultural distance" hypothesis, cannot explain why some cross-border M&A succeed and others fail. Whether cultural differences have a positive or negative impact on integration outcomes will likely depend on the outcome variables under investigation, the nature and extent of cultural differences, the integration approach taken, the interventions chosen to manage these differences, and a variety of other factors. Therefore, rather than asking *if* cultural differences have a performance impact, future research endeavors should focus on *how* cultural differences interact with other variables that affect productive vs. dysfunctional M&A outcomes.

Scholars in other management disciplines have increasingly argued that in order to comprehend complex organizational systems, perhaps new research paradigms need to be employed (Elliot and Kiel, 1996; Follett, 1951; Holland, 1995; Mendenhall, 1999; Wheatley, 1992). Each of the perspectives discussed above (strategic, organizational behavior, cross-cultural, and human resource management) are almost completely housed in, and founded upon, the scientific philosophy of logical positivism. Von Wright (1971) defined logical positivism as being "a philosophy advocating methodological monism, mathematical ideals of perfection, and a subsumption-theoretic view of scientific explanation" (Von Wright, 1971, p. 9).

Howard (1982) states that methodological monism is the assumption that "the methodologies appropriate to the cultural and natural worlds are essentially one" (Howard, 1982, p. 31). In other words, social phenomena are inherently the same as natural phenomena, and operate under the same laws; thus, "the philosophical problems of social science are those of all science... [and] the answers to these and related questions are essentially the same, whether we are studying the stars or mice or men...." (Brodbeck, 1968, pp. 1–2). The subsumption-theoretic view of scientific explanation holds that the laws that cause behavior of any kind, in any type of system (human or otherwise), can be uncovered through the use of logical positivistic forms of investigation. Logical positivistic philosophy and methodology were adopted early on by the social sciences, and form the lion's share of the research strategies by scholars studying M&A and other organizational processes.

There are, of course, other paradigms besides logical positivism that can be employed to study complex organizational systems like M&A. Two paradigms that are increasingly gaining interest among some social scientists are those of hermeneutics and nonlinear dynamics. An in-depth review of these two paradigms and their attendant methodologies are beyond the scope of this chapter (for reviews see Elliot and Kiel, 1996; Follett, 1951; Giddens, 1984; Gregersen and Sailer, 1993; Holland, 1995; Howard, 1982; Mendenhall, 1999). The overarching consideration before M&A scholars is the following question: If M&A is as systemically complex a process as the research findings are indicating that it is, perhaps it will be fruitful to bring to bear on it multiple methodologies housed not just in the paradigm of logical positivism, but from the paradigms of hermeneutics and nonlinear dynamics as well. By training the lenses of a multiplicity of paradigmatic views on M&A phenomena, perhaps the complexity of its processes will be clarified and exposed, and the paradoxes diminished as scholars are able to comprehend the processes that lay beneath them.

In summary, use of interdisciplinary approaches to the study of M&A is long overdue. The paradoxes discussed above provide a rich field for further research, and pose fascinating questions to be solved to both scholar and executive alike. Because of the complexity of systemic relationships involved in M&A, real insight will likely ensue only if research of an interdisciplinary nature, or research that is broad in its disciplinary orientation, is brought to bear on the M&A problem.

References

Angwin, D. (2004). Speed in M&A integration: The first 100 days. *European Management Journal*, 22(4): 418–30.

Bastien, D. T. (1987). Common patterns of behavior and communication in corporate mergers and acquisitions. *Human Resource Management*, 26: 17–34.

Brodbeck, M. (1968). *Readings in the Philosophy of the Social Sciences*. New York: Macmillan.

Buono, A. F., and Bowditch, J. L. (1989). *The Human Side of Mergers and Acquisitions*. San Francisco: Jossey-Bass.

Chatterjee, S. (1986). Types of synergy and economic value: The impact of acquisitions on merging and rival firms. *Strategic Management Journal*, 7: 119–40.

Elliot, E., and Kiel, L. D. (eds.) (1996). *Chaos Theory in the Social Sciences: Foundations and Applications*. Ann Arbor: University of Michigan Press.

Evans, P., Pucik, V., and Barsoux, J. L. (2002). *The Global Challenge: Frameworks for International Human Resource Management*. New York: McGraw-Hill.

Finkelstein, S., and Haleblian, L. (2002). Understanding acquisition performance: The role of transfer effects. *Organization Science*, 13: 36–48.

Follett, M. P. (1951). *Creative Experience*. New York: Peter Smith.

Giddens, A. (1984). Hermeneutics and social theory. In Shapiro and Sica (eds.), *Hermeneutics: Questions and Prospects*, Ameherst: University of Massachussetts Press, pp. 215–30.

Gregersen, H., and Sailer, L. (1993). Chaos theory and its implications for social science research. *Human Relations*, 46(7): 777–802.

Haleblian, J., and Finkelstein, S. (1999). The influence of organizational acquisition experience on acquisition performance: A behavioral learning perspective. *Administrative Science Quarterly*, 44(1): 29–56.

Haspeslagh, P., and Jemison, D. B. (1991). *Managing Acquisitions: Creating Value Through Corporate Renewal*. New York: The Free Press.

Hayward, M. L. A. (2002). When do firms learn from their acquisition experience? Evidence from 1990–1995. *Strategic Management Journal*, 23: 21–39.

Hofstede, G. (1980). *Culture's Consequences: International Differences in Work-Related Values*. Beverly Hills, CA: Sage.

Holland, J. H. (1995). *Hidden Order: How Adaptation Builds Complexity*. Reading, MA: Addison-Wesley.

Howard, R. J. (1982). *Three Faces Of Hermeneutics: An Introduction to Current Theories of Understanding*. Berkeley and Los Angeles: University of California Press.

Hunt, J. W. (1990). Changing pattern of acquisition behaviour in takeovers and the consequences for acquisition processes. *Strategic Management Journal*, 11: 69–77.

Jemison, D. B., and Sitkin, S. B. (1986). Corporate acquisitions: A process perspective. *Academy of Management Review*, 11, 145–63.

King, D. R., Dalton, D. R., Daily, C. M & Covin, J. G. (2004). Meta-analyses of post-acquisition performance: Indications of unidentified moderators. *Strategic Management Journal*, 25, 187–200.

Kogut, B., and Singh, H. (1988). The effect of national culture on the choice of entry mode. *Journal of International Business Studies*, 19: 411–32.

Lubatkin, M. (1987). Merger strategies and stockholder value. *Strategic Management Journal*, 8: 39–53.

Lubatkin, M., Schweiger, D., and Weber, Y. (1999). Top management turnover in related M&As: An additional test of the theory of relative standing. *Journal of Management*, 25: 55–74.

Mendenhall, M. (1999). On the need for paradigmatic integration in international human resource management. *Management International Review*, 39(3): 65–87.

Mitchell, D. (1989). The importance of speed in post-merger reorganization. *Mergers and Acquisitions Europe*, 1, 44–8.

Pablo, A. L., Sitkin, S. B., and Jemison, D. B. (1996). Acquisition decision-making processes: The central role of risk. *Journal of Management*, 22: 723–46.

Robino, D., and DeMeuse, K. (1985). Corporate mergers and acquisitions: Their impact on HRM. *Personnel Administrator*, 30, 33–44.

Schoenberg, R. (2000). The influence of cultural compatibility within cross-border acquisitions: A review. *Advances in Mergers and Acquisitions*, 1, 43–59.

Schweiger, D. M., and Goulet, P. K. (2000). Integrating mergers and acquisitions: An international research review. *Advances in Mergers and Acquisitions*, 1: 61–91.

Shelton, L. M. (1988). Strategic business fits and corporate acquisition: Empirical evidence. *Strategic Management Journal*, 9(3): 279–87.

Shrivastava, P. (1986). Postmerger integration. *Journal of Business Strategy*, 7, 65–76.

Singh, H., and Montgomery, C. A. (1988). Corporate acquisitions and economic performance. *Strategic Management Journal*, 8(4): 377–86.

Stahl, G. K., and Sitkin, S. B. (2001). Trust in mergers and acquisitions. Presented at the annual meeting of the Academy of Management, Washington, DC.

Stahl, G. K. & Voigt, A. (2004). Meta-analyses of the performance implications of cultural differences in mergers and acquisitions. *Academy of Management Best Paper Proceedings*, IM, I1–I6.

Stahl, G. K. & Voigt, A. (in press). The performance impact of cultural differences in mergers and acquisitions: A critical research review and an integrative model. In Finkelstein & Cooper (eds.), *Advances in Mergers and Acquisitions* (Vol. 3). New York: JAI Press.

Von Wright, G. H. (1971). *Explanation and Understanding.* Ithaca, NY: Cornell University Press.

Weber, Y. (1996). Corporate cultural fit and performance in mergers and acquisitions. *Human Relations,* 49, 1181–202.

Weber, Y., Shenkar, O., and Raveh, A. (1996). National and corporate fit in M&A: An exploratory study. *Management Science,* 4: 1215–27.

Wheatley, M. (1992). *Leadership and the New Science: Learning About Organization from an Orderly Universe.* San Francisco: Berrett-Koehler Publishers.

Zollo, M., and Singh, H. (2004). Deliberate learning in corporate acquisitions: Post-acquisition strategies and intergration capability in U.S. bank mergers. *Strategic Management Journal,* 25: 1233–56.

19 People and Cultural Aspects of Mergers and Acquisitions

What Are the Lessons... and the Challenges?

PAUL EVANS AND VLADIMIR PUCIK

What are the messages that this book leaves for the practicing manager and the academic? At the outset, a point made by Schweiger is worth highlighting. The easy and obvious benefits in value creation through mergers or acquisitions will not typically go to the acquiring company but to the shareholders who are selling, as buyers pay in advance for the synergistic premiums of acquisitions. What this means is that acquirers start the game with the cards stacked against them. Success depends on having a strategy or merger logic that goes beyond simple cost savings and rationalization, and more particularly on the capacity to realize those strategic benefits through the people and cultural integration processes that are the focus of this book. Consequently, the highest returns go to organizations that execute the post-merger integration process effectively.

Here, size and business focus *do* matter. There are winners in the merger and acquisition (M&A) game—GE and Cisco, to name two well-known examples that are discussed in this book, have made M&A into a core capability. Driven by a clear strategic logic, they tend to acquire smaller companies that are in the same business or one that is closely related. In general, there are many successful but unheralded deals where large companies acquire smaller firms, often family-owned, successfully integrating them into their own operations. However, there is no doubt that the merger where the initial odds are against success is the "merger of equals" between two large and equally sized companies, where each has a certain history of success that handicaps clear merger leadership and creates blockages to integration. These are the mergers that capture the attention of the press—and also of researchers—precisely because of the turmoil. The reader of this book should note that the "mergers of equals"—the

DaimlerChryslers, the Novartiss, and the Nordeas—are atypical of the merger scene.

The focus of this book is on the people and cultural aspects of M&A, and most of the articles start off by saying these are problematic issues. This is true, but they are not issues that have been neglected. For the last twenty years, there has been a growing literature on the importance of these people and cultural aspects of managing change. The popular press has made us well aware of this, and many students attending MBA programs have been through acquisitions, experiencing the cultural difficulties. Given the extensive coverage in the business press of mergers that falter or fail outright owing to people issues, be it ego battles between senior executives or large-scale cultural clashes, one would need to be quite isolated to remain in blissful ignorance.

Indeed, extensive research into the people issues of mergers has been conducted since the 1980s. The researchers involved have a wide variety of interests—corporate identity, cross-border cultural integration, the process by which employees come to terms with a merger (or fail to), the merits of alternative ways of retaining key talent, and more recently, the way in which knowledge gets transferred between two organizations. However, the complexity of the people and cultural aspects of M&A are such that there are few commonly accepted generalizations that one could make as a result of this attention. Perhaps, the only thing that unites all the studies is the general theme that people issues matter greatly in mergers, and that the failure to attend to them can turn otherwise promising mergers into failures.

With this background, what does this book teach us by way of a pathway, and what are some of the outstanding avenues for research and learning? Also, taking into account our own review of the literature from the human resource management (HRM) perspective (Evans, Pucik, and Barsoux, 2002), we single out six facets of the cultural and human resource challenge: (1) the importance of paying attention to the basics of HRM; (2) leadership, a neglected domain of study; (3) change management capabilities, because mergers are complex change processes; (4) communication; (5) cultural integration, where we suggest that the starting point for understanding the culture of another firm is knowing one's own culture; and (6) the important learning/knowledge transfer perspective that we expect will become a vital optic for understanding and steering M&A integration.

Paying Attention to the Basics of HRM

To begin with, the importance of paying attention to what we call the basics of HRM cannot be underestimated.[1] In this book, Schweiger summarizes the issues to pay attention to in the due diligence process—underfunded pension funds; differences in philosophy in compensation, training, and benefits; employee grievances, and the like—the typical list of topics on the HR due diligence checklist can easily run to several pages if the acquirer comes from North America.

Some of the HR basics, mentioned in passing by Schweiger and others, reflect the strategic intent of the acquisition, notably talent assessment and early planning of the retention and motivation of key staff in the human capital audit. The starting point for talent retention is the talent map developed during the due diligence stage, and after the deal, this needs to be refined quickly, using feedback from direct superiors, peers, and subordinates, past performance reviews, personal interviews, formal skill assessments, and direct evaluation of performance during the integration period (see Evans, Pucik, and Barsoux, 2002, for details). One of the most insidious ways in which value can be lost in a merger is through increased attrition of key staff such as researchers, managers, and salespeople. The momentum of the combined entity can be greatly lessened if many of the most talented staff leave because they are likely to have alternative options. In some cases, much of the value is bound up in the talent, so that the "assets walk out the door." Chaudhuri's study of Cisco and IBM emphasizes the role of HRM in retention, as well as the integration of capabilities embedded in people in high-technology acquisitions.

The failure to establish sound criteria for talent management is one of the notorious handicaps for mergers of equals, appointments being made from top-down on a representative basis (another HRM problem is compensation differences, the focus of much postintegration at DaimlerChrysler (see Kuehlmann and Dowling's account)). In this book, Engeli, Chua, and Stahl emphasize the attention that Novartis paid to establishing transparent criteria for new jobs, associated with a stronger performance culture to be established in the merged firm, thereby contributing greatly to the integration process, along with rigorous selection of the best people for these new jobs (30 percent of them being new hires). There may also be a serious problem among those who stay. Their motivation may drop because the merger process is de-energizing, or because new reporting relationships are less attractive than the ones they replace.

Leadership

One of the cultural and people dimensions that various chapters in this book highlight is the importance of leadership. The popular press loves to highlight mergers in terms of the leader personalities, equating GE with Jack Welch or DaimlerChrysler as the clash between Jürgen Schrempp and Robert Eaton. Mergers are portrayed as being driven by CEO ego, and there may be some truth to this. On the other hand, an absence of clear leadership may handicap the integration process, as indicated by Olie's study of Dutch–German mergers in this book.

However, as Sitkin and Pablo emphasize in their contribution, the literature on M&A largely leaves leadership out of the picture, except in the case studies. They argue for a more multidimensional view of leadership, leadership in the plural rather than as the hero executive. Indeed, the case studies in this book testify to this. Daniel Vasella may be seen as the "leader" of the Novartis integration, but behind this is the relationship between Marc Moret from Sandoz and Louis von Planta from Ciba years before the merger. Carlos Ghosn may be the person associated with the Nissan turnaround, but what emerges in the case study of Korine, Asakawa, and Gomez is that the foundations were laid by the critical relationship between Nissan's Hanawa and Renault's Schweitzer. Beyond successful mergers are indeed the unvoiced work of hundreds of leaders in transition teams. In the failures, there is conflicting leadership—supposedly joint leadership at DaimlerChrysler masking the reality of power struggles at the top; or the tensions between different realities, leading to collective suspicion of the central office, as in Olie's cases of the Dutch–German mergers.

The multidimensional view of leadership in Sitkin and Pablo's chapter strikes as worthy of further attention. M&A are complex change processes, requiring different types of leadership—the personal leadership that fosters loyalty, the relational leadership that builds trust, the contextual leadership to reinforce community, and the supportive leadership for internalized self-discipline and stewardship. The important role of the integration manager does not receive sufficient attention in this book (see Evans, Pucik, and Barsoux, 2002).

Change Management

Related to leadership is the issue of change. Two problems interact. The first problem is the complexity of the change processes that are involved, as Sitkin and Pablo point out—even complex change *within* a large firm is a difficult area. Faced with the complexity, managers often tend to tackle it as a rational engineering problem, to be analyzed and planned. The importance of thorough homework and rational analysis should not be underemphasized because there are so many interdependencies and uncertainties, that the merger task needs to be carefully framed. But the theory of planned organizational change, with its roots in the Organizational Development movement, tells us that rational plans interact with acceptance and trust, the human side of the change equation. This is captured by the classic but simple $Q \times A = E$ formula underlying, for example, GE's "change acceleration" methodology, applied also by GE to acquisition integration. The "E" stands for the Effectiveness of a decision or a change process. Effectiveness depends on the Quality of that rational analysis (Q)—the clarity of the strategy, the assessment of how value can be created through the integration, the planning of the integration strategy, and the like. But it also depends on the Acceptance of the decision (A)—the understanding and acceptance of the merger logic, of the need for change, the strategies for dealing with resistance, the acceptance of new strategic goals.[2] Trust is perhaps the key indicator of this side of change, and Stahl and Sitkin provide us with an account of the factors that are associated with the capability to maintain and rebuild that trust.

Change theory argues that change processes will be fraught with difficulty if there is not an accepted and understood need for change, with accompanying urgency. So, one potential hypothesis here is that the probability of integration success depends on the awareness of the merger parties that there is little hope unless there is transformational change. Maybe the reality is that neither the folks at Daimler nor those at Chrysler saw any real need for change, whereas managers and staff at both Nissan and Renault knew that they would have a troubled future ahead without radical transformation.

The second issue concerning change management stems from the inevitable secrecy that surrounds merger deal making, which means that managers on both sides have little time to prepare themselves for the challenges ahead, especially if they have no prior experience and have not tuned into the research lessons. Many of the precepts of "A" technology do not apply to M&A. One cannot go about building an understanding of the need for change in advance, one cannot involve people in advance in building a vision for the combined enterprise. Nevertheless, we will suggest in a later section that firms that are well equipped to manage acquisitions have a degree of realistic self-knowledge so that they are well prepared to tackle the challenges of integration.

Managing integration involves many challenges of change—combating the winner–loser syndrome, preparing the employees for change, managing the dangers of the first hundred days, setting up a transition organization, putting in place the new structure, policies, and practices. Yet, these changes are quite similar to those that must be confronted with a major internal reorganization. We have argued elsewhere that organizations that have a good track record in managing the Q and A of internal change are those that are well equipped to manage acquisitions.

Complex organizational change processes are ill-studied and poorly understood (Evans, Pucik, and Barsoux, 2002, chapter 9). Even the most simple of mergers involves a sequence of different steps, where all too often the focus on one type of change at one step can create problems at the next stage. With the benefit of hindsight, many executives who have been through mergers talk about this as "the first wave of change" and "the second wave."

Initially, the obvious synergies that have been paid to the selling shareholders must be realized, with the need for rapid restructuring and cost savings that provides the initial justification for the acquisition. But if this is undertaken with excessive speed and rigor, this may handicap the more collaborative symbiotic integration in the longer second wave where real value creation should take place. As Engeli, Chua, and Stahl emphasize, once trust has been undermined, it takes a long time to rebuild. Indeed, there is a danger in the prevailing wisdom that speed in postmerger implementation is critically important. There may be some truth to this in purely absorption acquisitions, but most mergers involve some initial absorption and restructuring at the initial stage, followed by symbiotic integration. Success at the stage of absorption can create problems at the next stage of fusion if the absorption has undermined the necessary trust.

Skill in managing large complex projects may be another essential change management competence. This is particularly true in the case of mergers of equals or in the implementation of symbiotic/fusion strategies, where team processes are at the heart of the integration strategy. These require the creation of transitional spaces, where the process of moving from A and B to C can be worked through. We see this well in the cascading project team used in the CNH/Fiat New Holland merger, as outlined by Morosini, and in the transitional project structure that was set up in the new Novartis (see Engeli, Chua, and Stahl's account).

An adage about change processes that we like is that people do not resist change; they resist *being* changed. If people are not involved in the change processes, the integration process will be slow, and that involvement typically comes best through teams. Our studies of vision-building processes have shown that it is the involvement in the process that generates the commitment and positive energy. In the study of learning at Nordea, as described by Björkman, Tienari, and Vaara, the senior executives believed that crafting a value-based vision is important, although this did not appear to have much effect on the people who were not engaged in developing that vision.

Let us make a final comment concerning mergers as complex change processes. Rather than applying change theories and concepts to M&A, researchers might well think of mergers as an arena for the development of new theories of complex organizational change, pushing our understanding of change processes beyond the established notions that we have mentioned above.

Communication Processes

This is at the heart of the people side of all change processes, and much, of course, needs to be communicated in a merger process. This includes reasons for employees to stay with the employer and remain motivated, and indications of how the cultural integration should proceed (especially what the new corporate identity is and what it means for employees). Apart from these communications with a high emotional content, a great deal of humdrum but vital information about roles, processes, systems, and so forth needs to be conveyed.

In general, there is agreement that communications need to begin early, remain intensive throughout the merger process, and deal quickly with the matters that are important to people (such as whether they have jobs, what they will be doing and where, how much they will be paid, and to whom they will report to). A major role for communications is to reduce stress and maintain trust, as Stahl and Sitkin remind us. DeNisi and Shin, with their focus on realistic merger previews, emphasize that the aim of communication is not to avoid the painful realities of change in a merger, but to make this manageable. Indeed, one of the oldest models of change is the Lewinian unfreezing–changing–refreezing framework, and the communication strategy must minimize the perverse consequences of the necessary unfreezing (such as the best people leaving), leading to the new identity formation process that other authors in this book emphasize.

Communication to customers, suppliers, and partners is of equal if not greater importance, and there is a tendency to focus on the internal matters. Indeed, there is often a need for some creativity and subtlety in communications because what is said internally may have negative repercussions when it leaks to the critical external customers and suppliers.

Cultural Integration

Cultural integration is certainly the most challenging aspect of M&A. Almost invariably in a merger, two disparate cultures must come together, even though an important strategic challenge is to understand which parts of the culture to preserve separately (for example, research capabilities), which parts of the culture to absorb (for example, logistics) and which parts to fuse (for example, sales and distribution).

Sometimes it may appear that the cultures are highly compatible, but this is generally illusory. The illusion of cultural compatibility can lead to a dangerous complacency about the demands of cultural integration. This is one reason why mergers of companies with supposedly similar cultures are less successful than conventional wisdom would suggest—the similarity is often more apparent than real. Surface similarities in national cultures can hide the need to work at cultural differences. According to Bjorkman, Tierari, and Vaara, this has been one of the handicaps in the Nordea merger story. Management comes to believe in their own rhetoric that as we are all "Scandinavian," we are all the same, thereby shunting aside the many tasks needed to prepare for cultural integration.

Early research suggested that it was the differences that created the problems, but the evidence is pushing that aside. As Cartwright as well as Greenberg, Lane, and Bahde and others note, cultural differences should not be automatically associated with negative consequences (see also Child, Faulkner, and Pitkethly, 2001; Stahl et al., 2002). If we have the troubled DaimlerChryslers on the one hand, we have the successful Nissan–Renaults on the other. When there are clear differences in national cultures, management is more likely to pay attention to the "A" side of change management, with better communication and team processes.

Despite this, there is an appeal to the argument that we need to have scientific ways of mapping out culture and cultural differences. Cultural compatibility is difficult to assess in the due diligence process, and many people in this book have lamented the complexity and lack of tools to undertake cultural due diligence. Cartwright's discussion tackles the issue, and she shows the difficulties. We have no objective ways of mapping cultural dimensions, except perhaps at the deep but abstract level of values and assumptions. The interdependencies between dimensions that we may use (decision making, attitudes to authority, communication styles) are complex, and as Cartwright points out, many of the dimensions have no clear relationship to performance.

Perhaps the aim of developing simple tools to assess and guide cultural integration is itself illusory. Is there an alternative way of framing the challenge of cultural integration?

The traditional approach is focused on assessing the target company, but an alternative may be to twist this on its head and to take as a starting point one's own company. We would argue that the company that is in good shape to handle cultural integration processes is the company that knows itself well—the firm that can articulate its own culture, put it into words, and where there is a minimal gap between what is espoused and how people behave, where there is an honest understanding of the firm's strengths and weaknesses.

The metaphor of marriage is often misused when it is applied to M&A, hiding the fact that true mergers of equals are difficult to manage while most so-called mergers, unlike marriages, are acquisitions. But if we employ the marriage metaphor, this means that the marriage that is likely to be unpredictable and full of tension is between two people who have little self-understanding, who are unsure of themselves, who have ideal selves that are far removed from how they are seen by others. These are barriers to trust that will contribute to problems of communication and handicap decision making. Alas, this is often the case in mergers. Companies with distinguished pasts, arrogant self-images, widening gaps between words and reality, incapable of organic growth are sometimes those that jump on the merger bandwagon. Olie's study of the difficulties of mergers of equals between Dutch and German firms in transforming industries seems to fit this picture.

Rather than hunting for tools for "objective" cultural assessment of the target company, the starting point for the company that is on the merger or acquisition route may perhaps lie more with itself. This indeed is an important message in a forthcoming book by one of our colleagues, Maurizio Zollo, written with the head of McKinsey's M&A practice (Zollo, Price, and Fubini, forthcoming)—"Know thyself!" They argue that corporate self-knowledge is important throughout the merger process and not just at the time of deal making. This goes beyond strategy—the firm that is equipped to manage integration has a deep knowledge of its management processes, of its strengths and weaknesses, of its capabilities and its functional limitations, of its staff bench strength, and of its core and peripheral values.

The acquisition capabilities of firms like GE and Cisco appear to be rooted in such self-knowledge—both firms developed distinctive cultures, with self-assured capabilities. Similarly, BP's rapid and successful integration of Amoco must be seen against the backcloth of the transformational process of change that it went through during the 1990s, driven by newly articulated values, focused processes, and greater clarity on its strategy.

From this perspective, self-knowledge is an essential foundation for a successful integration process, and one that is likely to be enhanced by the merger process, especially through interactions within transitional teams. This is a potentially virtuous learning circle. Indeed, self-knowledge is part of the broader learning perspective on organizations, which is the last facet that we will highlight.

Knowledge Transfer and Learning

Many authors in this book note that the integration process is one of learning and knowledge transfer. Greenberg, Lane, and Bahde emphasize the importance of language, also in the broader sense of mindset, distance, structure, motivations, while Björkman, Tienari, and Vaara point out that mergers should be viewed as social learning processes. In his study of the acquisition strategies of Cisco and IBM, Chaudhuri rightly emphasizes that one should clearly distinguish between capability transfer based on explicit and tacit knowledge, respectively. Explicit knowledge, such as tight global processes in logistics or quality management, needs to be transferred rapidly with tight one-way transfer during the restructuring process. But tacit knowledge is transferred, extracted, and created through social interaction in a longer lasting two-way process—through project management, exchange, and interpersonal processes, partnering, and mobility. Our understanding of learning and knowledge transfer processes with respect to explicit and tacit knowledge will contribute to our ability to manage integration processes that are appropriately differentiated.

The learning perspective, with its focus on knowledge creation and transfer, is an important new perspective on acquisitions, building on self-knowledge. As the belief gains ground that the source of competitive advantage in a highly competitive global world comes from learning and knowledge transfer, and not from ephemeral products or markets, so this perspective will gain in importance. Greenberg, Lane, and Bahde argue that a newly merged organization will not learn unless the learning perspective is built into the stages prior to integration—we would go further and suggest that the learning perspective has to be built into the culture of the firm itself.

Conclusion

The perspective that stands out for us as most promising for future research as well as for providing practical insights on M&A is that of learning and knowledge management. As this gains ground *within* organizations, so it will also facilitate mergers *between* organizations. From this learning perspective, an important paradox is that merger capabilities start with learning about oneself—it is through learning more about oneself, including an honest and clear understanding of one's strengths and weaknesses, that one develops the ability to manage complex integration processes with an acquired company or merger partner. One of the tangible indicators of practical progress will, we suggest, be a decline in the "winner–loser," "we–they" syndrome that, as Larsson points out, characterizes almost all M&A.

Notes

1. We argue elsewhere that there are three different facets to human resource management—getting the ever-changing basics of recruitment, selection, development, and so forth in place; managing organizational change (what we call the change partner role); and the emerging facet of managing tension and contradiction between the dualities that characterize organizations in competitive environments. See Evans, Pucik, and Barsoux (2002).

2. See Evans, Pucik, and Barsoux (2002) for an outline of GE's change acceleration methodology. Beer and Nohria (2000) describe the Q and A in similar terms in their review of change management—as Theory E (creation of economic value) and Theory O (development of the organization's human capability to implement strategy and learn from change actions).

References

Beer, M., and Nohria, N. (2000). *Breaking the Code of Change*. Boston, MA: Harvard Business School Press.

Child, J., Faulkner, D., and Pitkethly, R. (2001). *The Management of International Acquisitions*. Oxford: Oxford University Press.

Evans, P., Pucik, V., and Barsoux, J.-L. (2002). *The Global Challenge: Frameworks for International Human Resource Management*. Chicago: McGraw-Hill.

Stahl, G. K., Evans, P., Pucik, V., and Mendenhall, M. (2002). Human resource management in cross-border mergers and acquisitions. In Harzing and van Ruysseveldt (eds.), *International Human Resource Management: An Integrated Approach*, 2nd ed. London: Sage.

Zollo, M., Price, C., and Fubini, D. *Merging Forward*, book in preparation.

Index

ACEM Corporation, 146
acquisition disaster, 57
acquisition in Northeast Asia, 81
adaptability of organization
  innovation, 261
  risk, 261
  speed, 261
agreement formation in partnering,
  364. *See* Renault and Nissan case
alliance formation process (Renault
  and Nissan)
  closure, 369
  commitment, 368
  conceiving, 366
  courting, 367
  timeline, 371
alliance formation process (Renault
  and Nissan) management
  closure as investment, 374
  commitment as risk-taking,
    373
  conceiving as believing in shared
    future, 371
  courting as intensive fact finding,
    372
appropriate cultures, 270

autonomy in organization, 261
autonomy, retaining, 90
avoiding integration approach. *See*
  soft integration approach

bank mergers in US, failures among
  cultural differences, 54
  defection, 54
  demotivating employees, 54
  inadequate due diligence, 54
  poor planning and execution, 54
  unrealistic targets, 54
barriers and bonds theory, 56
bidirectional knowledge transfer,
  78
binational identity in Dutch-German
  mergers, 329
  board leadership, 330
  company language, 331
  corporate identity, 330, 331
  head office, 330
  management board, 330
boundary-spanning managers, 61

capabilities, sources of, 279
capital markets, 4

Career Concept model, 195, 198
  expert, 194
  linear, 194
  spiral, 194
  transitory, 194
career motivational solution,
  195
cash flow
  leakage sources of, 27
  models (discounted), 19
change management, 415
Ciba-Geigy and Sandoz
  merger, 379. *See also* Novartis
    merger
  profile of, 394
Cisco's acquisition of Grand Junction
    Networks
  objective, 289
  product development, 288, 289
  sales people, 288
  tacit knowledge application, 290
  workgroup business unit (WBU),
    287
closure
  as investment, 374
  stage (alliance formation process),
    369
CNH Global case, 11, 302
  alliance with Kobelco Construction
    Machinery, 308
  construction equipment business,
    303
  construction equipment business,
    organizational changes in, 313
  merger & acquisitions, joint
    ventures and alliances, 303
  merger with Case Corporation, 308
  multibrand and multichannel
    strategy, 309
  strategic repositioning and
    economic results (1996–1999),
    312
co-competence and motivational
  approach

realization of synergies in M&A,
  195
to acculturation in M&A, 190
to career development in M&A, 193
to communication in M&A, 191
co-competence integration approach,
  188
combination phase, 58
commitment
  as risk-taking, 373
  stage (alliance formation process),
    368
common product platforms, creating,
  318
communication
  in learning process, 63
  interventions and priming effects,
    242
  processes, 417
  quality, 92
communication management
  communication media, effective, 37
  communication philosophy, 36
  communication plan, 37
conceiving
  concept of, 371
  stage (alliance formation process),
    366
consistency and cultural issues
  consistency, 109
  diversity, 109
  dominance, 109
  realization, 109
consolidation approach, 22
constitutional management, 269
constructivistic perspective,
  application of, 152
context-specificity of learning, 170
contextual leadership in M&A, 216
contingent human integration
  strategies, 286
controlling integration approach. *See*
  hard integration approach
coordination approach, 23

corporate academy in M&A, 202
  career development and succession,
    205
  change management coaching and
    training, 203
  e-learning and e-communication
    infrastructure, 206
  experience in assessment, 204
  relationships with leaders, 205
corporate cultural diversity, role of
  consistency and cultural issues,
    109
  culture matters, 108
  ethics of corporate culture transfer,
    115
  generic types of overall corporate
    cultures, 110
  knowledge flows, 119
  merger policy, 116
  modeling the choice, 116
  multidimensional differentiation,
    116
corporate cultures, 108, 204
corporate cultures, generic types of
  pluralist , 110
  universal, 111
corporate language policy, 165
corporate management structures, 78
cost-benefit profiles, 116
courting as intensive fact finding, 372
courting stage (alliance formation
    process), 367
cross-boder mergers and acquisitions
  barriers and bonds in learning
    process, 64. See also M&A
    learning process, barriers and
    bonds in
  examples of, 53
  from process perspective, 56
  learning and knowledge transfer in
    M&A, 59
  organizational learning, 53
  recasting M&A as learning process,
    62

cross-border merger case study. See
    DaimlerChrysler merger
cross-border mergers and acquisitions,
    integration process in, 323
  binational identity, 329
  consolidation of merger, 327
  evaluation of mergers, 345
  examples of, 325
  national identity problem, 325
  restraining and supporting factors,
    332
  two-tier board systems, 324
cross-cultural mergers, 154
cross-functional project teams (CNH
    Global construction equipment
    business), 315
cross-national mergers
  learning enhancement in, 171
  learning in organizations, 158
  learning on sociocultural
    integration, 162
  Nordea case, 160
  sociocultural integration, 155,
    157
cross-over mergers and acquisitions,
    77
cultural assessment of target, 31
cultural awareness, 167
cultural clashes, 186, 189
cultural compatibility
  concept of, 254
  in M&A, 338
cultural consistency, degree of, 110
cultural differences, 157, 167, 258
cultural distance hypothesis, 89, 404
cultural due diligence in M&A
  appropriate and inappropriate
    cultures, 270
  concept of, 258
  constitutional management, 269
  cultural compatibility, 254
  cultural fit assessment, 258
  culture fit and integration problems,
    260

cultural due diligence in
   M&A *(Continued)*
   framework development, 253
   functional and dysfunctional
      cultures, 269
   intercultural training and
      competence, 263
   potential integration problem areas,
      263
cultural fit assessment, 258
cultural homogeneity, 111
cultural integration, 41, 418
cultural similarity, 89
cultural tolerance and sensitivity, 91
cultural training programs, 169
culture fit
   assessment, factors for, 260. *See
      also* culture fit and integration
      problems
   concept of, 254
culture fit and integration problems
   adaptability of organization, 261
   autonomy and involvement, 261
   degree of internal integration, 260
   diversity, 262
   employee welfare, fairness, and
      trust, 262
culture, defined, 132
customer purchase decisions, 256
   country-of-origin (COO) effects,
      256
   product country image (PCI) effects,
      256

DaimlerChrysler management
   board, 356
   structure, 359
DaimlerChrysler merger, 351
   as business thriller, 352
   chronicle of, 353, 356
   human resource activities, 360
   human resource issues
      identification, 360
   sources for study, 352

DaimlerChrysler merger process,
   phases in
   closing deal, 355
   human resource dimension, 353,
      355, 357, 359
   negotiation, 354
   postmerger integration, 358
   targeting partner, 353
decision-making simulation, 95
discounted cash flow model, 19
distrust, definition of, 84
dual premerger identities, 240
due diligence
   cultural sensitivity and integration
      process, 272
   process, 57, 403
   team, 70
due diligence phase, language barriers
   in, 66
Dutch decision-making style, 339
Dutch-German Mergers. *See*
   cross-border merger and
   acquisitions, integration process
   in
Dutch–German mergers, comparison
   of
   Enka Glanzstoff, 345
   Estel, 345
   VFW–Fokker, 345
dysfunctional corporate cultures, 269

economies of specialization, 111
employee receptiveness, 392
employee relationships, 224
employee resistance, 189, 190
employee welfare, justice and trust,
   262
Enka Glanzstoff merger, 342
ethics of corporate culture transfer,
   115
   plasticity, 115
   reproducibility, 115
ethnocentricity (barrier to M&A
   integration), 262

explicit knowledge, 420
external stakeholders (role in
    mergers), 333

FFV Ordnance, 141
Fiat New Holland
    construction equipment business of,
        303
    dealer network restructuring (US),
        307
    joint venture with Hitachi, 305
    merger with Case Corporation, 308
    Orenstein & Koppel, acquisition of,
        306
    product range, 307
Fiat–Hitachi joint venture, 305
fit-model, 114
forecasted cash flows, 21
free cash flow, 24
functional corporate cultures, 269

gap analysis, 254
global acquisitions, joint ventures, and
    alliances, social capabilities for,
    302
global construction equipment
    market, 304
global managers, 315
global organization across boundaries,
    312
global product development
    platforms, 319
global product leaders (GPL), 314
global system motivation, 112
Grand Junction Networks (acquired
    by Cisco). See Cisco's acquisition
    of Grand Junction Networks
growth strategies, 23

hard integration approach, 187
horizontal M&A, 185
human integration
    contingent approach, 283
    degree of, 281

role of, 278
speed of, 281
human integration strategies,
    executing, 296
human resource integration factors
    (avoiding resistance), 189. See
    also employee resistance
human resource issues identification
    (DaimlerChrysler merger), 360
    communication about merger, 361
    HR management, involvement of,
        361
    merger candidates evaluation, 361
    merger difficulties, 362
human resource management basics,
    413
    benefits, 414
    differences in compensation, 414
    employee grievances, 414
    training, 414
    underfunded pension funds, 414
human resource practices (of buyer
    and target), 29
human resource selection factors,
    186
human resources management to
    capture capabilities
    case studies for high technology
        acquisitions, 277
    Cisco's acquisition of Grand
        junction Networks, 287
    contingent approach to human
        integration, 283
    human integration strategy
        implementation, 280, 295
    human integration, role of, 278

IBM's takeover of Lotus, 291
insights from IBM, 293. See also
    IBM's integration approach
IBM's integration approach, 293
    degree of human integration,
        295
    learning effort, 295

IBM's takeover of Lotus, 291
    group-ware, 291
    product development, 292
    sales function, 292
identity (or self), concept of, 132
inappropriate cultures, 270
informal coordination, importance of, 121
informal self-coordination, effectiveness of, 128
information-based communications, 251
inspirational leadership in M&A, 217
intangible synergies, 22
integration, 17
    decision making, 158
    HR practices in value creation, 27
    integration stage, 37
    perspectives on intrinsic value, 19
    price and value, distinguishing between, 19
    role of, 27
    standard approaches, 22
    synergy source identification, 21
    transaction stage, 27
    transition stage, 33
integration and HR activities, 38
    building teams and work units, 39
    capable and motivated people, 40
    cultural integration, achieving, 41
    key target people, assessing, 31
    leadership, 39
    speed management of Integration Process, 38
    staffing, retention, and redundancy, 42
integration and HR activities (transaction stage)
    culture of target, assessing, 29
    detailing, understanding, and comparing, 29

guide behaviors and attitudes of due diligence team, 32
guide behaviors and attitudes of negotiators, 32
integration and HR activities (transition stage)
    communications with stakeholders, 36
    integration guiding principles, articulation of, 34
    integration project plan development, 36
    integration transition structure, 33
    way to integrate, 35
integration efforts (motivational patterns), 194
integration guiding principles, 34
integration planning (Novartis), 382
Integration problem areas, 263
integration problems, culture fit and, 260
integration process variables
    communication quality, 92
    cultural tolerance and sensitivity, 91
    retained autonomy, 90
    reward and job security enhancement, 91
    speed of integration, 90
integration processes in value creation, 281
integration stage, 37
    integration and HR activities, 38
    objectives, 38
integration strategies, typology of
    absorption, 257
    preservation, 257
    symbiotic, 257
    transformation, 257
integration strategy for HR, 280
intercultural training and competence, 263

intergroup cognitions
  merger identity, 237, 238, 245
  organizational identity, 236
  psychological states and. *See*
    psychological states and
    intergroup cognitions
  realistic information and, 242
  self-categorization theory-based,
    232
  social identity theory-based, 232
intergroup cognitions in corporate
    mergers, 234
  ingroup favoritism, 235
  out-group discrimination, 235
internal integration, degree of, 260
internal stakeholders, 336
international mergers. *See* cross-
    border merger and acquisitions,
    integration process in
interorganizational trust, 84
intervention approach, 23

job security, 91

knowledge flows, 119
knowledge transfer and learning, 420
Kobelco Construction Machinery
    alliance, 308

language barriers in integration phase,
    66
language differences (cross-border
    acquisitions), 65
leadership in M&A, neglected
    importance of
  implications, 220
  in M&A literature, 210. *See also*
    M&A literature, leadership in
  in organizations, 208
  M&A as change, 209
  model, 213
leadership model applied to M&A,
    213
  contextual leadership, 216

inspirational leadership, 217
  personal leadership, 214
  relational leadership, 215
  stewardship, 219
  supportive leadership, 218
leadership, importance of, 414
learning and knowledge transfer in
    M&A
  knowledge transfer, 59
  lessons learned, 61
learning enhancement in
    cross-national mergers
  articulation and codification
    aspects, 171
  contextual nature of learning, 172
learning in organizations, 158
  focus of attention, 159
  memory of organization, 159
  power of individuals, units,
    coalitions, 159
  socio-psychological factors, 158
learning on organizational decision,
    159
learning on sociocultural integration
    in making of Nordea
  cultural awareness, 167
  language policy, 165
  shared corporate vision, 162
  virtual headquarters, 164
learning perspective on sociocultural
    integration, 154, 156. *See also*
    cross- national mergers
learning process (cross-boder mergers
    and acquisitions), 56
legal framework for Dutch-German
    mergers, 328
Lotus takeover by IBM. *See* IBM's
    takeover of Lotus

M&A (merger and acquisition)
  as change, 209
  as learning process, recasting, 62

M&A (merger and
  acquisition) *(Continued)*
  construction of social identities in.
    See social identities, construction
    of
  corporate cultural diversity in, 108
  cross-border, 53
  from HR Perspective,
    recommendations for success, 48
  neglected importance of leadership,
    208
  people and cultural aspects of. *See*
    people and cultural aspects of
    M&A
  psychological communication
    interventions, 228
  synergy realization in, 183
  trust in, 82
  value creation, critical link in, 17
M&A from process perspective, 56
  combination phase, 58
  postcombination phase, 58
  precombination phase, 57
M&A learning process, barriers and
    bonds in, 64
  motivation, 71
  organizational structure, 68
  space, 67
M&A literature, leadership in, 210
  lack of attention to leadership, 211
  leadership, addressing, 212
M&A management, 395
  effective HR policies, 396
  orientation loss by employees, 396
  speedy integration process, 396
  trust levels, 396
M&A strategic objectives, synergies,
    and integration
  geographic market, 24
  line of business, 26
  market consolidation within
    geographic area, 23
  multiple strategic objectives, 26

products, services or technologies,
    addition or extension, 24
  vertical integration, 25
management style and shared values
    (Novartis), 390
map alignment
  approach, 314, 316
  implementation, 314
merger and acquisitions. *See* M&A
    (merger and acquisition)
merger and integration process, 176
merger framework, 340
merger identity, 237, 238
merger logic, 335
merger of best, 176
merger of equals, 178, 324, 325
merger policy, 116
merger process model, stages in
  closing deal, 352
  negotiating, 352
  postmerger integration, 352
  targeting, 352
merger synergies (Novartis), 393
merger, basic feature of, 323
merger, consolidation of
  central management company, 327
  legal framework, 328
  organizational framework, 328
Merita–Nordbanken merger, 163
MNB–Unidanmark merger, 164
motivation (M&A learning process,
    barriers and bonds in), 71
multibrand and multichannel strategy
    (of CNH Global), 309
  common product platforms, 318
  cross-functional project teams, 315
  global organization across
    boundaries, 312
  map alignment implementation,
    314
  organizational building blocks, 317
  product differentiation, 311
multiculturalism, 91

multidimensional globalization, Porter's conception of, 117
multiple strategic objectives, 26
multiple synergies, 22

New Holland dealers, 308
New Holland, product development by, 307
NIH (not invented here) syndrome, 71
Nordea (Nordic financial services group) Case, 160
Novartis charter on integration process, 383
Novartis financial results, 394
Novartis managers
  candor/trust/integrity, 388
  commitment/self-discipline, 388
  communication, 388
  competence, 388
  customer/quality focus, 388
  empowerment, 388
  leadership, 388
  speed/action/simplicity/initiative, 388
Novartis merger
  announcement of, 381
  Ciba-Geigy and Sandoz merger, 379
  employee receptiveness, 392
  high-performance culture, 386
  human resource management, 379
  integration planning and implementation, 382
  leadership, role of, 379
  merger negotiations, 380, 381
  merger synergies, 393
  mergers and acquisitions, management of, 395
  performance, 393
  personnel selection, 384
  redundancy process, 384
  trust-based culture, 391
Novartis merger, objectives of, 386
  compensation system, 389
  incentive payments, 389

management style and shared values, 390
  pay-for-performance, 388, 389
  shared values, 387
  stretched targets, 387
Novartis Venture Fund, 386

Orenstein & Koppel, acquisition of, 306
organizational building blocks establishment (CNH GLobal)
  book of brands, 317
  DNA of brand, 318
organizational complexity, 118
organizational fit
  administrative practices, compatibility of, 338
  leadership styles, 338
  organizational cultures, 338
  organizational structures, 338
organizational identity, 236, 237, 239, 338
organizational integration factors, 187
organizational learning. See learning in organizations
organizational reorganization, 209
organizational structure
  hierarchy management, 68
  linking mechanisms, 68
  subunit establishment, 68
organizational theory, 5
organizational trust
  benevolence, 85
  competence, 85
  integrity, 85
  openness, 85
  value, 85

pay-for-performance culture, 389
people and cultural aspects of M&A, 412
  basics of HRM, 413
  change management, 415
  communication processes, 417

people and cultural aspects of
M&A *(Continued)*
cultural integration, 418
knowledge transfer and learning,
420
leadership, 414
perfect integration conditions
value creation, 20
value destruction, 20
value maintenance, 20
performance controversy, 184
personal leadership in M&A, 214
personnel management problems, 263
personnel selection management in
Novartis, 384
physical space, concept of, 67
pluralist corporate culture, 110
policy-capturing studies, 95, 97
postcombination phase, 58
precombination phase, 57
price and value, difference between, 19
priming effects, 242
product differentiation, need for
downstream, 311
upstream, 311
psychological communication
interventions in M&A, 228, 230,
240
and priming effects, 242
corporate mergers revisited, 240
favorability of merged organization
identity, 235
intergroup cognitions, 231, 235
psychological communications and
attraction, 244
psychological states, 231
realistic information and intergroup
cognitions, 242
realistic information and
uncertainty reduction, 240
psychological communications in
corporate mergers (flow chart),
241

psychological states and intergroup
cognitions, 231
intergroup cognitions in corporate
mergers, 234
psychological states in merger
processes, 232
self-categorization process, 232
realistic information
and Intergroup Cognitions, 242
and Uncertainty Reduction, 240
redundancy process in Novartis, 384
relational leadership in M&A, 215
Renault and Nissan case, 364, 366.
See also alliance formation
process (Renault and Nissan)
against received wisdom, 371
alliance formation process, 366
change inside company, 374
partnership, 365
restraining and supporting factors
(Dutch-German mergers), 332
business conditions, 333
cultural compatibility, 338
internal stakeholders, 336
merger framework, 340
merger logic, 335
organizational identity, 338
role of external stakeholders, 333
top management, 342
revenue growth initiatives, 21
reward enhancement, 91

self, concept of, 133
self-categorization process, 232
semantic priming, 244
shared corporate vision, 162
social capabilities building
social capabilities perspective, 320
value creation, 321
social categorization
defined, 233
of ingroup, 233
of outgroup, 233

social competition, 138
social creation of groups, 134
  definition of out-groups, 135
  self-definition of in-groups, 135
social creativity, 138
social identities, construction of,
    130
  empirical observations,
    interpretation of, 138
  identity or self, 132
  social creation of groups, 134
  social identity and social categories,
    135
social identity theory (SIT), 232, 255
sociocultural integration in M&A, 3,
    157, 401
  basic personnel practices, 403
  corporate language policy, 156
  cultural awareness programs, 156
  due diligence process, 403
  future research, avenues for, 406
  importance. See sociocultural
    integration in M&A,
    importance of
  in making of Nordea, 162
  integration level on criticality, 402
  learning perspective on, 154
  management efficacy and
    precombination factors, 402
  points of agreement, paradoxes, and
    avenues, 401
  shared corporate vision
    development, 156
  unresolved paradoxes, 403
  virtual headquarters, 156
sociocultural integration in M&A,
    importance of
  capital markets, 4
  economic performance, 4
  human resources, 5
  organizational theory, 5
  strategic management, 3
soft integration approach, 187

speed of integration, 405
standard integration approaches
  consolidation, 22
  coordination, 23
  intervention, 23
  standardization, 22
stewardship in M&A
  balance, 219
  personification, 219
strategic synergy factors, 185
supportive leadership in M&A
  developmental support, 218
  emotional support, 218
  financial support, 218
  procedural support, 218
synergy realization in M&A, 183
  co-competence and motivational
    approach, 190, 191, 193
  corporate academy, role of, 202
  human resource integration factors
    (avoiding resistance), 189
  organizational and HR selection
    factors, 186
  organizational integration factors,
    187
  performance controversy, 184
  strategic synergy factors, 185
synergy sources identification, 21
synergy, categories of
  cost reductions, 21
  increased market power, 21
  intangibles, 21
  revenue enhancements, 21

tacit knowledge, 278
  application of, 283
  engineering knowledge, 280
  learning effort, 285
  management skills, 280
  manufacturing knowledge, 280
  preservation, 283
  sales knowledge, 280
  transfer of, 283

tacit knowledge flow
  from acquirer to target people,
    284
  from target to acquirer employees,
    284
  retention rate of employees, 284
Tajfel's law, 137, 141
takeover friendliness, 87
takeover situation affecting target
    firm's trust
  cultural similarity, 89
  positive interaction history, 89
  power equality, 88
  relative target firm performance, 88
  takeover friendliness, 87
task integration, 279
top management in merger, 342
  ineffectiveness, 344
  lack of cohesion, 343
  lack of continuity, 343
transaction stage, 27
  integration and HR Activities, 29
  objectives. *See* transaction stage,
    objectives in
transaction stage, objectives in
  financial, 28
  legal, 28
  organizational, 28
  strategic, 28
transition stage, 33
  integration and HR Activities, 33
  objectives, 33
transnational merger, 113
trust in M&A, 82, 103–107
  acquiring firm management's trust,
    93
  critical Role, 95
  importance, 83
  initial takeover situation, 87
  integration decisions and actions, 93

integration process variables, 90
  target firm members' reactions to,
    93
  trust development, 86
trust in M&A, critical role of
  empirical evidence, 95
  implications for practice, 97
trust, definition of, 84
trust, model of, 86
  in postacquisition process, 86
  reciprocal and dynamic nature, 87
trust-based culture, 391

uncertainty reduction, realistic
    information and, 240
universal corporate culture, 111, 119
unresolved paradoxes (sociocultural
    integration), 403
  culture matters, 404
  experience, 405
  imperialism, 404
  speed, 405

valuation methodology
  estimated terminal value, 19
  forecasted free cash flow, 19
  risk-appropriate required return,
    19
value (function of cash flow), 19
value creation, 19, 27
value creation by integration (stages)
  application of knowledge, 279
  preservation of knowledge, 279
  transfer of knowledge, 279
value destruction, 19
vertical integration strategy, 25
VFW–Fokker, noncooperation in,
    336
virtual headquarters, 164
volition-based mechanism, 229

Printed and bound by CPI Group (UK) Ltd, Croydon, CR0 4YY

23/04/2025

14660938-0005